Sir
WILLIAM
LYONS

Sir
WILLIAM
LYONS

THE OFFICIAL BIOGRAPHY

Philip Porter & Paul Skilleter

Haynes Publishing

First published in September 2001
Reprinted December 2002
This paperback edition published in August 2011

ISBN 978 0 85733 106 9

Library of Congress Catalog Card Number 2011923599

Published by Haynes Publishing, Sparkford,
Yeovil, Somerset BA22 7JJ, UK
Tel: 01963 442030 Fax: 01963 440001
Int. tel: +44 1963 442030 Fax: +44 1963 440001
E-mail: sales@Haynes.co.uk
Web site: www.haynes.co.uk

Haynes North America Inc.
861 Lawrence Drive, Newbury Park,
California 91320, USA

Design and layout by Dominic Stickland
Printed in the USA by Odcombe Press LP,
1299 Bridgestone Parkway, La Vergne, TN 37086

CONTENTS

ACKNOWLEDGEMENTS

This has been both a fascinating and daunting book to write. Clearly it could not have been done without a great deal of help from many people and multifarious sources.

Sir William's daughters, Pat Quinn and Mary Rimell, spent many hours painting a detailed picture of family life and the private man. They also gave access to their family archives. Without their assistance this account would have been considerably the poorer. Other members of the family, including Michael Quinn, Jane Quinn, Carol Smetham, and Alan Docking also gave help and support. Alan Newsome had the unusual distinction of having been both a friend of Sir William's and a colleague and this book has benefited from his reading of the draft.

Sir William actually began writing his own memoirs and progressed as far as the early 1950s and naturally these have been very helpful.

In compiling the prewar chapters we are grateful for help from Arnold School's Headmaster W. T. Gillen and school historian Kenneth Shenton and also from Gilbert Mond, the Swallow historian, who has made a study of the early factories. Though no longer with us, Connie Teather, Jack Beardsley, Harry Gill and George Lee recorded much about Swallow years gone by. Josie Lyons (no relation, she thinks!) provided useful facts on the family in Blackpool.

Naturally, there are considerably more living witnesses to William Lyons and Jaguar during the postwar years and the authors were greatly assisted by a host of interviewees, both in recent times specifically for this book and through previous interviews. 'Lofty' England, Bill Heynes, Bob Knight, Walter Hassan, Claude Baily, Alan Currie, David Jenkins, and Jim Randle spoke for the senior management. Additionally, on the engineering side, Tom Jones, Cyril Crouch, Trevor Crisp, Norman Dewis, Sid Bevins, Frank Philpott, Jim Eastick, Paul Walker, Howard Snow, Ted Barber, and Jack Dunnett added their recollections.

Former Jaguar executives John Morgan and Bob Berry worked

closely with Sir William and helped enormously with amusing anecdotes and with a more serious analysis of Sir William's management style.

In America, Jo Eerdmans, Tony Thompson, and Les Bottrill were exceptionally helpful. Jack Jones, Moss Evans, Eric Titcumb and, above all, Ron Butlin were especially interesting on the trade union angle. Bill Cassidy, Harry Rogers, Pat Smart, Alan Hodge, Ron Beaty, Jack Gannon, and Bill Jones described various lesser-known aspects of Lyons's character. Bernard Hewitt recalled what it was like to be on Lyons's personal staff and Oliver Winterbottom, William Towns, Stephen Dudley, and Keith Helfet all contributed towards the styling story.

From the racing world, Tony Rolt, Duncan Hamilton, and Sir Stirling Moss shared memories. Ole Sommer of Denmark gave the importers' angle and Bob Bett recalled the advertising story. Ted Loades of Abbey Panels and David Owen of Rubery Owen provided insights and Ron Hickman covered Lotus matters. Of the many motoring journalists quizzed over the years, Gordon Wilkins, Stuart Bladon, Paul Frère, and Patrick Mennem particularly assisted. Various books and magazines have been quoted (see endnotes) and thanks go to the authors and publishers of these.

The financial story has benefited greatly from the shrewd analysis and comments of Peter Underhill. Chris Stonier provided information on company tax history. Rosemary Smith and Peter Whurr assisted with research. Farming became increasingly important to Lyons and his farm manager Bob Robinson gave a fascinating account of a very different side to Lyons's character. Other Wappenbury employees – Tom Sage, Denise Blackmore, and Frank Adam – described Lyons's acts of great generosity and his later years.

At publishers Haynes, the enthusiasm for this project goes all the way up to John Haynes himself. Editorial Director Mark Hughes, as always, has been a tower of strength and a source of support and sound advice. Warren Allport, himself a historian, has brought his editing experience to bear to good effect.

Personally, Philip and Paul would like to thank their wives, Julie and June respectively, for their patience, support and help.

The Sir William Lyons files, which are held by the Jaguar Daimler Heritage Trust, yielded a great deal of information and added immeasurably to the research. The Trust is assisted by several volunteers and they were particularly helpful in sorting and providing material. Chief Archivist Anders Ditlev Clausager, as well as being a distinguished author in his own right, has contributed very significantly to this volume, in terms of verifying, elaborating, tracing persons, and providing wise counsel.

At Jaguar Cars, the book enjoyed the enthusiastic support of John Maries, then Managing Director of the JDHT, and Stuart Dyble, a JDHT Trustee and then Jaguar's Director of Communications and Public Affairs, that extended beyond their professional duties.

INTRODUCTION

It is entirely appropriate that a biography should be published to mark the centenary of the birth of Sir William Lyons. The authors have benefited from the full co-operation of Sir William's two daughters, Patricia Quinn (formerly Appleyard) and Mary Rimell, as well as many others who knew him. We are also fortunate that the late Andrew Whyte, from the 1950s onwards, interviewed many early acquaintances and distilled their memories in his book Jaguar – The History of a Great British Car, first published in 1980. Similarly, authors Paul Skilleter and Philip Porter have researched many arcane aspects of Jaguar history for almost as long. Most of those who have been interviewed for this book knew Sir William only when he was elderly and as his juniors, in age as well as status, approached him deferentially – with a respect that many of them still feel. What is certainly clear is that he left a strong impression on those with whom he came into contact, whether they were members of his family, employees, or even those – such as Sir John Egan – who were effectively his peers.

Some of his personal records survive. His daughter Pat has his draft autobiography, compiled around 1976, which she has generously made available for this book. (It was also made available to Andrew Whyte for his Jaguar history.) The Lyons collection in the Jaguar Daimler Heritage Trust archive is extensive and while it consists mostly of business correspondence and documents, there are also many papers of a more personal nature. Sir William did leave some published material, although publicity managers such as Ernest 'Bill' Rankin and Bob Berry may have written some of it.

What then was Sir William Lyons's claim to greatness? There is no doubt that he was a successful businessman and that he had the vision necessary to create a legendary brand – one of the world's best known. He pursued his career with single-mindedness, skill, and determination. He was, in modern parlance, 'multi skilled' and understood all the disciplines required to make a success of car manufacture: organisation, finance, man management, marketing and publicity, salesmanship, customer relations, and an understanding of engineering (though he was not an engineer). He excelled above all in the styling of motor cars, in which he was an artist. In all of these fields he made a contribution, either directly or through shrewd judgement of whom to entrust with vital activities. Most importantly, he was an enthusiast for the product and a more than capable fast driver, even when quite elderly. He achieved his successes without any great amount of either formal education or vocational training. He learnt by doing.

It is interesting to compare Lyons with some other of the leading personalities in the young British motor industry. The one with whom he had most in common was perhaps Cecil Kimber, founder of MG and Lyons's senior by 13 years. Some of the parallels are astounding. Both came from the same part of the world (Kimber spent his youth in Stockport), were keen motorcyclists and later enjoyed driving fast sporting cars. Intriguingly, their paths might almost have crossed; in 1914 Kimber became associated with A. W. Reeves of Crossley – the firm to which Lyons was apprenticed briefly in 1917.[1] Kimber and Lyons both had a keen eye for body styling and both MG and SS Jaguar owed a great deal of their success to attractive coachwork – in effect they were stylists. Both men knew the value of publicity generated by success in competition, were salesmen, great organisers, and good man-managers. Their workforces treated both, in equal measure, with devotion and deference. Most astonishing, both men introduced very similar cars at the same time – the MG SA 2-litre and the SS Jaguar 2½-litre made their debut at the same motor show in 1935.

The crucial difference between them was that Lyons was an entrepreneur, always preferring to be his own man, while Kimber never cast off the shackles of employment. However much freedom Kimber had in the early years of MG, he always seemed happy to work for somebody else (William Morris, later Lord Nuffield) and never showed the inclination to break away and set up his own business – not even when he was sorely tried. By contrast, Lyons's entrepreneurial spirit was more like that of Kimber's boss, Lord Nuffield, or of the Rootes brothers.

Lyons's style of management was to give executives a comparatively free hand – once they had gained his trust – but he still became involved in seemingly trivial matters. For years, he supposedly reviewed all incoming mail personally. It could be argued that he was too involved in detail; certainly he kept an eye on things – either by his regular daily inspections round the factory, by insisting on being kept informed by written reports, or with copies of correspondence. The archival evidence betrays, on the whole, an extraordinary level of micro-management, appropriate perhaps to the small company that Lyons had started out with, less so to an enterprise the size of the Jaguar group of the 1960s. However, it is greatly to Lyons's credit that he never seemed to lose sight of the wood for the trees.

Apart from successfully managing his business, Lyons's great talent was his eye for producing attractively styled cars. Basically, he was responsible for the 'Jaguar look' and continued to exert an influence, even in retirement.

The picture that emerges of Lyons, the man, is of a cool, aloof, autocratic individual in public but a much more relaxed and warm person in the fiercely guarded privacy of his home. Above all he was absorbed in his work – he rarely stopped thinking about Jaguar. He was unostentatious, preferring discreet elegance to anything showy or flashy, and disliked personal publicity; over his lifetime he gave remarkably few in-depth interviews. Only rarely did he allow a newspaper to publish a feature about his home life. While both he and Lady Lyons sat for paintings, he did not wish to have his likeness sculpted and would perhaps have disliked having his biography written. He did not have the flamboyance of Sir John Black or of Lord Rootes but was justifiably proud of what he had achieved during his life. He accepted the honours that were offered to him – a knighthood in 1956, an honorary doctorate in 1969, and other accolades.

Yet, in the end, Lyons surrendered his autonomy and let his company be merged with a bigger concern. While this may seem a surprising U-turn after having fended off several predators over the years and having himself extended his empire through a series of takeovers, it appeared to him at the time as an unavoidable step to safeguard the future of his creation. Coupled with this was his age, 65 at the time, and the fact that he had lost his only son and putative heir ten years before. He was sufficiently realistic to appreciate that there would be increasing difficulties for a company the size of Jaguar that stayed completely independent in a world where the motor industry was contracting into fewer and bigger groups. So he sold out to BMC, which he considered to be a congenial and benevolent senior partner.

After the Leyland merger in 1968, he served as Deputy Chairman of the corporation to Sir Donald (later Lord) Stokes and secured a remarkable degree of autonomy for the Jaguar operation. However, this situation did not last long after Lyons's retirement in 1972. In retirement, with the honorary title of President of Jaguar, he was distressed to have to watch from the sidelines as Jaguar lost its identity in the maelstrom of British Leyland but he continued to take an interest in the company, especially in the design and development of new models. John Egan, appointed by Michael Edwardes as Jaguar's Chief Executive in 1980, met with Lyons's full approval and his delight when Jaguar regained its independence shortly before his death was palpable. How he would have reacted to the Ford takeover we cannot know but assuredly he would have been pleased to see the way that Jaguar has developed since and continues to develop in his centenary year. His daughters are convinced that he would have been delighted at the outcome. Jaguar is now realising the potential that Lyons always believed the marque could attain, by building cars that expand technology to its limits and have a strong emotional appeal. Equally, Sir William's influence continues to be felt in the culture of the Jaguar company.

The main reason for Sir William's success was his uncanny instinct for spotting what the public wanted and then giving it to them – at a price they could afford. There has never been a Jaguar that was a failure – only a few that, perhaps, were not quite as successful as the rest! It was Sir William Lyons who developed those fundamental values that still, after 70 years, make Jaguars stand out: sportiness, style and elegance, comfort, even luxury, and high performance, coupled with the safety that comes only from impeccable road holding and handling. In that sense, every Jaguar today embodies Sir William's legacy.

Anders Ditlev Clausager
Chief Archivist, Jaguar Daimler Heritage Trust

CHAPTER 1

Lyons finds
a Swallow

William Lyons – he was given no middle name – was born on 4 September 1901 into a new century that was to see unprecedented change. On the death of Queen Victoria early in January 1901 Britain had entered the Edwardian age, a new era which saw science and technology supplant steam and iron as the driving forces of the industrialised world. So rapid and far reaching were these changes that while the first true aeroplane had yet to make its tentative flight, in little over 50 years Lyons himself would be flying the Atlantic on a scheduled service. These same economic and social factors also allowed the popularisation of motor vehicles, resulting in a worldwide industry, which became the economic barometer of the developed nations. It was an industry to which Lyons was to make a unique contribution.

Little motorised transport existed back in 1901, when King Edward VII ascended to the British throne and Theodore Roosevelt became President of the United States. Then, even the few cars that were in anything like series production usually cost the equivalent of a small house and it was the relatively new bicycle that gave many thousands their first experience of mobility. However, that was soon to change: standardised components allowed cars to be assembled on production lines, which slashed costs and selling prices. The pioneering Ford Model T in North America (1909) and Morris Oxford in Britain (1913) brought motoring to that rapidly growing segment of the population, the middle classes. Not that British and North American production was in any way comparable: in 1913 just 25,000 cars were made in Britain against the 462,000 built in the US and there were one million cars on North American roads by 1914. Nevertheless the trend on both sides of the Atlantic was the same: more, better and cheaper cars.

So Lyons was born into a world that was becoming ever more mechanised and, from an early age, he was fascinated by this new technology – even though the horse and cart were still the primary means of road transport. This interest in engineering was pursued right from the start with the same unswerving determination that was to become such a hallmark of his personality.

Some 60 years later Lyons recalled an incident in his childhood that illustrates this well. 'When I was seven years old and at my preparatory school, I won a form prize. I was permitted to make my choice from books, football boots, cricket bats or pads.

'I chose, much to the astonishment of the master in charge, an enormous book, obviously intended for a boy in the senior school, entitled *The History of Modern Science and Engineering*. It was pointed out that the book was far too advanced for me, which indeed it was, but nothing would dissuade me from it. When I took it home I found little in it that I could understand, but my attention was drawn to a description of the working of the internal combustion engine: this completely absorbed me and aroused an enthusiasm for everything concerned with engines – first motor cycles and then cars...'[1]

This was no mere infatuation; the appeal was to grow ever stronger. 'There is something about vehicles,' he explained later, 'whether they be motor cycles, cars or trucks, which introduces a sense of excitement which does not exist in any other product. I believe it is because we are producing something which, if not alive, is the closest thing to it – it engenders a spirit of animation.'[2] Lyons once remarked that to him only the theatre provided the same 'excitement and glamour' as the motor industry.

Certainly the Lyons family had a connection, of sorts, with the performing arts. His father (also named William) was an Irish musician, who as a young bachelor had visited mainland Britain with a touring orchestra. He played in Blackpool – then, as now, the country's most visited seaside resort. The town sprawls along much of a sandy, seven-mile (11.2km) stretch of Britain's north west coast and, with its brightly-lit trams and bustling promenade dominated by the Blackpool Tower, it evidently captivated the young musician.

On tour, William fell in love. His feelings were reciprocated by the young lady concerned, who (family legend has it) was quite dazzled by this glamorous young musician entertaining audiences around Blackpool's pleasure spots. She was Mary Jane Barcroft and, on 5 June 1894, the couple were married by licence in the Roman Catholic Church of the Holy Name at Chorlton upon Medlock, some 50 miles from Blackpool. The venue was chosen, perhaps, because of its reputation for excellent music.

William was then in his 23rd year, Minnie (as she was usually known) in her 24th. The groom's father was noted as Michael Lyons, commercial traveller, and the bride's as James Barcroft, manufacturer. Mr Barcroft was a man of substance and the Barcroft family played an important part in the business community of Waterfoot and the Lumb valley, about eight miles (13km) from Rochdale, where they ran a string of mills making felt carpets. Described by his local paper as 'the beau ideal of the country gentleman,' James Barcroft was also a leading member of the Rossendale Hunt and kept a number of fine horses.

Perhaps because of his elevated position, Mr Barcroft was not amused at his daughter's choice of husband but the strong-willed Minnie had refused to break off the liaison. In true Victorian fashion James Barcroft promptly 'cut her off without a penny'. No one knows the real cause of Mr Barcroft's annoyance; as a churchwarden it may have been connected with William's Irish Roman Catholic antecedents.

Today the Lyons family knows little about its Irish roots beyond memories of grandpa (William Lyons, senior) saying mysteriously that they were all 'thieves and murderers'![3] There is no evidence that Lyons had any particular interest in his family background and he is not thought ever to have visited Ireland.

So William and Minnie made their own way in life, settling down in Blackpool where they opened their Music and Pianoforte Warehouse. Here they sold and repaired the instrument that was to be seen, and heard, in almost every decent drawing room of the time. It was a successful business but Minnie is remembered as the one who really ran the shop, leaving time for the 'dreamy' William to keep up his playing and even occasionally to conduct orchestras that were visiting Blackpool's concert houses.

William wrote music too, his compositions sometimes reaching dizzying, if temporary, heights. 'The King and a Waltz – Blackpool composer's success' reported the *Blackpool Gazette* of 26 March 1912 after he had sent his *Infatuation* waltz to no less a personage than King George V. The King's private secretary was 'commanded to thank him for the same,' the letter from the royal household stating that the waltz had been played on board *HMS Medina* while Their Majesties made their way to India.

This incident appears to have been the peak of William's musical career and his granddaughter, Mrs Pat Quinn, confessed: 'I think my parents were rather unkind about him – they used to treat his composing as a great joke! I expect it was very Victorian...'

William and Minnie Lyons's first child, a girl they named Carol, arrived on 31 July 1895. She was joined a little over six years later, on Wednesday 4 September 1901, by William junior. Their early childhood in Red Cottage, Newton Drive (near Blackpool's largest recreation ground) appears to have been tolerably happy. Later Lyons recorded that his mother and father were 'a most devoted couple and were hardly ever parted from one another' – in this respect at least creating a precedent for his own marriage.

This closeness did not mean complete harmony in the parents' household though; Lyons recalled that his father 'had quite a violent temper when aroused'. Indeed, as a child, Pat remembered her paternal grandfather being 'fierce and rather frightening – all he ever did was criticise!'[4] Lyons was evidently the favourite: 'I was always conscious that he treated my sister, the only other child of the family, less kindly than he treated me.'[5] Though William senior remained a professing Roman Catholic all his life and Minnie formally adopted the religion upon her marriage, the children were not brought up as Catholics.

As a boy Lyons attended Poulton-le-Fylde Grammar School, where by his own admission he was an average scholar and one who did not particularly enjoy studying. It was at preparatory school that young Lyons gained the engineering book prize.

The piano warehouse generated enough income for Lyons to attend Arnold House, a private establishment (later known as Arnold School) in Lytham Road on Blackpool's South Shore. He arrived there on 30 April 1914 as war clouds began to darken Europe. Again, his academic progress was mediocre despite his admiration for the headmaster, F. T. Pennington, 'probably because he was a man of outstanding stature and dignity albeit of frightening severity'.[6]

Frank Pennington (1872–1938) had founded his own school in 1896 and in 1901 took over Arnold House. It soon became recognised as a leading school for boys in the area: the prime destination for the sons of minor solicitors and upwardly mobile artisans. Pennington himself was regarded locally as a fine businessman and something of a dictator. While Lyons was never regarded as 'frightening' by his staff at Jaguar, nevertheless his word there was absolute and maybe his bearing at the works was unconsciously influenced by the 'stature and dignity' of his revered headmaster.

Lyons's studies at Arnold House may have suffered because of his 'devotion' to sport, particularly running, though he admitted to being a 'dismal failure' at cricket. Out of school he was popular with some of the boys as he enjoyed repairing their bicycles; his true enthusiasm, however, lay with motor cycles. The school's official history relates that he 'tended to irritate the headmaster,' with

Pennington telling the boy 'that he would never get anywhere messing about with engines'.

Too young to ride himself, in his early teens Lyons cultivated friendships with the motor cycle-owning elder brothers of his class mates, with 'one of whom I spent a great deal of time as a hanger-on in his garage where he pulled his motor cycle to pieces and put it together again'.[7]

But in August 1914 what was to become known as the First World War began and, although Lyons was too young, many of the older students marched off to France. During the conflict, 285 boys from Arnold House joined the armed forces, most of them as volunteers.

Thirty-seven boys – most of them were little more than that – died but one survivor, Arnold Breakell, sold young Lyons his first motor bike. This 1911 Triumph he proceeded to rebuild, not to standard but 'to my own ideas' – surely the first instance of Lyons's desire to improve on the ordinary. The bike was sold for 'a substantial profit' after the Armistice, 'helped, of course, by the rise in motor cycle prices after the war'.[8]

Meanwhile, his period at Arnold House concluded with a special crammer course during his final term; this helped the young man pass what he found was the difficult apprenticeship examination for the Vickers shipbuilding yard at Barrow. But on leaving school in July 1917, aged not quite 17, there came a change of mind. Lyons's heart was not in shipbuilding so, taking advantage of his father's chance acquaintance with A. W. Hubble, Managing Director of Crossley Motors Ltd, he took up an apprenticeship with that Manchester firm instead. Part of the arrangement meant that he also studied engineering at Manchester Technical College, not far from the Crossley works in Gorton.

During the First World War the powerful and reliable Crossley 20/25hp model became a mainstay of the British forces; the Royal Flying Corps adopted it as a staff car and the chassis performed valiant service in light truck and ambulance guise. When Lyons joined towards the end of the war these latter variants dominated production and the young trainee 'felt very remote from cars in which I had such an intense interest'. He decided to leave; again something better had beckoned.

This did not go down well at home. Having failed to take up his apprenticeship at Vickers, in the space of months Lyons had quit the job he had obtained. Now he was to start another one – this time as, essentially, a motor car salesman.

Lyons's later accounts of how this came about are contradictory:

his unpublished memoirs written circa 1976 state that he simply left Crossley without finding another job. However, a more detailed account of the same period, written in April 1961, seems likely to be the more accurate. This tells how, while on a weekend home from Crossley, he was approached by J. E. Mallalieu with the offer of a job. Jack Mallalieu was well known to Lyons as the long-standing General Manager of Jackson Brothers, a local motor dealer. The First World War had just ended and the brothers were the distributors for Sunbeam in Blackpool; they also raced the cars on the nearby Southport sands.

But the job offered by Mallalieu was not primarily with the Jacksons. He had acquired the Metropole Garage (next door to Blackpool's Metropole Hotel in General Street) and was forming a new motor business with a Mr Brown from the Bolton textile industry. (Coincidentally the previous occupant of the Metropole Garage moved to the same building in Cocker Street from which Lyons himself would be operating a few years later.)

The wide-ranging position with Brown & Mallalieu seemed much more exciting than anything Crossley could offer, as above all it meant working with cars – now firmly established as a parallel interest alongside motor bikes for Lyons. 'I jumped at the idea and spent several happy years steeped in those workshops and showrooms,' he wrote in 1961.

Clearly the young man was perfectly able to 'stick at it' provided the work held his interest – that was key for Lyons. Later he said that his job with Mr Mallalieu was 'difficult to describe'. This explains, perhaps, the similar absence of rigidly defined job descriptions at SS and Jaguar for many years. He certainly learned the value of flexibility, another Jaguar virtue, for at Brown & Mallalieu he was expected to be everything: junior salesman, storekeeper, mechanic, and even charabanc driver. In 1919 the job also took him to London, where he helped at the first postwar motor show.

All went well for a time but any relief felt by his parents turned out to be relatively short-lived. 'I was, of course, still very young, but I worked immensely hard and took over, or was given, more responsibility than perhaps I should have been given,'[9] he confessed later. Jack Mallalieu engaged Charles Hayes as General Manager of the fast-growing business and virtually his first act was to strip many of these responsibilities from Lyons. This was a rude shock to the young man, who had relished the variety and the relative independence he had been given. He did not take to working under Hayes's strict control and no longer found the work a pleasure. 'We parted company,' he explained later. This slightly ambiguous turn of phrase supports the contention made by Harry Gill (one of Lyons's first employees) that Lyons had told him how, on returning from an excursion to the Isle of Man to see the TT motor cycle races, he found himself sacked!

There is also some doubt as to whether Lyons left Brown & Mallalieu for the express purpose of starting his own business or (as he wrote in 1961 and appears much more likely) without any firm idea about what he would do next. Somewhat grudgingly he filled in by working in the family business. The shop also sold gramophones and the young Lyons did toy with the idea of manufacturing these. He had neither any enthusiasm for, nor saw any future in, the mainstream business, observing: 'pianos are not things which people usually bought more than once in a lifetime, if then'. In fact probably the most successful aspect of the business was the workshop where pianos were repaired and renovated; it was here that Lyons worked rather than serving customers out front in the Bank Hey Street shop.

Evidently something from those days spent languishing amongst dusty pianos stuck, though. His nephew, Alan Docking, recalled an occasion many years later when, during a family gathering at Pat Lyons's home, 'my uncle asked me to play something'. He did but quickly found that the piano was in a bad way: besides being out of tune, some notes stuck or made no sound at all. 'Uncle Bill said: "Let's have a look." In minutes, not only were the lid and front removed, but the keys were being hauled out, together with the dampers and springs, and in fact the whole thing was pretty much dismantled. I was astonished as my uncle was rather noted for not being a DIY sort of person. But then I remembered that his working life had started in his father's piano shop, and he clearly recalled much of what he knew some 50 years earlier...'

For Lyons, the only good thing about this period in the doldrums was that it allowed him much more time to indulge in his main passion – motor cycles. These, of course, had long been a consuming interest and even before he was 20 he had owned more than 20 different types. Motor bikes were, after all, the cheapest way young men of the day could buy speed and excitement. It was probably thanks to his father's generosity as much as to the proceeds of his spasmodic employment that, from quite early on, Lyons was able to afford some quality machines. He told Andrew Whyte in the late 1970s: 'I bought an Indian and a couple of Harley-Davidsons. One of the Harleys came from Bert Houlding who made motor bikes himself, called Matadors. It was one of three Daytona models in England, and I did quite well with it, especially in hill climbs; I think my best result was when I won at Waddington Fells, on the moor above Clitheroe. My later motor cycle was a Levis two-stroke.'[10]

His enthusiasm for bikes had indeed spilled over from tinkering with them at home to competing with them; this activity extended from the end of the First World War into the first few years of him starting up in business for himself. At Blackpool, there were motor sport venues almost on his doorstep. Besides timed hill climbs, the wide expanse of smooth, hard sand left at low tide along the west coast made sand racing a popular local sport. But those temporary courses were unreliable – it was not unknown for everyone to turn up and discover the day's sport foiled by an unexpectedly early tide. This once denied Lyons a competitive outing on the AJS sidecar combination brought to Blackpool by works AJS rider and TT winner Jimmy Simpson; Lyons was to have ridden it at Morecambe but the course was waterlogged and the meeting had to be called off.

At least the surface was kind to both the elementary suspension systems of the time and the riders who might 'come a cropper,' as did the intrepid Lyons at least once. He was persuaded by the competitions representative of Wood Milne tyres to fit one of its covers to his Norton at one Southport meeting. The Norton was doing around 80mph (130kmh) on the first run when, recalled Lyons, 'the back tyre came off – and so did I!'[11]

But messing about with bikes did not conform to William Lyons senior's ambitions for his son. Alderman Jacob Parkinson recalled in 1950 being told by Lyons senior: 'I am worried about Billy. I wish I could get him interested in the shop. I don't know what he is going to do, I really don't.' Then in the early summer of 1921 something happened which changed all that.

By this time the Lyons family had moved to King Edward Avenue, which led from Queen's Promenade on the sea front, a mile (1.6km) or so from Blackpool town centre. On the right-hand side of King Edward Avenue, coming from the sea, some of the comfortable, red brick Victorian houses (mostly semi-detached or terraced) had small rear gardens backing on to a service lane. Number 23 was one of those which boasted a garage as well – though this was really more of a glorified shed, perhaps 14ft by 20ft (4.2m by 6.1m). Built of brick and adjoining a similar building next door at number 21, it had a pitched slate roof and doors that opened on to the lane.

Nearby (Lyons never stated exactly where) another garage was being used by the Lyons family and was where he overhauled and tuned his motor cycles. What happened next, that crucial meeting between two motor cycle enthusiasts, ultimately resulted in the Jaguar of today – one of Britain's largest car producers and among the world's most famous luxury marques.

The exact circumstances of this encounter are best related in Lyons's own words, perhaps a little stilted but authentic, penned in April 1961: 'One day I saw a very smart combination, as we used to call them, that is, a motor cycle and sidecar, standing in a garage not far away. I got into conversation with the owner, who informed me that he had made the sidecar himself and he was in fact making another one for a friend... Our garages being close together, we naturally had many conversations. I learned that he came from Stockport, and I introduced him to the local Blackpool and Fylde motor club, of which I was one of three founder members. In consequence, we saw a great deal of one another.'[12]

The new neighbour was also called William – William Walmsley. Together with his wife Emily Letitia, he had moved with his parents from Stockport, Cheshire, after his father (Thomas) had decided to relinquish the family's old-established coal merchant's business and retire to Blackpool and the seaside.

Earlier, during the First World War, William Walmsley had served in the Cheshire Yeomanry and, surviving the conflict with an injured leg, had returned to the family home – a detached house in a leafy suburb of Stockport. Blessed with a gratuity, a wealthy father, and an easygoing temperament, Bill Walmsley was quite content to indulge in his hobby of motor cycles and making things rather than pursue a career. He had acquired a liking for using his hands when, after leaving school, he had joined the family business. There he invented a horse-brass polishing machine and learnt the basic principles of coachbuilding from the horse-drawn coal carts and railway wagon bodies that were made 'in house' by the family firm.

His flash of inspiration – if it could be called that – was to apply his skills to the design and construction of a sidecar; it was to go with his ex-War Department Triumph motor cycle, one of a number of dismantled machines he had bought for reassembly and sale locally.

The prototype sidecar, given the racy name of 'Ot-as-Ell' by Walmsley, went on the road in 1920. With its bullet-shaped nose and gleaming, polished aluminium panels, it was dramatically different from anything else to be seen on British roads. (The nearest to it was probably the cigar-shaped sidecar being marketed by Harley-Davidson in America, although it is unlikely that Walmsley knew of this.)

Whether or not Walmsley built this first 'chair' expressly with a view to selling replicas is not known; but having built it, he certainly found a ready demand. So, in an informal partnership with his brother-in-law Fred Gibson and with the aid of one or two casual helpers, he set about making a few more sidecars – some in the shed at the rear of Fairhaven (his parents' house) and some in a lock-up garage a mile (1.6km) nearer Stockport.

By this time, at least, it is clear that Walmsley was very aware that he had a commercial proposition on his hands: on 7 April 1921, through the offices of patent agents F. Rosshardt of Corporation Street, Manchester, he had the sidecar design registered officially. He also had a photographic postcard printed giving basic details of the product – priced at £28 on its Watsonian chassis, with hood, screen, lamp and wheel disc £4 extra. It was described as being made to 'sit in, not on'.

A little over two months later, in June 1921, Walmsley was impressing a new set of motor cycle enthusiasts with his dashing combination, this time in Blackpool as he settled into 23 King Edward Avenue with his parents and Emily. Sidecar production now recommenced in the garage at the rear of number 23, with Walmsley himself, it appears, cutting the eight panels from sheet aluminium, shaping the ash frame and then pinning and gluing the whole assembly together. Much of the trimming was done by Emily. But even though home-built, what he now called the 'Swallow' sidecar looked a thoroughly professional job and a particularly impressive device for an established rider or for a young blade to carry his girlfriend in.

There was no advertising but orders came regularly and outstripped Walmsley's leisurely production rate of, at best, one a week. Walmsley's younger neighbour was deeply impressed and Lyons bought a Swallow himself. If Lyons had not been convinced of the Swallow's commercial potential before, he was then. People would wait in the street by the 'chair' and ask where they could get one. He quickly realised that, right on his doorstep, here were the makings of a real business: a well-designed product that was so attractive and so distinctively different from its competitors that it sold itself. Just as importantly, it lay in exactly the field that he was most fascinated by – motor cycles.

Lyons reasoned that to be a commercial success the Swallow sidecar just needed to be put into quantity production and sold to the motor cycle trade country-wide, as opposed to only local private owners. This was surely his big opportunity to break away from the constraints of being employed and a major step towards him being master of his own destiny. There were no dreams of great wealth: 'I don't think making a lot of money was in my mind when I started. I had to make a living for myself and get married.'[13]

The biggest obstacle initially was Bill Walmsley. He had been through a terrible war, was not by nature an entrepreneur, and now simply wanted to have some fun. Starting a 'proper' business with a partner, with all the work and disciplines that this would entail, held no immediate attraction for him. Anyway, he had tried something similar with his brother-in-law in Stockport and it hadn't worked out. Much better that the Swallow remained a hobby. Nor did he need the money. His father not only had the means to provide him with a good allowance but was, as Lyons recorded later, 'only too pleased to have his son home from the army and enjoying himself'.

But it was through putting 'persistent pressure' on Walmsley's 'old man' that Lyons finally achieved his objective. In 1922, after long discussions in the kitchen of 23 King Edward Avenue and at motor cycle club events (he had persuaded Mr Walmsley to join as well), Lyons was successful. Thomas Walmsley 'came round to the idea that it would be a good thing for his son to employ his time to some more useful purpose'. After all, William was now approaching 30 years of age and Emily was soon to have a child. Finally, probably not without some misgivings, William Walmsley agreed to his father's wishes. A partnership there would be and the Swallow sidecar would be put into series production.

The 'ways and means' were left to Lyons – as they often would be. Although Walmsley senior was a relatively wealthy man (easily able, and presumably willing, to have bankrolled the operation's start-up), as a first principle Lyons was determined that 'it must be a 50/50 project'. So after 'much talk', the enterprise was financed by a £1,000 overdraft at Williams Deacon's Bank in Blackpool, the facility being guaranteed to the extent of £500 each by the two fathers.

Lyons senior might not have been as wealthy as Walmsley but that £500 equates to some £12,000 today so he was obviously moderately well off; he also had useful local contacts and these he willingly made available to the partners: one was a Blackpool solicitor, T. E. Jesson. When the two budding manufacturers – probably in mid-August 1922 – asked Jesson to draw up a partnership agreement, he immediately pointed out a snag: Lyons was not yet 21 and, until his birthday on 4 September, would not be able to sign any legal documents such as the intended partnership agreement. This was a considerable disappointment, especially to the go-getting Lyons who was itching to get stuck into the new enterprise. However, 'we decided to carry on as though the partnership agreement had been signed; nevertheless I was not altogether happy.'

Premises were the next essential item and again, Lyons senior contributed by referring his son to an accountant, Mr Haworth. He in turn recommended they speak to a Mr Outhwaite, 'who owned an electrical appliance business which he ran in a little factory in Bloomfield Road, some three hundred yards [270 metres] from the Blackpool Football Club'. It was a tall, gabled and somewhat unprepossessing building but the two upper floors of number 5 were not being used by Outhwaite and were available to let. Lyons felt things were now progressing: 'This was a heaven-sent opportunity and so we decided to take it.'[14] However, with the partnership agreement still not ratified the lease could not be concluded officially and it was only through Haworth's influence that they were allowed in several days early, to clean up and prepare the working areas.

Monday 4 September duly arrived but the partnership agreement still had not been signed and sealed. This did not happen until 21 November, with the official commencement of the partnership being backdated – not to Lyons's birthday but to a week after, Monday 11 September. The reason is not known. Possibly, despite his misgivings about the delay, Lyons was so involved in the start-up of the business that neither he nor Walmsley found the time to visit Jesson for the formal signing. Perhaps they worked on a draft agreement dated 11 September while the solicitors worded the final document, or maybe the local bank took a while to have the overdraft facility cleared by its head office.

As the first legal cornerstone of the multi-billion pound business that is today Jaguar Cars, the 'Agreement of Partnership' between 'Mr William Walmsley and Mr William Lyons' is worth examining in detail. The document was just eight pages long and written in surprisingly straightforward English. It recorded that the two men would become partners 'under the name and style of "Walmsley and Lyons" [note that Lyons, some ten years Walmsley's junior, is the second placed name] and to carry on as such Partners the trade or business of Body Manufacturers for Motor Sidecars subject to the following terms and conditions...'

It stated that the business would be carried on at 5 Bloomfield Road, Blackpool 'and at such other place or places as may be hereafter agreed upon' and confirmed that the capital of the partnership would be £500 in shares each. Profits and losses were to be shared equally.

'Each partner may draw out the sum of Ten Pounds by way of salary' and afterwards also his share of the profits.

The following few clauses outlined book-keeping procedures (the books could be examined at any reasonable time by either party) and although the agreement stated 'Either Partner shall engage or dismiss' any employee or enter into any bond or similar without the consent of the other Partner, almost certainly the Jessons clerk slipped up here and missed the 'N' from 'Either'! Certainly the next clause went on to say that *neither* partner could incur liabilities exceeding £20 without the consent of the other. The signatures of both parties were required for cheques.

A further clause, which no doubt Lyons had cause to mull over later on, stated: 'Each partner shall devote the whole of his time and attention to the Partnership business...' The agreement continued with definitions of values, including the shares – 'the Profits gained during the preceding one year shall be deemed to be the value of the goodwill of the business'. Should either partner fail to meet the required conditions, the defaulting partner was prohibited from engaging in any similar business within 20 miles (32km).

Of course, all this had been agreed in advance between the two men, including paragraph three whereby Lyons was obliged to pay Walmsley the sum of £50 'in respect of and the agreed value of the benefit of Registration number 682070 now registered in the name of the said William Walmsley in respect of a sidecar, the benefit of such registration thereby becoming a partnership asset'. But at Jessons on that Tuesday in November, there was one surprise in store for Lyons: 'I received a bit of a shock at the signing when Walmsley produced a bill for his tools, for which I was to pay half; this was quite fair, but I had so little money that the twenty odd pounds I was to find out of my own pocket seemed a large sum.'[15] One can imagine William Walmsley thinking: 'Well, young Lyons, you wanted a partnership; now you have one...'

Nowhere on the agreement was the name Swallow mentioned but right from the start the partnership traded as the Swallow Sidecar Company; the exact day can only be guessed. Although the partnership began officially on 11 September, the company's first cash-book (remarkably, it survives at Jaguar) started on Wednesday 20 September. The very first entry was a deposit of £3 10s (£3.50) for a sidecar. The Swallow Sidecar Company was in business, with Lyons just a couple of weeks into his 22nd year.

As well as fixing the premises and the paperwork, Lyons and Walmsley needed to recruit the necessary labour. A trimmer, Arthur

Hollis, had already been used by Walmsley at 23 King Edward Avenue and was retained part time on a piecework basis, while an advertisement in the local paper brought Richard Binns – by a day or two the company's first full-time employee.

Dick Binns was a joiner with pattern-making experience and his job would be to make the sidecar body frames – after he had been told to construct the workbenches! Dick Binns was 'a very good man' according to Lyons and his wage was '£3 18s 4d [£3.92], less 1/8½d [8p] for a National Insurance stamp'. He was to stay for five years.

However, the necessary tinsmith to work with the aluminium panels proved elusive. Finally, Lyons approached a young man he knew at a local tinsmiths, where he had taken motor cycle petrol tanks to be mended. The shop owner was not at all pleased and Lyons, showing early on his acute sense of fair play, felt uncomfortable. 'It was the first and last poaching I was to do,'[16] he stated afterwards. Joe Yates was joined by another tinsmith, Jim Greenwood, and by a painter, Cyril Marshall (whom Walmsley insisted on calling 'Sam').

The final member of that little team formed during those first few days at Bloomfield Road was a 'boy'. He was given the title of apprentice but 15-year-old Harry Gill received no formal craft training, instead picking up skills from the older men with whom he worked. Harry's tasks also included running errands for Lyons: 'When I started I used to have to take the cheques to his father in the music shop at Bank Hey Street to sign, because he wasn't old enough to sign [them] himself.'[17] This certainly indicates that activities were under way well prior to either Lyons's 21st birthday or the official commencement date.

An office was needed and a corner about 6ft by 8ft (1.8m by 2.4m) was partitioned off. 'Walmsley built a desk and Hollis covered it with Rexine,' Lyons recalled. 'We acquired a second-hand typewriter and a filing cabinet, printed notepaper, optimistically invoices, cash book and sales ledger.'[18] The helpful Haworth supplied accountancy services and later on was able to recommend the first female employee: 'a Miss Atkinson, a funny little thing – very prim with thick glasses…she could not only do shorthand and typing but understood the books even if she did them rather untidily.'[19] Lyons himself kept the cash-book at first.

The basic infrastructure was now in place but this meant wages to be paid and running expenses to be met. It was vital that the sidecars should be sold in relative quantity, the business plan being based on at least ten a week. Exactly how this could be achieved fell to Lyons.

The division of duties between the partners meant that Walmsley, with his hands-on knowledge of sidecar construction, supervised manufacture and the other practical aspects of the business (he even coachlined the sidecars himself). This left Lyons – already showing a flair for organisation – with pretty much everything else: the office paperwork, wages, sales, advertising, and promotions.

Lyons's earliest attempts at the last two were undistinguished. In virtually the first week of business he fell victim to 'a very enterprising young man' by the name of McDougal, who persuaded him to take advertising space in the local Booth's Café menu; Lyons paid cash in advance. 'After many visits to the café and failing to see our advert, I enquired from the manager when the menu with our advert would appear, and was advised that no space had been booked.' A small annoyance only, maybe, but Lyons's sense of rightness and efficient use of money is revealed when he recorded: 'I kept a look-out for MacDougal for many years but never found him or our £4.'[20]

The first Swallow catalogue was an even greater disaster, for not only did the local printer make a 'shocking job' of it but also the wretched publication nearly brought about a court case. 'We had a letter from a firm of solicitors demanding the withdrawal of the catalogue as the "device" of a swallow, as they termed it, was an infringement of their client's registered device "The Swift Motor Co., Coventry".' On advice from Mr Jesson the catalogue was withdrawn, 'which was perhaps as well as it compelled us to do something better'.[21] Although variable in scope, some of the Swallow, and later SS and Jaguar, sales catalogues were magnificent in appearance and quality. For the first few years, before an advertising manager was hired, it is fairly certain that Lyons himself had a hand in their design.

The original catalogue had been mailed, together with an introductory letter, to most of the prominent advertisers in *The Motor Cycle* magazine. (Lyons guessed this was how Swift had got hold of one.) Additionally, Lyons placed an eighth-page advertisement in both this paper and *Motor Cycling*. 'The response to these appearing were quite encouraging and I followed up by doing a trip round the biggest motor cycle dealers, so we got off the ground, so to speak...'[22]

Lyons also felt it imperative to display the Swallow sidecar at the Motor Cycle Show in London (due to open on 25 November), mainly because it would introduce the sidecar to the trade. But again, the learning curve was steep. A polite reply was received from Mr Timerick on behalf of the organisers stating that Swallow needed to be a member of the British Cycle and Motor Cycle Manufacturers and Traders Union – and anyway, applications for stand space had closed the previous April...

But Lyons was not deterred and 'without delay set off on my Brough to Coventry' with Walmsley to persuade Mr Timerick just how important it was that Swallow should be allowed to exhibit at Olympia. Timerick, later to become a 'kind and helpful friend,' eventually agreed that the rules could be bent if a Show stand became available. 'I think he must have taken pity on us because we achieved what we would most certainly have failed to do in following years...'[23]

Fortunately, a last minute cancellation meant that a space did become vacant; Stand 180 was a tiny corner plot but that 'did not temper our jubilation'. It was an exciting, if exhausting, occasion for Lyons and Walmsley. 'I will always remember the night before the opening day,' Lyons reminisced in 1947, 'polishing the sidecars by the light of a policeman's lantern well after ten o'clock when the hall lights were extinguished, and being ordered out by Mr Phillips, the exhibition manager.'[24] No doubt tired but elated, they returned to Mrs Shirley's digs in Russell Square. (Mrs Shirley was a 'dear old Irish woman' Lyons had stayed with when attending the 1919 show for Brown & Mallalieu.)

The show, 'crowded to suffocation,' was a success and the partners, as they pointed their Brough Superiors towards Blackpool some 250 miles (420km) away, could feel well satisfied with their efforts. But they came back to the usual cash-flow problems of a rapidly growing but under-financed small firm. Lyons found it 'a desperate struggle after having financed the show, material stocks, and work in progress, to raise the wages each Saturday, and many a time I had to ask for the manager when I went to the bank, and persuade him to advance the money on the strength of our assets.'[25]

An examination of that first cash-book, almost certainly written up in Lyons's own hand, very much supports this: the show appearance was certainly costly with BCMT Union membership £7, stand space £4 5s 6d (£4.28), lighting £7 7s (£7.35), Mrs Shirley's accommodation £9 4s (£9.20), plus £50 for various other expenses, all adding up to more than £77. There were endless other bills to pay, too: wood, iron, sheet aluminium, tyres, and electrical equipment for the workmen.

Although that first show appearance might have produced some good contacts, it certainly didn't result in a stream of orders. The pressure on the overdraft became ever more relentless: income for

September had been £4 8s 5d (£4.42), with outgoings of £200 14s 6d (£200.73). In October just £30 came in, with £173 11s 8d (£173.58) spent. For November, when the partners were preoccupied with the Motor Cycle Show, income was zero! In fact, it wasn't until after the 1923 show that the cash flow situation began to ease. Lyons had good reason to be grateful to the accommodating Mr Francis at Williams and Deacon's Bank.

The next 12 months saw much hard work: 'Walmsley and I put our heads together to produce a range of models' (just two were on offer in those first few months) and more people were taken on. These included several who would form Lyons's first team and become key figures in the Jaguar organisation later. In April 1923 Harry Teather joined, starting as a 15-year-old general assistant; ultimately he became Purchasing Director of Jaguar. Arthur Whittaker arrived the same year. Aged 17 and a former Blackpool Grammar School boy, he had been an apprentice at the local Imperial Garage and was taken on as Swallow's first salesman. He covered many miles on motor cycle and sidecar visiting the trade but quite soon was put on to purchasing. Later, at Jaguar, he became Deputy Chairman.

Swallow had a much more impressive stand at the 1923 Motor Cycle Show and, significantly, Swallow sidecars were now to be seen on the stands of various leading motor cycle manufacturers including Brough, DOT and Matador. This was a 'tremendous help' because it gave Swallow great exposure without the cost of transporting the 'chairs' to Olympia.

Just as importantly, Lyons was extending his range of contacts among both trade and press. He found a particular friend in Raymond Bailey, Northern Manager of Iliffe & Sons Ltd, which published *The Autocar* and *The Motor Cycle* – two of Britain's leading weeklies. Bailey spent much time introducing Lyons to dealers from the North and it was through him that Lyons met Advertising Manager Claude Wallis (later to become Chairman of Iliffe) and G. Geoffrey Smith, then Managing Editor of *The Autocar*. 'These were the earliest friends I made,'[26] recorded Lyons. Similar close friendships were to spring up with those at Iliffe's rival publishing house, Temple Press. In turn, the serious-faced but energetic young Lancastrian was himself becoming a recognised figure on the scene.

It was probably at the 1923 show that Lyons had something of a run-in with George Brough, a similarly strong-minded individual. Lyons and Walmsley were already convinced enthusiasts for his high quality motor cycles, introduced in 1919; one of the few indulgences the partners had allowed themselves during the first couple of years in business were new Brough Superiors. Two identical SS80s were supplied to Swallow on 2 February 1923 and were replaced by two of the same model on 26 April 1924. (Brough devotees included Lawrence of Arabia who owned eight between 1922 and 1933. He is reported to have said to Mr Brough: 'If there was a better bike, I should buy it!')

For the 1923 show George Brough wanted a Swallow sidecar to display with his 'star exhibit' – the new SS100. This was excellent news for Swallow but 'it caused us a lot of anxiety because George was quite fanatically critical,' related Lyons. The complication was that he required the sidecar to be painted at a time when the products were normally finished in polished aluminium. It was with some apprehension that they delivered the specially painted and trimmed sidecar to the Brough stand. The anxiety was 'not without reason – we had barely arrived at Olympia...when I was faced with a storm of abuse from George, who had always been most friendly.' He told Lyons that the colour was wrong and the West of England cloth trim, which had replaced the usual Rexine, was dirty. 'How did I think he could put this on his beautiful S.S. 100?'

Fortunately Lyons had brought along the pattern they had worked to and everything was in fact to specification. The 'wrong paint' turned out to be the artificial lighting at Olympia, while the cloth trim was easily cleaned with petrol. Mr Brough was happy 'and the Brough Superior stand, with our sidecar in pole position, was the greatest attraction of the show'.[27]

So it didn't seem too bad when on the way home Lyons (with helpers Whittaker and William Docking, who was to become Lyons's brother-in-law) broke down. They had to remove a piston on the Talbot borrowed from Lyons's father and limped home on three cylinders during the early hours.

By now, the Swallow Sidecar Company was truly on its feet and the Bloomfield Road factory was 'a hive of activity'. Sidecars were being sent all over the country and, increasingly, to Europe. Additional space was taken in two other local buildings but sales would shortly be constrained by lack of space – a surprising achievement in view of the fact that the artificial boom, which had followed the Armistice, had long gone and Britain's economy was becoming increasingly depressed.

Things were certainly going well enough for Lyons to consider marriage. In 1923 he became engaged to Greta Brown, the daughter of Albert Jenner Brown, a schoolmaster in Cuddington near Thame. The Browns had moved to Blackpool when Greta's grandfather, who had been headmaster of St John's Church of England School in Blackpool, died and Albert Brown took over his job. Greta herself became a teacher, joining the staff at the Northlands High School

Lyons had met Greta in 1921 at a school friend's party. She later recalled: 'It was one of those silly dances where you exchanged labels and danced with whoever had your counterpart...and he couldn't dance at all – it was terrible! The first time he asked me to go out with him was pillion riding on the back of his bike and I had to meet him at a certain place, and I remember my parents said, "Why doesn't he call for you here?" and he explained afterwards – the bike would only start at the top of a hill going down, so that was why we had to meet there.'[28]

The wedding, on 15 September 1924 at St Stephen-on-the-Cliffs, was described by the *Blackpool Gazette* as 'quiet' and 'of more than usual local interest'. Both families were extremely well known, said the report, and 'the bride and bridegroom are popular with a wide circle of friends'. Lyons's schoolmate Arnold Breakell was the best man.

The honeymoon took the form of a motor tour of Scotland in the same Talbot 10/23 tourer that had let Lyons down the previous year. It did not fail this time although, on an impulse, Lyons bought a puppy on the journey up. The animal caused chaos at hotel stopovers and in the end was sent home by train but this did not diminish the couple's lifelong devotion to dogs.

On returning to Blackpool – rather earlier than intended because 'our money did not last long enough' – the newlyweds initially set up home in a flat, though shortly afterwards they moved to a bungalow (Westbourne) in Bispham Road. William and Emily Walmsley also moved to Bispham Road from Handley Road.

In 1924 Swallow first entered competitions. A cornerstone of the local motor cycle club, Lyons actively competed on various machines, although never with his own sidecar. He was, however, fascinated by the 37-mile (60km) Isle of Man road course, closed each year for the Tourist Trophy meeting, and when a sidecar TT was introduced in 1923 he regretted that Swallow didn't have a competition model to enter. It was irksome that Hughes of Birmingham, one of Swallow's chief rivals, did.

The next year, however, an opportunity arose. Swallow had purchased an oil-cooled Matador motor cycle for Whittaker direct from its maker in Preston and Lyons had come to know Matador's Managing Director, Lewis. So when in 1924 Lewis entered a Matador-Blackburn in the sidecar TT, Lyons persuaded him to specify a Swallow 'chair' instead of his usual Hughes. Privately, Lyons was 'not at all sure we could do something better or even as good'!

Accordingly, a special competition model was produced by Swallow, of which just three would be made; it did in fact turn out well and during practice for the Tourist Trophy proved entirely satisfactory. Lyons was too busy to go over to the Island before practice but when he did arrive, he 'was furious to find that a Hughes sidecar had been fitted to the Matador for the race... I found this out before I had seen Lewis and I immediately went to his hotel to accuse him of breaking his agreement with me...'

Lewis claimed his racing manager had insisted on it; Lyons accused him of being 'very naive' and stated that the outfit had gone well in practice and he should stick to his agreement. 'To do the poor man justice he agreed... I never heard the reaction but I have no doubt someone was on the fiddle.'[29] This episode showed Lyons the commercial hazards of motor sport and revealed his already highly developed sense of fair play. To Lyons, an agreement was always an agreement, even when it was not in writing.

The Matador-Swallow combination finished a respectable third, though a single special competition model failed to finish in the 1925 (and last sidecar) TT. For several years afterwards, Swallow's competition sidecars (some known within the factory as the 'Scrapper') performed well with various riders and in 1926 Dougal Marchant took a clean sweep of 16 world sidecar records, during which his Chater-Lea-Swallow combination achieved 86.35mph (138.96kmh) for the flying kilometre (1,093 yards). It all helped sharpen the Swallow image.

By 1926 it was becoming clear that Bloomfield Road and the various annexes were now, four years on, completely inadequate. More than that, Lyons was showing his instincts for always pressing ahead: he now had his sights on something more – coachbuilding.

Triggering this particular ambition was the Austin Seven, introduced in 1922 and (like the Mini 37 years later) a 'real' car in miniature. Lyons had bought an early example soon after he had married, though it was not his first car – that had been a temperamental Buckingham purchased from a sales representative when he had been working for Brown & Mallalieu. The little Austin's box-like shape hardly did Herbert Austin's 'masterpiece' justice, Lyons considered. Harry Gill recalled him being most impressed by a pretty, round-tailed Gordon England-bodied two-seater Austin Seven that turned up at the Bloomfield Road works one day. It showed what was possible with the car and Lyons became 'fascinated' with the prospect of a Swallow-bodied Seven.

But any thought of entering the coachbuilding trade, even on the most modest level, was out of the question at Bloomfield Road. Then in the late summer of 1926 he heard that a building erected purposely for coachbuilding was coming on to the market in Blackpool's North Shore district. The previous occupant, Joseph Street, had run into trouble and, after being used briefly by the Jackson Brothers, the property was now up for sale. Ideal though it might have been, it appeared to be beyond the partnership's means. Then, 'out of the blue, Walmsley's father, who had sold his prosperous coal business and was looking for somewhere to invest the proceeds, heard of our interest in this property and offered to lease it to us.'[30] The partners jumped at this offer 'with grateful thanks'.

So Walmsley senior bought 41 Cocker Street and rented it to the partnership; the lease, dated 9 September 1926, was for 21 years at an annual rent of £325. The move from Bloomfield Road was accomplished over a weekend – the cost of using removers was avoided thanks to the unofficial help of the driver and truck, which on the Friday had delivered new sidecar chassis frames from Haywards of Birmingham!

After the narrow confines of Bloomfield Road, the Cocker Street works, about 72ft by 45ft (21.9m by 13.7m), seemed vast. The main sidecar assembly area was on the ground floor along with the coachpainting booth. On the building's upper floor would shortly be Jack Beardsley's small smithy, accessed by stairs and a hefty open lift quite capable of taking the largest car. (Joseph Street had installed it for buses.) Emblazoned on the building's red brick exterior in capital letters was the business's new title: the 'Swallow Side Car & Coach Building Co.'.

While car trimming and bodywork repairs were taken on, the coachbuilding aspect of the title had to be justified. As this was 'an art about which I knew nothing,' Lyons's priority was to recruit 'someone who did'.[31] Interestingly, even at this initial stage he resolved to find a man 'with factory experience in quantity production'. Clearly Lyons intended that Swallow bodies were going to be made in series following the great names in coachbuilding – Hooper, Park Ward, H. J. Mulliner, James Young and so on – rather than as one-offs to individual customer requirements. Relative volume should result in lower selling prices and thus greater demand: that was to be a mainstream Lyons tenet.

Meanwhile, the sidecar business was doing fine and would have satisfied most people: Swallow was now the country's leading brand with over half a dozen different models on offer, the most popular, the Model 4, selling in its hundreds every month. 'But for the Model 4,' stated Swallow apprentice George Lee, 'I don't think we'd ever have had a Jaguar car. This model paid the wage bill for the early development of the Austin Swallow.'[32] That, in fact, was the next big leap forward for Lyons, who, though still aged only 25, was now co-managing a business with an annual turnover, in today's terms, approaching £1m.

CHAPTER 2

SWALLOW ALIGHTS
IN COVENTRY

The seaside resort of Blackpool, though it did have one or two small coachbuilding businesses, was not exactly crowded with men capable of designing and building motor car bodies. So shortly after moving into Cocker Street during September 1926, Lyons advertised in papers appearing in the heart of the British motor industry – Birmingham, Coventry, and Wolverhampton. The copy described the jig-making and panelling skills required, using 'jargon I made up after nosing about and finding out what was required,' admitted Lyons. With Lyons knowing so little about coachbuilding, things could have gone badly wrong but he was fortunate that the first applicant interviewed seemed 'almost to good to be true'.[1] Cyril Holland, then aged 34, had served an apprenticeship with Lanchester (one of Britain's oldest and most respected car manufacturers) and worked at a number of Midland firms including Morris. However, he came from the Mead & Deakin factory, which was then making bodies for Rhode cars.

Holland, it seems, answered the advertisement almost out of curiosity. Lyons questioned him closely and outlined his plans to manufacture bodies. 'Holland had the answers,' Lyons recounted with enthusiasm years later. 'He said if we could give him a sketch, he could frame up a body with the appropriate jigs for making the panels, panel the body, and finish it ready for paint.'[2] Holland was asked if he could start the next week.

Several other bodymakers came with him from Mead & Deakin and before the end of 1926 the Austin Swallow project was under way (though the first car bodied by Holland at Swallow is thought to be a Talbot-Darracq, a sand-racing casualty). Lyons had persuaded Parkers, the Austin dealer that already sold the Swallow sidecar range from its Bolton and Manchester premises, to supply him with an Austin Seven running chassis. This was against Austin policy but the 'carrot' for Stanley Parker was the promise of a northern distributorship for Swallow-bodied cars, which Lyons made it plain he was determined to build. On 21 January 1927 the invoice for

£114 5s 0d (£114.25), including carriage, was sent discreetly to Lyons's home address at Bispham Road.

It was while living there that Lyons became a father; his daughter Patricia was born on 23 April 1927. Connie Dickson (later Mrs Teather), a young secretary at the factory, remembered seeing Pat as a babe-in-arms there – a beautiful child with fair, curly hair.

Lyons found Holland a joy to work with. He 'not only lived up to his claims, but proved to be one of the quickest men to carry out his job that I have ever known. What delighted and impressed me the most was his ability to work with nothing more than a rough sketch of what he had to do.'[3] In Cyril Holland, Lyons had found someone who could interpret his ideas; Holland would listen to what Lyons had to say, look at his outline sketches, and almost instinctively create in metal the shape Lyons had envisaged.

The Austin Seven Swallow two-seater was therefore the first instance of the collaborative process by which Lyons would eventually produce some of the most beautiful cars the world has ever seen. Lyons usually knew to the nearest ¼in (6mm) what he wanted but he was incapable of producing anything like a styling drawing, nor could he work with his hands. He could only direct and suggest, relying on an empathy with skilled craftsmen to reproduce physically what he required.

Not that the little car which emerged from Cocker Street looked exactly as Lyons had expected. Maybe a little had been lost in the translation of Holland's patterns into aluminium panels by Musgrove & Green in Birmingham – especially the rounded tail, which had a slightly drooping look. 'I must say my spirits fell. I began to wonder whether I really had the ability to guide Holland to produce what was in my imagination.'[4]

Nevertheless, the body was put into production and the first announcement of the Austin Swallow two-seater appeared in *The Autocar* of 20 May 1927. The price was a modest £175 and, together with good proportions and bright paintwork schemes, made it a competitive offering amongst the growing number of other special-bodied Austin Sevens on sale.

Lyons had certainly chosen a good sector to be in. Fuelled by the popular Austin Seven, sales in the up to 8hp bracket – which really meant engines up to about 750cc (45cu in) – were rising sharply in Britain and would jump from 25,966 (16.3 per cent of all UK registrations) in 1927 to 42,199 (25.4 per cent) in 1929. Initially Swallow contributed little to these totals; hardly more than a car a day left Cocker Street during those early months.

Lyons now set about marketing the new product. Parker was signed up and so was his old firm Brown & Mallalieu in Blackpool but there was the rest of the country to be considered. Accordingly he made an appointment to see Frank Hallam in Birmingham; Hallam had bought a Model 1 back in March 1923 and subsequently had become a Swallow sidecar distributor in this key area. However, when Lyons arrived at the due time with the prototype Swallow Seven, he was told Hallam was 'out' and no one knew when he would be back. After an hour Lyons, tired of waiting, decided to go down the road to P. J. Evans, Birmingham distributor for Standard since 1912. In 1927 it was being run by Stanley Rodway and Norman Steeley, who proved to be 'most enthusiastic and agreed to give me a contract for 50 cars'. In return Lyons gave them exclusive distribution rights for Swallow over a large area of the Midlands. P. J. Evans became 'one of the most loyal and successful'[5] distributors for Swallow, SS and Jaguar; Hallam, said to have been in the pub, had missed the chance of a lifetime.

Next, the all-important territory around London and in the South needed representation. None of the sidecar outlets there was suitable and so Lyons contacted Henlys Ltd at 91 Great Portland Street, London. This turned out to be one of the most important business moves Lyons ever made.

H. G. Henly & Co had been founded by 'Bertie' Henly, who was ten years older than Lyons, in 1917 and shortly after starting the business he went into partnership with Frank Hough, formerly a motor cycle trader in Walsall, near Birmingham; both agreed that 'Henlys' sounded the better name for the business. By the time Lyons made his approach in January 1928, Henlys Ltd was well established with concessions for numerous makes including Austin. However, it was the firm's extensive advertising for one of Lyons's favourite cars, Alvis, that had caught his eye. Here was a thrusting and expanding business that appeared ideal to handle the Austin Swallow in London.

Not knowing the partners, Lyons first contacted Charles Hayes, who had made life uncomfortable for him at Brown & Mallalieu; Lyons discovered he was now General Manager of Henlys. Evidently there were no hard feelings between the two men and Lyons wrote to Charlie Hayes asking if Henlys would be interested in selling the new Austin Swallow. Hayes reacted immediately, telegraphing a surprised Lyons with the request that he personally be appointed as sole agent in London 'and would I meet him with a car in Fitzroy Square two days hence'. Lyons took care over his words when replying, making plain that he had contacted Hayes in his capacity as sales manager of Henlys as 'it was their resources I was most interested in'. By the time they duly met in Fitzroy Square, Hayes had undergone a change of mind. Realising that a 'lone deal' with Swallow was unlikely, he had decided to act privately as a middleman. 'It was some years,' wrote Lyons disapprovingly later, 'before I found that he was paid quite a large sum for what he claimed was his introduction of the Austin Swallow. In my opinion, as an employee of Henlys he was entitled to nothing for what he did. He was already getting paid a substantial salary.'[6]

Hayes had already primed Henly and Hough when they met Lyons at Great Portland Street later that day and they had a ready-made proposition for him. To Lyons's astonishment, Frank Hough said Henlys would place an order for 500 chassis with the Austin Motor Company, from which Swallow would produce 20 finished cars a week. Lyons, probably expecting a deal along the lines of P. J. Evans's 50 cars if he was fortunate, was completely taken aback. However, any delight was tempered by alarm, as scheduled production of the Austin Seven Swallow was five a week with little thought of any increase. The situation called for steady nerves and Lyons, still only 27, decided he 'must show no sign of inability to meet such a programme and that a way must be found...'[7]

Over lunch other facets of the deal were discussed: in return for the order, Henlys required distribution rights 'for the whole of the territory south of a line drawn across the map from Bristol to The Wash'. As Henly and Hough enthusiastically discoursed on their plans to appoint dealers and embark on an advertising campaign, Lyons began to feel more at ease. Here was the greatest opportunity the company had been offered since its inception. It just had to be taken up; that there was nothing in writing yet did not deter him at all. (The formal agreement with Henlys was signed on 18 January 1928, with Henlys receiving a 25 per cent discount on the Austin Seven Swallow two-seater catalogue price; the first delivery of an Austin Swallow to Henlys was on 21 January 1928.)

No doubt the little Austin Swallow seemed to sing as it travelled the A5 on the 200-mile (321km) journey to Blackpool. The six or more hours it must have taken – the car was hardly capable of much over 45mph (72kmh) – gave Lyons some valuable thinking-time. What would he say to Walmsley and how could they quadruple production?

Walmsley's reaction was predictable: he considered Lyons 'mad' and at first refused to co-operate with the expansion programme. He probably felt Lyons was running out of control and that his over-ambition would ruin the company. Cyril Holland, though, 'grasped the situation quickly' and, with the help of further workers brought in from the Midlands, production of the Austin Seven Swallow two-seater was raised to some 12 a week by mid-1928. One limiting factor at Cocker Street was the painting process; cellulose had yet to be adopted and the varnish took over a day to dry.

Gearing-up production achieved economies of scale, though, as increasingly Swallow was able to purchase parts direct from the manufacturers rather than local wholesalers. Much of Lyons's time was taken up in meeting an increasing stream of representatives but this helped him to begin establishing a network of friends and contacts within the industry that would stand the company in good stead over the coming years. Several of these visitors became friends too and some went right to the top like Ray Brookes, the Guest, Keen & Nettlefolds representative. Later Lord Brookes, he became Chairman of GKN, still today one of Britain's largest companies and a Jaguar supplier.

Lyons was also steadily building up his own team as well, including in the office (where Walmsley rarely worked and usually visited only to talk). 'Not only was I spending quite a lot of each day with Holland on the shop floor, but I was dealing with all the correspondence involved – sales, purchases, advertising, in fact the whole of the administration,'[8] recorded Lyons. He even designed the stylised wings that graced the early catalogues.

Fortunately, Lyons was increasingly able to leave young Miss Fenton to handle much of the office work. Alice Fenton, aged 18, had joined shortly before the company moved from Bloomfield Road; she had been working in the Lyons's music shop but Minnie Lyons thought she was capable of better things and recommended her to her son. Alice (full of personality, with vivid colouring and striking red hair) had considered taking a job offered to her by the Blackpool opera house but chose Swallow instead. This decision benefited Swallow, and later Jaguar, greatly. Alice turned out to be 'a demon for work and she was no more satisfied than I was myself to go home at night until we had got through all the necessary day's work, and this was to go on for the next 25 years,'[9] wrote Lyons. Miss Fenton, as she was always known, still managed to enjoy a vibrant social life; her main hobby became ballroom dancing because, she said, it was the only thing that was available after she finished work!

Arthur Whittaker was now office-based; following the appointment of distributors countrywide, he no longer had to put in the miles selling. Instead, Lyons placed him in charge of material purchases, a field in which he was to excel. From April 1928 Whittaker had his own secretary too: Constance Dickson. This shy little 17-year-old from nearby Fleetwood had recently lost her first job and queued as usual in the library to read the 'situations vacant' column in the local paper. (Her family, like many others at the time, was too poor to buy its own copy.) There she spotted an advertisement for an office junior at Swallow.

She well remembered being interviewed in the little office by Lyons; he was wearing plus-fours and had a 'very superior and autocratic' manner. After giving her some peremptory typing, decimal and fraction tests, he offered her 5s (25p) a week to start right away – increased to 10s (50p) when a nervous Miss Dickson managed to say that it would cost her half that amount to travel the ten miles (16km) from Fleetwood. Afterwards she learned that on the previous Saturday the office had been flooded with applicants. 'I can only think that as usual he was very, very busy...and when I passed the test it was an easy way to finish the matter so he could turn his attention to more important business.'[10] Lyons told the staff that 'at least she didn't smell of scent'.

Another Cocker Street recruit was local lad George Lee, just 14. He had joined Swallow as an apprentice coachbuilder in January 1927 and was soon working with Fred Perry, one of the Midlanders. He was to stay with the company almost 50 years. Lee's recorded memories of those early days at Swallow cast valuable light on early working practices there. Questioned about quality control, he replied: 'it existed from the operator. No such thing as an inspector – you were responsible and you knew it!' Each body number would be recorded at the works against the name of the man who made it 'and if it came back and there was anything wrong with it, he felt really guilty'.[11] Later, maintaining quality would be one of Lyons's worst frustrations; today, the wheel has come the full circle and assembly line workers at all Jaguar plants are once more responsible for their own quality.

The team-building continued with the enlistment of men such as Sheffield-born Jack Beardsley. He started at Easter 1928 as the company's first metal worker (actually a whitesmith); one of his first jobs was to flatten car springs to make the vehicle sit lower – the newly-introduced Morris Cowley Swallow being the first to undergo this modification. He also made all the bracketry and anything else in metal that was not bought-out. (Later it was Jack who built up Jaguar's first machine shop and was eventually in charge of 4,000 men.)

It was hard work at Cocker Street, but it was a happy place too. 'It was a free and easy "young" atmosphere,' Connie Teather (as she became in 1937) recalled, and often musical: 'Jack Beardsley, in charge of the anvil, belonged to a choir and had a very fine voice, and I enjoyed listening to the men and boys in the "shop" whistling the popular tunes.'[12] In that distant summer of 1928, *My Blue Heaven* and *Bye, Bye Blackbird* were the current hits and *The Desert Song* was among the many shows entertaining Blackpool holidaymakers. Connie teamed up with Alice Fenton to go dancing in the Winter Gardens 'in dresses two inches [5cm] above the knees...a "den of iniquity" my father called Blackpool'.[13]

To Lyons, Blackpool was now a straitjacket. With the sidecars still in full production, space was the fundamental problem. Cocker Street just didn't have the room to produce nearly enough Swallow open two-seaters for Henlys, let alone produce the Swallow Seven saloon, which Henlys now also wanted, or seriously pursue the potential which Lyons was sure existed for putting bodies on other makes of chassis. Not only that but Austin Seven chassis were arriving at Blackpool railway station a couple of blocks away 'in embarrassing numbers' and the stationmaster was 'complaining bitterly' to Lyons about the congestion in his goods yard. They did their best to collect as many as could be accommodated at Cocker Street. 'Why we didn't run into trouble with the police I will never know, for we brought the chassis away from the station by hooking together six at a time and towing them behind a car. Even at peak traffic hours...'[14]

It wasn't good for customer relations either. Most cars and virtually all the sidecars were delivered via dealers (most sidecars were dispatched from the works by rail) but for those who did collect, Swallow was invariably behind; the aspiring owner would have to wait, often with number plates tucked under an arm, all day. In some cases, customers had to be asked to come back the next morning.

Export orders added to sidecar volumes as well. Some overseas agents were appointed and letters from various parts of Europe came into the Cocker Street office.

It all added up to a move into larger premises. Initially a larger building locally was considered but that would not have overcome the other problems of being in Blackpool: extended lines of communication with suppliers and, above all, the lack of skilled labour. So finally, having talked Walmsley round to the idea, in the autumn of 1928 Lyons once again headed for the centre of the British motor industry.

There is evidence that he and Walmsley made a number of sorties looking at possible sites, including a serious prospect in Wolverhampton, but the breakthrough came when Lyons checked in alone at the Queens Hotel in Hertford Street, Coventry. There, 'by good fortune,' he got into conversation with a Mr Aylesbury of the Midland Bent Timber Company who, when he learned of Lyons's mission, introduced him to Charles Odell, a leading Coventry estate agent. Odell gave him details of various factories but these were all for sale, not to let: 'my first disappointment, because we certainly had no finances with which we could purchase anything bigger than perhaps a large hencote.'[15]

One property, however, seemed particularly suitable and that, Lyons learned, was owned by the Whitmore Park Estate Company, a syndicate of Coventry businessmen. It was headed by George Gray, who as a small building contractor had made his fortune by successfully tendering to build the new Courtaulds factory in Foleshill – the district of Coventry where the Whitmore Park Estate lay. Aylesbury, obviously a mine of local information, told Lyons that Gray and his colleagues were very approachable and advised him to contact Noel Gillitt, the estate's solicitor. Lyons met Gillitt the next day. He 'promised to recount to Mr Gray my interest' and secured Lyons an appointment with the syndicate directors following a board meeting.

Gillitt took him to the estate early that day so he could examine the buildings, which were approached by a private, unsurfaced turning off Holbrook Lane, the main road from Coventry city centre about a mile (1.6km) distant. On entering the estate, the White & Poppe engine works was on the right while on the left was the Dunlop Rim & Wheel Company. (Out of sight behind Dunlop was Motor Panels, a concern that would come into Lyons's sphere later on.) A little way further down the somewhat muddy road, on the right, were the units that interested Lyons. These were in four 'double H-section' blocks 30ft (9.1m) apart, each block therefore having eight shops each of 5,000sq ft (464sq m). Commissioned by the Government as reserve shell-filling factories, they had been completed early in the First World War. The first two were occupied by Holbrook Bodies, which was making fabric bodies for Hillman, but the third and fourth were empty. The third one appeared ideal for Lyons's purposes, even though it had suffered from being disused since 1919.

Encouraged, Lyons was taken by Gillitt for lunch back at the Queens Hotel; they found the bar crowded with, Gillitt informed him, Riley distributors and dealers. All were enjoying free drinks courtesy of Riley (Coventry) Ltd, which apparently extended this hospitality to anyone visiting its factory at Foleshill. Lyons was quite shocked: 'This, I thought, seemed an extraordinary way of conducting a business... I enjoyed the conviviality of the Queens bar during my short stay at the hotel, but I made a point of paying for my own drinks.'

They returned to Whitmore Park at precisely 4pm for the meeting with the syndicate board. It must have been a fairly intimidating experience for Lyons, entering the room to be faced with all the directors sitting around the table. George Gray, the Chairman, turned out to be 'a large quite formidable looking man with large bushy eyebrows, but with a kindly voice'. Could Lyons elaborate, asked Gray, on his interest in the block the estate wished to sell not let? Outlining Swallow's history and the objectives behind the intended move to Coventry, Lyons emphasised that he could not enter into a commitment to purchase but only take a lease with an option to purchase. The reaction did not appear favourable but Gray asked for a few minutes alone with the board, 'which caused me to think there was some hope'.

It appears that for all Lyons's low-key manner – sometimes even bordering on the dour – the sincerity and conviction in the way he expressed himself convinced people that this young man with the piercing grey-blue eyes and soft Lancashire accent knew where he was going and was a person of integrity too. Evidently this was the impact that Lyons made on the Whitmore syndicate. Gray returned to Lyons and offered to make an exception to its policy. He could lease the block for three years at £1,200 per annum, with an option to purchase the freehold later. Effectively Lyons, who had only just celebrated his 28th birthday, was now in control of a full-size manufacturing unit.

Lyons departed 'highly delighted' and asked Gillitt to have dinner with him at the Queens Hotel. Gillitt, it turned out, was married to the daughter of Jack Starley of Rover and told Lyons all about the Coventry motor industry and its moguls, including Reginald Maudslay, the founder of Standard. (Not surprisingly, the useful Noel Gillitt was invited to join the Swallow Coachbuilding board in due course.) Then 'after dinner we walked around Coventry and he showed me the Cathedral and St Michael's Church. I must say that I did not think that the city had anything else of interest...'[16]

There followed a number of visits to Coventry by both Lyons and Walmsley in preparation for the move. Lyons was becoming concerned at the expense of the Queens Hotel 'but the contacts I made there were very valuable'. Soon they took cheaper lodgings in St Paul's Road, Foleshill. The factory, disused for almost ten years, needed complete refurbishment inside. Having rejected a quote of £800 by George Gray's son, Bernard, to clean and whitewash the walls, Lyons asked Walmsley to supervise it using local labour. 'As I thought, Walmsley warmed to the idea...a job I knew he would do very well as an ex-army sergeant.' The labour exchange promised to send 12 men the next morning: the extensive unemployment locally was revealed when to Lyons's astonishment, 50 men turned up. 'I used one of the Austin component part boxes which had come down from Blackpool as a desk from which each man was interviewed.'[17]

The man engaged to help organise the gang, Chandler, proved able to turn his hand to anything and was hired full time. 'Proof of his value was that we never employed an outside contractor' – another plank in Lyons's policy of minimising costs. Maintenance and even minor building work would be done 'in house' for years, sometimes using assembly line workers during seasonal slack periods (though these were much rarer at Swallow and SS than at most other motor companies of the time).

Meanwhile the lease had been drawn up by Gillitt and was signed on the night of 8 October 1928 by Lyons and Walmsley at the Queens Hotel; it was in their names, not Swallow's, so was an onerous personal commitment. The Blackpool employees first learned of the impending move when a notice was pinned to the time clock saying that the firm was going to Coventry and that those wanting to come should sign their names below.

Cyril Holland had already asked if the move was definite and it was a 'terrible blow' to Lyons when he said he did not want to leave Blackpool: Lyons was depending on him to help develop new models. Although Lyons became increasingly worried about moving without Holland, he knew it was the only way ahead for the company. About 30 employees agreed to relocate – to the recruits from the Midlands it was 'going home' – and after much preparation and careful pre-packing of car sets (so production could begin at once), the move took place between September and November 1928. The only major hitch came when, to the partners' dismay, the new electric power cable from Holbrook Lane to the factory was stolen; it cost many hundreds of pounds to replace. However, with so little machinery to be installed, completed cars were entering the dispatch shop within just two weeks.

The Blackpool people did not find Coventry particularly wonderful at first. Harry Teather, then in charge of the stores, recalled: 'I was one of the last to leave Blackpool on the 7th November 1928 and my first impression on that cold and murky November afternoon was that the Midlands in general, and Foleshill in particular, were just about the most depressing areas I had ever seen.'[18]

Jack Beardsley, trying to get his smithy going, also remembered those miserable early days at Foleshill: 'There was no lighting – nothing... I moved down on November 11th, and it was the coldest winter I'd ever experienced. It was terrible – we had no lighting and no heating. But people didn't grumble – we'd got 10-gallon [45-litre, 12-US gallon] oil drums and knocked holes in the side and filled them with coke and that was the heating system.'[19] George Lee found other contrasts with Blackpool: 'What amazed me on the first morning was...thousands of pushbikes in Holbrook Lane, for nobody had a car then.' One problem Lee and the other youngsters faced was the extra expense of living in Coventry: 'We weren't earning enough money to pay for our lodgings and our parents had to send money down to pay the landlady.'[20]

While the Blackpool brigade had to acclimatise to Coventry, some of the newly hired Coventry labour had to get used to Swallow's working practices. It was the wing fitters who brought about the first labour crisis Lyons was to face. The piecework method of payment had been carefully explained to them: each car was accompanied by a small book of tear-off vouchers – one for each pre-priced operation that a man would carry out. At the end of the day everyone handed in the vouchers they had accumulated and at the end of the week the wages clerk simply added up their value to determine how much each man was to be paid.

When the wing fitters examined their first pay packets on the Friday night, 'we encountered our very first labour trouble which amounted to a riot,' recounted Lyons. Despite repeated warnings that their rate of working was not sufficient, the men were not prepared for the effect this would have on their earnings. They expressed their displeasure by invading the stores and dumping most of the contents on the floor!

Lyons went to the stores and spoke to the man who appeared to be the leader. 'I told him that he and his colleagues had only themselves to blame, they had treated a simple job with indifference and had not even tried to earn the money available to them, even though they had taken the job knowing what they had to do to earn good wages. At first I had no success. I was met by angry growls and threats.' As a concession, Lyons said that provided they did their best the following week, he would make an exception and call the first week a training period and pay them day rate for it. He left them to talk it over.

'Monday morning saw only half of these men turn up for work and the atmosphere was very different... The mood in the shop was very good and it was clear we had lost the trouble makers. By the end of the week, each man received a wage packet which gave him well above day rate and we had no more trouble...the men were happy to find they had a good steady job with good money at a time when there was a lot of unemployment.'[21]

However, this was not the only body shop problem afflicting Swallow as it struggled to get production under way at Coventry. Lyons had been intrigued by tales from Mr Aylesbury (of the Midland Bent Timber Co) of a much quicker body-framing technique. Instead of each wooden frame being built-up individually, this new (to Swallow) scheme involved using specialised machinery to precision-make all the frame components in quantity so these could be assembled on a jig, without any additional handwork, to form a complete body – side, roof and so on – ready for panelling. What the Midland Bent Timber Co brought to this process were steam-bent curved components – much cheaper than cutting them out of solid timber or laminating. It was decided to adopt this new process from the start at Coventry.

Aylesbury had introduced Lyons to Frank Etches, a steam-bending expert. He was working at the Triumph Motor Co Ltd's new car factory but was clearly not happy there and came to work for Swallow. The necessary machines were bought and installed within ten days but the first components produced 'would not fit in the assembly jig'. There were some 60 joints and 'the problem of finding where the errors were reduced Etches to almost a nervous wreck'.[22] The major problem was that the steam-bent timbers were unbending. For a week poor Etches struggled but in the meantime the bodymakers had used up all the body kits that had been brought from Blackpool and body assembly was in danger of being halted. Then one morning Etches did not appear, having made himself ill, whereupon the bodymakers expressed the view that if they persevered with the new method it would ruin the company. Lyons appreciated their concern but was convinced by the principle of jig assembly; it had to be got right.

There was one man he was sure could sort it out – Cyril Holland. A discreet message was sent via a mutual acquaintance to Holland in Blackpool to the effect that if he happened to approach the partners with a view to returning to Swallow, this would be welcomed. Contact was established, Lyons agreed to a hefty wage hike and Holland gave up his job at the Burlingham coachworks and moved to Coventry. To Lyons's delight, within a few weeks Holland had the jig assembly process working perfectly, replacing the steam-bent timbers with parts made up from composite pieces. Now one team of bodyframers could produce one frame an hour, reducing its cost by 50 per cent and easily swamping the panellers next in line. Production of the Austin Swallow saloon and two-seater quickly rose to 40 or more a week. The whole experience taught Lyons 'not to discard or change anything until you are satisfied with its replacement'.[23] However, it was not advice to which he would always adhere!

Lyons probably took costs much more seriously than any similar company of the period. The voucher system of paying the assembly workers not only fixed the cost for building each car but also provided what today would be called a weekly 'real time' analysis of labour costs. Add in the small amount of daywork paid, material costs and overheads such as rent, rates, heating etc and Lyons always had a remarkably accurate financial picture of the business.

Assisting in such matters was the new Company Secretary recruited at Foleshill, Edward Huckvale. Formerly Cashier and Chief Clerk at Daimler, Huckvale was selected from a large number of applicants by Lyons and Walmsley, the latter impressed because he was the only one not to have walked up the muddy road to Swallow with a neatly rolled umbrella! For Lyons, Huckvale was a man who 'shared my views about the danger of extravagance, the attempted sponsors of which, in the form of so called experts, were to pass briefly in various capacities through the senior realms of the staff during the years ahead'.[24]

Lyons had been concerned that the greatly increased overheads at the new Coventry works might eat up the small profit margin on the cars: their selling prices had been based on Blackpool costings. But the first check made with Huckvale on costs at Foleshill showed that the increased output more than offset the higher overheads 'and the profit picture looked good'. The cash-flow situation was good too and was helped by Henlys purchasing the chassis on which Swallow built its cars. This, and the funding by Henlys of virtually all advertising and promotions, was acknowledged by the large margin it enjoyed as Swallow distributor – 25 per cent against a more normal 17½ per cent.

So on 29 September 1929, probably sooner than they expected, Lyons and Walmsley jointly bought from the Whitmore Park Estate

Co not only the block they were in but also the empty fourth block further along. The price was £18,000 for the two, raised by means of a mortgage with the Coventry Permanent Building Society. Swallow now had 80,000sq ft (7,432sq m) of floor space.

However, these advances did not make Lyons complacent. 'I realised that there would be nothing easier than to allow non-productive costs to grow...so the strictest possible control was placed on every requisition.' For years he was fond of quoting as an example how at this time, when asked to approve the purchase of a new wheelbarrow by Harry Teather, he rejected it with the instruction to 'make do for the time being with a bucket'. This was not meanness for its own sake: the objective was to keep costs down, allowing the cars to be priced as low as possible and so 'stimulate the demand'. This remained one of Lyons's fundamental principles, which over the years guided his whole thinking.

The strategy was very suited to the late 1920s and early 1930s and helps to explain why Swallow flourished at a time when Britain's economy was fragile. By 1929 the country's manufacturing output had just about struggled back to 1913 levels, only to be badly hit by the worldwide recession which followed the Wall Street crash of October 1929. Unemployment in the early 1930s approached three million in Britain but, for those in work, the situation was not too desperate. To some of these, a Swallow offered highly individual motoring at an affordable price and perhaps provided an attractive and face-saving route for anyone in 'reduced circumstances' needing to trade down. The pretty little Austin Swallow also appealed to girls – as *The Autocar* said in 1930: '...there is no wonder that so many youthful belles find a Swallow just the very thing to make life complete and well worth living.' It has been said that the depression actually helped Swallow and there is probably some truth in this assertion.

With the return of Cyril Holland, Lyons now had his ace experimental body man back and new models of various sizes, all similar in style to the Austin Swallow Seven saloon, appeared in quite rapid succession. These used chassis from Fiat, Standard, Swift (John Price of Swift chose never to mention the unfortunate catalogue dispute!) and ultimately (from January 1931) Wolseley. These opportunities were often suggested by Henlys, to which advertising and promotions were still left (it even supplied road-test cars to the press). Floated in 1928 as a public company, Henlys continued to be 'magnificent in their support' as Lyons put it, backing Swallow's first Motor Show appearance in October 1929 with advertising in *The Autocar* and *The Motor*. (At the time of the 1928 show, the Austin Swallow had been displayed opposite Olympia at 71 Hammersmith Road; this was a common ploy for those who could not get, or afford, space in the show itself.)

'The Show was a great success,' said Lyons, 'but I knew that I should not be content to stay in the coachbuilding section, in spite of our prospects as only builders of a body on someone else's chassis.'[25] For some time Lyons had been mulling over creating a car of his own, one of distinctive and sporting appearance. George Lee recalled: 'When we came to Coventry I think his target was to make a car that would see the Alvis off on the road.'[26] Both Lyons and Walmsley owned an Alvis and liked the car.

The time when Lyons could act on this intention was not far off and it was through Standard that the route would be found. The Standard Nine Swallow, first seen at the 1929 Motor Show, had been given a new Lyons-designed radiator grille early in 1930 and it was this that brought Lyons into contact with the man who eventually would make it happen, Captain John Black of the Standard Motor Company.

Some six years older than Lyons, John Paul Black had entered the motor industry after serving in the First World War. He became a director of Hillman (and married one of the Hillman daughters) but left after the Rootes takeover. On 1 October 1929 he joined the Standard Motor Company as assistant to Standard's Managing Director (and founder) Reginald Maudslay. Black energetically tackled the problem of an outdated range of cars and old-fashioned management techniques. He was so successful that in February 1930 he was elected to the board on a larger salary and with a generous profit-sharing incentive. It was probably the same month that Lyons received his first telephone call from Black, who stated somewhat imperiously that he had seen the new Standard Swallow radiator and would like to have a sample to look at. In fact he had already sent somebody to collect one! 'I had some difficulty in being polite,'[27] recalled Lyons. Eventually Black got his radiator shell and soon the production Standard appeared with a grille very much like it. This first encounter did not appear propitious but from it much would come.

That month was important in the Lyons calendar for another reason. On 24 February 1930 the family was increased to four with the arrival of Pat's baby brother, John Michael. The Lyons were then living at 5 Eastleigh Avenue, Earlsdon, Coventry but they were all to move within a year or so to a larger detached house called Woodside in Gibbet Hill, Coventry.

The adoption by Swallow of Standard and other chassis came about partly because Lyons was unsure about the supply of chassis from Austin. 'I had known for some time that Sir Herbert Austin did not look favourably on the Austin Swallow'[28] because Austin was short of chassis for the best-selling Austin Seven itself. His fears about the continuity of supply were to prove justified but for an unexpected reason: Swallow very nearly became involved in a bribery scandal!

Lyons spoke to Chris Buckley, then Assistant Sales Manager at Austin, about his concerns over chassis supplies. Buckley told him of an investigation that had just taken place following Sir Herbert's discovery that Austin's Sales Manager, Sam Holbrook, had been taking bribes from the Rootes distributorship for priority deliveries. Holbrook was sacked and Rootes's franchise withdrawn. Worryingly, Buckley informed Lyons that Sir Herbert had already asked him whether the chassis delivered to Swallow were involved in Holbrook's illicit transactions – Holbrook himself ran an Austin Swallow, which in the circumstances did not help. Buckley assured him that they were not but Lyons felt that the situation was 'precarious' and asked Buckley to make an appointment for him to see Sir Herbert.

'Buckley rang me up at my home to say that Sir Herbert would see me in the morning and would I arrive about 10 o'clock and go to his office. I duly arrived on time and was told the great man had just gone into the drawing office where he was known to remain for indefinite periods... I sat reading magazines until one o'clock when Buckley came in, full of apologies, saying I should be wasting my time to wait any longer, as he was sure Austin would stay in the drawing office all afternoon and then go straight home. I was, of course, most indignant at the discourtesy I had been shown'[29] – so much so that Lyons now cared little about putting his point of view to Austin. In any case, 'with Buckley's help, no crisis arose' and Austin Swallow production continued unabated.

Herbert Austin (later Lord Austin) never figured very highly in Lyons's estimation. Even during his very last recorded interview, for a 1984 BBC television documentary on the motor industry, Lyons remarked: 'Austin was a bamboozler – he sort of pushed his way across everybody.'

Lyons admired Austin's great rival, William Morris, considerably more. He had started from scratch in the way Lyons was proud to have done and, although on a different scale and in a different market, Morris's strategies were not dissimilar to Lyons's. The former bicycle mechanic from Oxford had had the 'temerity' (as Miles

Thomas, later to manage the Morris empire, put it) to produce a car made almost entirely from bought-out components, leapfrogging the need for expensive plant and so challenging the established manufacturers, which were making nearly everything themselves. His strategy also involved volume to cut unit costs and allow a low selling price, another Lyons practice. The Morris Oxford of 1913 was reliable and excellent value; the company flourished and in 1925 Morris produced 54,000 cars, more than any of its competitors.

By 1930 Morris had grown out of being an assembler and had acquired most of its suppliers, while in 1927 it had outbid Austin for the bankrupt Wolseley concern. Lyons became 'very enthusiastic' about a new Wolseley model, the Hornet; this, with its advanced little overhead cam six-cylinder engine, he considered 'would make an ideal base for a sports model...the general conception of the chassis followed an enlarged MG and it promised to have comparable success.'[30]

The MG marque had evolved from modified versions of the Oxford created by Cecil Kimber, General Manager of Morris Garages. The 1929 pointed-tail MG M-type (based on the Morris Minor) is recognised today as Britain's first practical and affordable sports car. Lyons was certainly aware of the MG's merits and of Cecil Kimber's too.

With Wolseley had come a talented ex-Vickers engineer, Oliver Boden. Lyons went to see if he could obtain his blessing for a Swallow-bodied Hornet. 'Contrary to Austin's attitude,' Lyons reported, 'Boden was both enthusiastic and helpful.' A Hornet chassis was obtained through Henlys, which was a Wolseley distributor along with everything else. 'It took a few days working with Holland to outline what turned out to be an attractive and successful two-seater.'[31]

The Swallow Hornet is significant in the Lyons story as not only was it his first real sports model but its shape was arrived at using a process that from then on became Lyons's standard method of working. 'This was done,' explained Lyons later, 'without any drawings or even a sketch by using a 5/8ths [16mm] aluminium moulding section formed by hand to the contours guided by eye to produce a pleasing line. There really was no limit to the lines which one could develop with this moulding, both longitudinally and horizontally, to give a complete formation of a body outline, but in practice a skeleton like framework sufficed from which a wooden panelling jig could be made. This practice was followed through the development of every car body produced up to the XJ6 except the "E" and "D" types...'[32]

In the early days that wooden jig was built up by Holland and used to take patterns for the panel-makers. Later it became simply a support for panels fashioned out of sheet steel by skilled panel-beaters to replicate a full-size car. Lyons would then refine and modify these styling prototypes until he had achieved exactly the effect that he was seeking. It was probably a unique design process and it was one from which Lyons never deviated.

Exactly how much men like Holland contributed to the creative process is difficult to judge; certainly he had to steer Lyons away from the impractical on occasions. Holland also felt he earned his money, as he explained in a 1981 interview with Swallow historian Gilbert Mond: 'He used to come with these ideas when we were supposed to be finishing work. It got to the point that if I got away at 8 o'clock at night I'd got half a day off!'

The Wolseley Hornet Swallow was announced in January 1931 and was followed by four-seater and higher-performance 70mph (112kmh) versions on the Hornet Special chassis released by Wolseley in 1932. The car was the last Swallow to use a proprietary chassis. Lyons had set his sights higher and, with the company turning over the equivalent today of around £1.5m annually, he now felt he had the resources to take the business on another major step forward.

This, for Lyons, was 'the urge to produce a more individual car of our own design'. He approached John Black at Standard and was surprised and delighted to find Black, now General Manager of the Canley firm, 'most enthusiastic' about his proposal. This was for a unique Swallow chassis, which Standard would build up and deliver as a running unit to Foleshill. The frame itself, it was decided after discussion, had best be designed by Swallow and made by Rubery Owen, Standard's normal supplier.

Undeterred that no one at Swallow knew anything about chassis design (there was not even a resident draughtsman – Standard was relied upon for the few drawings required), Lyons got the sawmill to make one in wood as a pattern for Rubery Owen. His key objective was to lower the standing height as much as possible 'to enable us to design a body with a very low profile'. Then, as now, 'low' meant 'sporting'. Apart from the new frame, running components were normal Standard 16 (a Swallow version of which had been in production since May); Edward Grinham, who in January 1931 had become Standard's Chief Engineer, oversaw the mechanical aspects of the project for Swallow.

It was now around late summer 1931 and Rubery Owen – one of Britain's largest family companies – was in turmoil. A. E. Owen had just died and his son Alfred, aged 21, had been recalled urgently from his studies at Cambridge to run the company. Yet Alfred contacted Lyons almost at once. 'I remember I was quite astonished that he should find time to deal with something so comparatively insignificant, when having only just come to the company...but this was typical of him.'[33] Alfred Owen was to deal with 'practically every detail' of his business personally, Lyons noted with admiration, even to the extent of approving every company invoice. This accorded with Lyons's own instincts; even if he did not see each individual invoice at Jaguar later on, almost every staff and engineering memo or report passed across his desk.

While Rubery Owen manufactured the first frame, Lyons started on the body. Various ideas had already been discussed with Henlys and the design process included Donald Reesby, head artist of an Iliffe studio in Coventry. Given a rough sketch by Lyons, 'he produced a coloured drawing which surpassed my wildest dreams.'[34] When scaled, unfortunately the resultant car would have been 18ft (5.4m) long and 4ft (1.2m) high, but it proved a good inspiration. So did the big and somewhat flashy £600 Vauxhall Kingston coupé that Walmsley and, a little more reluctantly, Lyons had both bought to replace their Alvises. Lyons's Vauxhall was registered to him on 12 May 1930 at 5 Eastleigh Avenue, Earlsdon.

With Holland's help, Lyons now styled the 2+2 coupé and the patterns were sent to Motor Panels. The first body was under construction at Swallow when Lyons, who had begun to complain of acute stomach pains, was rushed off to hospital by ambulance – protesting to Greta that he was only suffering from indigestion. It was, in fact, appendicitis.

When Lyons returned to work after the operation he was shocked to find that Walmsley had raised the new car's roofline. 'Apparently, when my partner, Walmsley, sat in the car he decided that the headroom was inadequate and he was, I am sure, right. I had obviously allowed my desire to give the car a low profile to outweigh the need to provide the necessary headroom.' The higher roof spoiled the car's proportions but the Motor Show was less than a month away and there was no time for alterations. 'I hated it and felt very depressed,'[35] Lyons recorded but he was encouraged by Frank Hough, who persuaded Harold Pemberton, the well-known motoring correspondent of *The Daily Express*, to come and see the car.

Lyons found it impossible to detect from Pemberton's deadpan manner, as he walked round the prototype taking notes, what he thought about it. To Lyons's relief he did not bring a photographer so Pemberton was given the Reesby concept sketch. Lyons 'considered the ethics' of using exaggerated illustrations – including for advertisements – but consoled himself with the thought that it was common practice in many industries, including fashion, which depicted 'models 10 foot high with 12 inch waists'. Harold Pemberton wrote a story that astonished and delighted Lyons and gave the new car a splendid pre-Show launch the day before Olympia opened. Prominently on page 11 of *The Daily Express* (then Britain's biggest-circulation newspaper) was the headline 'Dream car unveiled – The £1,000 look'. It was wonderful publicity for Swallow even if the copy did go on to ascribe the car's design to 22 salesmen. (Frank Hough had obviously briefed Pemberton – though to be fair, the specification had been much talked-over with Henlys.)

The new car, called the SS1, aroused great interest at Olympia in October. Its striking, long-bonneted styling aped coachbuilt sporting thoroughbreds, which did indeed cost £1,000 (and more); yet it was priced at £310 (or around £10,000 in today's money). Yes, some considered it too extreme, others strongly doubted its pedigree but there was no denying its impact. 'It struck a new note,' as *The Motor* later put it.

The SS1 and the somewhat overlooked SS2 (a smaller and better proportioned version of the SS1) were displayed in the coachwork section: Lyons suspected that Sir Herbert Austin was preventing the company's election as a member of the Society of Motor Manufacturers and Traders (necessary for exhibiting in the manufacturers' section). However, Lyons acknowledged that his first application was 'optimistic' as membership of the SMMT had become 'closely guarded' following the collapse of so many of the small companies that had sprung up after the First World War. But he was disappointed that SS Cars was not admitted until 1934, regarding this delay as a serious setback in his plans to develop the company.

Lyons, writing privately a few days after the show had closed to thank *The Autocar* staff for its coverage, stated that the event 'has resulted in business far in excess of our most optimistic anticipation. Not only have we received hundreds of letters of congratulation, but orders are pouring in from all parts of the country, to the extent which causes us some alarm.'

The 1931 Show was also useful in attracting new dealers and distributors, including some from overseas; not all proved satisfactory but Emil Frey, who had handled Swallow sidecars in Switzerland since 1926, was among those that were. Frey became one of the first European agents for the SS1. The majority of Swallow sales, including the still active sidecar division, might have been in the UK but exports were certainly not unimportant to the company. Soon there were agents in a variety of European countries, many recommended by Ben Mason, Standard's Export Manager.

As for the SS name, this was certainly inspired by the Brough Superior SS80, which Lyons used to ride; it was also an important step in his determination 'to establish a marque of our own'. Only later would these same initials become associated with the cruelty of Hitler's SS troops.

In fact, 'SS' was arrived at only after 'a long argument' with both Maudslay and Black; what, if anything, the initials stood for was left diplomatically indistinct by Lyons: John Black could believe that they meant 'Standard Swallow', those at Foleshill 'Swallow Special'. Their true meaning 'was never resolved'[36] according to Lyons.

That first SS1 was not a particularly good car but it was strikingly different and modestly priced; again Lyons had produced the right car for the period. Britain's economy was still struggling but at least manufacturing was back to nearly 84 per cent of 1929 levels and rising (in Germany and the US it was still little more than half) and average incomes were increasing in real terms. Not many people actually purchased this eye-catching but rather impractical motor car (only about 500 were sold during 1932) but they could dream realistically of doing so.

Lyons, back to full health, ensured that a completely revised SS1 appeared for 1933, a longer, better-proportioned car being displayed at the October 1932 Motor Show. It was beautifully timed to catch an upswing in Britain's economy: wages were rising, the cost of living was falling and, having stagnated for two years, new car registrations leaped from 143,053 in 1932 to 178,574 in 1933. The new SS1 was able to double the company's sales that year, up from 777 units to 1,526; the coupé was soon followed by saloon, tourer, and Airline versions.

However, Lyons was frustrated that production was handicapped by delays at Standard. Typically, he wrote on 3 November 1933: 'Dear Black...while appreciating the difficulties which you are experiencing in obtaining supplies, you will understand that I am now very concerned due to non-delivery of chassis... We have, at the present time, few short of 1,000 orders on our books, and the difficulty we are now experiencing in giving information to our dealers and customers will, I am afraid, if we do not get going very quickly, result in a large number of cancellations.'

On the shop floor, however, there were grumbles even about the current level of production, especially in the body and trim shops.

Many of the men there (and some of the women, too, who had been recruited for trim work) had now been working long hours for four years, with only a week's break at the beginning of August.

Lyons detected, or was told about, the mood on the shop floor and one evening (related Connie Teather, née Dickson, in the 1980s) as the men were going home, he called them all together and gave what became known as 'the swimming pool speech'. He spoke in a friendly way about how he understood how tired they were (so was he) and what a marvellous job they had all done since they had joined the firm. Lyons continued: 'Forget your wives, forget your children, forget your gardens, and all the things you want to do – if we can just get this SS1 off the ground and make this our own car firm you will have big houses, big cars and swimming pools.' Connie commented: 'The thought of any of them owning a swimming pool filled them with amusement and they all laughed, the tension was over and the meeting broke up – and the men carried on working.'[37] Well might they laugh – the average weekly wage in 1934 was little more than £6.

The office in which Connie Dickson and Alice Fenton worked was hectic too as they tried to keep pace with the sales, general invoicing, correspondence and all the other paperwork being generated as the business grew. Dictation did not start until the phones quietened down at 5.30pm so Connie and Alice rarely left before 7pm or 8pm, sometimes later. At one point Lyons had the notion that the firm would look more efficient and businesslike if the girls wore black skirts with white collars – 'like Lyons waitresses' Alice said (referring to the popular chain of teashops, which were then in almost every big town). It was a little while afterwards that Alice's younger sister Nancy came from Blackpool to work for Swallow too; the pair were quickly dubbed 'SS1 and SS2'.

Arthur Whittaker, for whom Connie worked, was usually busy seeing representatives and every year there would be crucial meetings with the major suppliers like Wilmot Breeden or Lucas. After much discussion in the smoke-filled corridor, Lyons would be brought in to conclude the deal. Alice Fenton continued to handle sales; a sales manager as such was not appointed until 1935 when Eric Warren came from Brown & Mallalieu. When Lyons had left the Blackpool dealership, he had promised that one day he would send for Eric Warren...

CHAPTER 3

BIRTH OF THE JAGUAR

William Walmsley has not featured a great deal in the narrative following the establishment of the SS1; the reason is that the bigger the company grew, the less part he took in the running of it. Lyons increasingly resented any 'interference' from Walmsley after the SS1 roof incident but in any case Walmsley preferred to spend his time on his hobbies or driving around the countryside. This did not pass unnoticed by the workforce. Harry Gill remembered: 'He used to go on long weekends, Friday to Friday.' Walmsley would disappear with a four-seater SS tourer and on returning he would ask Harry to take him round the factory and show him what had been going on during the week. He did not always like what he saw: 'Who the bloody hell told you to do that?' he would ask Gill. When informed it was Mr Lyons, Walmsley would say: 'Don't mention that bloody man's name again to me!'[1] Shortly afterwards Harry would hear another fierce row going on in the office.

Quite trivial things widened the growing rift between the partners. Lyons habitually arrived at the office at 9am; Walmsley came in earlier, as most of the workers did, at around 8am. Just once, Lyons came in to find that Walmsley had opened all the letters. It infuriated him. 'If you open any more before I come in, you'll answer them!' he told Walmsley, who was never known to write a letter himself at Swallow.

Walmsley's more routine intrusions into Lyons's time were also resented. Speaking over 50 years later, Lyons recalled: 'He used to come into my office and I used to [think], "Oh, how long is he going to take?" and he'd talk for half an hour about nothing.'[2]

Another irritant, and one that became quite disruptive within the works, was Walmsley's model railway, which he was constantly expanding at home. Not only did he ask the paint shop to paint items but also he made increasing demands on Harry Teather in the stores for materials. Harry had no objection to the odd piece of brass or a handful of screws but when it came to boxes of screws and armfuls of brass strip it was a different matter; he had to account for his stock. It became serious enough for Teather to consider resigning and he went to Lyons and told him that he couldn't work for two masters. Lyons told him to bide his time.

Of course, the whole company was changing as it grew and the original Blackpool people, caught up in the stimulating rush of progress and expansion, found almost before they realised it that the family atmosphere of the early days was fading a little. But the business always retained a uniquely personal feeling while Lyons was in charge. There were few people at the top and changes in the executive (as much as there was one – Lyons alone made the major decisions) were rare. People were used to working with one another for decades. Although there could be frictions, this produced a generally very cohesive team and allowed the rapid deployment of ideas; everyone understood each other.

But while Lyons was regarded with huge respect by the old Blackpool hands, and those who came to work closely with him in Coventry, he was not considered without flaws. Asked once whether there was a streak of ruthlessness in Lyons, George Lee (who had joined at the age of 14) replied: 'I would say, yes, he was a clever man and ruthless with it, and I suppose that's really necessary when you've got a job up top, isn't it? It's no good being kind to everybody and the business going by the board, is it?'[3] George spoke with experience: on one occasion Lyons came unexpectedly into his part of the factory and noticed a man standing round apparently idle. He demanded that he be sacked. In fact the operator had come to George with a problem and he was sorting it out with him. George Lee simply told the man to stay out of sight for a while until things died down and no more was heard about it.

There is no doubt either that people like George Lee knew that they were, to an extent, simply being used by Lyons to achieve his objectives. Lyons considered that he was paying a fair day's wage for a fair day's work; most of the key men were on a bonus scheme, which allowed them to earn considerably above the average. (Later they were to feel that the bonus element of their money was too great and the salary part was too little.) Lee commented: 'I don't think he realised that a lot of his staff were as interested in the firm as he was...'[4]

However, Lyons undeniably had a special regard for those who came with him from Blackpool for what Connie Teather called 'the Great Experiment' (for no one, not even Lyons, knew if setting up a big factory in Coventry was really going to work). He could be generous if they required help and when one Blackpool man, Donald

Brown, had to leave the company for unexpected reasons, Lyons later secured him a Jaguar franchise.

Some of the Blackpool émigrés earned another small distinction. Lyons became famous through his formal manner towards even his closest colleagues, almost all of whom were addressed by their surnames. In fact, this was a democratic way of addressing people and it avoided implied favourites. There were just a few exceptions to this otherwise ironclad rule: when speaking (at least in private) to Cyril Holland, Jack Beardsley, Harry Teather or (later) Fred Gardner, Lyons used their Christian names. But they were about the only ones.

The next fundamental problem facing Lyons in the early 1930s was that although the coachwork was now 'right', the cars' performance was not and the SS was regarded with considerable scorn by owners of established sporting marques like MG and Riley. Their views were given some credence when, in the company's first official venture into international competition, two of the three works-prepared team of SS1 tourers ended the 1933 International Alpine Trial on the end of a tow-rope. Reliability was better in the 1934 event but, while the team did not disgrace itself, a lack of power and a number of chassis deficiencies were still evident. As for the ordinary customers, sometimes they had to contend with poor cold starting, stiff steering and overheating.

It was not all bad news, though. On 3 April 1933 Frank Hough had written to 'Dear Billy' about the Henlys demonstrator: 'I thought it might interest you to know that on Saturday last this motor car, after having done 10,000 miles, was sold outright for £295, cash. This goes to prove the popularity of the model and I think that this year you will find they unquestionably hold their second-hand values far better than they did last year, although even today we are getting £195–£220, which, in comparison to other makes, is certainly not a bad figure. I am pleased to inform you that the new models are still selling extraordinarily well...'

The difficulty for Lyons was twofold: the limitations of having to use virtually off-the-shelf Standard components and the lack of an in-house engineering capability. 'It was obvious if we were going to get anywhere we must do something about the engines, but I did not know how we should do it,'[5] Lyons recorded. He was, in fact, floundering. Various schemes were considered during 1934 including supercharging the existing 2.2-litre (130cu in) Standard side-valve unit or even fitting a Studebaker engine. (Henlys was an agent for this make and an American power unit was a popular choice of specialist manufacturers in the 1930s.) Then in June 1934 a Surrey firm (Gillett, Shepperson & Co Ltd of Bookham) quoted for a '20hp high performance engine'. (This might well have been the Blackburn engine that had been redesigned with a 1.6-litre [97cu in] capacity and a twin overhead camshaft cylinder head for AFN's Frazer Nash TT replica.) Initially Lyons had expressed serious interest in this unit but ultimately none of these avenues led anywhere.

Salvation came in the shape of Harry Weslake, who was introduced to Lyons by the foundry that was making the existing SS cylinder head. This blunt West Countryman had built up a considerable reputation tuning motor cycles at Brooklands. In the 1920s, while Lyons and Walmsley were launching their sidecar, he had invented a system of measuring airflow and thus the efficiency of cylinder heads – knowledge he applied to good effect on W. O. Bentley's Le Mans-winning cars. However, he was regarded as something of a maverick in the industry because, Lyons felt, chief engineers did not like someone coming from outside and improving on their work.

According to Harry years later, he told Lyons at their first meeting: 'Your car reminds me of an overdressed lady with no brains – there's nothing under the bonnet!'[6] They were then supposed to have had 'a first class row,' retired to a pub for a drink and become 'the best of pals ever since'. Lyons, not noted for being fond of brash characters, came to respect Weslake very considerably, largely because he delivered on his promises. Harry would work closely with Jaguar until the 1970s.

Weslake usefully improved the existing side-valve engine but urged that an overhead-valve cylinder head was the real answer. He claimed he could design one that would fit the existing 2.7-litre (162cu in) Standard block that SS was using and give another 25bhp. Lyons was interested but sceptical; he said he would pay only on results, though he did pay Weslake an interim retainer. The agreed target was 95bhp, some 25bhp up on the SS1's output. In May 1935 the new head was tried out on the test bed: result, 104bhp. Lyons considered this 'better than anything we could have wished for,' later describing the moment as one of the best breakthroughs the company ever had. The prospect of real performance to underwrite the SS's good looks had finally arrived.

Elsewhere, there had been progress too. Holbrook Bodies, which owned the first two blocks next to Swallow on the Whitmore Park Estate, was in the hands of the receiver. In October 1931 Gillitt tipped off Lyons that Bernard Gray (son of the Whitmore syndicate boss) was interested in buying the seven-acre (2.8-hectare) property for £12,000 if Swallow wasn't. He added that Lyons should 'appreciate the fact that there are many other people in this neighbourhood who also have a keen eye for a bargain'.

Uncharacteristically Lyons appeared to sit on this news – probably due to the hectic aftermath of the Olympia Show that month and the urgent need to get the first SS1 into production. However, he was 'provoked into action' when Stanley Gliksten, Swallow's timber supplier, remarked during a visit in 1932 that he had offered £18,000 to Lloyds Bank for these two empty blocks – simply for the timber they contained. 'I told Stanley that I had hoped to buy it, and to my surprise, he very generously said that if that were so he would step down and withdraw his offer.'[7]

Lyons was then faced with a slightly awkward banking situation, which arose from his loyalty to those in Blackpool who had helped get the business started. He still retained accountants O. & W. B. Haworth (whose Alan Mather became a Swallow Coachbuilding director) and Williams Deacon's Bank remained Swallow's bankers – at the time of the move in 1928 Lyons had arranged for the local Lloyds branch to act as agents for the Blackpool bank. Three years later, Huckvale was reporting increasing reminders from Lloyds that it was unusual for this sort of arrangement to continue for so long, especially as the account was now a large one.

Lyons considered that any offer he put to Lloyds Bank would be more acceptable if it was handling the Swallow account permanently 'but I was so indebted to Francis in Blackpool that I did not feel I could do this without his willing agreement... So I drove up to Blackpool to explain the position to Francis. He could not have been more charming...'[8]

Making up for lost time, Lyons went directly to Lloyds Bank's headquarters in London to see its Chief General Manager, Mr Wilson. He seemed impressed with the progress Lyons outlined: the company was on course for a £22,000 profit to July 1933, up from £12,000 in the previous financial year. Lyons then told him that he intended to transfer the company's account to the Lloyds branch in Coventry and offer £8,000 for the ex-Holbrook Bodies' buildings.

Lyons came away from the meeting with 'no idea' of Wilson's reaction to this proposal but about a week later a letter came from Wilson accepting his package deal. Well might Lyons write later: 'This gave me a lot of joy.' What he had succeeded in doing was to purchase all eight ex-Holbrook shops (the two blocks of four) plus the Holbrook sawmill for £10,000 less than he and Walmsley had paid for their original two blocks! The transaction was finalised on

9 December 1932, the money being raised by an overdraft at Lloyds, offset by the credit in the Swallow Coachbuilding Company's current account.

The company's structure also underwent important changes in the early 1930s. It is known that Swallow Coachbuilding had become a limited company in April 1932 but the earliest surviving company minute book dates from 5 May 1932. The entry on that day records a meeting at which Lyons, Walmsley, Gillitt, and Mather (of the accountancy firm O. & W. B. Haworth) 'resolved that the goodwill and registered trademark Swallow should be sold to S.S. Cars'. This indicates that SS Cars certainly existed as a functioning legal entity at that time even if it was not a limited company. (SS Cars Ltd was not officially incorporated until 10 October 1933.)

Clearly the intention behind the new name was to get away from the coachbuilding image. One of the new names considered for registration was the Swallow Motor Company Ltd and in May 1933 Noel Gillitt reported that 15 limited companies commencing with the word Swallow existed but that only the Swallow Motor Cab Co Ltd appeared to conflict (and that was in course of dissolution). This approach was not proceeded with.

The business became known as SS Cars Ltd, which became the vehicle used by Lyons for his biggest step forward yet: flotation as a public company. In all probability this would have occurred in the natural course of events but it happened when it did because at last Walmsley 'expressed a wish to retire,' as Lyons put it later. The partnership was finally at an end and, as the business was half Walmsley's, a large amount of cash needed to be realised (Walmsley took few if any shares as part of the settlement).

The sale of shares in SS Cars Ltd opened on 11 January 1934; offered were 100,000 6½ per cent cumulative preference shares of £1 each at 21s 6d (£1.07) per share and 140,000 5s (25p) ordinary shares at 10s 6d (53p) per share. The flotation created nowhere near as much interest as when Jaguar Cars Plc was put on the market in 1984; in 1934 *The Financial Times* merely observed that the preference shares appeared to be a high yielding investment of their class, while the ordinary shares had 'possibilities'.

Lyons became Chairman and Managing Director; the other directors were Noel Gillitt, Thomas Wells Daffern (a director of the Coventry Permanent Building Society) and Arthur Whittaker – a mark of Lyons's regard for his General Manager. That was all: no bankers, no one from financial institutions, no impressive list of lords, knights, or barons. The 'favoured few,' those who had also thrown in their lot with Lyons and come with him from Blackpool, received a small packet of shares each.

William Walmsley left a wealthy man. With the company enjoying increasing profits, a solid asset base and a healthy bank balance, he must have departed with a sum that today would be worth millions. It was an outcome he could hardly have foreseen when he put that first sidecar together in his garden shed in Stockport.

It might have been surprising that the partnership lasted as long as it did but Lyons would have bought Walmsley out much earlier had he possessed the funds. The relationship had broken down years before: the two men had such different outlooks and objectives. Lyons, tenacious and energetic, had the extra incentive of needing to make his own way in the world financially. The easy-going Walmsley, due to inherit his father's not insubstantial estate, had no such spur. For Lyons, the achievement of one objective was simply the signal to set another. Walmsley was usually quite content with things as they were, so long as the business was doing 'all right'. Some of the conflict arose over money: while Lyons consistently wanted to re-invest profits, Walmsley's attitude was more 'now we've made some money, let's spend it'. At least that was the impression that Pat Lyons had gained from her father before the Second World War – though, in fact, Lyons did not like Walmsley's name being mentioned in the house.

Perhaps because of his more relaxed attitude, Walmsley was sometimes the better liked of the two within the company. Yes, everyone acknowledged Lyons as the driving force behind the firm's progress but he kept his distance, socially, from his employees. Walmsley, on the other hand, would happily stop off at the pub after work and enjoy a 'gill' with the lads – unthinkable except in the most rare of circumstances with Lyons.

William Walmsley died at Poulton-le-Fylde on 4 June 1961, just short of his 69th birthday. Some measure of the rift between him and his erstwhile partner is shown by the fact that Lyons did not attend the funeral but instead sent Arthur Whittaker and Edward Huckvale to represent Jaguar. Walmsley's remarkable sidecar had opened up the commercial world to Lyons and without it there might be no Jaguar cars today; that is surely Walmsley's best epitaph.

For Lyons, an irritant had been removed. The future was his own to mould and with the successful flotation of SS Cars Ltd behind him, the sky was now the limit.

Lyons was already planning a major new model for the traditional October Motor Show launch period. Heart of the car would be the

100bhp Weslake-modified engine, which John Black (now Managing Director of Standard following the death of Maudslay) had agreed to manufacture – even to the extent of putting in the necessary plant at his own expense. Black also agreed, verbally, that this engine would be supplied exclusively to SS but Lyons, already wary of Captain Black's volatility, 'decided that complications and differences arise so I insisted on a written agreement'.[9]

On 1 April Lyons made one of his most important appointments. William Munger Heynes, aged 32, joined SS Cars Ltd as its first Chief Engineer. Heynes came from Humber where he had been apprenticed in 1923, working later for Leslie Dawtrey and Edward Grinham. After the Rootes takeover of Humber, both these men defected to the Standard Motor Company, Grinham becoming Chief Engineer and Dawtrey his assistant. When they heard Lyons was seeking an engineer for SS, they remembered this quietly spoken, confident young man and recommended him. No harm either for Lyons having a Chief Engineer respected at Standard.

Much was at stake and Lyons took his time choosing from a variety of candidates. Heynes remembered being interviewed five times before he was offered the job. The challenge Lyons threw down was immense: he told Heynes that his eventual aim was to produce one of the world's finest luxury cars. After the stifling atmosphere at Humber ('they didn't want anything new,' Heynes recalled) this was heady stuff. Bill Heynes was amazed at the confidence Lyons placed in him 'but it had the desired effect of making me self-reliant and at the same time duly careful when I knew that the work I was doing was going straight to the customer.'[10]

Heynes turned out to be an inspired choice and he was to build up an engineering team that, by the 1950s, was probably the best of any specialist car company in the world. To Lyons, Heynes was the engineering equivalent of Cyril Holland, able to discern what he wanted and make it a reality. 'Build up' was the operative phrase because SS did not even have a drawing office. This, with just one draughtsman initially, was quickly established by Heynes, who set to work on the chassis for the new car. He added professionalism in other areas too, telling Arthur Whittaker bluntly that the nuts and bolts he was buying were 'rubbish' and that in future supplies must come from GKN.

Lyons, meanwhile, set Holland to work on the body design for the new car and spent 'a great deal' of his own time on it too. A running prototype was finished just in time for the trade launch at the Mayfair Hotel, London on 21 September 1935. It was called the SS 'Jaguar'.

Lyons talked of its market positioning at SS Cars Ltd's second AGM on Friday 11 October. He said the Jaguar was intended to have a much wider appeal, to 'a market not so susceptible to trading conditions as the specialist two-door body upon which the company had always concentrated'. It also offered quality and performance 'hitherto associated with only the most exclusive type of car – at a moderate price'.

Visually the car was, in fact, a miniaturised Park Ward Bentley (Cyril Holland claimed Lyons had directed him towards the imposing Bentley radiator as the inspiration for the Jaguar's). A mid-sized sports saloon, it was much more mainstream than the previous SS1 and, while not possessing the refinement of the larger Derby-built car, was less than a third of the price. Lyons had asked the dealers at the launch convention to guess the figure: the average of those (quite informed) guesses was £600 (this figure was given in a 1947 address by Lyons – in his later accounts of the same occasion it varied), so Lyons knew he would spark amazement when he revealed that the retail price was £385.

Backing-up the mainstream 2½-litre (162cu in) saloon were a scaled-down, cheaper 1½-litre (108cu in) version and a new two-seater sports car, the glamorously styled SS Jaguar 100 – this was low on volume but high on ability and finally gave Lyons a car which could win international rallies.

Then there was the success of the name 'Jaguar' itself. The South American feline evoked all the qualities that Lyons would like customers to consider were inherent in the car: speed, sleekness and silence. However, it was a last minute choice by Lyons: his new range for 1936 was very nearly named Sunbeam.

In the mid-1930s Sunbeam was a prestige, if slightly faded, marque that had built some very advanced racing cars and held the World Land Speed Record five times between 1922 and 1927.

When, therefore, Sunbeam-Talbot-Darracq (the companies had combined in 1920) went into receivership early in 1935, Lyons saw an opportunity to buy a ready-made and highly credible sporting-luxury brand name, ideal for his intended new range of cars. At the end of May 1935 Lyons began negotiating with Alfred Herbert Ltd, the Coventry machine tool company; apparently its offer for the STD assets had been accepted by the receiver.

These negotiations were going so well that on 6 June 1935 Lyons wrote to Alfred Herbert Ltd: 'As agreed today, the writer confirms arrangements made between us, in reference to the acquisition by us of the Name, Goodwill, Patents and Drawings, of the Sunbeam

Motor Car Company Ltd.' A cheque from SS Cars for £200 was enclosed and it was also understood that all the existing stock of Sunbeam cars would be purchased by David Rosenfield Ltd of Manchester (of which Bertie Henly was a director). The arrangements were even leaked to the press, which reported that SS 'will produce a range of Sunbeam cars at their modern factory in Coventry'.

However, shortly after Lyons returned from an SS Car Club rally in Blackpool late in June (the club had been formed the previous year), he was profoundly surprised to find that the deal was off. The Rootes brothers had snatched Sunbeam to further swell their haul of other makes. Lyons reported to his board on 3 July that negotiations for the Sunbeam Motor Co Ltd 'had ceased and were unproductive'. That the secretary of the SS Car Club had absconded with the money collected to pay the Imperial Hotel, leaving Lyons to foot the bill, concluded a difficult few days for the boss of SS!

The biggest problem was the need for another name for the new cars, with barely two months remaining before their announcement. With Bill Rankin – the company's first Press and Public Relations Manager, who had joined in 1934 – Lyons explained events to William and Bob Bett's Nelson Advertising firm. Founded by William Bett (ex-Henlys) in 1929, the agency now handled advertising accounts for SS Cars as well as Henlys.

'I asked our publicity people to let me have a list of the names of animals, fish and birds. I immediately pounced on 'Jaguar' for it had an exciting sound to me, and brought back some memories of the stories told to me, towards the end of the 1914–1918 war, by an old school friend who, being nearly a year older than I, had joined the Royal Flying Corps. He was stationed at Farnborough and he used to tell me of his work as a mechanic on the Armstrong Siddeley 'Jaguar' engine. Since that time, the word Jaguar has always had a particular significance to me and so SS 'Jaguar' became the name by which our cars were known.'[11]

That school friend was Arnold Breakell, who thus takes some responsibility for Lyons settling on a name which so suited the car and which – it has been said – sounds good in any language. The SS Jaguar, though, sold on its own merits as a highly competent luxury sports saloon of modern and attractive appearance. Magazine road tests were genuinely enthusiastic about its all-round virtues and ecstatic about the 100 two-seater's 95mph (152kmh) performance. With the Jaguar, Lyons's cars became credible by any yardstick and the expansion of production that followed was increasingly at the expense of other manufacturers who attempted, and failed, to offer similar value for money.

The SS Jaguar range had a massive impact on the company's sales. While 1,724 cars were built in the 1934–5 season (Jaguar's financial year then ended on 31 July), production rose to 2,467 in 1935–6 and to 3,637 in 1936–7. Again Lyons's timing was right; the company was helped by Britain's improving economy, reflected in growing UK new car registrations: in 1932, the first year of the SS1, these stood at 143,053 but in 1936 the figure was 295,967.

These increased levels of production were made possible by the new chain-driven 'conveyor' assembly line, brought in after a crude but effective time-and-motion analysis of how long it took a team of men to fit-up a painted body. Normally a moving line of this type was the preserve of specialist installers but, having established that the cost of the parts needed was 'so reasonable,' Lyons discussed the matter with Jack Beardsley. He 'expressed the view which was typical of him "there was nothing to it"… It proved to be one of the most successful things we ever did for it saved several thousand pounds and lasted without trouble for very many years.'[12]

Despite all the hard work by Jack Beardsley, Harry Gill (who devised the mechanism), and others, it had taken until January 1936 for the new moving assembly line to be fully effective. But Lyons was still able to report in October 1936 at SS Cars Ltd's third AGM that trading profit for the year ending 31 July 1936 was £30,258, up from £27,960 the previous year; a dividend of ten per cent was once again recommended. The adoption of the new assembly line reflected in the accounts, with investment in plant doubling in one year. A considerable increase in stock and work in progress, perhaps caused by the production problems, was financed by a near trebling of monies owed to creditors. In spite of this, the directors' fees doubled in a year! Tax on profits was, however, at a modest rate of just ten per cent.

As ever, Lyons's private life was subservient to the demands of the business. His daughter Pat recalled that when she was a young girl it even dominated holidays, her father driving the family to the beach and then saying he would have to get back. 'I remember feeling disappointed that he never seemed to be with us.' While there was no doubting that Lyons had a deep-seated affection for his family, this lack of time and his impatience for results certainly impacted on the children. 'He did his best, I'm sure, but he didn't spend a lot of time with us really,' said Pat. 'One of my earliest memories was when I was quite little and he tried to teach me the days of the week, and I always forgot Thursdays – which absolutely exasperated him and I remember him saying, "you stupid little thing!". I can remember that to this day. I can remember him trying to teach me to ride a bicycle, a two-wheeler, but he didn't really allow much time – he got very impatient with me because I couldn't balance on it in two minutes!'[13]

Among the few relaxations Lyons allowed himself during the busy 1930s was golf; he had started playing in Blackpool, where he had been a leading member of the local club, and his passion for the game increased. Pat again: 'My father used to play golf as often as possible and was no novice. Golf was second to motor sport and he always used to say that had he had more time, he would have been a better golfer – though I'm not sure he actually would have been. I don't think he had the right temperament.' In fact Greta was rather better and she later played for her county.

Lyons's decision not to spend a lot of time on the golf course – or on other diversions from work – was a conscious one and it was not taken entirely without regrets. Pat heard him talk about it: 'He used to say how much he'd had to give up in those days. A lot of his friends would go off and play golf and have fun and he was so determined he'd get this going, and he was obviously quite torn as to whether to join his friends or stick at it. Sometimes he used to say – not in a grudging way, but he definitely felt he gave up quite a fair bit to get where he got. In fact he used to be a bit irritated with people who moaned about not being successful, because they didn't put enough effort into it.'[14]

One essential in Lyons's life was his annual pilgrimage to the Isle of Man for the Tourist Trophy motor cycle races. Also, he and Greta would follow motor rallies (in which the SS100 sports car was doing increasingly well). These events provided an important opportunity to meet friends and the press – though such excursions were not so popular with the Lyons children. 'I remember all those jolly parties,' said Pat, 'with them all going off to the RAC Rally and we were left with some horrible governess... But they had a lot of fun with those rallies...'[15] She would herself, too, in due course!

Besides rallies, Lyons was also interested in *concours d'élégance* – beauty contests for cars. Some rallies would include these, but there were also regular and highly fashionable *concours* meetings – seaside resorts like Bexhill, Brighton and Bournemouth were popular venues. Lines of highly polished and often embellished motor cars of all descriptions, including exotic coachbuilt and foreign ones, would line up for judging. Lyons keenly examined the latest or more interesting cars and even filmed details on the company's Bolex. On returning to Foleshill he would scribble features for Cyril Holland and Harry Gill to bear in mind for the next new Jaguar model.

Motor shows were another source of styling inspiration to Lyons and Cyril Holland, made to accompany him, became quite embarrassed as, unabashed, Lyons would stop by a stand and say in front of the stand's personnel: 'I like that, Cyril, you want to remember that when we do one of our next jobs!'[16]

As there is plentiful evidence to prove that Lyons was at his happiest when designing cars and none to suggest that he felt unconfident in his abilities by this time, it is perhaps strange that during 1935 he appeared to investigate the appointment of a stylist. On 6 July 1935 Mr H. A. Nabi had written to Lyons from 47 Museum Street, London: 'Following our several interviews concerning the re-organisation of your coach work, as I regret Mr Van den Plas cannot give you full satisfaction under the conditions of agreement with Messrs Wendover Ltd, during my last visit to Paris, I interested my friend, Mr Figoni, who is well known in the coach building world, both in name and capacity, in your scheme. He is prepared to give you exclusive rights in time and type in all England, and to accept the responsibility of the technical direction of your coach building and creation of models for the sum of £15,000 per annum.'

Whatever had been Lyons's motives in talking with Mr Nabi (sheer pressure of work, perhaps?) and despite his admiration for continental styling, the sum mentioned was not much under half of the entire annual profit of SS Cars at the time! The negotiations therefore came to an abrupt conclusion and Lyons replied with typical politeness three days later: 'The salary to which you refer is considerably in excess of the value which we may put on the services of Mr Van den Plas or Mr Figoni...'

It was only as the 1930s drew on that Lyons began to feel any sense of personal financial security. It has always been his family's contention – broadly supported by the pattern of his life – that achieving great wealth was never Lyons's prime objective. That eventually he did so was almost a by-product of what he enjoyed doing most, which was (as he later said to Bob Knight at Jaguar) simply 'making nice cars'.[17]

As a boy he had often listened to his mother talking of her way of life before she had married impecunious William Lyons senior. The Barcrofts had been well off and young Lyons was much taken with her tales of living in a big, fine house – Edgeside Hall, which James Barcroft had purchased in 1869. So much so that later in life, Pat felt, he 'wanted to get back to that nice comfortable feeling that you didn't have to worry about money'.

Until the mid-1930s Lyons did not have that particular feeling, and probably not without reason. For one thing, the Swallows and the early SS models were 'fashion' cars and fashion has a tendency to change. Up until quite a late stage before the company was floated, Lyons and Walmsley supported the business personally and any major catastrophe – the wrong model or a disastrous failure of a major supplier – could have proved fatal for the business. After all, a long list of better-known makes than SS ran into serious trouble between the wars – AC, Bentley, Lea-Francis, Sunbeam, Lagonda and even Riley. Despite his company's rapid progress, there probably lingered in Lyons's mind the fear that the business was still on a knife-edge. The family felt this underlying concern and it filtered through to a pre-teenage Pat. 'He was very concerned about having enough to keep us all, because in the early days he took such a risk that he was seriously worried as to whether he was going to make enough money to bring up his children. It was quite an obsession – he worried a lot.'

Although it did not threaten the business, it was at about this time that the company experienced its first strike. This took place in the sawmill, where the body frames were made and where Fred Gardner was now in charge. (Later he would replace Holland as Lyons's styling prototype builder.) Gardner's brother-in-law was working in the sawmill but although there was no closed shop, the other machinists objected to the fact that he was not in their union and threatened to strike if he was not dismissed. Lyons recorded: 'Gardner reacted as he did for the next 50 years. He said "not on your life"…whereupon all the men, with the exception of the one involved, walked out and the woodmill came to a standstill.'[18]

To his surprise, Lyons discovered that, despite the unemployment rife in Coventry, no wood machinists were available; but he heard that the situation was different in Scotland. Accordingly, early that Monday morning he telegraphed a recruitment advertisement to the *Glasgow Herald*, instructing those interested to telephone Fred Gardner. 'The response was beyond anything we had hoped for.' Gardner was able to pick the best and the sawmill was working again by Thursday.

The following Monday Miss Fenton showed a union official into Lyons's office. 'I enquired what I could do for him. He replied that he had come about the strike in the mill. I said that we did not have a strike. The men who did strike were no longer in our employ and had been sent their cards and the money due to them.' Lyons showed him the sawmill in full swing. The man said little and nothing was heard of the matter again. 'To the best of my knowledge, the great majority of the new men in the mill remained happily with the company for many years,' wrote Lyons in 1976. 'I have no doubt that the way the situation was dealt with would today give rise to considerable criticism from trade union quarters;'[19] that was probably one of Lyons's better understatements!

The results for the year ending 31 July 1937 showed further progress. Profit was up by around 50 per cent to £41,632. Reflecting sensible management, stock was down, as were creditors but the bank balance had more than doubled to £86,650. There was increasing investment in plant and the dividend paid was up a healthy 25 per cent.

It was during 1937 that Lyons was sufficiently confident about his personal finances to purchase Wappenbury Hall, a traditional if initially a rather gloomy 'Victorian pile' not far from Leamington Spa and some 20 minutes' drive to Foleshill. It was, Pat recalled, quite a dramatic change from the comfortable but modest mock-Tudor house in Gibbet Hill, Coventry where they had lived previously. The house appears to have been chosen by Lyons with minimal reference to his wife, the clincher being the large billiards room! The move was all part of Lyons's unspoken desire to 'live like people used to live,' complete with butler, head gardener and domestic staff. Alas, this gentleman's idyll was to last only until the start of the Second World War in 1939.

The year 1937 also saw the birth of the Lyons's second daughter, Mary, on 23 July. She was to be their last child.

Ironically, virtually coinciding with the move to Wappenbury, came exactly the sort of unpredictable catastrophe that perhaps Lyons had feared. Yet again it concerned a new method of body construction. Lyons had planned a new range of cars for 1938 that would finally dispense with coachbuilding – however streamlined, the wood framing process for the bodies was too slow and expensive for the quantities of Jaguars that Lyons felt the market would take.

A new all-steel bodyshell was designed at Foleshill and, as SS could not afford to commission a complete body-in-white from a major specialist like Fisher & Ludlow, was made up of a number of quite small panels that would be assembled at the SS works. Also, in true SS fashion, few drawings were made; instead patterns were taken from the styling buck for the various outside contractors. The problems arose when these individual panels began to come back: they would not fit together.

By then the coachbuilt assembly lines had been dismantled, so for a disastrous few months virtually no cars at all left Foleshill. It was not until October 1937 that production slowly got under way and it took until May 1938 for the full rate to be achieved. For a while, things looked grim; compensation from the firms involved (Rubery Owen and Joseph Sankey) seemed likely but did not mean that the company's lost market share would be regained automatically.

The new cars had received an enthusiastic reception when displayed at the October 1937 Motor Show – held in London's recently built exhibition centre at Earls Court. Although a new 3½-litre (212cu in) engine was now offered, making the '100' sports model Britain's cheapest 100mph (160kmh) car, it was the remarkably low-priced 1½-litre saloon (actually 1,776cc, 108cu in) that caused just as much interest. It seemed hardly possible that such a car, with all the expensive leather-and-walnut interior appointments of its two larger-engined sisters, could be built for £293 and still return a profit. The answer was, it couldn't. Lyons's bold strategy was to market the 1½-litre model virtually at cost. In this way he achieved enough volume to defray overheads and reduce unit costs on the many components shared by the 2½- and 3½-litre (162 and 212cu in) cars. It was these larger models, priced at £395 and £445 respectively, which contributed the profits.

Once production difficulties were overcome, this policy was a big success and in the year to 31 July 1939, SS Cars' workers (now 1,500 strong) for the first time built more than 5,000 cars in 12 months – 5,320 in fact. Of these, no fewer than 3,152 were 1½-litre (108cu in) saloons.

Profits for the 1938 financial year were down a quarter at £29,727 but represented a good recovery from the near-disaster of the steel body introduction. These problems impacted heavily on the accounts with a massive increase in stock (presumably unfinished cars), again funded by creditors, and the dividend was cut, which showed prudent management. However, these accounts indicate that Lyons was not a production man and that clearly he needed a good production engineer.

The new range of cars made a significant impact not only on the car-buying public but on other manufacturers too. While the established names might laugh-off Lyons's pre-Jaguar offerings, the 1938 Jaguars were serious motor cars. In the late 1930s BMW's advanced 2-litre (120cu in) 328 sports car (sold in Britain as a Frazer Nash-BMW) was the 100's chief rival, though at £695 (including 33 per cent import duty) it cost much more than the £445 Lyons was asking for even the 3½-litre (212cu in) 100 two-seater.

During an urgent attempt to reduce costs, Rolls-Royce undertook a costing exercise on the 3½-litre Jaguar, comparing it with the 4¼-litre (259cu in) Bentley, a car that Lyons himself much admired. While the Jaguar saloon cost only £445 complete, the Bentley had a chassis price of £1,150 and cost £1,510 with a Park Ward saloon body. The report concluded that while 30 per cent of the Bentley's extra chassis cost could be justified by better design and materials, 70 per cent could not and was attributed to SS Cars' 'good manufacturing technique backed up by sound purchasing of fabricated parts'. It was not that the Jaguar was better than the Bentley, because it was not. The worrying aspect for Rolls-Royce was how closely Lyons's Jaguar approached Bentley standards of comfort, performance and handling for so little money.

It was in a 1938 Jaguar 3½-litre (212cu in) drophead that the Lyons took a rare motoring holiday in France; they went with Jack Bradley (the family doctor) and his wife, Eileen. They drove down to Juan-les-Pins on the Côte d'Azur, recently made fashionable by the Duke and Duchess of Windsor. There, Lyons became fascinated by the new sport of waterskiing. He even tried it, Pat thought.

This excursion illustrates the sharp division between Lyons's personal and business life. At work, he did not regard any of his staff as friends in terms of meeting them socially, let alone holidaying with them. Even those who had joined him in Blackpool had little if any knowledge of Lyons's personal life and few ever saw the inside of Wappenbury Hall. The only exception in this respect was Alan Newsome; he was to act as solicitor for both the company and Lyons personally and would eventually take a seat on the Jaguar board. Alan was certainly part of the Lyons's social circle and so was his more extrovert brother Sammy – proprietor of the Coventry Hippodrome, SS dealer, and amateur rally and hill climb driver.

Other close friends were Bob and Marjorie McKeown (Bob was MD of a Courtaulds subsidiary), and Stanley and Pauline Hattrell. Stanley Hattrell, an architect, did have a business connection; he assisted Lyons both with alterations to Wappenbury Hall and with extensions to the factories, especially during and after the Second World War. However, their friendship certainly did not stop Lyons frequently challenging Hattrell's bills and he also objected to some of Alan Newsome's! He did not like paying for 'intangibles' such as advice, Newsome recalled.

As has been mentioned, Lyons formed particularly strong ties with the motoring press; it in turn was far from averse to becoming close to this remarkable young man and his ever-newsworthy company.

Iliffe and *The Autocar* have already been mentioned; Lyons became friendly not only with Managing Editor Geoffrey Smith and successive Editors of *The Autocar* but also some of the staff – including the famous artist F. Gordon Crosby and Technical Editor Douglas Clease. However, according to Christopher Jennings of *The Motor*: 'The person who had the best relationship, by miles, with Jaguar was Tommy Wisdom – he had been a friend of Bill Lyons and Greta ever since they were at Blackpool. There was nobody who had quite as much influence with the manufacturer as Tommy, but we came close behind.' In the 1930s Tommy Wisdom was the motoring correspondent for *The Daily Herald* and *The Sporting Life*. A competent driver, Wisdom, with his wife Elsie, gained Lyons his first international competition victory when he took one of the first SS Jaguar 100s to a Best Performance in the challenging International Alpine Trial of 1936. Later, he won a race at Brooklands in the same car.

In 1938 Lyons himself entered a motor race, a so-called 'trade race' at the May SS Car Club meeting at Donington Park near Derby. Lined up in three identical SS100s were Lyons, Heynes and Sammy Newsome. *The Motor* reported: 'W. Lyons, MD of the SS Company, simply couldn't wait on the starting line and was twice hauled back by the starter. When he did get it right he drove with the most awe-inspiring determination, and despite having tossed up for cars was soon in the lead.' Lyons surely set a strange kind of record with his Donington win: there can be few people who have won the very first motor race they entered – and then have never driven in another! More significantly, Lyons put up a faster lap that day than any other SS100 driver – and they included some of the quickest of the period – in any of the other races.

There is no doubt that Lyons, had he wished, could have become a successful racing driver, certainly at club level. That he was accomplished behind the wheel also meant that he was (as he later put it) sensitive to the handling qualities of a car and therefore able to assess what his engineers were doing. Not all managing directors in the car industry had this ability and often the products suffered as a consequence.

It was during a visit to another racetrack, Brooklands, in September 1938 that Lyons asked Tommy Wisdom for his opinion of a race engineer called Walter Hassan. Yes, Bill Heynes needed more help on the engineering side but the underlying reason for the enquiry was Lyons's ambition to enter 'the top bracket of world high performance cars'.[20] Hassan, whom Lyons had never met, appeared to have the qualifications to take SS forward in this direction. He had been one of W. O. Bentley's first employees at Cricklewood, London and later contributed much to Bentley's Le Mans wins. He had then worked for Woolf Barnato, creating some record-breaking Brooklands outer-circuit cars, before joining Thomson & Taylor's competition workshops at Brooklands.

A couple of years earlier, Lyons had entered into an agreement with that remarkable driver and Riley tuning exponent, Freddie Dixon. They had known each other from the days of Dixon's earlier motor cycle racing career. Dixon was a somewhat eccentric character and the arrangement lasted barely four months, although Dixon continued to try to interest Lyons in the Le Mans 24-hour race. Lyons knew full well that the SS100, while competitive in road rallies, would be outclassed in endurance racing but he did indeed become determined to one day produce a car that could hold its own in the world's most famous sports car events. The recruitment of Hassan was a step on the way to achieving this.

Hassan appeared a much less erratic character than Freddie Dixon and he joined SS in 1938 as Chief Experimental Engineer; he turned out to be everything that Lyons had hoped for. As for Hassan's opinion of Lyons, he stated towards the end of his career that 'like WO Bentley, Lyons was not really an engineer, but he was able to choose his team, to pick people out... If you were honest with him he appreciated it. A lot of people told him things were going well when they weren't but he always found out... You had to have the courage of your convictions. If you didn't think he understood what you were getting at, you had to put it to him clearly, and generally speaking he accepted it... It always paid to be fair and square with Sir William. That was best in the long run.'[21] While he did devote some time to race-tuning the 100 sports car, Hassan worked mainly on a new SS chassis with independent front suspension. In any case, thoughts of sports cars or motor racing receded rapidly as the political situation in Europe grew ever more serious.

In the late 1930s Lyons was among those in Britain who considered that a war with Germany was a distinct possibility and 'apart from the fear we all had of war, I was very depressed about the outlook for our company. I tried desperately to find some work which we could do so that we would have a start if war broke out and car production had to stop. Our machine shop was almost non-existent so I realised our only hope would be to obtain some airframe contract.'[22]

On 11 November 1938, Lyons reported to the board on his latest visit to the Ministry of Aircraft Production (MAP). He had driven to the Ministry's Harrogate contract department where he was referred to Short Brothers at Dorchester some 350 miles (560km) away; he presented himself there without an appointment the next day and was rewarded with a contract for Stirling bomber wing components. The board also discussed delays in plans for the 1940 model range but could reflect on record sales and a bank balance that stood at an extremely healthy £76,800.

Despite his concerns about a possible war, the favourable situation at the bank undoubtedly influenced Lyons's decision to purchase Motor Panels (Coventry) Ltd. This was acquired during the 1939–40 financial year. The company was also on the Whitmore Park Estate and had long supplied panels to Swallow and SS. It had been founded by a group of metal workers but, despite their undoubted abilities and all the business from SS, Motor Panels does not ever seem to have been in good shape financially. In fact SS had been supporting the concern covertly with loans from 1936, when it had also investigated taking a 50 per cent stake. A major shareholder was Mulliners, the large Birmingham bodymaking firm. Lyons's logic in acquiring a panel-making facility could not be faulted. If Motor Panels could be developed, SS might be in the highly desirable position of self-sufficiency in body supply. Unfortunately, world affairs would ultimately foil this plan.

The political situation was now much worse and was brought home chillingly to everyone at Foleshill when, during August 1939, work started on air raid trenches between the factory buildings. Orders for cars had by now slackened dramatically, although the directors (meeting on the last day of August) learned 'the remarkable fact that collections had been maintained'. They also discovered that Motor Panels was proving difficult to assimilate, with Lyons reporting that 'he had been very concerned for some time with the progress of the company and he found it difficult to keep on top of the situation' – a rare admission!

Even more seriously, the balance at the bank was now down to just £4,078; clearly, with drastically reduced sales the company's finances were haemorrhaging, and the Chairman and Secretary had to make the necessary arrangements with the bank. Fortunately Mr Cherrington at Lloyds proved to be 'exceedingly helpful' about the overdraft – at first. Sufficient defence contracts were proving difficult to secure and Lyons wrote to Austin's aircraft department emphasising his readiness to take on work 'to your complete satisfaction'; another begging letter was sent to Crossley Motors asking if it required bodywork.

On 3 September 1939 – the day before Lyons's 38th birthday –

Britain declared war on Germany. At SS, car production was winding down, with just existing stocks of parts being used (though an unexpected late order from Henlys in January 1940 meant that cars were still leaving the plant during most of that year). As the buildings received their camouflage paint (one job not carried out by maintenance!), Lyons arranged for David Rosenfield Ltd – the company that had taken up those obsolete Sunbeams in 1935 – to buy the stocks of unsold new Jaguars. The £42,331 received temporarily cleared the overdraft but at the company's first wartime AGM, held on 30 November 1939, shareholders were told that in spite of record sales the previous financial year, no dividend could be paid. The last few months had seen a drastic downturn in the company's fortunes. From a profit in 1938–9 of £48,787 on sales of £1.4m and a bank balance of £86,860, both sales and the cash reserves had plummeted. The directors reported that the large extension to the factory, planned well before the war, had been completed and that war contracts had been obtained.

In truth, these contracts were nowhere near enough to keep the wolf, or wolves, from the door. One predator was John Black who, in mid-December 1939, pointed out to Lyons that the SS account with Standard up to 30 November was £15,275 19s 4d (£15,275.96), exclusive of spares amounting to some £3,500. 'In addition to this we also have a large number of completed engines, gearboxes and a lot of other units which we have already paid for.' The pressure was building...

As aircraft work slowly got under way, a useful contract was secured by the sidecar division. This was thanks to H. R. Davies, who had founded his own motor cycle company (HRD) in 1924 and had won the Senior TT in 1925 on the same machine. Howard Davies had relinquished the failing business in 1928 but in the 1930s had been placed in charge of sidecar sales and development for the Swallow Sidecar Co (1935) Ltd. (This company, wholly owned by SS Cars Ltd, had been formed after the flotation to look after the sidecar interests.) Swallow had continued to produce hundreds of sidecars a month and Lyons designed most of the new models with Davies.

Howard Davies had a contact in the War Office and volunteered to introduce Lyons. The result was a large contract for sidecars of various descriptions (over 10,000 would be built by the end of the Second World War). Unfortunately there followed a disagreement about commission, Lyons complaining (not for the first or last time in such situations) that Davies was earning more than *he* was. Davies left but it is evident from the state of the company's finances at this time that in reality there was little cash to pay large bonuses. Contracts for many tens of thousands of trailers were secured too 'but we had a long way to go to avoid a critical financial situation,'[23] recorded Lyons.

As 1940 began, it seemed certain that SS was going to get a contract to build parts for the new Avro Manchester bomber. This was secured through Lyons having met Frank Spriggs, Managing Director of Hawker Siddeley, while playing golf with Frank Hough of Henlys before the Second World War! However, in May this fell through when the Manchester was cancelled due to engine problems. This was serious for SS, as although it still had a contract to repair the ancient Armstrong Whitley bomber, which temporarily replaced it, this in no way compensated for the lost Manchester job – especially as money had been spent on more new buildings for this contract.

It was now December 1940 and SS Cars' financial position was parlous. At the AGM held on 12 December, the company regretted not being able to produce the accounts for the year ending 31 July 1940. When they were subsequently completed, they showed a loss – the first since the company's formation – amounting to £22,660. Turnover was down 80 per cent and the overdraft stood at £23,200, ironically the approximate sum paid for Motor Panels. Also substantial expenditure had been incurred in building the new extensions. Not surprisingly, Lloyds Bank was getting restive over the size of SS Cars' overdraft and Lyons had to disclose the lost contract. 'As a consequence, I was asked to give my personal guarantee which was very worrying as it involved all my holding in the company and everything else I possessed.'[24] The amount Lloyds required Lyons to guarantee was £32,000 – or about six times the value of the family home.

There is no doubt that Lyons felt let down by Lloyds and it was nearly two years before he was released from his guarantee. After 18 years of hard work, it certainly must have been dispiriting to see everything that had been gained now under threat. Lyons, however, simply went on battling for contracts. By mid-1941 it had been decided, after much boardroom discussion and without Lyons voting, that the company should take out a debenture with Lloyds to secure a larger overdraft against the company's assets. The better news was that the lengthy task of putting the factory on to a war footing was now complete and the company was making a day-to-day profit. Indeed, by the end of July, the annual accounts for 1940–1 showed an impressive recovery to profits of £40,419, though the overdraft was now up to £70,511 with stock and work in progress up 64 per cent to £216,251. Motor Panels and Swallow Sidecars were contributing to the profits by way of rent and dividends.

Meanwhile, work had begun on the old Armstrong Whitleys and SS discovered that making aeroplane parts was vastly different from building motor cars. 'I have a vivid recollection,' Lyons wrote of the period, 'of the arrival of the first Whitley bombers at our Foleshill factory, as they went past my office window on a convoy of "Queen Mary" transporters. I followed them into the factory and was surprised how little they appeared to be damaged. Together with the works manager and chief inspector, I examined them carefully, and I made a remark to them – which I will never forget – "We'll have these repaired in under a month." Some of them were still there a year later. I was at the time ignorant of the stringent Aeronautical Inspection Directorate requirements.'[25] But Lyons and the workforce learned to work to the AID's standards and in the end SS was responsible not only for the repair of the aircraft but also for getting them flight tested at nearby Tachbrook aerodrome. More aircraft work was acquired gradually and over the course of the next five years various parts for the Spitfire, Lancaster and Mosquito were made too.

The year 1941 saw the worst period of the Coventry blitz. Bill and 'Dutch' Heynes lost their first son and on the dreadful night of 14 November, when Coventry suffered particular punishment, the Foleshill factory was damaged also. The occasion was memorable for Lyons for many reasons, one trivial on its own but to Lyons expressing the spirit of Coventry people at this time. Just after dawn he had made his way through the city 'amongst terrible devastation' and arrived at the works. 'As I stepped out of my car at the gates, I met a little man whom we employ as a works barber. Where he had been I do not know, but he touched his cap and said, "Sharp this morning, sir".'[26]

The Lyons's family life was disrupted along with everyone else's. All the domestic staff disappeared and Greta Lyons suddenly had to cope with managing the vast Wappenbury Hall alone. However, she wasn't alone for long as when the air raids on Coventry began, the house became full of refugees from the bombing. Amongst Mary Lyons's earliest memories are a Mr and Mrs Knight: '...they had the servants' hall as their sitting room and he was a shop steward at Standard's. I adored Mr Knight... I can remember spending more time with them than I did with mummy or daddy. Mummy was busy doing voluntary canteen work at Anstey aerodrome and daddy was at the factory most of the day. Apart from the Knights in the house, there were other families, some in the attic. These were people with nowhere to go. I can remember mummy telling me that after one of the worst blitzes, they drove into Coventry and there were people just walking out of Coventry. She would stop and say, "Where are you going?" "We don't know." So she'd pick them up and take them to Wappenbury.'[27] The stables and large coach-house at Wappenbury were put to good use too, being packed with car chassis and engines removed from the Foleshill works for safety and to release factory-floor space.

Pat had been sent to a boarding school in Wales but recalled in the holidays all the family cycling into Leamington, about five miles (8km) away, to go to the cinema because her father would not use the car for leisure purposes. Mary remembers this too: 'He was very conscientious. He was obviously allowed a bit more petrol than most people. We often used to say, "Oh, can't we drive to Leamington?" But he would never do it. Not because he wasn't going to risk being caught, but from principle.' Mary also remembers around this time a rare incident of her father becoming involved in domestic matters: 'Mummy must have been away when daddy suddenly decided he was going to make some crab apple jelly. I got very excited about this. We went and picked some crab apples and got our *Mrs Beeton's* and made this crab apple jelly which I might add was very good. I remember mummy coming back and being absolutely furious. He had used the entire month's sugar ration. The whole lot...'[28]

Work went on at Foleshill and in the autumn of 1941 a contract was obtained to make various Armstrong Siddeley Cheetah aircraft engine components. This came about through another of Lyons's fortuitous acquaintanceships, this time with Chris Oliver, General Manager of Armstrong Siddeley (owned by Hawker Siddeley). Lyons explained the difficulties he faced getting contracts because of his lack of a machine shop. Oliver was able to help. He had been told to disperse some of his activities from the Coventry factory, so he gave some of the Cheetah engine work to SS and helped it set up the necessary machine shop. Lyons had located a run-down shoe factory away from the air raids at South Wigston, near Leicester. This factory was requisitioned and was organised and run by Jack Beardsley. The machine shop helped SS gain other specialist war work and, moved to Foleshill after the war, was to form the core of the company's peacetime machining capability.

In April 1942 Lyons received an unexpected proposal which, had it come to fruition, might have changed the face of the British motor cycle industry after the war. He was contacted by Edward Turner, then probably Britain's leading motor cycle designer. In 1935 Turner, born a few months earlier than Lyons in 1901, had taken charge of the Triumph motor cycle concern after it had been split from the Triumph car company and bought by Jack Sangster. Turner produced 'ground-breaking' designs, which made Triumph a world leader in its field. His Triumph Speed Twin of 1937 has been described as the most important motor cycle of its decade and Lyons thought that the motor cycle company had earned Sangster £100,000 in a year. However, Turner was of almost artistic temperament and very much his own man, so not many were surprised when, in 1942, he fell out with Sangster over design royalties and was sacked.

His main proposal to Lyons, apart from offering his services to SS Cars generally, was that they should 'start a new venture in which the equity was shared between you and me'. The operation would be set up at Motor Panels and begin by manufacturing a sidecar chassis for Swallow's existing military contracts. This would have formed a 'nucleus of production' that, with some bought-out components and an engine Turner would design, could then move on to making motor cycles – initially for the Government but with an eye for the 'immediate post war potential'.[29]

There was no better man than Lyons, still the keenest motor cycling enthusiast, for Turner to have approached. Turner then lived at Lyons's old house, Woodside at Gibbet Hill. (Could he have bought it from Lyons?) On 27 April 1942 Lyons wrote to Turner saying that he would very much like to go into the matter further. However, he wanted Turner to 'prepare the most comprehensive plans and estimates for not only are these a very valuable guide as a programme for procedure, but they also provide a check in the progress achieved, and are a very good indication of the extent to which departure from the programme increases the financial commitment of the undertaking.' (This also provides an interesting illustration of how Lyons controlled the costs of new projects.)

A satisfactory response must have been received as Lyons drafted a letter in June 1942 confirming Turner's appointment as 'Technical Engineer of our subsidiary company, Motor Panels (Coventry) Ltd'. The draft agreement included: 1) 'It is agreed that a motor cycle business shall be formed, on the termination of hostilities, or such earlier date as may be mutually agreed, having a share capital of £10,000 to be held equally between SS Cars Ltd and yourself. 2) Expansion shall be financed by equal investment by both parties, otherwise from profits, or by loan, 3) Turner to be MD at a nominal salary of XX, the chairman to be myself or nominees of SS Cars, without remuneration unless paid by SS Cars, 4) Neither to dispose of part or whole of their share holding without the consent of the other.'

The letter was never sent. On 22 June Turner wrote to Lyons regretting that he had to inform him that he had 'accepted an appointment with Birmingham Small Arms Ltd. May I here say how much I would have liked to have joined with you in business and to thank you for your kindness and courtesy during our negotiations.'

On 24 June 1942 Lyons replied to his letter: 'Dear Mr Turner, I am not surprised to receive your letter advising me that you have joined BSA. I do hope that you will find that you have made the right decision. One cannot dispute that it is the safest one. Please accept my very best wishes. Yours sincerely, W. Lyons.'

Whether a partnership between Lyons and Turner – both strong-willed individualists – would have lasted will never be known but a Jaguar-owned Triumph in the 1950s and 1960s remains a tantalising proposition. The Turner story does not quite end in 1942, though. In 1960 Jaguar bought Daimler from BSA; its Chief Engineer was Edward Turner, who in the meantime had designed two highly effective Daimler V8 engines. Turner left upon the takeover but his 2½-litre (155cu in) V8 went on to power some successful Jaguar-bodied Daimlers into the late 1960s.

Meanwhile, back in the early 1940s the financial pressures on SS Cars were easing as contract work increased. Also Lyons had pleaded successfully with Sir Archibald Forbes at the Air Ministry for bridging finance in connection with the new buildings that the company had erected in anticipation of the Manchester contract. These had been erected on a 19-acre (7.7-hectare) site purchased by SS Cars from the Whitmore Estate in March 1937 for £7,965. The new factory, completed during the Second World War, almost doubled the company's floor area.

There was certainly no spare money around when another unexpected opportunity arose in 1942. In October John Black of Standard offered to sell SS the 'exclusive' engine plant, on which the company's 2½- and 3½-litre (162 and 212cu in) engines were made. The reason given by Black for his decision was that he did not want to make the engines again for SS after the Second World War. Lyons jumped at the chance, especially as 'before the war, Black had given me reason for a great deal of anxiety' about the exclusive nature of the engine arrangement. 'Several other makers had asked him to supply them, and I had not found it easy to prevent him doing so.' Moreover Lyons saw the offer as 'a great step forward towards our becoming the self-contained manufacturing unit at which I aimed'.[30]

Black put the plant value on Standard's books at £16,351 but he would be prepared to sell it for £10,000, with payment deferred until after the war. Lyons managed to negotiate this figure down to £6,000 and decided to try to pay the whole sum within 12 months. 'I am arranging for the plant to be removed as early as possible,' he told the board on 1 October 1942. The urgency was due to Lyons's mistrust of Black; this later turned out to be justified. 'It was not long before Black proposed that we should revert back to the old arrangement and return the plant to Standards. I said "No, thank you, John, I have now got the ball, and I would rather kick it myself." He pressed me very hard, even to the extent that we should form a separate company together, but I was unwilling to accept his proposals, even though I so much appreciated his help in the past.'[31]

Considerable self-sufficiency in engine supply – SS would still be reliant on Standard for the 1½-litre (108cu in) engine after the war – was a step towards manufacturing autonomy. A step backwards was the sale of Motor Panels. This was after considerable effort had been put into making it an effective operation but, with the company's overdraft still massive and after discussion at the April 1943 board meeting, an offer of £2 per share from Rubery Owen was accepted.

Lyons knew exactly what he was having to do and much regretted it. He wrote later: 'I have often thought what might have been if the war had not broken out, for we would have gone ahead developing it [Motor Panels] and we would have built up a very substantial body plant. It might have altered my outlook on a lot of things, and the whole history of the company might have been different... We just didn't have the money so I sold Motor Panels to Rubery Owen.'[32]

It is very possible the bank was pressing him to sell Motor Panels. Although the 1942 results showed an increasingly healthy pre-tax profit of £67,152, the overdraft was now within £25 of £88,000. With stock up to almost £300,000, creditors way up again, and tax on the profits now increased to 43 per cent, the company was clearly not generating sufficient funds, making the sale of Motor Panels advisable. Also in the years 1940–2, some £30,000 had needed to be spent on air raid precautions, the equivalent of £700,000 in today's money. However, it has further been suggested that a militant unionised workforce at Motor Panels also acted as a catalyst in Lyons's reluctant decision.

Greater control over finances came during 1943 when Arthur Thurstans joined from Lockheed to take up the newly created post of Chief Accountant. He quickly set up more professional systems throughout the company and Lyons came to have a high regard for him.

In July 1943 Lyons reported on negotiations with the Gloster Aircraft Co. This concerned one of SS Cars' most interesting wartime tasks, the building of the first Meteor jet fuselages. It took some months for this to get under way, due to the delay in receiving the necessary special tooling from Standard. The job had overtaxed Standard's capacity, according to Lyons, but Black 'fought hard to keep it for himself'. Only at the beginning of 1944 was satisfactory progress achieved.

Regrettable though the decision to sell Motor Panels had been, Lyons had doubled his money and Rubery Owen's £50,000 certainly reduced the overdraft, which was down to £49,656 in the 1943 accounts. Encouragingly, profits had almost doubled to £118,314, although a wartime tax rate of no less than 70 per cent took some £82,230. The benefit of Arthur Thurstans's greater control of the finances was illustrated by a reduced stock figure.

At the 1944 AGM, held in May, the Chairman looked forward to peacetime production, emphasising that the plant's capacity was now nearly twice as great as it was in 1939, 'almost all the building at the Company's expense'. Behind closed doors at Foleshill, low-key development work on the postwar range of cars had in fact been taking place for some time and significant progress had been made in various directions.

One wartime duty at Foleshill was night time fire-watching in case of an incendiary raid. Not being one to waste time or opportunity, Lyons soon ensured that the Sunday evening shift consisted of himself, Bill Heynes, Walter Hassan (who had returned to SS after a spell with the Bristol Aeroplane Co) and Claude Baily. Engine designer Baily had joined the company in 1940 from Morris Engines. Hassan, who had considered Lyons somewhat stiff and formal when he first joined the company, now found that his boss began to unbend somewhat as they all discussed postwar plans.

Uppermost in Lyons's mind was a completely new engine, which eventually would supersede the now rather ancient Standard-based units. He favoured the racing-type twin overhead camshaft cylinder head as used on many of the best competition cars and motor cycles before the war – such as, he told Hassan, 'the Peugeots and the Sunbeams'.[33] Not only was this type of valve layout efficient but (and this was expressly required by Lyons) it reflected this efficiency visually when the bonnet was opened.

Walter Hassan and Claude Baily were more sceptical, as this advanced, complex type of engine was not common in production cars at the time. But Lyons found a powerful ally in Bill Heynes, who had been wedded to the overhead camshaft concept since his engineering apprenticeship days. The ohc lobby won and so was born the famous XK engine, which appeared in 1948. Powerful, refined and reliable, it was to be at the heart of Jaguar's success on road and track for 30 years. Yet the decision to adopt it was a brave one; unreliability in service could have been ruinous for the company.

While the new engine concept was being developed discreetly at Foleshill, Lyons was planning the investment that would be needed to manufacture it and to acquire some of the machines then on loan from the Government. The Second World War was now clearly going to be won and Lyons, in common with most car manufacturers, wanted to be ready to take advantage of the pent-up demand for new cars, especially from overseas. So in addition to the existing £100,000 facility at Lloyds Bank (relations were once again cordial), he arranged for a further £100,000 of credit (later increased to £150,000 though, in the end, not all was used). Wartime levels of taxation were extremely high and though the company made a profit of £164,919 in 1944, some 75 per cent was taken in tax. By July 1944 the company was at its strongest financially since formation, with net current assets of £322,432, stock and work in progress of £300,439, and was again in credit at the bank.

During 1944 John Black once more came into the picture. This time it concerned the Triumph car company, which in 1939 had gone into bankruptcy (competition from SS was probably among the reasons!). Lyons had examined the books in 1939 but had felt that to bring Triumph back into profit would jeopardise his own company. Now Black was investigating the purchase of Triumph himself 'but would not do so if I changed my mind and join forces with him'.

Although in October 1935 Lyons had assisted Black in purchasing 20,000 shares in SS Cars Ltd for £5,000, before the Second World War he had always rejected suggestions of a joint venture and now he did so again. An annoyed Black retaliated by telling Lyons that 'he would buy Triumph and go into competition with us. He said he could not see us surviving it...'[34]

Lyons was not in the least perturbed and sure enough, although Standard did acquire Triumph in November 1944, nothing ever emerged from Canley that offered a challenge to Lyons's products. 'In spite of our differences,' Lyons wrote later of Sir John Black, 'I would like to pay tribute to him for his great energy and the success he made of the Standard Motor Company in the early postwar years.'[35] In fact, the two men enjoyed perfectly cordial relations in their later years.

Of much greater concern to Lyons than any threat from John Black was the news towards the end of the Second World War that SS Cars Ltd would be among those companies not qualifying for any of the very limited supplies of steel which would be available postwar. This, thought Lyons, was because SS was not viewed by the Government as an exporter; with Britain in desperate need of foreign currency, there was clearly going to be an 'export or die' policy. Certainly, before the Second World War the company's resources had not stretched to setting up an export organisation having, in Lyons's words, 'barely established our home market'. Considering that the first Jaguar appeared towards the end of 1935 and that four years later the country had been at war, this was entirely true.

As ever, Lyons took immediate action. Inspired by 'elaborately prepared brochures' which SS Cars had itself received from various companies during the Second World War, he prepared his own very comprehensive brochure detailing the company's postwar plans. This included the intended export programme and the tonnage of steel required for the new model proposed, 'which I named the "International", thinking it would have a psychological effect.'[36] This document Lyons delivered personally to Sir George Turner, then Permanent Secretary to the Ministry of Supply, emphasising verbally the major points in the brochure. But it was a long two weeks before the letter came agreeing to the entire allocation of steel that Lyons had requested – as he had pointed out, this was tiny compared with the quantities needed by mass producers such as Ford, Austin, and Morris.

When peace was declared on 8 May 1945, and VE Day was celebrated, the company could look forward to producing cars once more. Just beforehand, though, an important technical change took place: on 9 April 1945, the company officially adopted the name Jaguar Cars Ltd. There were a number of good reasons for this change; not the least being that the original name would always evoke memories of the SS troops that, in another of Lyons's understatements, were 'a sector of the community not highly regarded'.[37] But it also avoided confusion, especially overseas, over what the car was really called – was it an 'SS' or a 'Jaguar'?

It had been back in September 1937 that Lyons had proposed that Jaguar Cars Ltd be formed 'for the purpose of preserving our interest in the name Jaguar'. Jaguar Cars Ltd, number 333482, was successfully incorporated on 11 November 1937. At various times subsequently, particularly during the war years, the adoption of

Jaguar Cars as the company's title was discussed; then, in April 1945, the time was finally right.

As a courtesy, Lyons checked with Armstrong Siddeley about the change: 'In spite of our already having used the name, I asked Sir Frank Spriggs, then managing director of Armstrong Siddeley and with whom I had become friendly during the war, if he had any objection to our doing it. He said they had no intention of using the name and agreed to our proposal both verbally and in writing.'[38]

Some traditional aspects of Lyons's organisation did not continue with him into the postwar world. One much-regretted departure was Cyril Holland; he had been made Body Shop Manager but was not happy directing large groups of men. Also, while Lyons had offered him a much bigger salary than he had anticipated, he did not offer Cyril the written contract he wanted. He left to run a number of successful small companies of his own and Fred Gardner took over his role as Lyons's styling 'interpreter'. Harry Gill had also left, feeling he had been sidelined at Motor Panels where he had been sent; he too succeeded in his own businesses.

Then the Swallow Coachbuilding Company (1935) Ltd had also gone. War contract work had tailed off and Lyons did not want to resume making civilian sidecars. The Helliwell Group of Stratford-upon-Avon, which amongst other things had made windscreens for Swallow sidecars and for the early SS (and had undertaken aircraft work during the war), agreed in December 1944 to buy the share capital.

It took more than 12 months for the deal to go through, although Helliwell were given the nod to begin trading under the Swallow name in the meantime – resulting in a slight mix-up when SS Cars received an order from a company in South Africa for 2,000 bicycles! The delay had been caused by Helliwell's legal advisers who were unhappy with certain aspects of the proposed agreement, concerning possible wartime taxation liabilities, and also the nature of financial transactions between Swallow Coachbuilding and the parent SS Cars Ltd company going back to 1935. The sale finally went through on 4 December 1945; the last link with Swallow had been severed.

CHAPTER 4

XK120 – AND
AMERICA BECKONS

In common with most (but certainly not all) British motor manufacturers, Jaguar's first postwar products were slightly modified versions of its prewar cars. To restart production, much effort was needed to locate and refurbish long-disused tools and jigs, while the engine manufacturing plant obtained from Standard had to be installed. By July 1945 the assembly line had cranked into action once again although it was not until 1946 that the full range of 1½-, 2½- and 3½-litre (108, 162 and 212cu in) saloons – now with plain 'Jaguar' instead of 'SS Jaguar' radiator badges – began to leave the works in any quantity.

As far back as 1943 Lyons had briefed Mr Cherrington at Lloyds Bank of his intention to introduce two new small (10hp and 12hp) Jaguar cars within a year or so of getting back into production with the 'old' range after the war. His reasoning had been that in postwar Britain, economic conditions and petrol rationing would mitigate against the thirsty, big-engined Jaguars – as previously noted, even the '1½-litre' was in fact 1,776cc (108cu in). It was because overseas markets, especially the United States, still favoured larger engines that Lyons shelved (and soon abandoned entirely) his small-car plans – though a family of small-capacity engines was kept in the frame for some years as a precaution.

Also, it had become clear during the contest to obtain steel supplies that the export market would become increasingly important. Britain, brought almost to its knees by the war effort, desperately needed foreign currency, especially US dollars. This was emphasised sternly by Sir Stafford Cripps, who insisted on a 50 per cent export rate if car companies were to receive their steel allowance. (Cripps then headed the Board of Trade in Clement Attlee's new Labour Government, which had unexpectedly swept aside Churchill and his coalition in July 1945.)

Even then, Jaguar's export deliveries did not get under way properly until the latter part of 1947, partly because of coal and materials shortages in the dreadful winter of 1946–7 but also for historic reasons. Before the war, Lyons had regarded exports as mere icing on the cake: in the company's best prewar 12-month period (1938–9) only 226 out of the 5,454 Jaguars delivered went overseas. The home market absorbed everything that could be produced 'so we did not go to the expense of establishing export outlets,'[1] admitted Lyons later. This left the postwar Jaguars Cars Ltd somewhat poorly prepared to tackle exports.

Therefore, with some urgency, reliable outlets (with the adequate service and parts facilities upon which Lyons insisted) began to be established or reinforced in various key European and New World countries. Often these concerns were run by colourful characters, none more so than Joska Bourgeois in Belgium. Described as 'a young woman of imposing countenance and unavoidable presence,'[2] she took up the Jaguar cause during 1947 with great determination. When later that year the Belgian Government prohibited the import of cars costing above £500, she helped Jaguar establish a local assembly plant with Van den Plas. (Madame Bourgeois later made an even greater fortune when, in 1967, she obtained one of the first Toyota distributorships in Europe. We will return to this legendary figure in the industry later; she did not enter the public eye until her involvement with the one-time Chairman of Jaguar Cars, Geoffrey Robinson MP, became well known in the late 1990s. She died in 1994.) Elsewhere in Europe, Emil Frey continued (with Marcel Fleury) in Switzerland, Georg Hans Koch remained in Austria, and J. W. Lagerwij looked after Holland. There were also Charles Delecroix in Paris and Erik Sommer in Denmark, though for a while France and Denmark were among those countries that barred the import of cars from Britain – they too had their currency problems.

In Australia, Lyons had been disappointed when his prewar distributor in Melbourne, Crosby Brothers, forecast selling only 100 cars a year. So when a cable arrived from Jack Bryson offering to contract for 2,000 cars a year if he was given the distributorship, Lyons was impressed – this was the sort of entrepreneurial spirit to which he could relate. Having checked out its references, in the summer of 1946 he gave Bryson Motors (hitherto a small-time importer of Morgans and Ariel motor cycles) its opportunity. 'We made the appointment and it was only because we could not supply them with the full 2,000 cars, that they did not reach this target,'[3] recounted Lyons with some admiration years later. Certainly Australia and, to a lesser extent, New Zealand were to be prime markets for Jaguar.

Despite these efforts, exports built up only slowly. By far the greater number of early postwar Jaguars, mostly 1½-litre (108cu in) saloons, went to the car-starved home market – from total sales of 4,342 in 1946–7, just 910 went overseas. Like all manufacturers, Jaguar could sell everything it could build. Even so, Lyons adopted a long-term view and, talking confidentially at a Motor Trade Luncheon Club engagement in April 1947, showed an advanced appreciation of the vital need still to put the customer first: 'There is in some quarters,' he said, 'an inclination to regard the customer as a nuisance... I think this arises from the fact that so many salesmen consider that the customer is fortunate to be able to obtain a car of any kind, any how, and is therefore inclined to treat him as someone who is receiving a favour. In my opinion, during this time of a seller's market, now is the opportunity for making friends for the future... I do feel that this question of the relationship with the customer is a vitally important one.'[4]

This regard for the customer, if not unique in 1947, was probably ahead of its time in the motor industry; it also extended to the quality of the product, about which Lyons sometimes despaired. For instance, in May 1946 he drafted a memo to Works Manager Ted Orr and Production Manager John Silver: 'I am very perturbed at the number of complaints which we are receiving from our agents who call at the works. Almost every one I see refers to bad workmanship and carelessness, such as parts unpainted, nuts loose etc etc. It is a disgraceful thing that a company of our reputation should turn out cars which, our agents advise us, require overhaul before being delivered to our customers... It is no use striving to obtain a large output if we are to lose our reputation.'

Six months later the situation had improved very little and Lyons issued a further memo, this time about the number of complaints being received from owners: 'in spite of every pressure I have put upon the Inspection Department, these complaints are increasing in dangerous numbers...' Lyons felt that those responsible 'would better appreciate the seriousness of the position if they themselves received these complaints personally.' While he did not think that was possible, Lyons did attach a typical letter 'which I am sure you will agree we should be ashamed to receive'.

Such matters were taken up in the first *Jaguar Journal*, the house magazine launched in October 1946; its Editor was press and public relations man Ernest 'Bill' Rankin but its editorial leader smacks of Lyons. Quality, it said, 'was never in greater demand than it is today. Weary of shoddy makeshift articles which were tolerated only under the stress of war, the buying public is manifesting a strong reaction in demanding not only more goods but better goods.'

Volume One, Number One, which sold out within an hour, also contained a long (5½-page) report of a 'unique' mass meeting of employees and management, which had taken place in the main assembly shop at 4.30pm on 24 September. Almost all the workforce seemed to have been present – some 1,400 people – while on the platform were Lyons, Charles Gallagher (Chairman of the union shop stewards' committee), Works Convenor P. Bentley, Works Manager Ted Orr and 25 shop stewards.

Since the end of the Second World War labour relations at Jaguar had deteriorated. As Mr Gallagher explained from the platform, there had been a number of minor unofficial stoppages and 'discord' between management and unions. This had resulted in a 'no punches pulled meeting' between management and shop stewards the previous week and the mass meeting had been called, in the presence of Lyons, to ask the workforce to endorse the policy which that meeting had formulated. 'To my knowledge,' continued Gallagher, 'in no other factory in Coventry has the managing director come on the platform to afford the workers an opportunity of putting questions to him.' He then called on Lyons to address the meeting.

Lyons said that it had been his intention to tell a few home truths but admitted that he had rather altered his views after a remark that Mr Gallagher had made. 'He said something I have looked forward to for years. I have long hoped that one day one of the workers would say something nice about management!'

He went on to point out that the company was anxious to arrange piecework prices so that good money could be earned but conceded that lots of differences and 'irritations' had sometimes resulted in stoppages and walk-outs. Now, there would be regular meetings with shop stewards each Wednesday and if matters raised could not be settled by Mr Orr then he, himself, would be 'quite willing' to become involved. He wanted to establish confidence in the shop stewards, while the re-established Joint Production Committee would view all production problems 'as a whole'.

'I am convinced that we have a better opportunity now than ever before,' concluded Lyons, 'of earning money, good money, if you will only go for it…so let's get cracking and go all out for 150 cars a week…work as one unit and you will find it will lead to continuous and well-paid employment.' At which, said the report, there was 'spontaneous applause'.

Questions from the floor included the 40-hour week and a guaranteed wage, to which topics Lyons responded with the need, as he saw it, for realism and to 'hold our own against competition... The American trouble has been a blessing to this country but it can't go on for ever.' Reiterating a philosophy he had held since the earliest days of Swallow, that reward should be linked to production, he assured his listeners 'I am prepared to let you earn through the roof if the price is right'.

The formal proposals were then put to the meeting. Key points were: constitutional procedures should be followed for all negotiations between management and works; any matters not covered by procedures should be raised at the Wednesday meeting; the desirability of further mass meetings of all workers, shop stewards and management 'with a view to obtaining confidence and co-operation'; and that workers should be asked for a vote of confidence in shop stewards. In response to a question about the choice of shop stewards, Lyons advised: 'It is absolutely essential that you pick a man who really knows his job. He must be a craftsman...do not be influenced in this very important matter by political motives.'

Gallagher summed up. 'The object is to prevent, as far as it lies in our power, needless stoppages. If you accept the policy you will place in the hands of your shop stewards the opportunity of doing this. You will not be giving away the right to strike.' There was unanimous approval from the floor of the motions. 'I hope,' concluded Gallagher, 'that this meeting will be a landmark in the history of this company.'

This whole incident has been worth dwelling on for several reasons. Firstly, it confirms Lyons's core policy when dealing with strikes or walk-outs, a policy he adhered to almost without deviation until his retirement: no negotiations without a return to work. Secondly, the matter highlights Lyons's sense of fair play. He failed to understand why, if there were agreed procedures in place, these should not be explored fully before strike action was resorted to. Neither could he understand the lack of appreciation by unofficial strikers that loss of production cost sales, which in turn damaged the company's progress and jeopardised the very creation of the revenues on which the workers' wages (and wage increases) depended. To him it was all a matter of common sense.

His daughter, Pat Quinn, remembered his attitude well. 'He could never understand why they [the workers] were being so stupid in more or less destroying their own jobs. I used to say, when I was going through a very socialist phase, "well, it's all right, they should have more money" or whatever. He used to say, "well, if we distributed the profits and they all got a penny each extra it wouldn't make much difference to them, but the important thing is to keep the business going." He always used to say it wouldn't help by just giving them more money.'[5]

In some ways the unions, which did not want their positions to be undermined by the bypassing of procedures, were in the middle of all this. Before 1940 they had not really achieved prominence at SS Cars but, as skilled craftsmen from new trades entered the company's employ during the Second World War, by 1943 they had finally obtained a foothold.

Only reluctantly did Lyons come to accept them, however. Jack Jones, of the Transport and General Workers' Union (which he was later to head), had known Lyons before the Second World War. Aside from his TGWU position, Jones was Secretary and leader of the Confederation of Shipbuilding and Engineering Unions and so was in contact with the sheet metal and vehicle builders' unions, giving him a good overall view of union relations at SS and Jaguar.

'He [Lyons] was very much anti-union initially but we managed to convert him. He was very antagonistic. This was in Holbrooks...a rather Heath Robinson-type of factory, I am afraid. He kept the trade union movement out wherever he could, particularly the sheet metal workers' trade union, and my own union, the Transport and General Workers...'[6]

Jones recalled Lyons's hands-on approach. 'Although he was top man, he was obviously interested in all the operations in the plant. So, when there were occasional disputes about piecework prices [it was essentially a piecework factory], I'd be talking to the works manager Teddy Orr and suddenly Billy Lyons would appear...he'd be the most difficult man to convince...' Incidentally, while Lyons was constantly around the factory, Jones did not find that he was anxious to identify with the shop-floor workers in the way that he recalled Captain Black of Standard did. He remained 'austere, almost aristocratic'[7] according to Jones.

Jones also remembered Lyons's 'strong line' against some of the shop stewards. In one instance a young shop steward, who was very active in promoting the union and 'perhaps taking more time than he should going round the plant,' was sacked. There were repeated appeals to reinstate him but Lyons simply kept the man at home on full pay 'for weeks and weeks on end'.[8] He would not back down.

However, Jack Jones acknowledged that 'against that there was this general background of immense activity on his part and one felt he was a man who had built from the ground upwards.' Overall, Jones considered that the unions' relations with Lyons were 'quite good, but he wanted every ounce of flesh' and that while Lyons was a man of his word, he gave this only 'very reluctantly'.[9]

That mass meeting of union officials, workers, and management in September 1946 had been good-humoured and constructive. It seemed to have ended on a note of genuine rapprochement between Lyons and the workforce. Unhappily, though, this apparent spirit of co-operation and trust lasted only a few weeks. By 10 October 1946 Lyons was involved in a dispute over hourly rates agreed back in July. 'I have personally assured a representative gathering of shop stewards that it is the company's policy to ensure that the workers earn the highest rate it is possible for the company to pay,' wrote Lyons on that date, 'and I very much regret that the company's production and the workers' earnings are again, after a few weeks' successful effort, jeopardised by unnecessary agitation and strike action.'

So Jaguar was not after all to be spared the series of unofficial stoppages that, though usually of short duration, all too often prevented the company realising its full sales potential worldwide during the following 35 years.

Even back in 1946, of all the countries that appeared to offer export opportunities, it became increasingly clear to British car makers that none was more important than the United States. Yet this vast market was under-exploited – in 1946 Britain's most valuable exports to the US were certainly not cars: they were led by textiles (£5.5m), whisky (£5.2m), and linen (£3.1m). Cars accounted for little more than £500,000 and of the 359,000 made in the UK during 1946, 147,000 might have been exported but few went to North America.

Yet a set of conditions there had produced a wonderful opportunity and, for once, British industry was ahead of the game. The US had been at war with Japan until August 1945, when the atomic bomb finally concluded the matter, and American industry was taking a long time to change from a war footing to peacetime production. It was not helped during 1946 by a series of countrywide strikes, which affected coal, steel and the railroads, as well as automobile manufacturers and their suppliers. For a while (reported *The Autocar* in October) it was common to see new cars driving around New York with painted wooden bumpers. There was an acute shortage of new automobiles in the showrooms (only two million cars were made in the US in 1946 against expectations of double that quantity) and for the first time many Americans were prepared to try even 'funny foreign cars' – if they could get them.

Austin – followed by Morris, Ford of Britain and Standard-Triumph – did begin to make some inroads but Jaguar was held back by materials delays and the lack of a sales organisation in the US. In fact Lyons had to contend with a negative – a prewar distributor was claiming a percentage on all Jaguars sold in North America, having apparently registered the name there. This was overcome towards the end of 1946 but only after Lyons hired solicitors recommended by Studebaker (a marque then being sold by Henlys). They put forward the argument that as the 'distributor' had not imported any Jaguars since the war, his claim had lapsed. This was not challenged and Lyons was free to sell his cars in America unhindered.

In some ways the Jaguar of this time might have appeared unsuitable for this sophisticated market. After all, the car's design dated back to 1937 and even then it had appeared old-fashioned with its traditional upright radiator, cart-sprung solid axles, and quaint wooden dashboard – by that time most American automobiles had adopted faired-in radiators and boasted independent front suspension. In 1947, therefore, the Jaguar appeared positively antique, yet it was perhaps this very aspect that appealed to certain Americans – 'retro' styling decades before the concept was invented!

But the Jaguar 3½-litre (212cu in) saloon (and its drophead counterpart introduced at the end of 1947) nevertheless had a competitive, 90mph (145kmh), performance plus an undoubted presence. With the introduction of left-hand drive, exports to the US went up from just nine in 1947 to 245 in 1948 (financial years June to July). However, it would take something a lot more modern and exciting than these baroque old cars to bring Jaguar the success it would eventually achieve in America. And behind the scenes at Foleshill, exactly such a product was under development.

Jaguar was not one of those companies to have grown rich on war contracts. Indeed, as recounted the transition to war work had proved almost fatal. But Lyons's determined pursuit of contracts and the ability of the workforce to produce high-quality products had, by the end of hostilities, pulled the financial situation round somewhat. The balance sheet at 31 July 1945 looked robust; there was £38,856 in the bank and although profits, at £78,269, were less than half the previous year's figure, at least this meant a less punitive rate of tax of 'only' 47 per cent.

At the AGM Lyons also announced that the authorised capital of the company had been increased to £500,000 by the creation of 150,000 new 5½ per cent shares of £1 each. Only 100,000 had been issued, however, and this was to be the last issue of Jaguar shares for sale until the company emerged from the BL conglomerate in 1984 as a private company once more. After 1946, Jaguar always funded its cash requirements – including major acquisitions – from its own profits.

By now, while still a small concern, Jaguar Cars Ltd was being taken a little more seriously within financial circles – although Lyons took umbrage when he discovered that *The Financial Times* required a large payment to list Jaguar's daily share quotation. It took a veiled threat from Rankin about withdrawing Jaguar's advertising for the *FT* to reconsider; it did and Jaguar's share price was listed from February 1946.

Some important personnel changes took place during 1946. At the board meeting of 30 May Noel Gillitt's letter of resignation was read out. The solicitor who had been so helpful to Lyons back in 1928 had gone to Kenya on active service and stayed there. (Alan Newsome, who had been his assistant since 1936, now took over his role, although not yet his seat on the Jaguar board.) At that same meeting, Lyons proposed William Heynes as a board member alongside himself, Arthur Whittaker, and T. Wells Daffern. It was due recognition of Heynes's vital role in the company and of his quiet common sense in so many matters.

In September 1946 there arrived the final major component of Lyons's ace team, which would carry the company through into the 1970s: Frank Raymond Wilton England joined as Manager of the service department. After an apprenticeship at Daimler between 1927 and 1932, 'Lofty' (he was 6ft 4in [1.92m] tall) became a race mechanic and worked for such legends as Sir Henry Birkin of Bentley fame, Whitney Straight at Brooklands and, after a spell in Alvis's service department, for Richard Seaman and Prince Bira of Siam. He also raced motor cycles, his best result being third in the 1936 Lightweight Manx Grand Prix.

During the Second World War 'Lofty' flew Lancaster bombers and returned to civilian life as Assistant Service Manager at Alvis again, while also trying his hand at motor racing. But he could not see 'any great future' in the car side of Alvis and so, through his 'old chum' Walter Hassan, obtained the job at Foleshill. 'Lofty' soon ensured that the service department became a useful profit centre, initially due to the efficient rebuild service it offered to the many owners of older Jaguars who could not get hold of a new car.

LEFT: *William Lyons senior, the young musician who came to Blackpool from Ireland and stayed.* (Mrs Pat Quinn)

ABOVE: *William Lyons developed a passion for motor cycles early on. At the age of 18 he had this Sunbeam that could be started on petrol and then run on paraffin, a wartime idea.* (Mrs Pat Quinn/JDHT)

BELOW: *William Lyons was an average scholar but enjoyed success in sports. Here, aged nine, he receives a prize for running at Poulton-le-Fylde Grammar School.* (Mrs Pat Quinn/JDHT)

LEFT: *'We worked hard, but we played hard too,'* remembered Sir William. *This Harley-Davidson was one of his favourite motor cycles and he had several competition successes with it.* (Mrs Pat Quinn/JDHT)

ABOVE: *The partnership begins: this 1923 snapshot from the Lyons family album shows William Walmsley astride his SS 80 Brough Superior with William Lyons, ten years his junior, in the Swallow sidecar. The location is King Edward Avenue, Blackpool. Lyons would not often be in the passenger seat…* (Mrs Pat Quinn).

BELOW: *The original Bloomfield Road premises, photographed by William Lyons c1937.*

ABOVE LEFT: *Portrait of William Lyons as a young man – perhaps just into his 20s, when he was establishing the Swallow Sidecar Company.* (Mrs Pat Quinn)

ABOVE RIGHT: *Early days with Greta Brown: the young engaged couple together with Greta's sister.*

BELOW: *This photograph, dated 9 July 1925, shows Lyons (middle row, far left) with some of his closest friends and associates. Next to him is Jack Mallalieu, Walmsley is second from the right in the same row, and Lyons's school friend Arnold Breakell – in some ways responsible for the Jaguar name – is third from the left in the top row.* (Mrs Pat Quinn)

LEFT: *Cyril Holland, photographed when in his 80s alongside an Austin Swallow saloon. Holland was the key figure in helping Lyons enter coachbuilding.* (Andrew Whyte)

ABOVE: *Three Swallow stalwarts photographed in the 1970s (from left): Jack Beardsley, George Lee and Harry Teather. Their practical and organisational skills helped Lyons get off the ground at Blackpool.* (Paul Skilleter)

BELOW: *Parenthood for William Lyons came in 1927 with the birth of his daughter Patricia, pictured with Greta in the couple's Blackpool home.* (Mrs Pat Quinn)

ABOVE LEFT: *Swallow sidecars under construction at Swallow Road.*

ABOVE RIGHT: *John Black at his desk at the Standard Motor Company. Without his help, Lyons might never have progressed to making his own car. This photograph is signed and dated September 1933, just two years after the first SS1 appeared.* (Mrs Pat Quinn)

BELOW: *Lyons (right), aged 33, with the works-prepared SS1 tourer and its crew for the 1935 Monte Carlo Rally – driver Brian Lewis and (left) co-driver Reuben Harveyson. Note Swallow Coachbuilding and SS Cars Ltd plaques, and the impressive 'sun burst' Foleshill office doors.*

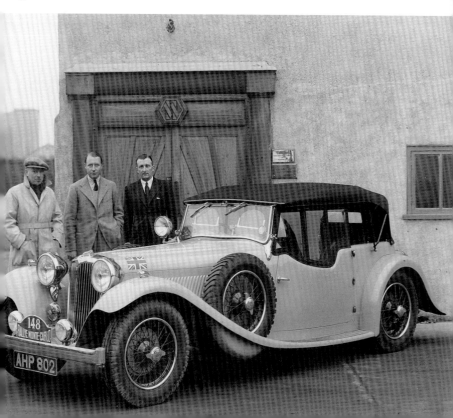

LEFT: *Lyons at the announcement of the 'Jaguar' at a convention at the Mayfair Hotel, London, for SS car dealers on 21 September 1935.*

BELOW: *Along with the new Jaguar saloon came a scintillating sports car – the SS Jaguar 100. Here at the Olympia show, almost certainly in 1935, Sir Malcolm Campbell (in pinstripe suit) and Lyons examine its new Weslake overhead-valve 2.7-litre engine.*

RIGHT: *On holiday! This was taken when Lyons took an SS Jaguar drophead to the South of France. Yes, Lyons then smoked – but was soon to give up as it affected his throat.* (Mrs Pat Quinn)

FAR RIGHT: *Lyons in his late 30s at a seaside concours or rally meeting, talking to, almost certainly, Douglas Clease, Technical Editor of* The Autocar. *Concours events were a source of styling inspiration.* (Mrs Pat Quinn)

BELOW RIGHT: *An improved version of the immensely successful SS Jaguar saloon was shown at the 1936 dealer convention. Lyons is seen with (from left) Bertie Henly (on whom he relied so much), the Hon Brian Lewis (later Lord Essendon), Bill Bett (of Nelson Advertising) and Claude Wallis (of Iliffe, publisher of* The Autocar).

LEFT: *A man about to win his first, and only, motor race! A pensive-looking Lyons waits on the grid at Donington Park, 1938, with Bill Heynes (wearing helmet) and Sammy Newsome (centre).*

ABOVE: *France, 1938: William Lyons with Eileen Bradley, wife of the Lyons family doctor, Jack Bradley.* (Mrs Pat Quinn)

BELOW: *In the late 1930s Wappenbury Hall became the family home. An imposing Victorian edifice, it was often used by Lyons as a location to view new models in 'normal' surroundings.* (Alan Docking/ courtesy Mrs Pat Quinn)

ABOVE: *William Lyons kept a remarkably consistent and quite small circle of friends; none was employed at Jaguar and few had any direct connection with the firm. In the bottom row are (from left) Bob McKeown, Pauline Hattrell, Louise Rendall, Marjorie McKeown and Lyons. In the top row are Greta Lyons and Stanley Hattrell. The photograph was probably taken by Philip Rendall, husband of Louise.* (Mrs Pat Quinn)

BELOW: *Just sometimes, Lyons found time to play with the children on holiday. This is at Poole, near the home of Lyons senior, with Pat aged about 8 and her brother John.* (Mrs Pat Quinn)

FAR LEFT: *Granny and Grandpa Lyons in their garden at The Orchard, Elm Avenue, Parkstone in the late 1930s, together with John and Pat.* (Mrs Pat Quinn)

LEFT: *Lyons at work in the office at Foleshill. If not by this time (the late 1930s), then in due course that intercom box on his desk had the facility of cutting into the lines to any of his executives, regardless of whether they were on the phone to somebody else.* (Mrs Pat Quinn)

BELOW LEFT: *Switzerland, shortly after the war. With William and Greta on a skiing holiday are John and Mary.* (Mrs Pat Quinn)

ABOVE RIGHT: *William Lyons presents Ian Appleyard, his son-in-law to be, with a replica of the SS 100 with which the young rally driver drove to an Alpine Cup in the 1948 Alpine Rally.*

RIGHT: *Family gathering on the Isle of Man, where Lyons loved to watch the motor cycle races each year. John, Pat and even Mary are there too. This might have been the year Lyons nearly tried out the winning bike over the TT course.*

BELOW: *When Pat Lyons married Ian Appleyard it was a great occasion, if somewhat dominated by Jaguar people. Here the proud father 'assists' Pat from the church. 'It was raining', recalled Pat, 'but I was not very happy about him bundling up my train!'*

LEFT: *Ian and Pat Appleyard and their famous white XK120 became Europe's most competitive rally team in the early 1950s.* (Paul Skilleter collection/JDHT)

BELOW: *Driving an XK120, Stirling Moss brought Jaguar its first truly significant race win in the Dundrod TT race in September 1950. Bill and Greta pause with him in the paddock.* (Mrs Pat Quinn)

TOP RIGHT: *Sales of British sports cars, including Jaguars, boomed in the USA after the war. While in Los Angeles in 1950 Lyons met XK120 owner Clark Gable.*

MIDDLE RIGHT: *In 1950 Lyons purchased what had been a derelict café on the Devon coast at Salcombe. This became The Bolt, seen in its 1960s prime with an extra storey and fully landscaped grounds. It was the Lyons's favourite retreat for many years.* (Mrs Pat Quinn)

BELOW RIGHT: *How Lyons styled cars: this Mk VII is purely a shell made of panels formed to Lyons's instructions.*

LEFT: *Assembly lines at Browns Lane in 1952 showing Mk VII saloons and XK120 roadsters under construction.*

BELOW: *'Bill Lyons's proudest moment' reads the contemporary caption on this photograph of him receiving the Dewar Trophy from Wilfrid Andrews, President of the Royal Automobile Club. It was 'awarded to Jaguar for the most outstanding technical and engineering development of 1951', recognising Jaguar's historic Le Mans win and many other race victories.*

BOTTOM: *The North American market was vital to Jaguar but was fraught with distribution problems early on. Jaguar's original East Coast distributor was Max Hoffman (right), who was highly able and, Lyons was to find, skilled in litigation too! This is September 1952 at Watkins Glen, where Lyons watched C-types racing.* (Mrs Pat Quinn)

BELOW LEFT: *Here, during an October 1953 visit, Lyons and 'Lofty' England (right) meet with Charles Hornburg in Los Angeles. Hornburg, like Hoffman, caused difficulties for Lyons, but was considered much more loyal to Jaguar than his opposite number in New York. The car is an XK120 roadster.*

ABOVE: *In the Jaguar pit at Le Mans in 1953, the year of a second C-type victory. On the left are Joe Wright and Harold Hodkinson of Dunlop, Jaguar's partner in the development of the disc brake for cars. Bill Heynes is holding stopwatches, like Lyons. Standing is R. J. 'Bob' Knight, one of the C-type designers who went on to engineer the XJ6 with Heynes.*

BELOW: *At Le Mans in 1953 a happy Lyons celebrates victory with Bill Heynes and drivers Duncan Hamilton (centre) – a Lyons favourite – and Tony Rolt (right).* (Paul Skilleter collection)

ABOVE: *After the C-type came the D-type. Lyons watches as Norman Dewis in the unpainted prototype prepares to demonstrate the new 165mph Le Mans car at MIRA in 1954.*

BELOW LEFT: *Happier times in California. It was comparatively rare for Greta to accompany her husband on business trips but she did on this occasion, and Pat too. Here they enjoy a round of golf with San Francisco dealer Kjell Qvale at Pebble Beach.* (Mrs Pat Quinn)

BELOW RIGHT: *John Lyons as a young man. His tragic death in 1955 probably changed the course of Jaguar history, and Bill and Greta never entirely recovered from the blow.* (Mrs Pat Quinn)

'Lofty' England was to become perhaps Lyons's most trusted aide and on his retirement in 1972 took over as Managing Director of Jaguar. However, at first he was not too sure what to make of his new boss. 'After I had been at Jaguar some six months I went to see WL and asked him if I was doing things to his satisfaction. He replied "I'll tell you when you go wrong." So I never asked again!'[10]

England discovered a very 'lean' regime at his new company. 'Jaguar operated with an absolute minimum of managerial staff and had no-one who spoke any foreign languages except Bill Rankin who with the help of one girl was advertising, exhibitions, public relations and press relations manager. So I was called in when we had visits from European distributors who could not speak English, and also to man the Jaguar stand at Earls Court, through which WL concluded I had some organisational abilities.'[11]

'Lofty' found that Lyons had a sense of humour, 'which a lot of people didn't realise and which I think contributed a lot to the fact that I got on well with him...and because I also had the good luck of going around with him a lot when we were setting up the European and American markets.'[12]

A snapshot of Lyons and Jaguar at this time comes from a visit made to Foleshill on 14 November 1946 by *The Autocar*'s staffman John Dugdale, not long back from a trip to the US. (Eight years later Dugdale would be Jaguar's West Coast Sales Manager). He was shown around the factory by Rankin who, Dugdale recorded in his private notes, 'was not too sympathetic' about the delay in producing new models and considered that firmer deadlines needed to be given to the backroom boys. Dugdale also noted that the female content of the workforce was higher than he had seen elsewhere. (Many women had been taken on by SS during the Second World War and had remained, especially in the trim shop.)[13]

Interviewing Lyons, Dugdale found that he had visited the Paris Motor Show, where he had seen and disliked the new Raymond Loewy-designed Studebaker; new models he did like included Packard and Buick. However, Lyons expressed concern at how individual marques were going to be distinguished from one another (the new all-enveloping streamlined style had done away with the traditional radiator). Lyons was also pondering on which distributors to appoint in the US and was leaning towards Rolls-Royce and Bentley outlets. As for expanding the company, Lyons felt that it was being held back by the austerity Labour Government.

Dugdale had further contact with Lyons in 1947 after he had written a series of articles on a trip he made to Italy, from where 'all the innovative new car styles seemed to be coming'.[14] Lyons phoned and expressed his interest and Dugdale sent him photographs of the latest creations from Carrozzeria Touring, Stablimenti Farina and the 'innovative' Pinin Farina. Also included were pictures of new Alfa Romeos sporting an elegant, upright, oval radiator grille.

All these impressions went into the melting pot as Lyons evolved his first new postwar styles. The key project was the new 100mph (160kmh) saloon, for which the equally new twin overhead camshaft engine had been designed, but while the power unit was virtually ready, there were considerable delays with the body. This was because for the first time, the company was abandoning self-assembly and was going outside for a complete body, to be delivered ready for painting and fitting-up. While this would incur heavy tooling charges, over a period the cost per body would be much reduced. The risk was that the lower unit cost would be achieved only if a certain production level could be attained. A lot hung on this car, which would be called the Jaguar Mk VII.

However, Pressed Steel at Oxford was quoting ever-longer delivery times and by 1948, Lyons (in consultation with Bill Heynes) had decided to hold over the all-new saloon and launch an interim model. This would utilise Heynes's new independent front suspension chassis designed for the Mk VII but would retain the existing pushrod engines and be clothed in a modernised version of the existing body, handbuilt at Foleshill. It would go some way towards catching up with manufacturers like Armstrong Siddeley and Riley, which had been much quicker off the mark with genuinely new models after the Second World War.

Of course, Jaguar's grindingly slow progress in terms of both production and new models was in some measure due to the outside forces that Lyons had to face. The winter, which extended into 1947, was said to have been the worst for 50 years and Jaguar was hit further by a major fire on Friday 31 January. Some 8,000sq ft (743sq m) of the 'new' factory were destroyed and much trim material lost. New supplies were brought in over the weekend and no production was lost but within days the factory was at a standstill due to power cuts.

These also meant that early in March much of the factory lacked heating; hot drinks were served but, a works notice warned sternly, 'the service will be withdrawn if employees take advantage of the position and crowd around the trolley'! In fact 1947 was a miserable year: Britain, struggling to repay huge US wartime loans, was forced to introduce rationing even more stringent than during the Second

World War; potatoes, bread and sweets were all on the restricted list. Petrol rationing continued until 1950.

Financially, however, the company was now emerging into strong profitability as production rose, from 2,928 in 1946 to 4,356 in 1947. Although the annual accounts for the year ending 31 July 1946 showed profits down at £32,717, they also reflected a huge £207,469 investment in plant. The following year, profits were up to a record £190,424 and the position at the bank remained healthy despite further large-scale expenditure on facilities to manufacture both the new engine and new models. In each year a modest ten per cent dividend was paid.

The cash flow was good enough for Lyons to consider an acquisition for the first time since he had examined the Triumph books in 1939. In August 1947 he reported to the board that he had made an offer of £85,000 for Lagonda and its assets, and a reply was awaited. Lagonda had been founded in Britain by an American, Wilbur Gunn, at the turn of the century but had been owned since 1935 by solicitor Alan Good. The company produced small numbers of expensive, sporting-luxury cars (though some at SS Cars had rather dismissed the Lagonda people as 'playboys'). However, Good had appointed W. O. Bentley as Technical Director – giving rise to the intriguing prospect (had this 1947 takeover been agreed) of Lyons employing the great 'WO' himself – whose name was perpetuated on the Bentley cars (now built by Rolls-Royce) that the postwar Jaguar models still so much resembled!

But either the deal was rejected or Lyons was deterred by the report made by Edward Huckvale and cost accountant John Witherall after they had visited Feltham and met with 'WO' and Alan Good. Instead, industrialist David Brown purchased Lagonda and effectively merged it with Aston Martin, which he also acquired in 1947. (Much later both Aston Martin Lagonda and Jaguar were purchased by Ford – the consequent cross-fertilisation resulting in the Jaguar-powered DB7 of 1996, the most successful Aston Martin ever.)

At the beginning of 1948 John Dugdale paid another visit to Foleshill. This time Lyons showed him a prototype of what would become the Mk VII (except that it sported an 'Alfa' grille at this stage). 'Lyons made a habit of showing his new car mock-ups to journalists, to business friends, or to owners whom he trusted,' Dugdale wrote in 1993, 'in order to bounce ideas off them. He was careful to reserve his own opinions and decisions...'[15]

Dugdale noted privately at this time Bill Rankin's comment that Lyons did not like personal publicity 'but in my experience of human vanity, I doubt this, nor can a man in the public eye object to the public description of his success, if fairly done'.[16] There was still no Sales Manager at Jaguar; Miss Fenton continued to combine the role with that of secretary to Lyons, who 'looks at all the mail himself, adding attention notes,'[17] recorded Dugdale. On Lyons's office wall hung a 1934 Gordon Crosby drawing of the SS1 tourers on the Alpine Trial.

Also not published in *The Autocar* were Lyons's observations on other makes: the new Bristol 400 he dismissed as too heavy and a poor performer, the new Studebaker he now liked, and he criticised Alvis – once his aiming point – in terms of strategy. 'We don't try, like Alvis, to get as much as we can for our cars, we price according to costs... Alvis calculate they are getting so much profit per car but they fail to get the necessary production to make the job worthwhile. You have got to have quantity.'[18]

Those comments on Alvis underscore key features of Lyons's own strategy over the years: that the selling price of the cars must be kept down to achieve volume. Volume amortised overheads and reduced unit costs, allowing competitive pricing and thus completing a virtuous circle. The historically low price of a Jaguar compared with the opposition often caused amazement. However, the discrepancy did not always stem from Lyons's keen pricing but was also due to the greediness of some other manufacturers, which tended to price their cars on what they considered the market would bear – not on cost. To Lyons this policy was short-sighted; that Jaguar outlived almost all other British luxury makes surely proves him to have been correct.

Amid all the hard work needed to get the business functioning properly again after the Second World War, in 1945 Lyons found time to fulfil his ambition to enter farming. He had been influenced in this regard, thought Pat, by the Rootes brothers; both had farms and Reginald's herd of Jersey cows was world famous. He was also anxious to own the land around Wappenbury Hall and the two aims coincided neatly, as he related years later to Bob Robinson (his farm manager for 25 years).

Lyons had been taking his dog for a walk one morning when he met the owner of the farm next door to Wappenbury Hall, one Mr Davis, leaning on a gate. 'I said "Look, Mr Davis, if ever you want to sell your farm, I'll be a good customer for you. Let me know." He was getting to retirement age. I only walked up to the wood and back with the dog and he was still leaning on the gate, and he said, "Well, you'd better have it, Mr Lyons. I've decided I'm going to pack up." I sent my agent in and they did the valuation next day and it was all settled up. That's how I started farming.'[19]

Farming became Lyons's major leisure activity in his retirement. At first, though, he could devote comparatively little time to it and began modestly with just three Jersey cows. However, daughter Pat soon took a keen interest in the venture.

At the end of the Second World War, two of the three Lyons children were still at school. Pat, however, was 17 and had left at the end of the 1944 summer term. In 1939 she had been sent to Lowther College in North Wales (for safety, though it transpired that most nights had to be spent in the air raid shelters because of German bombers passing overhead en route for Liverpool!). After about a year she went to Wycombe Abbey near High Wycombe but within a couple of terms the girls were unceremoniously bundled out when the school was requisitioned, without warning, for the American air force headquarters. So Pat ended her schooling at Cheltenham Ladies' College. Mary, some ten years younger, went to Godstowe when she was ten; this was the preparatory school for Wycombe Abbey to which she moved in 1950 (staying until 1954). John (less than two years younger than Pat) had attended a preparatory school in Warwick before going to Oundle – this well-known public school was chosen largely because of its historic links with engineering. He was there for most of the 1940s.

As soon as travelling was practicable after the Second World War, the Lyons family went for a skiing holiday in Switzerland. At Arosa, Lyons hired a private guide to teach them all skiing and became quite proficient himself. Afterwards, he insisted that Pat went to a finishing school in Lausanne, chiefly because he 'was very keen for me to learn French. Well, he was always very keen for me to do everything, actually!'[20] It was not a happy time for her and, meeting her father at the Geneva Motor Show (where she recalled 'going round the show looking at Alfa Romeos with him'), she asked if she could leave Switzerland provided that she got digs and took French lessons. Her father agreed.

Returning to England, Pat found that London beckoned and she attended a secretarial course in South Kensington – 'secretarial work was about all that one could think of for girls to do in those days... Quite honestly, there were no such things as career departments, it was all complete chaos really at the end of the war. Nobody was very interested in what teenagers were doing.'[21] The course was not a great success, if only because Pat came off her horse and damaged her right hand, making typing virtually impossible!

However, the farm had caught her imagination. She particularly enjoyed working with the animals although her father, intent on applying the same business principles he used when running Jaguar, was soon asking her to prepare budgets and work out costs. That was not what Pat wanted to do: 'I wasn't interested in learning how to do budgets, I was interested in the animals.' Nor did her parents particularly approve of Pat going down to the pub with the farm hands; it came too close to consorting socially with the workers, something which Lyons, even in Blackpool, had avoided.

Then it became apparent to Lyons that just three cows made no economic sense, 'so overnight there were suddenly 53,' recalled Pat. 'I couldn't get to know 53 and somehow it all changed, a manager came in and I began to lose touch with it. I wasn't able to look at it as a business, which was the only way my father would have given me the chance to get more involved.'[22]

Pat would have liked to have studied at an agricultural college but this was unusual for a girl in the 1940s and it was not a career path her parents actively encouraged. Today, she admits that, had she been more determined, they might not have stood in her way. As it was, she had many local friends '…and I remember Daddy grumbling at me going out every night.'[23]

This family interaction was of a very typical nature and Lyons was a conventional father in most respects; although he was open to discussion with his children, he was among the last of a generation that had been brought up to have very definite views. Pat commented: 'I remember having quite strong arguments with him about what is right and what is wrong. To him, it was always quite clear. I used to argue, certainly when I was in my teens, that there were shades of grey. He wouldn't have that at all. Everybody knew what was right and what was wrong, people's conscience would tell them that, and it was all quite clear. He set very high standards and expected people to stick to them.'[24]

Mary agrees: 'He was perfectly straightforward and you always knew exactly where you stood with him. He made his views abundantly clear. If you didn't agree, then you had to have the courage to go and do your own thing without his approval.

'He was not always a good listener if the subject was of no interest to him. I can remember when my brother was alive, I needed some more pocket money for school at which he expressed surprise tinged with disapproval. I started off with a long list – notepaper, toothpaste… I had hardly got to the third item when he said, "All right – that's fine". John, who had obviously experienced similar practical problems, immediately interjected and said, "Go on, make him listen". Father was very anxious that we should learn the value of money from an early age but his lessons were somewhat inconsistent. His mind was usually still at the "works". However, he was very supportive when I wanted to continue my education in Paris at the Sorbonne and...in Madrid. He made all the necessary arrangements.'[25]

Pat also remembers her father as being 'scrupulously fair. It was something he was absolutely adamant about, that you must always be fair. Obviously he was the one who decided whether it was fair or not! But it was what he strove for.'[26]

Pat was still preoccupied with the farm to a degree when she celebrated her 21st birthday with a family party at Wappenbury Hall on 23 April 1948. This was the year she met her husband to be, Ian Appleyard; for some years after that, rallying took over from farming as her chief enthusiasm. (Pat finally achieved her ambition to farm later in life, establishing a herd of pedigree Longhorn cattle and a flock of Cotswold sheep in 1977. Today she farms 65 hectares in Gloucestershire and in 2000 her cattle won the Male and Female and Supreme Champion at the Royal Show; further successes were Reserve Champion Ram at the Royal and Supreme Champion Ram at the Three Counties show that same year.)

For Lyons and Jaguar, 1948 was to be a significant year. It saw the dramatic announcement of the new XK engine and the beginning of Lyons's first serious attempt to establish the marque in the United States. Lyons and Bertie Henly sailed on the *Queen Elizabeth* in March specifically to set up the urgently needed sales and service organisation in North America. Ironically, just a few weeks before, Bill Rankin had to counter newspaper rumours that Jaguar was 'earmarked for extinction' as a car manufacturer, with its steel allocation to be withdrawn due to a poor export performance. 'Such statements have no authority and are entirely without foundation,' stated Jaguar emphatically.

Some groundwork had already been done in the US. The original idea of using Rolls-Royce distributors had been dropped and Bertie Henly, who had previously visited the country on Studebaker business, had persuaded Lyons to retain Max Hoffman, an Austrian emigrant, to handle sales on the East Coast. However, this choice – made on the basis of Hoffman's plush Park Avenue, Manhattan showroom and Henly's opinion that he was a good salesman – would not prove particularly auspicious. Hoffman had been importing Jaguars since October 1947 but already, noted John Dugdale after his interview with

Lyons in January 1948, he 'lives from day to day and cars are kept in bond until he can produce the cash'.

The appointment during Lyons's visit of Charles H. Hornburg on the West Coast proved to be more successful but it too came about somewhat haphazardly. Hornburg, a friend of the Earl of Warwick, had been visiting Warwick Castle and made a speculative visit to Jaguar's Holbrook factory where he met Lyons. Despite Hornburg not even being in the motor trade, Lyons was quite impressed with his manner and promised to short-list him as Jaguar's West Coast representative.

Lyons's previous experience of Americans had not been extensive. The first encounter must have been in the summer of 1917 when US troops were billeted in Blackpool and, as a schoolboy, he would have watched the 'doughboys' drilling on the beach. Then during the 1940s Lyons had struck up a friendship by correspondence with Richard A. Hutchinson, President of the Studebaker Export Corporation in South Bend, Indiana, after an introduction by Bertie Henly. Lyons had found Dick Hutchinson a useful confidant and source of advice on various occasions including the thorny question of Jaguar's trademark in North America. Now he assisted with Lyons's itinerary in the US.

It is some indication of how relatively unknown Jaguar was there in early 1948 that Hutchinson, when writing a letter of introduction for 'his old friend Bill Lyons' to the President of the Studebaker Corporation, C. K. Whittaker, felt it necessary to describe the car. 'I am sure you are familiar with the Jaguar, but if you are not, it is an outstanding job and is entirely different from most of the British cars. It is more or less along the lines of the Rolls-Bentley job, although it is cheaper, but has as good performance, looks, etc...' Within four brief years, Jaguar would be the hottest imported car in America.

Landing in New York in mid-March for the five-week visit, Lyons first contacted Hoffman. 'He was very small,' recorded Lyons, 'and of a type I found it difficult to imagine could fill the role of a good salesman. I was later to find that he had some exceptional qualities, although they were to prove by no means favourable to my interests.'[27] Indeed, Lyons was doubtful also that the premises Hoffman showed him (a disused furniture warehouse in 'deplorable condition') could be converted into the service area stipulated by the contract. However, Hoffman told him that he had engaged a contractor, who would start the following day with 60 workmen and complete the job by the time Lyons had returned from the West Coast in two weeks' time.

Lyons enjoyed 'a good and interesting flight' right across North America, catching his 'first sight of the magnificent display of the millions of lights of Los Angeles. The huge expanse of these lights stretching as far as the eye could see made a deep impression. In those days there was no fog which in later years invaded this area so badly and I landed to a beautiful clear sky and clean air.'[28]

He and Bertie Henly stayed at the Beverly Hills Hotel where they saw, but did not meet, some film stars; Lyons did meet a Mr Rummins, who turned out to be 'the MG representative on the same mission as myself' – to arrange franchises. At that time MG was better known, in California certainly, than Jaguar as the neat little TC sports car, introduced in 1945, had achieved fame beyond the small numbers (2,001) exported to the US; it introduced to American enthusiasts the joy of driving a responsive two-seater. However, a Jaguar sports car was not in the company's immediate model plans; Lyons had come to establish bases from which he could sell his saloons and convertibles.

After being unimpressed with proposals from a Packard dealer, Lyons plumped for Hornburg. Despite no track record in the industry (he had been a salesman for *Time & Life*), Lyons decided that 'his personality confirmed to me that he would make a good representative for us'. In this he was encouraged by Henly, who later told John Morgan (who joined the company many years later) how he had said to Lyons: 'Well, come on. He's hungry and he's very smart, and I think he'll do a good job for you.'[29] Lyons granted Hornburg the Jaguar franchise for a large part of the west of America on a commission basis, thereby linking remuneration to sales; the formal agreement was typed up there and then, on 22 March 1948, by the stenographer at the hotel.

Although some problems would emerge later, Hornburg did indeed turn out to be a good salesman, establishing a 'small but attractive' showroom, which exists to this day, on Sunset Boulevard. While Lyons and Henly were still on hand, he arranged a display of Jaguars in Hollywood with Clark Gable (already an MG TC owner) placing the first order, for a drophead coupé. Lyons also visited the studio to see where Gable worked and described the tea there as 'terrible'! Soon some worthwhile dealers in the West were appointed, including the enterprising Norwegian Kjell Qvale (who established an outlet in San Francisco) and others in Santa Barbara, Dallas and Seattle.

Returning to New York, Lyons was 'quite astonished' to find that the new service depot had indeed been completed within the fortnight. The achievement impressed Lyons. 'The Americans are remarkable,' he wrote later, 'the way they seem to work in a haphazard fashion yet one sees an old sky scraper being demolished and only a few weeks later a new one is half completed in its place. It certainly is an eye-opener.'[30] Lyons and Henly also fitted in a visit Canada and to the Studebaker and Chrysler plants to study their assembly methods.

In hindsight, the crucial appointments by Lyons of Hoffman and Hornburg were probably made too hastily and the contracts drawn up without the benefit of proper legal advice. Hoffman in particular was to cause Lyons and Jaguar considerable grief before, after some years and at great cost, the contract was rescinded. However, one has to remember the pressure Lyons was under to establish, as quickly as possible, sales outlets in this vital new market. The entire future of Jaguar hung on its ability to export and there was no time for months of research.

Lyons and Henly travelled back to the UK on the *Queen Mary* and at the Jaguar AGM on 6 May Lyons reported that profits for 1947–8 had increased by a healthy 39 per cent to £264,229. Income (company) Tax, Profits Tax (the same thing under a different name), and Excess Profits Tax would reduce this figure by 48 per cent! The bank balance had increased to £129,519.

For Lyons on his return there was also the personal satisfaction of becoming a Vice-President of the Society of Motor Manufacturers and Traders. He was now clearly part of the establishment even though his greatest achievements were yet to come.

There was a postcript from America: with rationing still making life difficult in Britain, Dick Hutchinson sent Lyons some suits. When thanking him, Lyons had to admit: 'I took these to Tepesch the other day but I am afraid that I must have put on a lot of weight when I was in America and Tepesch says it is impossible to make them fit me, so I am passing them on to some poor people which I am sure is what you would have wished.' In return, Lyons sent Hutchinson a Rolls razor.

At Foleshill, Lyons was also once more embroiled in the fight for quality. 'I do not recall ever having seen cars in the condition of those which I have recently inspected,' he wrote to John Silver in August. 'On most of them it has not taken ten seconds inspection to disclose glaring examples of shocking workmanship and lack of inspection. The faults are too numerous to detail but some are so bad that customers find it difficult to believe that the cars could have left the works in that condition.' This was despite his repeated instructions that cars should not be handed to the dispatch shop until complete in every detail. He then instructed Silver that a large inspection label must be displayed on the screen and the inspector in each department must sign his name. If a car did not pass it needed to be sent back to the beginning of the line and come down again.

On 30 September, ahead of the October motor show, Bill Rankin organised a dealer launch for the new Jaguar Mk V saloon – the interim model with the modernised prewar body mounted on the new chassis. With typical ingenuity and economy, Foleshill's social club was sumptuously decorated using red moquette and calico drapes that would eventually end up in Mk V seats! William Pethers and his Hippodrome Orchestra (organised by Sam Newsome) played *Lovely To Look At*, then Lyons introduced the car and explained how it was designed for the export market.

However, behind the scenes frantic work was going on to complete an even more exciting car – Jaguar's first sports car since the SS100, which had ended production in 1940. At the last minute Lyons had decided that Jaguar needed something spectacular at the all-important Earls Court Motor Show in October – and if his all-new 100mph (160kmh) saloon, the Mk VII, couldn't be shown, then at least its engine could.

Heynes and Hassan co-operated enthusiastically. They welcomed the chance of a low volume sports car in which to launch the new XK engine; this would ensure any bugs could be ironed out before the make-or-break Mk VII was released. Also sports car owners would be a lot more tolerant of any early problems (though in the event there were virtually none).

While a Mk V chassis frame was shortened and adapted, Lyons evolved a flowing, two-seater body of extreme beauty, a superb translation of the all-enveloping body style that the major Italian coachbuilders had been refining since the late 1930s. One of the greatest sports car designs of the century, the XK120 is all the more remarkable for the speed with which it was produced. Lyons himself recorded: 'it was done more quickly than anything before or since, and I could compare weeks, almost days, with years and it was not altered from the first attempt.'[31] In fact Lyons claimed to have arrived at the basic body shape in under two weeks.

His nephew, Alan Docking, recalled a visit to Foleshill at this time: 'I was taken into the 'holy of holies' where the prototype XK120 stood in almost complete form, but without radiator grille. At least half a dozen grilles were presented up to the car for Uncle Bill's approval, all basically similar but with minor differences in bar thickness, the number of bars, and the oval shape. They all looked good to me, but it was " No, no, no...yes! That's the one!" This was for me an early example of his absolutely correct feeling for style – a question of pure instinct rather than logic or engineering.'

With the departure of Cyril Holland, Fred Gardner was now his chief interpreter. He and Lyons were to form a unique partnership within Jaguar. Gardner, who in November 1949 would be appointed superintendent of the saw mill and prototype body department, looked after what was called the body development shop. He was a rough character who could be foul-mouthed and physically intimidating to those who dared invade his 'kingdom'. Yet he and Lyons got on famously in a clear instance of how Lyons would tolerate, and even find amusing, behaviour that he would not have countenanced had that person lacked the special qualities that he admired and needed.

Many years later Lyons was asked about his styling methods: 'The lines of our cars are arrived at by the direct shaping of panels until they become pleasing to the eye,' he explained. 'I have a fairly clear idea of what I want to see and I get the best results working in the full size and assessing the effects and the car itself in its natural environment. Only then can the proportions and detail of the car be determined exactly and these, to me, are of paramount importance.

'I believe a car should be attractive to the eye, well balanced and free from unnecessary embellishment. It should be capable of giving pleasure to the owner over a long period of time. Totally new concepts in styling, like fashion, can often be short-lived in terms of satisfaction and pleasure.'[32]

Norman Dewis, who joined the company as Chief Tester in 1952, further explained how the styling was done: 'Lyons had to have something he could look at. He used to have lights shining on it and he worked on light lines. He would stand and look from different angles – front, side, three-quarter – and he could follow the light line, and where there would be a break, that was a bad shape so he would modify the shape to continue the light line.'[33]

The first XK120 body was produced by the Abbey Panel and Sheet Metal Co. Originally a four-man partnership, Abbey Panels was wholly acquired later by Edward Loades, one of the partners. The company has considerable importance in the Jaguar story. After selling Motor Panels, Lyons had few in-house skilled sheet metal workers and those that he did have were among the most militant in terms of industrial action. They certainly did not appreciate Lyons's habit of working all hours on styling projects. But Abbey Panels kept an open shop and employed only free-spirited men who,

Ted explained, 'wouldn't be forced by the trade unions – they were too good at their job'.

This attitude Lyons found refreshing so instead of employing just his own men for prototype work, four or more on the Abbey Panels payroll were always there, shaping the styling prototypes. Effectively, therefore, Abbey Panels became Jaguar's in-house styling department, while Abbey's Exhall factory also built low-volume Jaguar production bodies (including the first XK120s, the C-, D- and lightweight E-types, and later, such as the XJ220). Edgar Williams was the leader. Bill Jones, who worked in the department, recalled: 'Lyons would say: "Right, put me a roof panel on and I want so much shape in it." They'd get a lovely, highly polished piece of aluminium and roll it, and put a nice gentle shape in it. He would come back and say: "Just a fraction more". That's how all these lovely shapes came about.'[34]

On Friday 20 October there was a press preview of the new XK120 at the Grosvenor House Hotel in Park Lane, London. Seven days later the public saw the car as the Earls Court doors opened at 10am for the SMMT's 33rd London Motor Show.

This was a highly significant event for Britain, the first since the 1939 Show had to be cancelled because of the Second World War. Efforts had been made to revive the show in 1946 and 1947 but Lyons had been one of those who argued against this, Jaguar being among those manufacturers which would have had nothing new to display. But in 1948, Lyons was ready and made sure the public knew it. Nelson Advertising had secured every poster frame from the Underground station to the exhibition and some 750 London buses were also emblazoned with Jaguar advertising. Clearly, Jaguar meant business.

Preceded by a press day, the Show ran from 27 October to 6 November and the pent-up design talent of the European motor industry was finally released as a torrent of new models received their first motor show airing. Amongst the 43 distinct marques and 21 coachbuilders represented, Morris displayed three new cars including the remarkable Minor, while Land-Rover displayed a new cross-country vehicle that, conceptually, was to outlast all the cars at Earls Court.

But when it came to sheer crowd-pulling glamour, little could compete with the sleek bronze Jaguar roadster on Stand 146. The equally new Mk V saloon looked good but it was the XK120 Super Sports that captured the imagination of press and public. For the first time, Lyons had produced a car that was ahead of the opposition in both style and performance – '120' indicated the car's 120mph (193kmh) top speed, a rate of progress associated in 1948 only with racing cars or the most expensive Italian exotica. Yet this supercar was not the preserve of millionaires: the price tag of £998 (before tax) meant that someone like a doctor or a modestly successful businessman could realistically contemplate affording an XK120. Theoretically, that is, for all the production was earmarked for export and, in any case, deliveries would not commence until the latter half of 1949.

In a jaded Britain, 90,000 people flocked to Earls Court on the first day alone for their glimpse of the future – or even normality. On the Saturday, Jaguar workers were brought down by coach and by special train to see 'their' cars in an interesting early experiment to allow the shop floor to view the results of its labours.

Besides coping with the sensation caused by his new sports car, Lyons also had official duties to discharge as an SMMT man; a letter of 12 December to Dick Hutchinson at Studebaker confirmed Lyons's difficulty with small talk. 'The Motor Show was just one mad rush,' he wrote, 'and, apart from the ordinary routine of the show I had to spend a lot of my time, as vice-president of the SMMT, entertaining people in whom I was not really personally interested.' Hutchinson might have already heard Lyons talking about the Show – an interview with Richard Dimbleby had been broadcast by the BBC's American News Service and in it Lyons described the Show as 'an unqualified success'.

It was also a severe shock to Lyons and all at Jaguar, even if a welcome one. Charles Hornburg visited the Show from the US and alone offered to take the first year's production of XK120s. This plus the colossal interest in the car generally made it clear that there had been a complete underestimation of the car's impact and the demand that it would generate – especially in the US. Even while the prototype was being still gawped at over the hastily positioned posts and ropes at Earls Court, Lyons was negotiating with the Pressed Steel Company for a steel body to replace the coachbuilt aluminium one he had planned for the XK120. Some 200 or so XK120s had been scheduled prior to the Show; eventually, over 12,000 would be produced. No wonder the staff Christmas party – attended by Lyons and the other directors – was a particularly jolly occasion.

In February 1949 the International Automobile Exhibition was held at the Armory, Lexington Avenue, New York – the first of its kind and solely for imported cars. Austin was prominent (all part of Len Lord's ambitious $600,000 drive to establish the A40 saloon on the US market) but Jaguar had the biggest stand, organised by Max Hoffman, and Ernest Rankin and 'Lofty' England flew out. The star attraction, of course, was the XK120, further fuelling Jaguar's export orders.

At Foleshill, Lyons was still having to cope with the perennial problems of labour and quality. He brought in a bonus scheme, based on the numbers of cars leaving the factory, which meant that an operator's basic weekly wage of around £8 could be increased by as much as £30. But the sheet metal workers were still being difficult: on 21 March 40 of them went on strike over the use of a machine.

As for quality, Lyons continued his habit of selecting cars from the dispatch area and driving them home. Typical is the memo he wrote on 3 May 1949: 'The following are the superficial faults which I noticed on the car I took home last night (black/pigskin 3½). Brakes pull badly to nearside. Bad engine roughness at 2,400. Indicators do not cancel. Rim of steering wheel not to specification. Spokes of steering wheel not vertical and horizontal. No stop on instrument panel door. Numerous creaks.'

At the AGM three days later, Lyons reported record orders and that the new factory extension was practically completed, with new plant installed. However, he believed that the industry would soon meet serious competition and there were signs that a buyer's market would force prices down. A net profit of £136,361 was recorded and a ten per cent dividend was paid. (Perhaps the company's satisfactory financial outlook encouraged the modest philanthropy that Lyons announced at the 10 June board meeting, where it was agreed to covenant £400 a year to the Lynwood home at Sunninghill, set up to assist retired motor industry people.)

Concrete evidence of the XK120's speed came on 30 May 1949 when Ronald 'Soapy' Sutton, Jaguar's test driver, took an XK120 along the *autoroute* near Jabbeke in Belgium at almost 133mph (214kmh). Lyons was there together with journalists flown over in a chartered Douglas DC3; they were also flown back so they could file their stories that night. In proving that it was even faster than its type name, the XK120 rightly took the title of 'the world's fastest production car'; the resulting publicity in the evening and morning papers further elevated Jaguar's rapidly climbing image.

An interesting light is shed on Lyons's attitude to the shop floor workers by an incident that occurred in June. His frustration at the workers' attitude to pay and quality has been recorded already but it is clear that he was capable of sympathising with them on other matters. The incident also illustrates the harsh regime of the foremen (sometimes amounting to tyranny) under which the assembly line operators often worked in the motor industry at that time (and for many years afterwards) – something worth bearing in mind when considering stoppages.

Lyons had met with the shop stewards on 15 June and recorded the result in a memo to John Silver (copied to Ted Orr and Bill Heynes). The stewards, he said, expressed criticism of methods used in the factory and 'I could not help but feel that there was considerable justification for this'.

It centred around the fact that when workers complained about certain assembly methods being uneconomical or that the jigs provided were completely unsuitable, 'no action was taken to effect remedies'. Lyons pointed out to the stewards that everyone was working under very serious difficulties and many items required attention. 'This they appreciated but it was stressed that it would do much to help the spirit of the workpeople if some answer was given to them. In this I upheld them one hundred per cent, and expressed the view that I regard it as of the greatest importance that foremen or chargehands should react co-operatively to any suggestions or criticisms raised by workpeople. Unfortunately I know from experience that more often than not, they are antagonistically received.'

He went on to state that he took a very serious view of this matter and desired a continual investigation into methods. 'It is a foolish policy not to invite and give serious consideration to criticisms or suggestions put forward by the workpeople in regard to instructions, methods, or tools given to them.' Clearly Lyons recalled the time when the company was small and he was involved on a day-to-day basis with shop floor matters. It also reveals that he was keen to encourage criticism if it would improve the process and he saw that the workers were best-placed to evaluate their own methods and tools. In this respect he was ahead of reality at Jaguar by some 45 years; not until the 1990s were Jaguar workers empowered by management to help arrange their own tasks and assembly procedures.

The summer brought a further challenge to Lyons: motor racing. The British Racing Drivers' Club announced it would hold a production sports car race at its Silverstone airfield circuit on 20 August 1949 and Jaguar was immediately in a dilemma. Lyons had always been circumspect about racing (as opposed to road rallies) but if the XK120 did not show, suspicions would be aroused among the press and the public that maybe it wasn't all it was cracked up to be.

Finally, Lyons agreed that three cars could be entered (in the names of individuals) provided it could be demonstrated to his satisfaction that they would almost certainly win. Accordingly, a test session was arranged at Silverstone under 'Lofty' Engand's direction. During this Lyons turned up and insisted on trying the car himself. He set off at a rapid pace with the long-suffering Ernest Rankin in the passenger seat. 'Hey, Rankin,' said Lyons, 'I've left my specs behind – tell me where the corners are!' Walter Hassan related how a somewhat shattered Rankin stumbled from the XK when Lyons pulled in. However, the objective had been attained: the lap times were as quick or quicker than anything else likely to be entered. And so it transpired: despite spirited competition from Frazer Nash, XK120s finished first and second in this, the car's (and the XK engine's) first competition appearance. Leslie Johnson drove the winning car.

The well-publicised victory further fuelled demand for a car that was virtually impossible to obtain: not until the spring of 1950 would the 'productionised' steel-bodied XK120 come on stream and in the meantime the original aluminium-bodied versions were trickling out of Foleshill at a painful six or so a week. In early October 1949 Hoffman was cabling from New York to say that the Florida season started in December and while he was taking orders, he did not know what delivery date to quote. 'Unless definite dates quoted many orders will be lost. Very important you answer immediately.' There was little that Lyons could do, although an increased build rate for the existing XK120 was achieved from early in 1950.

It was the slow model changeover that resulted in a dramatic 52 per cent drop in profits, said Lyons reporting on the 1948–9 financial year at the AGM. Even then, 49 per cent of the £125,000 profit was plundered by the Revenue – money that Lyons would dearly have liked for growing the company faster. He was investing as much as he dared, though, with tooling costs up 250 per cent as Jaguar strove to bring the XK120 into series production and to bring the Mk VII to the market.

No wonder that Lyons had a jaundiced view of the British Government. In June he had written to Dick Hutchinson: 'The general conditions, from a political point of view, are becoming very tense. The Labour Party are undoubtedly beginning to realise that their policy of more for the workers, which they have flogged since they came into power, is not altogether a sound one...the workpeople themselves are beginning to smell a rat and realise that the Arcadia to which the Labour Government promised to lead them, is now a distant vision.' At least the Government's dramatic devaluation of the pound in August 1949 gave a boost to the competitiveness of British exporters that was to last 20 years – and from which Jaguar benefited more than most.

The XK120, although still beyond the reach of British purchasers, was once again mobbed at Earls Court in October and the Jaguar stand was extensively filmed by newsreel cameras and shown on BBC television. At the Scottish Show, the Jaguar dealers north of the border presented Lyons with a large cake decorated by a representation of the Silverstone racetrack, complete with three correctly coloured models of the XK120s that had triumphed there back in the summer.

However, while the XK120 had indeed won the race, it was clear that the car's performance was now well ahead of its brakes – at least in competitions. This was no doubt strongly in Lyons's mind when, with considerable foresight, he wrote on 9 November to G. Edward Beharrell, Managing Director of the Dunlop Rubber Co: 'You may remember the last time you were at our works, we discussed the question of brakes. Since then, I understand you have made great strides with the disc brake for aircraft, and I am wondering whether you have decided to produce this for cars. I am sure it would be a great boon to the British industry if you were to do so and I feel you would receive practically a hundred per cent support. I will be interested to learn if you have any such plans.' That is how Lyons and Jaguar became crucial partners with Dunlop in developing the disc brake – one of the important automobile engineering advances of the 1950s.

At the November board meeting, though, it was the forthcoming Mk VII that was a major topic. The tooling, Lyons stated, was costing £250,000 but Pressed Steel had agreed to spread this very considerable sum (far more than Jaguar had ever paid for previous types of body) over two years. Lyons also suggested that a further building licence should be applied for 'as more space would be required for storage of bodies for next year's output'.

Towards the end of the year HRH Prince Edward, the Duke of Kent, visited the factory (for the second time). Accompanied by his tutor, he was entertained to lunch by Lyons in his private dining room and was later taken for a run in an XK120 by 'Lofty' England. Unfortunately Jaguar has no photographic record of this particular royal occasion – the glass plate negative was dropped while being developed!

CHAPTER 5

LYONS GOES TO LE MANS

For Jaguar 1950 was an important year: some of the XK120's huge sales potential was realised, the XK also tackled the world's most famous motor race (Le Mans), and in the autumn Lyons's all-important new saloon, the Mk VII, was launched at the London Motor Show. Yet these achievements represented just the beginning of a quite remarkable string of successes from a team that would continue into the 1970s. In January 1950 even Lyons himself could not have predicted the heights Jaguar would reach, yet he was well aware that the people he had brought together were capable of exceptional achievements. 'I believe the executive staff we now have,' he said at a staff dinner that month, 'is, in spite of the existence of some discord last year, quickly becoming co-ordinated into a team of great strength, which will carve the company's success indelibly on the history of the motor industry.'[1] Was this merely a bold rallying call or did Lyons truly have a feeling of destiny?

Later in January, with a general election in prospect, Lyons was soliciting the same staff for help in counterbalancing shop-floor support for the Labour Party. His memo stated: 'If, therefore, it is your intention to vote Conservative, which I assume it is, the Party would greatly appreciate your help.'[2] That 1950 election saw Labour's majority cut to five and it was forced to the polls 20 months later when Churchill and the Conservatives were returned to power. Lyons was not, however, a great political activist by nature but he remained a solid Conservative Party supporter all his life and during the 1950s ensured that the company donated small sums to the local Conservative association annually.

As for those shop-floor workers, Lyons addressed them through the January 1950 *Jaguar Journal*, where he took up a familiar theme: 'The need for exports is only too well known to us all, but it does not require a great deal of intelligence to appreciate that the way to meet competition abroad is by reducing prices...' Devaluation and the Korean War meant that material costs were rising steeply and, as lowering wages was unacceptable, Lyons argued that increasing production was the only answer. His concern was that if the seller's market ended, reduced home sales would lower production, negate economies of scale, and force up export prices – reducing sales still further. Additionally, home sales were much more profitable and these profits were helping to sustain the export drive necessary to obtain steel.

In March Lyons made his usual visit to Switzerland and the Geneva Show, where he took careful note of continental styling trends and gave a speech to dealers. It revealed that he had not forgotten the attractions of a smaller model in the range: 'Jaguar is not unaware of the ready market for a cheaper car,' he said, adding that he saw it as a 'profit earner'. Then so confident was he of Jaguar's future that he made an extraordinary prediction: the company 'will have established for itself an unchallenged supremacy outside the cheap car market, and that it will, in consequence, prove to be one of the most valuable agencies which a distributor can hold.' Lyons's prediction of the ultimate worth of the Jaguar 'brand' (though in 1950 this description had yet to be applied to cars!) was uncannily accurate.

At the same time, the first steel-bodied XK120s were leaving the factory and at last some inroads could be made into the backlog of orders from North America. This happily coincided with the second annual New York imported car show, now held at the Grand Central Palace on Lexington Avenue. It was also now all-British – though this did not stop the show's prime mover, Sir William Rootes, inviting Alfred Sloan of General Motors and Henry Ford II to make the introductory speeches! But the US domestic industry took a benign view of imports in the early 1950s as Lyons himself knew – Dick Hutchinson of Studebaker had emphasised in a letter: 'The US auto industry always encourages foreign auto manufacturers as competition is always good for the industry.' (A grass-roots protectionist movement did emerge in the 1950s but it wasn't until the Japanese invasion of the 1970s that the US auto industry really changed its tune!) In any case, according to SMMT figures, British imports to the US were no more than pinpricks, amounting in 1950 to 19,980 cars, of which just 912 were Jaguars. That compared with US domestic production of 6.3 million.

Lyons visited the show, this time choosing the still-novel adventure of crossing the Atlantic by air. This made a big impression on him and he devoted considerable space to it in his unpublished memoirs. He evidently travelled by BOAC Stratocruiser as he described 'sleeping bunks situated in an upper storey...the noise from the engines was incredible making it impossible to get any sleep.'

After 11 hours they landed at Goose Bay, Canada. 'One's first impression after touching down was of bleak desolation and it was quite easy to imagine one had landed on the North Pole,' he wrote. The unfortunate passengers were taken across the snow 'into a large wooden shed in the centre of which was a large coke stove which all the passengers immediately surrounded...' They re-embarked after an hour and landed at La Guardia Airport, New York, three hours later. Lyons's stamina, already legendary back at Foleshill, is indicated by the fact that after arriving at the Waldorf Astoria at 9am, he stopped simply for a cup of coffee before going to meet Hoffman in Park Avenue.

Lyons also visited Hornburg and Qvale on the West Coast. Hornburg threw a big party and Lyons was photographed with Clark Gable who was taking delivery of his first XK120. (Hornburg was canny in persuading high-profile film stars to buy Jaguars, knowing the association would do much to glamorise Jaguar's image.) However, the lavishness of Hornburg's parties backfired as Lyons decided that he was making too much money out of Jaguar! Later, as a consequence, his margin was reduced from five per cent to three per cent.

Lyons made a decision to return to England earlier than expected and, unable to get a flight with BOAC, booked with KLM. He found this airline 'lacked the air of efficiency of BOAC' (!) and the steward's method of demonstrating the use of the life jacket did nothing to allay the fears of any nervous passengers – his announcement commenced: 'Well, folks, in case we fall in the drink...' There was a stopover at Shannon where the aircraft landed 'in an alarming series of hops and jumps. When the shaken passengers were gathered in the departure lounge the aircrew passed through and the captain in a loud voice announced, "Sorry about the landing, the co-pilot was taking a turn."'[3]

Back in the UK Lyons reported to the board on the success of the New York Show but, surprisingly perhaps, he felt the sales situation was 'precarious and we should have to rely mainly upon the XK model...for future business in America'. Evidently the traditionally styled Mk V saloon was not proving sufficiently attractive – or more accurately, by far the greater demand was for the XK120, which could not be built in sufficient numbers. This was to cause all sorts of problems.

Although the Mk VII (when it finally arrived) sold well, there is no doubt that in the early 1950s the XK120 was the defining Jaguar in North America. While a few US servicemen posted to the UK during the war had discovered the SS100, for most Americans the XK120 was the first Jaguar sports car they had ever seen. Also, Lyons had succeeded in creating more than just a fast two-seater; he had re-written the sports car rule book. Not only was the XK120 extremely quick but it was smooth, comfortable and docile too – attributes not previously associated with sports cars. Together with its stunning looks, this helped the XK120 impact deeply on the American psyche, sparking a love affair between Jaguar and America that has lasted to the present day.

This was far from being a one-way love affair but early on the marketing arrangements for North America certainly caused Lyons much anguish. Already far from satisfied with Hoffman's behaviour, in June Lyons had the embarrassment of receiving a letter from the British Consulate General in New York accusing Hoffman of making rash and unrealistic delivery promises to his dealers, whose customers were now contemplating legal action against him. This would be very bad publicity for British firms, pointed out the Consulate General, which considered that 'it looks as though Hoffman is capable of sharp practice'.[4]

Lyons replied that he had addressed the Jaguar dealers during the New York Show and explained that it was not possible for the company to supply XK120 and Mk V convertible models alone. Distribution had to be on the company's production ratio of all models which, he said, was clearly understood by everyone. However, in September the British Embassy was again reporting that Hoffman was creating problems, making impossible promises yet still taking deposits. He was now having to use any XKs he received to stave off lawsuits. Additionally, Hoffman was signing up dealers, authorising them to accept XK orders and *then* telling them they had to take one saloon for every XK.

Attempting to justify his selection of Hoffman to the Embassy, Lyons responded: 'although when appointing the Hoffman Motor Company as our distributors for Eastern America, they were not ideal for our representation, it was recognised that Mr Hoffman was a man with experience, very go-ahead and quite outstandingly preferable to any other sales organisation which was available to us. We have endeavoured to assist the Hoffman Motor Car Company to establish itself on a sound financial basis as we believe that when this is achieved, they will prove a first class distributing organisation.' For once, Lyons would be proved wrong.

Of course, those who actually managed to obtain a new Jaguar were usually delighted. The June issue of *Jaguar Journal* carried a photo of Ray Milland in his new XK120, the picture endorsed 'To

Bill Lyons, This is a picture of a happy man! Many thanks, Ray Milland.' The same issue had a photo of Lyons standing with Clark Gable (described as an 'ardent Jaguar fan') alongside his 120.

It was in the late spring of 1950 that Lyons was elected President of the Society of Motor Manufacturers and Traders. In view of his struggles in the early 1930s for his company to be accepted for SMMT membership, this appointment meant a great deal to him – not just in terms of personal gratification but as final proof that his company, Jaguar, was now recognised by its peers as fully part of the establishment. The only downside was that Lyons, who disliked public speaking and suffered from nerves beforehand, had to make many more speeches in his new capacity. However, colleagues noticed that the extra practice helped and Lyons became a considerably more confident speaker during his term of office, even if he still did not relish such duties.

At the factory Lyons still had to contend with unofficial industrial action, doubly frustrating when the shortage of new Jaguars was contributing to the problems in the US. A notice, signed by Lyons, went up on the works noticeboards in May: 'It is a matter of great concern to me that stoppages of work occur from time to time without legitimate reason and I have come to the conclusion that they must be the result of some subversive influence, for knowing as I do the sound common sense of the majority of workers, I cannot imagine them cutting off their earnings with no hope of advantage.'

He appealed to all conscientious workers to resist attempts to bring about stoppages and reminded them that the company had never changed its policy as a result of stoppages, and it never would. He pointed out that the recent incidents had cost the men the equivalent of 3d (1p) per hour per man for 3½ months, and thus they would have to earn that amount more just to recover the money they had lost. 'And it's just got us all nowhere,' he concluded. 'Ridiculous, isn't it?'[5]

Quality was, of course, Lyons's other major continuing concern and, in mid-June, he circulated all his staff about complaints from the US. 'As you know, on my return from America, I took strong measures to tighten up the quality of the work, and I believe it had some effect, but I am still far from satisfied...' He said the tragedy was that the problems came from an 'accumulation of a lot of small things' not the basic design of the car. He continued: 'it is disgraceful that when we have a car which is accepted as fundamentally good, our production should suffer because of carelessness and a complete lack of interest on the part of all those concerned.'[6]

It was partly to improve design and test reliability that earlier in 1950 six XK120s had been prepared at the works and handed over to private entrants. They would compete in a wide variety of events, mostly racing, in Lyons's most ambitious, if still covert, sortie into motor sport yet. The veteran Italian driver Clemente Biondetti was spectacular in the Targa Florio and Mille Miglia but mechanical problems meant that Leslie Johnson's fifth place in the latter event was the best result obtained in these first sorties. (It was also to be the highest place ever recorded by a British car in the Mille Miglia, which was discontinued after a bad accident in 1957.)

However, much had been learnt prior to the ambitious entry of three XK120s (all in their drivers' names, not Jaguar's) in the Le Mans 24-hour race. In 1950 – perhaps still today – the Grand Prix d'Endurance de 24 Heures was the world's most famous motor race and had been established by the Automobile Club de l'Ouest back in 1923. From the start the British were amongst the event's staunchest supporters and the five wins by Bentley between 1924 and 1930 had become the stuff of legend. Until the XK120, however, Lyons had never produced anything suitable for this most gruelling of races. Now, he sanctioned a low-key entry of three cars – the beginning of an unique association between Jaguar and Le Mans.

For a first attempt, the marque did remarkably well, with Leslie Johnson and Bert Hadley on course for third, if not second, place before succumbing to clutch problems three hours from the end. Lyons did not attend, emphasising that this was not an official Jaguar effort; instead, he kept his usual appointment with the Isle of Man Senior TT motor cycle race.

His enthusiasm for motor cycles was still unabated and 'Lofty' England recalled Lyons telling him that after the 1950 TT 'he had persuaded Gilbert Smith of Nortons to let him do a lap of the TT course on the winning bike early the next morning. He said "I was really looking forward to it but by 10pm my wife had convinced me that I would be a fool to do it!"'[7]

One of the six works-prepared XK120s had been allocated to Francis Ian Appleyard for rallying. Ian, the son of a Leeds Jaguar dealer, had already made a remarkable Best Performance in the 1948 Alpine Rally using a thoroughly obsolete 3½-litre (212cu in) SS100. That made him a worthy candidate for receiving a works-prepared XK120 but so too, perhaps, did the fact that he had just married Lyons's eldest daughter Patricia! The wedding had taken place in May 1950 at Wappenbury parish church, the reception being within walking distance at Wappenbury Hall. 'Actually, it was more of a

Jaguar occasion than anything else,'[8] said Pat, as most of the guests seemed to be from the factory, overseas distributorships and the motor industry generally.

Pat also recalled that the wedding day was set with the date of the Alpine Rally in July firmly in mind. The newlyweds duly 'cleaned' that Alpine, the toughest event in the European rally calendar, gaining a Coupe des Alpes with their XK120 (registered NUB120). They would achieve a clean sheet in the next two years as well, this hat-trick gaining them the first Alpine Gold Cup ever awarded. It is true to say that Ian and Pat Appleyard were the outstanding rally pairing of the early 1950s.

Jaguar's other big competition success that year came in September when a brilliant up-and-coming young driver called Stirling Moss won the Tourist Trophy sports car race at Dundrod, Northern Ireland. Tommy Wisdom had entrusted the 20-year-old with his XK120, another of those six team cars. The race was run in appalling conditions and Moss's victory was not only a big boost to his career but also to the XK120's reputation as a serious sports car. 'Mr Lyons came to me that night,' said Moss, 'and asked me if I would lead the team next year.'[9] It was this win, plus the promising performance of the XKs at Le Mans, that finally persuaded even the cautious Lyons to enter motor racing officially for the first time, and with a full factory team.

On the business side, the accounts for 1949–50 revealed an impressive 149 per cent increase in profits to £311,000, mostly due to the Mk V, though tax once again took an investment-sapping 49 per cent. The cash balance was up from £41,841 to £192,275 and investment in plant and tooling had increased by £100,000 during the year. The dividend reflected this solid performance and was increased by 50 per cent to a generous (by Jaguar standards) 15 per cent.

With the new Mk VII imminent, in August Lyons wrote to the Ministry of Supply on the still-critical subject of steel allocations. He suggested Jaguar should be treated differently from other firms because his company had an exceptionally high export rate – 80 per cent, or $500,000 in the last month, he claimed. It was very important, he argued, to be able to price the Mark VII, 'which we are pinning great hopes on,'[10] as competitively as possible, and he needed to know the steel allocation in order to calculate production. (Ultimately Lyons's pleas were heeded: in early December the Ministry of Supply agreed to an extra 500 tons of steel for Jaguar's export programme.)

As a member of the National Advisory Council for the Motor

Industry (Lyons was a member of NAC until 1952 and again from 1955), he spoke at a meeting in October about steel quotas being cut by five per cent. Discussions also took place about the supply of vehicles to the car-starved home market in 1951; 'Mr Lyons stressed the importance of not waiting until export demand fell drastically before giving consideration to the needs of the home market.'

October saw Earls Court as the venue for another triumphant launch of a new Jaguar, the Mk VII saloon (the Mk VI designation was skipped because Bentley had used it). Princess Margaret opened the show and toured the stands in the company of Lyons in his role as President of the SMMT. *The Daily Mail* commented that she appeared to show special interest in the new 105mph (170kmh) Jaguar. Everyone else certainly did, including the motor industry moguls. Engineer Bob Knight recalled standing near the metallic silver blue MK VII set on a sea of red cloth. 'It was an absolute show-stopper. The Rootes brothers peered at it, and it was priced at £998, and I remember one saying to the other, "Huh, they can't make it for that, that must be the export price."'[11]

Even factory personnel found the price hard to believe. Peter Craig, later to be Plant Director, said of that £998: 'I told Sir William many times he could have put a two or three in front of that figure – he could have sold that car with a three in front of that figure. But he didn't do it – he kept it at £998. But I say that if he had put a two or three in front of it, he wouldn't have made it for the years that he did. So you get the length of run out of the tooling... We certainly made improvements but we didn't change a Jaguar every other year.'[12]

Lyons made a last-minute decision to take all the employees down to Earls Court to savour the public reaction, though it was carefully pointed out in the *Jaguar Journal* that this was not setting a precedent! He gave them each ten shillings (50p) spending money too. A crowd of workers was photographed arriving at Euston Station carrying 'JAGUAR' placards and banners – a masterstroke by Lyons, for not only was he engendering a spirit of enthusiasm in the employees but was also showing press and public that the workers were proud of their company.

The workers were duly appreciative. Afterwards, the *Jaguar Journal* carried a letter from the shop steward's secretary thanking Mr Lyons on behalf of all employees 'for the very splendid gesture in inviting everyone to the Earls Court Exhibition... It just proves that if Jaguar intends to have a go, nothing is impossible. If we can only be assured of this excellent spirit throughout the whole works, then there is no limit to our achievements.'[13] Alas, that spirit did not last long...

As soon as the show ended, the display car was shipped to New York, where it created an equal stir in the Waldorf Astoria. Over 500 retail orders were taken, claimed the press release issued by Ernest Rankin, adding to the $20m US trade orders taken at Earls Court. Americans certainly took to the Mk VII: by their standards it was not over large, it looked great, it had the XK120's engine, and it handled superbly. Lyons had another winner on his hands that, in volume and profit terms, was much bigger than the XK120.

Now, all Jaguar had to do was make enough Mk VIIs but more space was needed for this. For some time Lyons had been discussing with the Ministry the Daimler Shadow No 2 factory in Browns Lane – a largely residential road at Allesley, a village a few miles from Coventry city centre. Having been refused permission to enlarge the existing factory in Swallow Road, and being unwilling to move to a depressed area despite Government incentives (though he had sent investigative teams to Scotland, Wales, and even Northern Ireland), Lyons felt this fine modern factory would be ideal. However, he had to exercise all his negotiating skills to persuade the civil servants to let him have it on his terms. Most of the negotiation would be with Sir Archibald Rowlands, the Permanent Secretary, and it helped that Lyons knew and liked Archie Rowlands, who was Chairman of the National Advisory Council on which Lyons also sat.

There followed much tough bargaining and at various times both the Ministry and Lyons threatened to pull out of discussions altogether. But the country desperately needed to earn dollars and Jaguar was doing exactly that, which may have clinched it. An agreement was reached with the rent for the five years fixed at £30,000. The only drawback proved to be that Daimler, although tailing-off production of the Ferret armoured car, was very tardy about vacating and the move to Browns Lane took a year to complete.

In the meantime, Lyons had approached Rae Geddes, Chairman of the Dunlop Rim & Wheel Co, to propose that Dunlop buy the existing Jaguar factory opposite it on the Whitmore Park Estate. Geddes agreed.

It was during 1950 that Lyons acquired a new property himself. The family used to rent a house in the small coastal town of Salcombe, Devon for holidays and Lyons discovered, high above the bay, a derelict café with wonderful views across the water. During the Second World War the property had been commandeered by the War Ministry and three gun emplacements were still in the grounds. It was a case of love at first sight and, after some difficulty, Lyons managed to purchase The Bolt, as it was appropriately named.

Renovating the property proved difficult and expensive, not least because so soon after the war there were still many restrictions on materials. It was to become the Lyons's holiday home and favourite retreat; a swimming pool was built and the grounds were kept immaculate by a resident gardener. Lyons's small circle of close friends established before the war would be among the visitors, including Bob McKeown (of Courtaulds) and his wife Marjorie, Jack Bradley (the family doctor) and his wife Eileen, and architect Stanley Hattrell and his wife Pauline. Lyons's other friends also included members of the press – Tommy and Elsie ('Bill') Wisdom, Claude Wallis from Iliffe, and Eric Adlington from Temple Press amongst them. Naturally, family members and their offspring would stay as well, so The Bolt often echoed to the shouts of children while Bill Lyons poured tea on the terrace.

Lyons undoubtedly deserved some time to relax. It had been an astonishing year, which had seen a massive increase in production (from 4,190 cars in 1949 to 7,206 by the end of 1950) and the launch of a new luxury sports saloon that was pretty much the equal of anything built the world over. The only sad aspect had been the departure of Walter Hassan to Coventry Climax; with Bill Heynes firmly entrenched as Chief Engineer, Wally could see no prospects of immediate advancement at Jaguar. His leaving was much regretted by Lyons.

The following year (1951) began with Lyons attending an NAC meeting in January where he expressed the need to keep down export prices despite increasing costs. Clearly he felt the export boom was a freak situation that could not last and, when that dried up, a strong home market would be crucial to survival. He also saw a threat from a reviving European car industry: 'Already it is disturbing,' he wrote in the *Jaguar Journal*, 'to say the least of it, to see Germany displace our industry from the position of leading exporters to Switzerland.'[14]

On the technical front, Jaguar was now actively working with Dunlop on developing the disc brake but Lyons was obviously anxious that another manufacturer might reap the benefit commercially. Writing on 1 February to G. Edward Beharrell of Dunlop, he emphasised that the disc brake testing was 'very encouraging' and that he understood Dunlop was granting manufacturing rights. In view of Jaguar's long-standing interest in the brake and the testing it was doing, he hoped 'we are given the opportunity of being first in the field'.[15]

Exactly a month later members of the National Union of Vehicle

Builders (NUVB) went on strike after alleged victimisation of two shop stewards. The strikers claimed that normal redundancy procedure had not been operated by the firm. Management replied that redundancy procedure had been followed to the last detail, to which the strikers retorted that they believed 'the intention of the management has been to try and destroy the trade union organisation in the factory'.[16] The dismissal of the two shop stewards, they maintained, 'is the first step in that direction'.

'This is absurd,' countered Lyons in a summary of the strikers' statements. 'All other unions have publicly refuted this allegation... Assurances have repeatedly been given by union permanent officials that no preferential treatment is expected because a man is a shop steward.'[17] Unsurprisingly, the May 1951 *Jaguar Journal* carried the headline 'Strike Tragedy' and spelt out the terms of the agreement: 'Until the procedure provided above has been carried through, there shall be no stoppage of work either of a partial or a general character.'[18]

The strike developed into one of the most serious and long lasting ever seen at Jaguar. As it entered its seventh week, with 325 NUVB members on strike, nearly a thousand workers of the Amalgamated Engineering Union and the Transport & General Workers' Union were laid off. Another thousand workers were still employed on engine production but Lyons feared that this could not continue for much longer.

Lyons wrote to Archie Rowlands at the Ministry of Supply that Jaguar had offered 'to allow the matter to be determined by a single arbitrator whom the strikers themselves could appoint, not connected with industry or labour... Unfortunately, there is a strong communist influence which takes very good care that the workers... are not given any fair opportunity of considering any proposals which the company may put forward...the Ministry of Labour has made no attempt to deal with this illegal strike... I might mention the members of the AEU and T&GWU are most anxious that the company should stand out against what amounts to tyranny.

'The tragedy of the whole thing is that we are losing most valuable dollar business...it is estimated we have already lost roughly two million dollars worth of business. Our principal American distributor, Mr M. E. Hoffman... has advised us that he is so very much dependent on Jaguar, it is impossible for him to continue with the expensive sales organisation which he has built up during the last few years. His showroom in Park Avenue alone costs him $4000 a week. This is a most serious aspect. It has taken us a long time to build up the sales organisations in America... I regard it as being of the greatest importance that the strike should be settled during the present week and I shall be very grateful if you will be good enough to do what you can to influence some action immediately.'[19]

Three days later a meeting was held at the Ministry of Labour at which the men agreed to return to work for constitutional procedure to operate. It might have been a victory for Jaguar and common sense but it had cost the company dearly. The only good to come out of the matter, Peter Craig recalled, was that it at least allowed time for a problem with the Mk VII's door hinges to be sorted out with Pressed Steel!

In spite of the unfortunate strike, the 1951 annual accounts showed continuing progress, with profits up to £336,000, although inflation was 8.3 per cent that year. Tax took no less than 55 per cent. Cash still stood at just under £200,000 but investment in plant and tooling was up a healthy 58 per cent to £628,573. Key directors were paying themselves generously with remuneration of £30,088 or approximately twice the dividend!

Meanwhile, on the racetrack Jaguar's discreet support of leading drivers in XK120s was bringing results. Headed by Stirling Moss, the first five places in the annual production car race at Silverstone were taken by the type. Lyons had personally arranged that Stirling Moss, uniquely among the drivers, should be paid starting money by Jaguar and Bill Heynes had to warn Company Secretary Huckvale that 'it is regarded as most vital that this information does not come to the knowledge of any third party'![20]

After Jaguar's exploratory foray to Le Mans the previous year, after much pressure from Heynes and England, Lyons had given permission the previous December for a purpose-built Le Mans car. Though undoubtedly a motor sport enthusiast, Lyons never let his heart rule his head when it came to motor racing – it had been the downfall of Bentley – but he knew that the French endurance classic was unique among European races in being widely reported by newspapers across America as well as in Europe. Victory would truly establish the Jaguar name in the company's key markets without the colossal advertising expenditure, which was beyond his means.

Under Heynes's direction, Bob Knight designed a tubular chassis to take a mildly modified version of the XK120's engine, while an aerodynamicist was taken on to design a body that would be efficient but still retain some resemblance to the XK series. Malcolm Sayer, whose background was in the aircraft industry, created a most beautiful shape and he would thereafter play a leading role in the unfolding Jaguar story.

That the C-type Jaguar did its job is well known, though only after an excruciatingly tense few hours for Lyons, watching in the pits. Moss and Fairman had set a cracking pace but then retired when an oil pipe fractured. When another C-type dropped out for the same reason, the tension was unbearable. Luckily Peter Walker and Peter Whitehead brought the third car home to the desired victory ahead of a dispirited and surprised opposition. It was an immensely satisfying occasion for Lyons.

'My proudest moment,' he would say years later, 'was in 1951 when my Jaguar first won the Le Mans 24-hour race. It was the first time a British car had won since the Bentley days.'[21] This was not quite true; he had forgotten Lagonda's victory in 1935! Certainly the effect of that first Le Mans on Jaguar's reputation cannot be underestimated. Before June 1951 there remained nagging doubts in some quarters about Jaguar cars: they seemed almost too good to be true. The Le Mans victory dispelled those doubts for good. Suddenly, Jaguar was elevated alongside Bentley in terms of sporting prowess, while the press counted the win as nothing less than a boost to national morale.

'Lofty' England, who had been delegated the job of organising the team (on top of his duties as Service Manager!), endorsed the impact the win made in North America. When he first started going to America, he said, 'if you were in a Jaguar car people would pull up beside you and say, "what is it?" But as soon as we won Le Mans people who were interested in motor cars immediately knew what a Jaguar was... The race that did the most for Jaguar was the 1951 Le Mans... It put us on the map.'[22]

The value of that Le Mans win in terms of column inches worldwide could probably be measured in terms of millions of pounds even by 1951 standards. Lyons did not allocate large sums to buy advertising space; he preferred to generate publicity and Jaguar's Le Mans programmes of the 1950s are the most high profile examples. Bob Berry explained that he differentiated very clearly between publicity and advertising. He was very keen on getting as much favourable editorial as possible. Firstly, it was free and, secondly, it was written by someone who was not employed by the factory and therefore was unbiased. 'He always said,' recalled Mary, 'that good editorial was worth at least two adverts. He was confident that a good product at the right price that was pleasing to the public would sell itself, but he certainly did not leave it to chance.'

Lyons's continuing difficulty, even without strikes, remained making enough cars. In that Le Mans month of June, Pressed Steel was still achieving only half the agreed delivery rate of 200 Mk VII bodies a week. Also, the Moss Gear Company in Birmingham just couldn't keep up with Jaguar's demand for gearboxes, creating another bottleneck. This motivated Lyons to agitate even more for an automatic gearbox, which he knew the American market wanted and which would ease the transmission situation. For almost a year, Jaguar had been in negotiations with the relevant Government department to obtain an import licence for automatic transmissions from America; this involved spending, rather than earning, dollars. US dealers were demanding automatics but it wasn't until 1953 that Jaguar launched the Mark VII with an automatic gearbox, first in the US, then also on the home market.

That Daimler was taking an age to evacuate the Browns Lane factory didn't help production either but Jaguar's gradual move was under way by June, supervised by John Silver and co-ordinated by Harry Teather (who 23 years before had orchestrated Swallow's move from Blackpool to Coventry). By autumn, the tool room, machine shop, and road test departments had been moved to the new factory. The removal contractor gathered together lorries from all over the Midlands at weekends and transferred whole departments over the two days. 'The great secret,' Lyons explained many years later, 'is to tell every man what he is supposed to do and where he is to go. In that way you don't have a lot of people wandering around looking lost and getting in the way.'[23]

As the year ended, Lyons had finally completed the Browns Lane rent negotiations with the Ministry of Supply. However, the shrewd Jaguar MD had arranged with Rowlands that if other Government factories were let on more favourable terms, these would be applied to the Browns Lane site. Lyons clearly now had the upper hand.

With the spacious Browns Lane plant secured, Jaguar could now look for new lines of business outside motor cars. Just before Christmas 1950, Lyons had written to the Ministry of Supply enquiring about engine or vehicle contracts. This bore fruit almost a year later when Jaguar secured a Ministry contract to manufacture Meteor tank engines (though this might have been linked to the deal to secure Browns Lane). At any rate, Lyons believed this contract could double the size of the business: 'We may be expected to produce 35 engines per week which should provide almost as much revenue as our car production.' By the end of 1952, however, an end to the Korean War was in sight and Meteor engine production was reduced drastically. However, it turned out to be almost a relief: the facilities were needed to build more Jaguars.

For Lyons, 1951 had been a year of monumental achievement. While still in his forties he had launched a brilliant new luxury saloon in world markets, successfully negotiated for a new million square foot (92,900sq m) factory, and seen a Jaguar win the Le Mans 24-hour race for Britain. Production at 6,496 cars might have been down on the previous year but that was because he had also stood firm against unwarranted strike action. Now, aged 50, he was as energetic as ever and looking for further progress.

It was in 1952 that motoring journalist Patrick Mennem had his first memorable meeting with Lyons. 'When I was a reporter on the *Coventry Evening Telegraph* in 1952, I was sent to interview Mr Lyons and I was told that, whatever you do, get there on time. I was 25 and with the arrogance of a 25-year-old, I thought I'd got it all sorted out in my mind what I wanted to ask him and hadn't really done enough preparatory work. I arrived at his office and was ushered in.

'"Mennem, sit down," and I sat down. He was absolutely immaculate and looked as though he had been scrubbed that morning, beautifully turned out. "And what do you want to talk to me about, Mennem?"

'I said, "What is your biggest problem at the moment?"

'He said, "Labour," and that was it – an absolute inky void... He didn't give you an ounce of help. It was up to you. And you were stretched to the limit to keep going. He thought it was up to you to ask him the right questions. If you couldn't do that, you weren't doing your job. That taught me a fantastic lesson. I thought, "Never again would I go in unprepared."

'His view of the union movement fell far short of idolatry! He thought they were screwing the whole business up, but he couldn't afford to say so outright. The place, in those days, was absolutely dominated by trades unionists, absolutely stiff with them.'[24]

Bob Berry, who had come to Jaguar in 1951 as an assistant to Ernest Rankin (and who would eventually head Jaguar's PR department), recalled Lyons's reaction to press interviews. He always remained polite and despite 'some incredibly crass things being said to him, he would never afterwards say, "Well, that was rubbish". He always respected someone else's point of view.' In fact, said Bob, 'He never expressed an opinion about any individual – whether he liked or hated them you had no idea by the way he spoke... He was very guarded that way. No, not guarded – it just wasn't him.'[25]

As for those infamous labour problems, Lyons did build a good working relationship with several of the more responsible union officials. One such was Ron Butlin, who became a convenor in 1952.

A mutual trust built up between the two men and sometimes Lyons would phone Butlin on the shop-floor. 'He'd then make various comments and say, "What do you think?" and I'd tell him. People wouldn't believe, as convenor of one of the unions, that I was advising the boss. They would say it was sabotage to representation on the shop-floor.

'But I didn't find him like that. I found him an honest, straightforward bloke with a good backbone and the principles that he'd stand by what he said. I always told him, "Whatever you do, stand by it. I'll stand by what I'm going to do, but if you let me down, I shall be destroyed." We had this understanding between us which was good. We saved many a dispute because he was involved.

'On one occasion one of our members was in the hospital and they sent him his discharge papers. I went to Mr Lyons and I told him. I said, "This is disgraceful." He sent an instruction down to management that never again would anybody be sent their discharge papers whilst they were under medical care. That was the sort of man he was.'[26]

While production in the new plant built up steadily – led by the Mk VII but with XK120 sales boosted by a new and delightful fixed-head variant – Jaguar's 1952 competition programme centred once more on Le Mans. All other races were incidental to the goal of winning the 24-hour event – including the Mille Miglia that year, on which Stirling Moss was dispatched in a C-type with experimental disc brakes.

Despite heroic efforts, Moss found he was unable to keep up with the new Mercedes-Benz 300SL coupé and, after retiring, cabled to Browns Lane: 'Must have more speed at Le Mans'. In a rare instance of near-panic at Jaguar, Sayer was instructed to revise the C-types' bodywork and the cooling system was adapted to suit. There was no opportunity for any proper testing and at Le Mans all three cars overheated and retired. The cruel irony was that the 1951 cars would have won easily.

When in a 1971 interview Lyons was asked what the biggest setbacks in his career were, he named this failure as one of two. It did not help that Mercedes, his *bête noire*, took the spoils. But his reaction to the debacle showed another aspect of his character. Despite the loss of worldwide publicity so important to what was still a tiny company, he did not rant or rave at those he felt were responsible. 'Never once do I recall him trying to apportion blame, or get angry or upset,' said Bob Berry. 'When we were all back at the hotel, he said, "we didn't do well at all there, did we?"… It was usually 'we' rather than 'you', but it was clear what he meant.'[27]

In the Le Mans month of June, the sale of the Swallow Road factory to Dunlop was completed and the £433,000 realised made a useful contribution to funds. With profits up 18 per cent to £396,000 and cash standing at £422,675, the company was looking very sound, though, worryingly, inflation was ten per cent that year. Tax was now an even more punitive 61 per cent. The accounts show that investment in plant and tooling only kept pace with depreciation, which is rather surprising, but both dividends and directors' fees were up by a third, the latter to £40,067.

The move from Swallow Road wasn't completed until the autumn of 1952 and Bill Cassidy recalled that his experimental department was one of the last to be installed at Browns Lane. Shortly afterwards he was given a surprise promotion. 'We didn't have a foreman then. I was working on a milling machine one day at 12 o'clock, and at ten past I was the foreman – that was how they worked!'

Cassidy had seen Lyons talk to body shop superintendent Bill Robinson and he heard Lyons say, 'All right Robinson, I'll leave that with you.' Robinson asked Cassidy whether he could run the shop. 'I replied that I'd effectively been doing it for some time. "Right," he said, "there's your office." That was it. Once you had Lyons's confidence, then you couldn't do anything wrong. But until you did, he was a very hard taskmaster.'[28]

With the move completed and Browns Lane fully functional, in late November Lyons was able to hold a convention of distributors and dealers, suppliers and press to show off the new facilities. The UK dealers were still being denied anywhere near enough new Jaguars and Lyons was fully aware that they were suffering while Jaguar had concentrated on growing exports – from less than ten per cent before the Second World War to no less than 84 per cent in 1951. This, he explained, had been vital for the survival of the company because the steel quota for purely domestic sales would have reduced production to 'a completely uneconomic level'. He asked suppliers to help on prices to ensure the final products remained competitive.

As for the overseas markets, North America was still the most important but also the most problematical. Then an article in *The Daily Express* caught Lyons's attention. Johannes Eerdmans, whom he had met during a brief wartime holiday at Woolacombe, Devon, had resigned from his position as Joint Managing Director of Thomas de La Rue and was going to America. Dutch born, Eerdmans had been responsible for building up the company's Formica division and had become a naturalised Briton. Lyons had been 'very impressed' with his personality and considered that he might just be the man to help him establish more direct control of Jaguar's North American affairs as 'there was no-one in the organisation I could spare who was qualified to undertake an assignment of such importance'.[29]

'Lyons saw it in the paper and 'phoned me immediately,' recalled Eerdmans. 'He said, "Can I see you? I'd like you to do something for me in America."'[30] They met at London's Dorchester Hotel and Lyons explained the problems with his two American distributors, Hornburg and Hoffman.

Lyons's relationship with Hoffman in particular had deteriorated badly. Earlier, Jaguar had begun to receive complaints from Hoffman's dealers that they were being forced to take two Volkswagen for every XK120 allocated to them. (This was before the remarkable Beetle caught on in America and it was a difficult car to sell.) Lyons decided to set up a dealer conference in New York over Hoffman's head 'for I had made no progress in my attempts to restrain him from pursuing this unacceptable practice'.[31] However, Hoffman was invited to attend. The night before the conference Lyons was visited by three dealers, who warned him that Hoffman had advised all the dealers to ignore any attempt to restrict his activities; the dealers hoped that Lyons would put an end to the imposition of VWs.

Over 100 dealers packed into the room at the Waldorf Astoria to hear Lyons say that he had advised Mr Hoffman that he should discontinue this condition. He then went on to compliment everyone, including Hoffman, on the sales success. 'To my astonishment,' Lyons recorded some 25 years later, 'what I said was received in silence and Hoffman mounted the platform and said he wished everyone to know he was the distributor with a contract which placed no restriction on his conditions of sale and any dealer who did not accept the conditions he imposed would receive no XKs at all and he would fight any attempt by the company to interfere... Hoffman had convinced and frightened everyone, apparently even those who had come to see me the night before, that he held the whip hand.'

Lyons consulted his lawyers the next day but found that any legal action against Hoffman, including cancelling his contract, would be extremely difficult. 'It was an insight into what a remarkable little man Hoffman was,' Lyons ruefully admitted later.[32] But he saw in Eerdmans someone with the strength of character to tackle such difficulties and Lyons gave him the job; it would prove to be an inspired decision.

The last day of 1952 saw a board meeting held at Browns Lane, where Lyons brought up the matter of solicitor's charges. Alan Newsome & Co had sent an account in the sum of £1,510 12s 6d (£1,510.63) for handling the sale of the factory. Lyons pointed out that the regular legal fee for such a sale in London would be £195 and in the provinces £295. Of course, Alan Newsome was a close friend of the Lyons family but this did not inhibit Lyons from pursuing what he felt was an unfair charge! Huckvale was instructed to write to Mr Newsome, who maintained that his fees were reasonable. They eventually reached an amicable settlement and, clearly, their friendship was never an issue. (A similar situation arose some 11 months later when Lyons disagreed with his old friend and sparring partner Stanley Hattrell, the architect, over his role in acquiring Browns Lane. This particular debate rumbled on for several years and did slightly mar relations between Lyons and Hattrell, according to Pat Quinn.)

Lyons further reported to the board that virtually all exports were going to North America and prospects looked very good. 'Mr Eerdmans will establish himself in New York and will be on the spot to deal with any matters that might arise...'

The meeting further noted that negotiations were taking place with Pressed Steel 'for the production of a pressed steel body for a new 2-litre [122cu in] car which we have in hand, and which it is hoped we should be able to sell for a price not exceeding £695 excluding Purchase Tax'. This project would eventually turn into the unitary-construction 2.4 (151cu in) saloon, a most significant model in Jaguar history.

In February 1953 Lyons and his new recruit Eerdmans travelled to America to visit both Hoffman in New York and Hornburg in Hollywood. Shortly afterwards Eerdmans set up an office at 487 Park Avenue, New York – pointedly adjoining Hoffman's premises. 'It was obvious that neither Hoffman nor Hornburg welcomed Eerdmans's appointment, but I was satisfied that he was capable of looking after our interests,' wrote Lyons.[33]

The new year brought Lyons little time to spend on his expanding farm with its herd of pedigree Jerseys; this was being run by a full-time manager, the first being a Mr Hitchman. He was succeeded, recalled Mary Rimell, 'by a delightful Irishman called Halligan whose daughter Patsy I taught to ride. Unfortunately Halligan hit the bottle at times and I don't think he was really qualified as a manager.'[34] Then in the mid-1950s Mr and Mrs Johns came.

The company was still expanding fast and Lyons evidently felt that the commission structure, which contributed to his income, was inappropriate. So at a board meeting in March he stated he had again decided to forego £10,000 of the commission due to him. Then, he proposed that the bonus Whittaker and Heynes received each Christmas should be replaced by commission based on two per cent of the net profits. This Christmas bonus for certain staff had long been a point of discussion, as in previous years people had found they depended almost more on the bonus than their regular wage. The link with profits for Lyons's two most senior men was generous and clearly demonstrates how valuable he considered them to be. However, as Jaguar's profits grew, Lyons came to regret this arrangement!

In June, faster, lighter C-types contested the Le Mans 24-hour race; this time they were well-tested (by Norman Dewis, who had joined the previous year) and had disc brakes. Against a line-up that included most of the grand prix drivers of the day – Ascari, Fangio, Hawthorn, and Villoresi amongst them – and most major manufacturers, the C-type of Tony Rolt and Duncan Hamilton took the honours for Jaguar and Britain in this, the Coronation year. They clocked the first ever 100mph (160kmh) average for the race and once more Jaguar garnered massive worldwide press coverage.

Lyons witnessed the triumph and after the race, said Tony Rolt, 'We took him to a fairly racy nightclub in Paris. He could let his hair down!'[35] Greta went too – she often accompanied her husband to Le Mans and was always very much part of the celebrations afterwards. The two race winners were among Lyons's favourite drivers. 'He always,' stated daughter Pat, 'used to rave about Duncan Hamilton and Tony Rolt in their heyday, what terrific people they were.'[36]

Back home, the victorious C-types paraded through Coventry and made a ceremonial entrance to the Browns Lane factory, where they were welcomed by virtually the entire workforce, assembled in the car park below Lyons's office. It was one of the few occasions on which Bob Berry recalled Lyons making an extempore speech. 'He would do an ad lib speech *in extremis,*' said Bob (who wrote many speeches for his boss), 'but he'd work very hard not to do it. The very nature of the guy meant that whatever he said had to be exact, precise, and therefore he would avoid any situation which would make that difficult.'[37]

The following weekend *The Sunday Times* carried an unattributed, but useful, profile of Lyons in his prime. After sketching in Jaguar's Blackpool origins, the feature went on to describe the Jaguar management team of which Lyons 'is the captain and the sole selector. To say he inspires it would introduce a note of mysticism foreign to his outlook. Nor does he drive it, for that is foreign to his own character. He directs it. But he directs it with a sustained and compelling intensity of purpose. His is an example of individual enterprise on a scale uncommon in these days of impersonal corporate undertakings...

'Personally trim, immaculate in dress, he has the aura of power but not the trappings. No entourage of secretaries and personal assistants trails his unceasing movements around the great modern factory... The men who work for him at all levels know him, but few at any level recall a conversation lasting more than ten minutes. His interest is precise, kindly and aloof.'

This paints a fine word picture of Lyons at Jaguar's helm.

That 1953 Le Mans victory had emphasised the worth of the disc brake, which Jaguar had done so much to develop with Dunlop. Lyons enjoyed a close relationship with Dunlop and was sent a copy of the minutes of a meeting held by that company on 1 July to discuss 'Disc Brakes for Road Vehicles,' the topic being 'to obtain the adoption of the brake for general use on cars and trucks'.

The minutes noted that 'no undertaking to develop brakes for cars in competition with Jaguar will be made without Mr Lyons's agreement at this stage. As he will be assured of every assistance in improving the performance of Jaguar cars for next season, it is hoped that he will not object to our collaborating with certain other racing interests who may approach us'[38] – by which Dunlop meant the American Cunningham team and Mercedes-Benz. In fact Lyons was not at all sure about the proposed recipients of the new technology and said so!

It would be several years yet before the disc brake appeared on a production Jaguar but nevertheless cars were leaving Browns Lane in ever-greater quantities. Lyons reported to the board in July that 250 cars were being produced per week. Also, reacting to continued pleas from UK dealers, Lyons felt that it was now possible to release more cars to the home market, 'without detriment to our export requirements, which would still average about 70 per cent of output'.

It was during 1953 that Lyons bought his first, and only, boat – an open, clinker-built craft constructed by a small shipyard near Salcombe. Patterned on the local working boats used to ferry people across the bay, it had a small inboard engine and was about 15 feet [4.5m] long. Its name was inspired by the car which had just gained Jaguar's second Le Mans win – *Sea-Type*! The craft provided much enjoyment for family and friends over many years and was often used to reach Salcombe from The Bolt. (*Sea-Type* was sold in more recent years but is thought still to exist.)

More production equalled greater profits and for 1952–3, these were up again at £438,000 pre-tax – but only by ten per cent, which probably reflected tighter margins in spite of increasing sales. Post-tax profits at just £190,187, combined with stock and work-in-progress being up £725,000 (45 per cent) and modest investment, accounted for a fall in the bank balance. The dividend was increased by a quarter to 25 per cent.

Occasionally business propositions would come Lyons's way. In early October the inventive engineer Harry Ferguson (of Ferguson tractor fame) proposed collaboration on a vehicle of his design. He was not prepared, until some agreement was signed, to disclose any detail apart from mentioning the 'Ferguson System' (an interesting four-wheel-drive arrangement). However, without full information, Lyons was not willing to proceed beyond a meeting of accountants. 'May I add that I do not in any way underestimate the genius which you possess for achieving great objectives,'[39] wrote Lyons diplomatically.

However, Ferguson's letters began to border on the abusive and negotiations – such as they had been – ceased. The car project, which Ferguson was proposing to a number of manufacturers at the time, was impractical but his all-wheel-drive system had real merit as Bill Heynes appreciated when asked to comment upon it. Many years later it was adopted by Jensen and while Jaguar fitted the system experimentally to an XJ-S and to the prototype V12 XJ220 in the 1980s, no Jaguar car appeared with all-wheel drive until the X-type saloon of 2001 (and that used a Ford-based system). Former Jaguar works driver Tony Rolt, who had worked for Harry Ferguson Research Ltd from 1950, later headed FF Developments, the company that was formed to develop and promote the Ferguson system. However, Jaguar was perfectly capable of being innovative on its own account, as 1954 would show.

CHAPTER 6

TRAGEDY AND A KNIGHTHOOD

The new small saloon was a prime item for the January 1954 board meeting, Lyons reporting that a £360,000 body tooling order had been placed. Increasing plant capacity would require a further £300,000. Every step, he said, was being taken to get prototypes on the road at an early date. By early 1954, the US market was getting much more competitive and Lyons relayed the news of price reductions in America to maintain sales.

Interestingly, later that month Lyons received a farewell letter from Sir John Black, just ousted as Chairman of Standard-Triumph. 'Looking back, I feel very glad that I had an opportunity of working with you in the early days,' wrote Black, 'and I have so admired the tremendous enthusiasm, courage and hard work that you have put in to bring your company to its extraordinary position in the industry today, and feel quite sure you will go on to even greater successes.'[1] It was a fine tribute from Sir John, who did not allow previous disagreements to cloud his personal appreciation of Lyons's achievements. He certainly contributed to these: without the ready assistance of Black and the effectiveness of Standard as a key supplier of parts and engineering back-up in the early 1930s, Lyons may never have progressed beyond being a coachbuilder. In turn, Lyons acknowledged the energy and effectiveness of John Black at Standard.

More memories of times past were evoked for Lyons when on 18 February 1954 he presented the prizes and certificates at the Arnold School speech day at the Palace Theatre, Blackpool. Addressing the pupils of his old school, he emphasised the importance of two precepts: 'I have learned that the two greatest essentials in life, from the point of view of getting on, are enthusiasm and determination. You must be interested and be prepared to put the maximum effort into what you do. I have found these qualities extremely rare.'

Lyons certainly possessed these attributes fully and, while making money was never his prime objective, his own 'enthusiasm and determination' were paying off as Jaguar flourished. At a board meeting, while renouncing £10,000 commission, Lyons still received a commission payment of £22,548. His two top men were being well rewarded too: Heynes and Whittaker each received bonuses of £3,962.

Meanwhile in the USA, Jaguar Cars North American Corporation (JCNA) had been formed officially, with Jo Eerdmans as President. He soon got to grips with the peculiarities of the US market. While John Dugdale (the ex-*Autocar* journalist, who in May 1954 had joined JCNA from Rootes in New York) might have stated correctly that the Mk VII and XK120 were the most desirable specialist cars in the USA, competition was looming. True, Ford's Thunderbird and GM's Corvette were dismissed out of hand by some hardened sports car enthusiasts – only an import would do for these folk – but finally Mercedes-Benz was entering the sports car field with the impressive 300SL coupé and the less impressive but more affordable 190SL open two-seater.

So it seemed surprising that early in 1954 Eerdmans wrote to Chuck Hornburg urging him to reconsider his decision not to take on a Mercedes-Benz franchise! Eerdmans was concerned that failure to do so could ultimately lose Hornburg dealers, as some might defect to Mercedes entirely. He pointed out that Max Hoffman sold Mercedes 'east of the Mississippi' and that did not seem to have harmed Jaguar. However, later it would be that same German make which would be the catalyst in Lyons deciding to make the final break with Hoffman.

At home, 1954 saw Lyons's growing eminence being recognised in various ways. He was now president of the Motor Industry Research Association (MIRA), Jaguar having been one of the key motor companies to have helped establish this test and research facility. Jaguar was also a major benefactor to the Motor Trades Benevolent Fund, of which Lyons also became President. However, he received one of his greatest accolades when he was appointed Royal Designer for Industry by the Royal Society of Arts; this was true recognition of Lyons's personal success in combining form with function in the Jaguar car.

Most unusually, the 20th AGM in May was marked by a voice of dissent from a shareholder. Mr Billington said he could not support the motion in favour of passing the accounts. In his opinion they were an example of 'unfairness and greed'. In support of his view he quoted the increase in the directors' remuneration compared to the dividend. He was also concerned that the shares were 'grossly undervalued' and that there was danger from speculators or from a takeover by another manufacturer.

Satisfying the shareholders was never Lyons's priority but he did take up Mr Billington's points. No director, he said, had received any salary increase for four or five years and added that increased earnings were due to increased profits. As for the dividend level, he felt this gave a good return on the original share price. He further pointed out that the motor car business was an expensive one to run and the company was committed to considerable investment in new tooling and needed to retain as high a proportion of profits as possible. Such a policy was in the interests of the shareholders, he said. As for a hostile takeover, Lyons had no fear of that: although he did not mention it, he had the controlling interest...

Jaguar Cars Ltd was doing well, however. The annual accounts to 31 July 1953 presented at the meeting showed a 27 per cent increase in pre-tax profits, up to £558,000, but the tax bill was a massive £341,070 (61 per cent), once again restricting the company's ability to reinvest. However, that year's figures were somewhat higher because they included an element of back tax and the cryptic wording of the annual report suggested the company had been under-declaring tax in previous years! The dividend to be paid was increased by 30 per cent and cash had nearly doubled to £703,996 but this increase was reflected in reduced stock and work in progress. Net current assets were virtually unchanged. With reduced investment in plant and machinery, this had been funded out of cash flow.

T. Wells Daffern retired at that AGM; perhaps Lyons felt he had discharged his moral debt to the Manager of the Coventry Permanent Building Society who had proved so helpful to him in the 1930s! Not that these 'outside' directors were well remunerated, Alan Newsome recalled. Daffern was replaced by Edward Huckvale, Company Secretary and himself a veteran of 25 years' service with Jaguar.

At about this time Bernard Hewitt, working for a small local firm, was looking for better prospects and wrote to Jaguar among others. 'To my utter amazement, my wife rang me up and said, "There's a Jaguar just arrived here with a letter." I was asked to go for an interview and I was shown up to Mr Lyons's office...we had a chat. I was completely amazed because he offered me the job on the spot. He wanted someone who could put into practice some ideas that he'd got.'[2]

Hewitt assumed an unique position within Jaguar as a personal assistant to Lyons, though he describes the post as more that of a special projects manager. So he joined Alice Fenton and Geoff Mitchell, the chauffeur, as only the third member of Lyons's personal staff. Not that the irascible Gardner was impressed when Hewitt was shown his province. 'When I was originally taken round and introduced to all the heads of department by "Pop" Shortley, the Commercial Manager, he said, "This is Bernard Hewitt. He's going to be working directly for Mr Lyons".

'"Well, don't go in my bloody mill without me saying so,"'[3] was Fred Gardner's response.

Bernard Hewitt has another anecdote of his early days at Browns Lane. 'Soon after I joined Jaguar I became a Freemason. The next morning, Lyons said, "I understand congratulations are due, Hewitt." I don't know how he found out. Nobody at work was involved. "I'm very pleased about that Hewitt but, remember, work first."'[4] Lyons was a Freemason himself but did little more than pay his annual dues to the local lodge; Pat Quinn recalled that he was not very impressed with the organisation. Undoubtedly he could see all sorts of potential improvements!

In the competition sphere, a replacement for the C-type would make its debut at Le Mans on 12 June. The new D-type was a remarkably advanced sports racing car, its semi-monocoque construction predating by some 15 years what was to become typical Formula 1 car practice.

It was, of course, disc-braked but Lyons had again begun to fear that Dunlop might supply this valuable weapon to some of his rivals. Accordingly, in February Lyons wrote to G. Edward Beharrell expressing his concern that, if Dunlop supplied disc brakes to the American Cunningham team for Le Mans, it would have the effect of 'loading the dice against a Jaguar win, a Dunlop tyre win and a British win'.

Beharrell was able to reassure him that Dunlop had been released from its commitment to Cunningham. As further proof of his company's loyalty to Jaguar, he added: 'If you are successful at Le Mans, as I hope you will be, there will be an increased interest in our brake for production cars on which you will naturally wish to be first in the field...our test work for production models should be completed as quickly as possible.'

With an even more powerful version of the XK engine, and with a Malcolm Sayer-designed body shape incorporating a distinctive tail fin for stability, the D-type possessed everything needed to win. However, Le Mans 1954 turned out to be a massive disappointment for Jaguar. Firstly the three D-types were delayed by sand in the fuel which caused blocked filters and cost valuable time. But Duncan Hamilton and Tony Rolt then put in a heroic drive in torrential rain to haul in the leading Ferrari and, when in the last hour the Ferrari failed to restart after a routine pit stop, the race seemed to be Jaguar's. However, with rather more than the regulation number of mechanics working on the car, the big 4.9-litre (302cu in) V12 was coaxed back to life and the Ferrari won by a mere 105 seconds. Clearly there had been an infringement of the rules and 'Lofty' suggested Jaguar should protest. Lyons would not hear of it. For all that a Le Mans win meant to Jaguar, he did not wish to win races that way.

At that year's Motor Show in London, the XK was seen to have been refined into the more practical XK140 range, while the large saloon was given more power and renamed the Mk VII M. The stock market approved – the 5s (25p) ordinary shares jumped from 50s (£2.50) to 70s (£3.50) – though rumours of a Chrysler takeover probably helped too!

Bill Cassidy remembered how seriously Lyons took these important annual shows. 'There were times when we worked till three o'clock in the morning, then back in again at eight o'clock, and sometimes right through the night for two nights without any sleep. I've been there with Mr Lyons at two in the morning on the show cars. He'd say, "I'll see you at seven o'clock, Cassidy." That was it. You were there, you didn't argue about it.'

'When we used to do a show car, he'd want it down as low as we could get it – the sleek look. In the early hours of one morning we put the car on a ramp and lifted it up to the height of the stand. We then clamped the suspension down. He said, "Now that's it, but what about those exhausts?" 'So I said, "Let's take them off and I can put two dummy tail pipes out the back." "Brilliant idea. You go ahead and let me see it." That's how you got his confidence.'[5]

It had long been Lyons's ambition to secure the freehold of the Browns Lane plant and in early December Lyons opened negotiations with Sir James Helmore of the Ministry of Supply for the purchase of the site. 'For the whole of the factory,' he wrote, 'including the portion of the factory and the offices at present occupied by The General Electric Company, we offer a figure of £958,300 being capitalisation of rent at 6 per cent per annum. From this we are entitled to deduct the amounts already paid out for bringing the factory into its present state, less the rent already due for the three years of our occupation...'

By this means he reduced the figure to £668,294. Lloyds Bank had agreed to finance the deal but by January 1956 had changed its mind. Not yet would Lyons achieve one of his main commercial objectives.

The company had progressed well under Lyons's astute but

cautious management since the difficult early postwar period. He had in his armoury the stunning XK sports car and a fine prestigious large saloon. However, the time was approaching for another bold step that would broaden the Jaguar range and appeal to a new, much larger market. The year 1955 was, however, to be a period of great personal tragedy and one which would have a dramatic impact on the whole history of Lyons's company.

First, the US sales organisation remained to be sorted out, with the principal need being to terminate Hoffman's distribution contract on the East Coast. The final straw for Lyons, according to John Dugdale, was when Hoffman allocated his Frank Lloyd Wright-designed showrooms in New York, intended for Jaguar, to his Mercedes-Benz franchise. Lyons journeyed to the US in January 1955 and on the last day of his visit put his dissatisfaction in writing to Max Hoffman. That Hoffman was considered a complete rogue by Lyons is reflected in the litany of complaints.

Lyons maintained that Hoffman had never shown any appreciation of the importance of a strong dealer organisation. His handling and distribution were a constant source of friction with owners and dealers, the latter not even having written contracts. There were continual disputes over territory among dealers, who felt a deep resentment towards him. He had refused to accept cars until given a further price concession. 'I have been shocked by the evidence that you personally and as a consequence your organisation have abandoned any semblance of loyalty to our products and instead have transferred your interests to other competitive makes of cars,' by which Lyons chiefly meant Mercedes-Benz. Lyons continued: 'You...have shown an indifference to Jaguar which has permeated your entire organisation which is now spreading at an alarming degree through the ranks of dealers and owners in your territory.'[6] He further accused Hoffman of consistently profiting by paying less customs duty than shown. Moreover, a 3½ per cent additional discount given for sub-distributors had mostly been retained by Hoffman and, when occasionally passed on, had been offset by new handling charges. Lyons also knew that Hoffman was now threatening to sue any dealer who bought cars direct from Jaguar's US company.

Hoffman's response to this justifiable tirade was immediate and typically aggressive: he had an injunction served on Lyons, preventing him from sailing home for several days. The effect of this episode would colour Lyons's views and attitudes towards the US market for the rest of his career.

Although Hoffman resorted to litigation, Lyons finally had his way and the distributorship was terminated at the end of 1955. At a July board meeting Jaguar's legal costs were disclosed: the affair had cost $24,226.76. On top of that, John Dugdale recorded, 'Hoffman received an "override" – a compensation payment on every Jaguar sold in the East for several years. He played the same game with Mercedes-Benz, Fiat and BMW.'[7] According to Alan Newsome, it cost $100,000 in total to get rid of Hoffman. Others put the figure higher.

Furthermore, not only Hoffman but also Hornburg was in Lyons's firing line as John Dugdale, running Jaguar's West Coast office at 9155 Sunset Boulevard, was well aware. 'It may seem strange that William Lyons, who face to face was always at pains to be courteous even when he was being blunt, was determined to break Hornburg. The Chairman had a bulldog quality and somewhere along the line he had become convinced that Chuck Hornburg had been less than straight with him.'[8]

There was certainly truth in the accusation that, like Hoffman, Hornburg had been making easy money selling the glamorous Jaguars while not investing enough in the vital service and parts facilities. Jaguar had to send out its own service representatives to improve the situation and customer relations were suffering. Aside from this and the need to reduce Hornburg's territory, the biggest bone of contention centred around import duties. Hornburg had successfully obtained a landmark ruling against the US Government and had received a large refund for over-payment on Jaguars shipped in; Lyons considered that a proportion of this belonged to Jaguar.

Hornburg in turn was unhappy about Lyons's front man Jo Eerdmans; Hornburg flew to Coventry and made a number of allegations to Lyons about Eerdmans, Dugdale, and Jaguar's US company in general. However, his attempts to influence Lyons backfired when the Chairman simply referred him back to Eerdmans. In turn, Eerdmans complained to Lyons via Dugdale (on a visit to the UK) about Hornburg's 'petty and unco-operative attitude during negotiations'. He would, he cabled, prefer it if Lyons did not consider Hornburg as a possible distributor after July 1956.

While the matter dragged on well into 1956, a compromise was eventually reached whereby Hornburg remained in the Jaguar fold but returned some of the overpaid duty to Jaguar and gave up a large portion of his territory in the west. Two more distributors were appointed and together with the removal at last of Hoffman on the East Coast, Jaguar could finally look at developing sales much more effectively in North America.

It had been a bruising episode all round but the US market was vitally important to Jaguar. Lyons's company had become Britain's biggest dollar earner and, indeed, the biggest dollar earner of any importer into the US during both 1953 and 1954. North American deliveries had increased dramatically from 729 in 1949–50 to 5,218 in 1952–3 (financial years), even if they had slipped back in the 1953–4 year (to 2,834 units) while the big distributorship shake-up went on. Sales rose during 1955 but Jaguar still lost out to Volkswagen as top-value importer that year, although the Coventry firm remained in a good second place. Mercedes-Benz was also making some progress, helped by the new 190SL, which (after a delayed start) had reached the market in January 1955 (1,727 were sold worldwide that year, against 1,451 XK140 open two-seaters).

Lyons, in fact, expressed his concerns about the Germans' progress at a 1955 NAC meeting, of which he was a member once again. Sir Patrick Hennessy (Ford of Britain's Managing Director and a friend of Lyons) had said the Germans were gaining on the UK with their prices not rising so quickly. The minutes recorded: 'Mr Lyons complained that all attempts to make economies in production were offset by rising costs. Mr Lyons said that British prices were likely to go up, whereas German prices were likely to go down.'[9]

It was in March 1955 that Lyons's only son John, 25 years old that January, joined the company. After leaving Oundle, John had served a three-year apprenticeship at Leyland Motors and then had carried out his National Service. Those two years were spent with the Royal Electrical and Mechanical Engineers, mainly in Germany; there he was involved in vehicle maintenance, tank recovery, and various engineering tasks. He was 'demobbed' towards the end of 1954, after which he spent six months in Paris with Charlie Delecroix, the Jaguar distributor there.

John Lyons was a highly personable and much-liked young man. 'Dutch' Heynes, Bill Heynes's wife, described him as having his mother's charm combined with his father's wisdom. He was popular, too, with his sisters and was particularly close to Pat during the war years. 'He'd got a lot of my father in him,' said Pat, 'but I wouldn't say he was entirely like him.'[10] She also recalled that he had 'a terrific sense of humour'.

Just after the war, she and John went on a 'mad excursion' to Rome across a war-torn Europe in a little two-seater Standard prototype, which had been stored at Wappenbury during the hostilities. They had just about enough money to get back home. Later, in February 1951, the Standard was replaced when his father provided John with an XK120 as a 21st birthday present. Unfortunately, a big allowance failed to come with it. Said Pat: 'I remember John joking once: "a fat lot of good it is to me, I haven't got enough money to buy petrol for it!"'[11] Also, when towards the end of his National Service John needed a new hood on his XK120, he didn't dare have one fitted because, on taking the car back to Wappenbury, his father would have seen it.

It was always accepted within the family that John would succeed his father at Jaguar. In mid-March 1955 he duly started work at the Browns Lane factory, with Lyons senior sending a memo to all staff explaining that his son would 'ultimately take a position of responsibility. His first assignment for the company will be to undertake an investigation into economies which can be achieved in the design, construction and manufacture of the Mark VII. I shall be glad if [you] will give him every possible assistance and co-operation.'[12]

It is difficult being the boss's son at the best of times and, while he experienced much goodwill at the plant, the cost-cutting job that he had been given was tough. 'My clear impression was that John had been given a task that would have daunted anybody in the business with many more years experience,' commented Bob Berry. 'He was pretty unhappy about the whole thing.'[13] Little was achieved; when for example John pointed out that there was no need for carpeting under the front seats, the trim shop misunderstood and simply snipped off the carpet and threw it away!

'He was a lonely man,' confirmed Bernard Hewitt; 'Sir William was in the end office, Alice Fenton's office was next, I was in the next one and John had the next one. Occasionally, he'd say, "Come into my office. Let's have a cup of tea together and a chat."'[14]

While at Oundle, John had created his own styling models and was now building himself some sort of single-seater racing car in the corner of the experimental shop. It was never brought to fruition. He also took a keen interest in the competition shop and would have seen the redesigned and much faster 1955 works D-types coming together ready for Le Mans on 11–12 June. Alas, he was destined never to see them in action on the Sarthe circuit, as on 6 June a tragic accident occurred that would also have far reaching consequences for Jaguar's future history.

Bob Berry and Norman Dewis were driving two of the D-types to Le Mans. (It was a principle at that time always to drive the works cars to Le Mans; it demonstrated they were true road cars, while the journey would also show up any incipient faults.) They reached

Southampton where they were to fly by Silver City Airways to Cherbourg. John, who was driving a Mk VII support car, was due to rendezvous with them at Southampton. 'We waited and we waited, and we finally decided we could wait no longer,' recounted Bob Berry. 'It was getting dark and the last thing we wanted was to drive these cars in the dark down to Le Mans, so Norman and I decided, having given up our slot and sat there and sat there, that we had to go.'[15]

John caught a later flight and then stopped at Montebourg, about 30 miles (48km) south of Cherbourg, at a petrol station on the left-hand side of the road. Shortly after pulling away from the station, on what Andrew Whyte describes as 'the straight but heavily cambered N13,'[16] he collided head on with an American service vehicle at the brow of a hill and died instantly.

This was not, according to 'Lofty' England, a case of John simply driving on the wrong side of the road in a fit of absentmindedness; he pointed out that John was a good driver and was very used to continental motoring, as he had spent almost two years in Germany while on military service. 'Lofty' thought that John hit a patch of oil in the wet and the car swung across the road into the path of the bus. Mary Rimell believes that the pronounced camber of the road encouraged drivers to keep towards the middle, so both vehicles might have been in the centre when breasting that rise on this switchback road (certainly the main impact was on the Mk VII's left front). Whatever happened, the accident cost him his life, William and Greta their son, and Pat and Mary their brother.

Shortly after 7pm that evening word of the accident came through to the factory. 'Lofty' was telephoned and he immediately got in touch with the British Consul in Cherbourg to check. 'I drove over to Wappenbury and broke the sad news to Sir William and Lady Lyons. Fortunately their phones were out of order so the press could not contact them. I took them to my house.'[17] 'Lofty' then went over to Cherbourg to deal with the formalities and arrange for John's body to be flown back to Birmingham on the Wednesday morning.

Needless to say, his mother and father were distraught, as his sisters recalled. Pat: 'One could say it wrecked their lives. It was just the most devastating thing ever. They were both absolutely heart-broken. I don't think my mother ever got back to how she used to be before.' Mary agreed but felt that, if anything, it was a harder blow for her mother. 'I think Daddy threw himself more into his work, whereas Mummy only had her bridge and her golf. I was 17 and still at home. I think Daddy retreated into his work. Even more.

He buried himself in his work, completely I think after that. For the next 10 years really.'[18]

There was great sadness at the factory too, where John had already become a popular and respected figure in those few short months. Jack Gannon was working in the experimental department: 'We were all absolutely devastated. John had been around and we got to know him. He would have been a wonderful replacement for his father. He had the same sort of attitudes. He was open, he would listen, he would ask a lot of questions – he wanted to know. But he had the sort of attitude that made you respect him. He wasn't just the kid that was following in Dad's footsteps.'[19]

Pat, though, is not so sure how it would have worked out in the long term and her mother, too, had been diffident about the prospect of John being expected to emulate his father at Jaguar. Would he have matched up to those famously exacting standards? Could he have accepted the inevitable restrictions and tensions of working for his own father?

'I think it is difficult to anticipate what would have happened,' speculated Pat. 'Obviously it was a terrible blow losing John, but whether it would actually have made any difference to Jaguar's future I don't know. If John had been at Jaguar he would have been faced with the same problems... It wouldn't have been plain sailing.'[20] In a most tragic manner, the family was spared the possibility of witnessing John trying, and perhaps failing, in the near-impossible task of following his wholly unique father.

On one point everyone is adamant. No one saw any emotion in Lyons at work. His strength of character and enormous self-control allowed him to submerge his deep hurt. To all intents and purposes, it was business as usual for this remarkable man. The next day he sent a memo to Bill Thornton in the prototype body shop: 'The small piece of plasticine which I have roughly put in the centre of the new Mark VII badge you are modelling has been put there because I think the step between the nose of the bonnet and the badge is too great.'[21]

However, in a broader sense, worse was to follow six days later. Three works D-types started at Le Mans but some 2½ hours into the 24 hours, the worst motor racing disaster ever occurred, resulting in the death of over 80 spectators and a driver. Up until then Fangio (in a works Mercedes-Benz 300SLR) and Hawthorn (in one of the new D-types) had been enjoying an epic dice for the lead, with Hawthorn setting the fastest lap. Then at about 6.27pm, Hawthorn pulled into the pits for a scheduled refuelling stop. An Austin-Healey behind him moved out towards the centre of the road and was struck by Levegh's 300SLR which was launched into the air. It broke up on crashing into a retaining wall and major components scythed through the crowd opposite the pits, with terrible consequences.

The organisers decided to continue the race on the grounds that to stop it would make the job of evacuating the wounded and removing the dead even more difficult. They specifically asked the competitors to keep racing but at midnight, on orders from Stuttgart, the Mercedes team withdrew while in the lead. Hawthorn and Bueb continued to what, inevitably, was now to be seen as a hollow victory. This was further tainted when afterwards some of the French press attempted to blame Hawthorn for the tragedy, with similar inferences being made by some of the Mercedes race personnel. Later, the official enquiry was to exonerate Hawthorn fully.

'Lofty' England was considerably upset that Mercedes-Benz had pulled out, especially after racing for a further six hours. The withdrawal had cast a shadow over Jaguar dutifully continuing as requested by the ACO. Of course, whether the German cars would have won had they stayed in the event is impossible to say for certain.

In commercial terms, the tragedy denied Jaguar much of the publicity that its efforts deserved. 'At the time,' recalled Bob Bett of Jaguar's advertising agency, 'we had all agreed that, whoever won, we would advertise the race. But when I came back and saw the headlines in *The Daily Express*, "Disaster at Le Mans", I changed my mind a bit.'[22] He discussed the matter with Lyons who, after some thought, concurred with Bett's view. The advertisements were cancelled.

It is an illustration of Lyons's single-mindedness that he still sent Rankin a lengthy memo shortly afterwards bemoaning the lack of publicity (as opposed to paid advertising) resulting from Jaguar's win. He felt that 'Hawthorne [*sic*] very clearly demonstrated that a British car was a match for the Mercedes which has had such a tremendous build up, not, of course, without some justification.

'The Mercedes attempt to dominate the sports car world has been just as intense as their attempt in the case of the Grand Prix car,' he continued, 'and the car they produced was, in fact, identical in most respects, to their Grand Prix car, produced at phenomenal cost.' He went on to say that it was strange to him that no reference had been made to Britain 'producing a car at least the equal of Mercedes, or even a superior one, as proved by Hawthorn lapping faster than Fangio.'[23]

It would be relevant to add here that Mercedes-Benz was part of Daimler-Benz, a massively larger organisation than Jaguar Cars Ltd, with hugely greater resources. Its manufacturing facilities had been largely devastated during the war but even by 1950, passenger car production had reached some 22,000 units compared with Jaguar's 7,206. By 1955 the gap was even more disparate: Mercedes-Benz produced 63,678 passenger cars that year against Jaguar's 10,868 – and this, of course, ignores all Mercedes-Benz commercial vehicles, Daimler-Benz aircraft work and various other activities. No wonder, then, that Lyons was so keen to drive home the point that his tiny company had produced a Le Mans car – the D-type – which to all intents and purposes was the equal of the best that the might of Mercedes-Benz could field.

Not that Jaguar lacked respect for Mercedes-Benz. 'Lofty' England had known the legendary Mercedes team manager, Alfred Neubauer, since before the Second World War and Bill Heynes was extremely friendly (Bob Berry's words) with its equally well-known chief engineer, Rudolph Uhlenhaut. But the 1955 Le Mans would rankle for years.

Lyons's other beef was that Britain's ineffectual Formula 1 cars were getting a disproportionate amount of column inches despite their failures, while sports car racing was being neglected despite British cars being successful there. This might have been an incentive for Jaguar to enter Formula 1. The ebullient cylinder head expert Harry Weslake was certainly game for it!

'There is one thing which has emerged from this ill-fated Le Mans race,' Harry wrote on 25 June to Lyons, 'and that is that a British firm can compete with the Hun when it comes to racing…I do not know what your feelings are about 2½ litre [grand prix] racing, but I think we could administer quite a shock to the German and Italian camps if we really set about it, and it should not cost a lot of money to achieve.'[24] However, while both Lyons and Bill Heynes toyed with the idea at various times, a Jaguar Formula 1 car never became a reality in their lifetimes.

On a lighter note 'Lofty' often used to tell the story of 'how you can do things correctly without spending a lot of money'. Before Le Mans, he received three telegrams. The first came from America and was along the lines of: 'President, Vice-President, officers, staff and employees of Jaguar Cars North America Inc., 427 Park Ave., New York, wish all members of the Jaguar team competing at Le Mans 24 hr race, June 11/12 1955: Best of luck.' The next one was from his own people back at Browns Lane: 'Good luck from all members of the Service Department.'

'There was a third which said: "Good luck, Lyons". And when we won, we got another one which said: "Well done, Lyons".'[25]

Away from the racing scene, sales were now climbing a little more slowly and the 1955 annual accounts showed slightly reduced profits of £526,000. However, in spite of a reduction in income (company) tax and the dropping of the excess profits tax, the tax bill still amounted to £265,939. The year had seen investment in buildings (£20,000) and plant (£220,000) but creditors had jumped by 50 per cent or almost £1m – this was probably due to gearing up for the new medium-size saloon.

Lyons himself was continuing to be well remunerated and the return for shareholders continued to be poor. Today, directors' fees would never exceed the dividend! Money had been transferred out of the revenue reserves into capital reserves and the number of shares in issue increased. These would have gone in ratio to the existing shareholders and would not, therefore, have altered Lyons's own proportional holding.

Throughout his career, Lyons considered reducing costs and improving efficiency almost as important as making profits and he pursued these goals with an almost fanatical zeal. Peter Craig, then a charge-hand, recalled an occasion in the mid-1950s when, as he had done before the Second World War, Lyons tried a time-and-motion experiment 'to get three cars off in an hour. He stopped everyone, blew a whistle to start them, then blew again twenty minutes later to see how much everyone had done!'[26] Also, the factory employed men known as rectifiers but Lyons found this difficult to stomach. 'I only pay for perfection,' he maintained, meaning that the operators themselves should not pass on faulty jobs. Years later, of course, Jaguar workers would control their own quality and today rectifiers and inspectors are almost non-existent at Jaguar plants.

Jack Jones of the TGWU also recalled how Lyons involved himself in everything. 'He was a very hands-on manager, very close to the shop-floor, rather austere, almost aristocratic, although he didn't come from that background. Nevertheless, he had his hand on the tiller, very much so.'[27]

'He was always prepared to be right in the centre,' confirmed Ron Butlin. 'Nothing to do with the periphery for him. He was right on the button. Absolutely hands-on all the way. There wasn't somebody telling him what to do. He could tell somebody else.'

According to Butlin, Lyons could be ruthless in his shop-floor dealings. 'He had a track manager that he brought from Blackpool with him, a Mr Hartshorn. I got on well with Bert. I was walking through the paint shop on one occasion. Sir William had already gone through and he told one of the labourers to put one of the bodies on one side because there was something wrong with it... Mr Hartshorn walked through and he told the labourer to put the body back on to the track to get it through. The labourer said, "I was told by Sir William not to do that." He said, "Well, I'm telling you to do it. I'm your boss."

'"Blimey," I thought when I heard this, "You're for the high jump." He sent for me to go into his office and when I went in, he was sitting at the table and he was crying. Sir William had sacked him.

'A lot of people thought he was ruthless, but to be a good businessman, there's two sides to every question and if he'd dealt with the management and the labour force differently, we'd soon have seen that weakness and the men would have played on it.'[28]

Meanwhile, the new 2.4-litre (151cu in) saloon was having a difficult and protracted birth. Originally scheduled for a spring 1955 launch, it finally appeared in October, with a convention at Browns Lane in September revealing the new 'compact' to dealers and press. This addition to the range was to be a most important step forward for the company, returning Jaguar to a market slot not serviced since the old 1½- and 2½-litre (108 and 162cu in) saloons left production in 1949. It would increase Jaguar production very considerably, bringing economies of scale to the organisation as a whole.

One suspects that Lyons had always had greater priorities than to sit for the completion of his portrait by Simon Elwes, which had been started towards the end of 1953. It had been funded by a group of friends and was finally delivered to Wappenbury Hall in time for Christmas 1955. 'A few think the background takes a little getting used to,' wrote Lyons to the artist, 'but they consider it is a very good likeness of me and all compliment you on your work.'[29] Today, the painting hangs in Mary Rimell's hallway.

The outstanding event for Lyons early in 1956 came when his knighthood for services to export was announced in the New Year's Honours List. Yet he received the news quite diffidently. 'He did seriously think about accepting it, because I don't think he felt very comfortable about it,' Pat Quinn remembered. 'A lot of people in these circumstances say they accept an honour on behalf of something or somebody else, and sometimes this is rather a put-on thing, but I think in his case it was very genuine – that it was an honour and that it gave the company status.'[30] That is certainly the line Lyons took when acknowledging the congratulations of his board, when he said he looked upon it as an honour bestowed upon the company. He wished everyone to take a like view and to feel that, but for their joint endeavours, this honour would not have been granted.

This was genuinely meant but some of the old hands found it difficult to assimilate the fact that their bossy young master from Blackpool days was now a knight of the realm. Many years later, Heynes recalled that Arthur Whittaker 'wouldn't call him Sir William. I said, "what do you call him?" and he said "I just don't, he knows my voice when I get on the telephone." And he would not call him Sir William. I suppose because Sir William always called him Whittaker.'[31]

One secondary reason for Lyons's reluctance to accept the knighthood was his dislike of public speaking, which now could only increase. 'He hated it,' said Pat Quinn. 'It was a nightmare, an absolute nightmare. I really admired him for that because it was purgatory for him to have to speak. There were some times when he wasn't really frightfully good at it, but he did make himself do it.'[32] He would certainly contrive to avoid the duty whenever he reasonably could and some colleagues understood. Stanley Clark (Chief Executive of the SMMT) wrote to Lyons around this period: 'As I felt you were reluctant to undertake the toast of the Chairman... I have approached Mr Waring who has consented to do this, and I hope you will now enjoy your lunch very much more.'

At any rate, from then on it was Sir William Lyons and Lady Lyons; but one thing was certain – no one noticed any accompanying affectation.

On the competition front the year had made a good start for Jaguar too, as Ronnie Adams and his crew in a works-prepared Mk VII won the Monte Carlo Rally. This event, one of the toughest of its type, attracted huge interest in the 1950s and enthusiasts would huddle over Raymond Baxter's radio reports late into the night. The success sat well alongside the big Mk VII's continuing domination of the annual saloon car races at Silverstone.

Those *Daily Express* race meetings, especially the earlier ones, were big social occasions too, much enjoyed by Lyons. 'I remember the parties at the end of Silverstone were absolutely fantastic,' said Pat. 'Giles the cartoonist, he was always there, and of course Tommy Wisdom was always the ring-leader. A whole lot of us used to be in the press tent and everybody kept saying, "it's no good leaving yet because you can't get out of the car park." We used to stay until it was practically dark.'[33]

With the right crowd, Lyons enjoyed socialising as much as anyone and he would also take endless trouble over preparations for the big parties held quite regularly at Wappenbury Hall. During or shortly after the war, Pat remembered, he had seen at a ball one of those rotating mirrored spot-lit globes and obtained one; he then spent hours before a party with 12-volt batteries and a couple of big Lucas P100 headlamps trying to recreate the effect at Wappenbury!

Lyons had been continually warning that the early postwar sellers' market was unreal and could not last. He was about to be proved right as the industry went into recession. During 1956 the Government imposed a credit squeeze and the minimum hire purchase deposit went first to 33.33 per cent, then to 50 per cent. Purchase Tax, just 33.33 per cent in 1946, was now 60 per cent for cars, against 25 per cent for items like cameras and domestic electrical appliances. This taxation made the home market considerably tougher for Jaguar.

This atmosphere contributed to Lyons stalling the negotiations to purchase the Browns Lane plant. In any case, Lloyds Bank was obviously becoming a trifle anxious about advancing the money – already Jaguar's overdraft was exceeding the agreed £1m limit.

There were further demands elsewhere on Jaguar's resources. The Cunningham Organisation had taken over as New York distributors from Hoffman; it was prepared to make a loan of $600,000 to fund the purchase of stock by Jaguar's US company from Hoffman but Jaguar had to organise overdraft facilities for what were now its two US subsidiary companies.

Perhaps because of the sharp share price rise the previous year, at a board meeting early in 1956 Whittaker asked if Lyons had given any thought to issuing special shares for employees; the matter would be considered, he was told. Heynes expressed a more worrying concern – the directors' position if Lyons should not retain control. None of them had service contracts. Lyons explained that 'in bringing Mr John Lyons into the company this position had been taken care of'[34] but, of course, with the tragic accident these plans were void. He did appreciate their apprehensions and confirmed that he would address the matter.

It was as a memorial to his greatly missed son that in January Lyons had offered £10,000 towards a new science block at Oundle School. He had in mind that part of it might be named the John Lyons Lecture Room but later, when invited to lunch during a visit to the school by The Queen Mother, he made clear that he did not want any personal recognition.

Not only were Jaguar's costs rising but there was now agitation for a large wage increase. Lyons told the workforce of his concern at the unions' request for a 15 per cent rise. It would have 'the most disastrous effect,' he claimed, and would cost the company a sum almost as great as last year's profit. That would mean no money for new models or plant. The alternative of increasing prices would also be disastrous; Jaguar had already held prices down in America, and given increased margins to dealers, to keep up the volume. 'Today, American business pays only a portion of the company's overhead charges.' He urged the workers to put long-term security first. Privately, he noted that a wage reduction might be more appropriate!

In late February Lyons wrote a curious but interesting little piece about the company, probably for a speech. It contains a number of clues to how Lyons achieved what he did and how he saw Jaguar positioned in the marketplace. Seemingly without false modesty, he denied that Jaguar was a personal success story. 'You know there really is no such thing. All an individual can do is to know what he wants, have a good enough idea how to get it, and then build up a team of first class people to do it, and in Jaguar this has certainly been achieved.'

He explained how Jaguar uniquely fitted between the mass-producers and the low-volume prestige manufacturers. 'I think the success the company has achieved has been due to the policy of aiming to make a first-class car by high efficiency methods. You see there used to be only two categories, the mass produced cheap car and the special luxury car made only in small numbers, which was expensive, not only because it was better but because of the limitations in the methods which could be used. Tooling and special plant were unwarranted. The Jaguar is a luxury car and it is produced in greater numbers than any other car of its type by high efficiency methods.'

He went on to talk of the value of motor racing but concluded: 'Yes, we have done everything we possibly can to develop our exports, and we are still today exporting 60 per cent of our production, nearly 40 per cent of it going to America where we have sold over $60,000,000 worth of cars since we became established there six years ago.'

The first visit to a Jaguar factory by Her Majesty The Queen and Prince Philip took place on the afternoon of 22 March. They toured the factory for two hours with Lyons. Prince Philip was very reluctant to leave the experimental department and had to be sent for by an equerry. Pat, though, was disappointed not to be presented to The Queen but her father had deemed it inappropriate – she was not, after all, even a company employee. However, she was given a prime position from which to stand and watch.

It was in March that Lyons created – that is the best word for it! – four new directors. For the first time there was female representation as the popular Alice Fenton was made Home Sales Director, recognition of her unique contribution to the business since the Blackpool days. Still unmarried, Alice continued her efficient management of the home market sales organisation (Ben Mason from Standard having taken over exports in 1950), liaised with the dealers and still acted as Lyons's secretary-cum-personal assistant. John Silver and Ted Orr became Production and Works Directors respectively, and 'Lofty' England Service Director. Not that these new appointees had much voting power on the board. There, Lyons remained utterly in control and, while board meetings often featured long debates, he alone made the final decisions.

An internal study at this time of profits per model and market confirmed Lyons's more public comments that the margins being earned on exports and on the 2.4 model overall were modest in comparison with home sales (production was now running at 380 cars a week, incidentally). Costs, therefore, began to assume an even greater importance. Asked in an interview about the cause of the present recession in the industry, he nominated the forcing up of car prices by continuous wage claims. 'It is disappointing that even today unions and workpeople do not understand that they have a responsibility to keep down costs and it cannot all be done by the much abused word "productivity".'

It was not just in public that Lyons was talking of costs. 'The necessity to drastically reduce the company's overheads is becoming a matter of grave urgency,' he told his executives and asked them to make 'drastic cuts' in their departments' expenses. On the assembly lines, most overtime was being eliminated and efforts made to reduce excess stocks of cars – for once, it seems, Jaguar production was ahead of demand, for some models at least.

In taking costs seriously, once again Lyons was demonstrating his grasp of the need for tight financial management. He considered that the lack of cost control was a natural result of expansion and increased staffing levels. Information was available but not being used. 'We have no co-ordinated team controlling expenditure,'[35] he wrote. Lyons proposed that the works estimating department would take on this role, analysing excess costs as shown by the weekly reports and then taking action in conjunction with the executives concerned.

It was indeed a difficult year for the whole industry. Further import restrictions in Australia (which had continued to be one of Jaguar's most important overseas markets after the US) and a fall in home market demand had led major manufacturers – including BMC, Standard and Ford – to lay off or make redundant thousands of workers. Jaguar, as a small specialist manufacturer with a large weighting of US sales, was cushioned from the worst effects to some extent. Many other manufacturers were on short-time working but Jaguar managed to maintain a five-day week for most of the year. However, on 29 November, just 24 days after France and Britain launched their assault on the Suez Canal, the following announcement was made: 'For the first time in the history of the company, Jaguar are to go on to a four day week.'[36] Fortunately, it was to last only two months.

With worsening trading conditions and a chaotic political climate on top of all the usual pressures of business, it is surprising that Lyons did not decide to withdraw from racing for that year. However, the writing was on the wall, the principal reason being that Jaguar's small engineering team was devoting too much time to race cars to the detriment of production car work – much as Heynes would deny it. The 2.4, with its new unitary bodyshell (Jaguar's first) and new suspension, had not been developed properly and many complaints were received. The first E-type prototype existed but it would be a long five years before it could be launched. The priority had to be the production cars or Jaguar would lose the pre-eminent position it had enjoyed since the beginning of the 1950s.

The 1956 Le Mans was the last that Jaguar would enter officially and nearly proved to be another calamity: two factory D-types crashed on the second lap and 1955 victors Hawthorn and Bueb in the third were badly delayed by a cracked pipe in the fuel injection system. Fortunately for Jaguar, the day was saved by the lone entry of privateers Ecurie Ecosse, David Murray's Scottish team taking a famous victory with its own D-type.

Lyons had expounded his views on motor sport when he contributed a chapter to a book entitled *Racing From the Manufacturer's Point of View*. A manufacturer, he wrote, had to remember that participation was for the benefit of the business and this attitude could dilute the pleasure. 'I must say, however, that I do get pleasure out of it, even if a great deal of it is spoilt by the anxiety which one cannot help but feel during an important race that one hopes to win. To hear one of the timekeepers in the pit announce that so-and-so who is in the lead is overdue compares unfavourably with the most hair-raising nightmare.'

He felt that motor racing could bring practical benefits to the products of those companies that produced performance cars, as Jaguar did. Grand prix racing, he felt, required a totally different approach. A manufacturer must 'depart completely from conventional design and ignore the characteristics of his normal production'. Lyons's talk of the risk of failure and of jeopardising one's reputation further explains why a Jaguar-built Formula 1 car never appeared.

Although the figures did not reflect the poor trading conditions in the second half of 1956, turnover for the year 1955–6 was said to be a third up but pre-tax profits were only slightly ahead at £551,008. Tax was marginally lower but still consumed a massive £224,332. The effects of lower margins, increased stock-in-trade, an increasing need for working capital to fund growth, increased investment and, presumably, the payment to Hoffman, meant that the company had at its financial year end an overdraft of £561,977, a net outflow of £1.25m. It is hardly surprising Lyons was concerned. However, showing his customary disregard for shareholders, he maintained the same dividend but increased his management charges!

In October Lyons became President of the Fellowship of the Motor Industry, a position normally held for one year, but he would hold it for three. Though Jaguar was a comparative minnow, its Chairman was considered the equal of anyone in the industry. Indeed, he and his company had a disproportionate stature and influence, also evidenced by his continued membership of the NAC.

All through the year, Lyons continued his practice of sampling both production and prototype Jaguars and in late November he took the prototype 3.4 saloon home for the weekend. This larger-engined version of the 2.4 was being developed primarily in response to demands for more power from the US market. On the Monday morning he sent Heynes and Knight his comments. As usual, he did not spare their feelings: 'Immediately on starting up the engine, it is obvious the noise level is quite unacceptable. It gives the impression of a solidly mounted engine without any dash or toeboard insulation. In this respect, I would say it is almost twice as bad as the 2.4. On starting off the initial top gear get-away is disappointing. In all other respects, the performance is very good indeed. The cornering characteristics I found peculiar, the initial turn giving the impression of slight understeer, changing rapidly as one gets deeper into the turn to oversteer, calling for quick correction.'

On the evening of Tuesday 12 February 1957, a potentially devastating fire broke out towards the north end of the factory. Some 156,000sq ft (14,493sq m) were badly damaged – so hot had the fire been that lead, melted from the glazing bars and flashings, ran through the rainwater pipes and filled the drains! Where inflammable goods were stored, the steelwork buckled and collapsed.

Though most employees had gone home, it was all hands on deck to remove as many cars as possible. Some 16 fire brigades attended the scene and battled to get it under control.

As could be expected, Lyons showed considerable fortitude in the face of adversity. Union convenor Ron Butlin remembers Lyons's reaction next day. 'When the fire happened, he walked through and reassured people we would rise from the ashes. He gave people the confidence that our jobs weren't finished and we weren't wasting our time.'[37] 'Lofty' England remembered him saying simply: 'We'll beat it.'[38]

Suppliers and local firms rallied round and offers of help poured into the works during the next 24 hours. Limited production began in just six days and, after 'first aid' repairs, it was soon back to normal levels of around 200 cars a week. The first load of new steelwork for the main rebuild was dispatched to the site on 1 April and the erection completed by 4 May, with the roofing finished by 8 June – just 14 weeks. Today, you would be unlikely even to obtain planning permission in that time!

Just before the fire, on 30 January 1957, the 160mph (257kmh) XKSS 'supercar' had been introduced – to produce a competitive car for Sports Car Club of America racing, using parts from a run of 'customer' D-types that had remained unsold. As a road car it was quite simply in a league of its own and a foretaste of the E-type to come. However, Rankin communicated his concern to Lyons that the car was receiving an 'unexpected degree of interest and publicity,' which might be 'very effectively stealing in advance the thunder we shall need for the XK150.' Rankin need not have worried; only a handful of XKSS cars was made, with the fire putting paid to any chance of continuing production of either the D-type or the XKSS.

More importantly, Jaguar had been gearing up to launch the 3.4-litre (210cu in) engined version of the 2.4-litre (151cu in) saloon; long demanded by the North American market, this additional model appeared on 1 March. The 3.4 immediately became the fastest four-door car in series production, capable of 120mph (193kmh), and would prove to be a very good further string to the bow.

In May, the XK150 was introduced in fixed-head and drophead versions. Essentially, this was a stopgap modernisation of the XK140 because, as Lyons later admitted, the company had lacked the resources to develop the entirely new sports car originally planned to bridge the gap between the XK and the arrival of the E-type. The XK150 was the first production Jaguar (and one of the first cars ever) to have disc brakes; this, along with its handsome, sophisticated looks helped make the car a greater success than perhaps Jaguar expected, including in the US. In fact on 26 June Jo Eerdmans was pleading with Export Manager Ben Mason for more 3.4 sedans and the new XK150: 'Almost every consignment is sold by our distributors to dealers, and by dealers to the public, before the ship arrives in port.' He went on to stress that Americans were not prepared to wait for the XK150 and would soon transfer their allegiance to other foreign makes, 'foreign cars being popular at present'.

In late March Lyons put together his reply to the union's latest wage demand plus a variety of statements made publicly by Harry Urwin of the TGWU. Lyons felt that, after four demands for increases in the past five years, the employers had to call a halt because of increasing costs. 'In case it may be thought these chaps (union officials) were always on wrecking sprees,' stated *The Financial Times* journalist Peter Cartright, 'I and colleagues were once present when Harry Urwin was trying to get his and other members back to work after a fortnight's strike... As usual the mass meeting was held at Hearsall Common. We stood on a low wall at the back of the platform. At one point a half brick was hurled at Harry as he tried to persuade them back – and hit my colleague from *The Daily Telegraph*.'[39]

At an April board meeting, the thorny subject of the staff bonus scheme, which Lyons had instigated long ago, arose again; this weighted remuneration towards the bonus and resulted in low basic salaries. Ted Orr made the point that when there was no bonus, in holiday periods for example, the staff found difficulty in managing. Both Heynes and Silver added that this was also a stumbling block when trying to engage new staff. Lyons said he would consider the matter. He was as good as his word; from 1 August 1957 staff salaries were raised by 40 per cent and the bonus scheme was revised. The total yearly pay was very similar but the change in emphasis was what everyone had wanted.

During April, Lyons and Ted Orr had what Andrew Whyte described as being a 'monumental row over a matter of principle concerning wage negotiations'[40] and the latter left. He was replaced as Works Director by Bob Grice, who had just rejoined Jaguar from BMC. Lyons told his directors that he hoped the standard of work would improve. He was also concerned that it was costing too much to produce the cars, in comparison with other manufacturers, and it was decided to acquire a Ford Zephyr for comparison with the 2.4.

The previous autumn the Mk VII M had been replaced by a plusher, upgraded version – the Mk VIII. In May Lyons reported to Heynes on his findings when trying the Mk VIII which had been sent for demonstration to HM The Queen. He said the suspension was noticeably harder, with 'greater road shock than on the Mark VII,' a high level of road noise, jerky gear change, unsatisfactory brakes and a slight smell of petrol. He gave a list of items for attention!

Meanwhile the quality of bought-out parts was causing concern (in fact, some of the defects on that Mk VIII could probably be laid at the feet of suppliers) and Lucas was contacted after the wiper motor failed on another car being sampled by Lyons. 'Far too many cases of this nature are being experienced on test cars and also in the hands of customers,' wrote Grice.

Bob Grice certainly appeared to be taking quality seriously, which must have pleased Lyons. His new Works Director supported the sacking of an operator for bad workmanship, which could have caused a fatal accident on the chassis line (though 'by mutual agreement' this sentence was commuted to one week's suspension). 'We are determined to raise the standard of the cars and regularly checks will be taken. Disciplinary action will be taken by the supervision should any further bad workmanship arise,' stated Grice. He also became very involved with labour relations, dealing with the shop stewards and taking a firm line, particularly on absenteeism.

As, officially, the factory had retired from racing, Jaguar relied upon Ecurie Ecosse at Le Mans in June 1957. Using works-prepared cars, the valiant Scots duly delivered Jaguar's fifth win there. It was one of Jaguar's most convincing victories yet, with D-types in first, second, third, fourth, and sixth places! It might have contributed to Lyons seriously contemplating a return to competition although, as he wrote to Harry Weslake: '...when we go back into motor racing we must be streets ahead of everyone else, as we were before.' It was the rapidly increasing rate of development in the sport that conspired to ensure that Jaguar was never able to build a car with that big advantage; so despite Heynes's enthusiasm, Jaguar itself would never field another Le Mans car.

The financial results for 1956–7 showed some improvement, which was impressive considering the difficult conditions in Britain. Pre-tax profits were seven per cent up at £589,638 but tax was still taking a staggering £274,317. The cash situation had improved considerably with the overdraft reduced to £83,446. The dividend remained unchanged although the management fees were up again. Stock was down by £600,000, probably as a result of the fire, and the big jump in debtors is probably explained by amounts owing by the insurers. Break-even was now reckoned to be 190 cars per week, whereas previously it had been 150 (1955) and 160 (1956).

Interestingly the Chairman's report, which previously had clearly been written by a salesman rather than a financier (ie Lyons!), now concentrated more on the business. Bob Berry recalled how Lyons took a great interest in the annual report; its production was a major event as Lyons pored over every word. In the 1960s Berry drafted the review and Lyons amended it. 'We'd spend hours in his office going through each word, almost.'[41]

In 1957, there were some good things to report. Exports were up six per cent, in spite of the fire and the continuing import restrictions in Australia and New Zealand. The company could claim to have exported to 84 countries during the year.

With the production workers paid on a piece-rate basis, every new model introduction led to arguments over setting the rates for every single operation on the car. The piecework system had enabled Lyons to cost the assembly of a car remarkably precisely since the 1920s but now the sheer complexity of the system made it a nightmare. Pricing the assembly of the new XK150 was no exception.

The trim shop disputed the time allowed to cut sets of leather trim. A price was offered and rejected. The men requested a fatigue allowance. The company offered a little more, which was actually higher than the factory average. It was rejected. A trial was agreed and the two men selected took over 70 minutes to carry out the job. The company had based its calculation on 51.25 minutes. A staff supervisor did the job in 42 minutes and used less leather. Lyons, of course, was deeply involved in all this. 'The company is willing,' he concluded, 'to demonstrate an average time of under 45 minutes for any reasonable period.'[42]

However, the battle continued. The NUVB Jaguar Shop Committee prepared 'An Open Letter to Sir William Lyons'. Lyons replied, taking each paragraph in turn, dissecting it, and demolishing it. 'There are very often two sides to a story but there is usually only one which is true. Surely, if there is honesty of purpose, both sides (I am sorry to refer to sides, we should be one) should accept whatever genuine evidence is obtainable to establish an agreement. Your refusal to accept a demonstration completely destroys your case, as it establishes that you know you are completely in the wrong, yet you persevere in your endeavour to force an issue which cannot do other than wreck the company's production and damage its future prospects, and all to no avail.'[43]

Next, the men concerned walked out, to which Lyons responded that 'the most regrettable aspect is, of course, as with all strikes of this kind, the failure to honour the agreement which exists between the employers and the unions, which provides for a procedure to deal with disputes. Until something is done to make the Agreement worth the paper it is written on, trouble makers will continue to disrupt the smooth working of our factories.'[44] Sadly for Lyons, it was 25 years before legislation backed up agreements between unions and managements.

CHAPTER 7

LYONS INTRODUCES THE MK 2 AND BUYS DAIMLER

Lyons had succeeded in broadening his range with the 2.4/3.4 saloon and volumes had almost doubled as a result. He now needed to consolidate and improve this important small saloon. Also, the rest of the range was starting to age and while long production runs contributed much to Jaguar's competitive pricing, he could not allow any of the models to become too blatantly outdated.

The year 1958 began with strong demand and the immediate challenge was simply meeting this. However, a myriad of minor disputes, both inside and outside the company, continued to make life difficult and much of Lyons's time would be taken up with labour problems rather than moving the company forward. To use a modern phrase, he was 'fire-fighting' too much of the time.

As always, Lyons did not spend long hours in his Browns Lane office, as Bernard Hewitt recalled. 'Whenever he was at the factory, twice a day, without exception, he came downstairs and went through the works...at quite a pace. To walk with Sir William, you'd really got to move... He'd go straight through the factory unless he saw "Charlie" doing something he didn't agree with. Then he'd stop dead and deal with it. That didn't go down too well with Superintendents at times. The mere fact that everybody knew he was going through that factory twice a day had its effect. Everybody was always working.

'He'd work long hours. I remember one occasion he saw me in the corridor at lunchtime. He said, "I want to see you before you go tonight, Hewitt". I waited and waited, and at seven I thought I would go and knock on his door. He had forgotten about it which was not typical of him, but he was still working very hard... His energy was amazing. I don't think he ever switched off.'[1]

Those brisk sorties might coincide with clocking-off time. 'There was a works siren to start and finish work,' recalled Sid Bevans. 'Lyons would expect people to start on the siren and to work until the finishing time, and no short-cutting on time. If there was a group of people waiting to clock out he would get quite angry about that. I've seen him walk up to a group of guys and actually say to them, "Go on then, clock out".[2]

Even when socialising, Jaguar was usually on Lyons's mind, as daughter Mary recalled. 'He wasn't terribly good at small talk. He had a very good way of switching off and not listening if he wasn't interested. I can remember a cocktail party they had at home. Afterwards, Mummy said, "Wasn't that story interesting that Marjorie McKeown was telling you?" Daddy said, "What, what, what?" I was actually standing next to him when Marjorie was telling him this story. He obviously hadn't listened to one single word of it.'[3] Old friend and company solicitor Alan Newsome had similar memories. 'He spent most of his time thinking about Jaguar, even when other people were talking about something else.'[4]

'He had no small talk whatsoever,' confirmed journalist Patrick Mennem. 'Unless you were saying something which he thought of importance, he lost interest.'[5] As Mennem had already discovered, he was a nightmare to interview; Bob Berry, who arranged some of the comparatively few interviews Lyons gave, concurred. 'Within 30 seconds he was interviewing them. He was more comfortable asking the questions!'[6]

During the late 1950s both daughters had spells working at Jaguar; predictably, perhaps, they did not stay. 'I was stuck in the Overseas Department where I filled in guarantee forms for six weeks,' remembered Mary. 'After six weeks, I thought, "He doesn't really want me here."'[7] She said her father had a rather Victorian view of women and had never really thought of his daughters – as opposed to his son – having serious careers. 'He simply assumed we would get married and be totally conventional.'[8]

Mary maintained that he was not prejudiced against women in the workplace, citing his regard for Alice Fenton. 'Anyone who proved their worth was appreciated and trusted,' she said, 'but you didn't get any help along the way. It was up to you to prove you could be successful. Had I been really interested in working at Jaguar I should have pushed myself harder. But I did not show real enthusiasm – horses were my first love.'[9]

Pat, who spent a considerable period at Jaguar's Piccadilly export offices, agreed, also making the point that neither she nor Mary possessed any relevant qualifications or training, so could hardly have been given positions of responsibility. Unlike John, they had not been groomed for great things.

While Mary was working at the factory, Pat Smart occasionally escorted her to Jaguar functions, collecting her from Wappenbury in his heater-less MG TF. 'It was a cold, frosty February night and of course the old gravel crunched well, and I crept in and got the car as near as I could to the door. Knocked on the door – and the cook's name was Mercedes, which always amused me – Mercedes came to the door and I said I'd come to collect Miss Mary. She told me to step inside the porch – not inside the house – and wait, and I heard a voice, obviously from the banisters upstairs, "Tell that racing driver to be careful!" And I'd crept in at around 5mph [8kmh]!'[10]

Lyons's sampling of the product continued unabated and focused increasingly on press cars. A critical report of a Jaguar test car in the *Sunday Express* merited an explosive memo to Rankin: 'Will you please let me know how it is that such a shameful state of affairs can exist.' Rankin investigated and found that the faults were relatively unimportant but promised: 'In future all press cars will be double-checked by myself and Berry before collection or despatch.' Grice did not escape, either, when Lyons tried the Mk VIII owned by Lord Louis Mountbatten and compiled a list of faults that he had identified.

In March the roadster edition of the XK150 finally joined the fixed-head and drophead models; together with an optional high-performance 'S' engine for the XK150 range, the new two-seater variant was aimed very much at North America. There, the horsepower race was in full swing and General Motors was gaining credibility with its own all-American sports car: Briggs Cunningham was soon to send Jaguar a cryptic note warning that, in sports car terms, the Chevrolet Corvette is 'our biggest competitor in the American market'.

Other Jaguar distributors relayed their opinions, often helpful, on various subjects to Jaguar. In March, Kjell Qvale in San Francisco sent a number of suggestions, which Heynes forwarded to Lyons: power-assisted steering was essential on the 3.4, the Mk VIII needed much higher performance, and a modern transistor radio was vital for America. He thought that, with Cadillacs costing $5,000 to $7,000, the Mk VIII could be put up to between $6,000 and $7,000 without losing sales, especially if it was given Rolls-Royce type rear seats.

The final comment from the coolest city in California was that a better heater was required. We do not know what response, if any, Lyons made to Qvale on this point but on one visit to New York, the founder was button-holed by an owner who certainly considered his XK's heater ineffective. Tony Thompson, then a Jaguar employee in the US, related the story. 'The car was started up, and the car had, if you remember, a Smiths heater with two little doors on it, and a control on the dash. I smoked and so he [Lyons] told me to light a cigarette. He held the cigarette – I'd no idea what he was going to do – he held it beside the heater and the smoke very gently wafted away. "Look," he said, "it works perfectly."' The owner protested: 'Sir William, temperatures get to 15 below zero.' Lyons admonished him: 'Young man, you just put on an overcoat.'[11]

The USA remained a vitally important export market for Jaguar and merited increasing attention from Lyons; he now regularly went to the US, often at the time of the New York Motor Show. On 7 April 1958 he arrived in New York having sailed on the *Queen Mary*; this time, Lady Lyons and their two daughters came with him. At the Show, Lyons met with all the local Jaguar hierarchy (Jo Eerdmans, Briggs Cunningham, Chuck Hornburg from LA, and Frankie Watts from Miami) but also found time for lesser mortals as Les Bottrill discovered.

Bottrill had worked in the experimental department at Browns Lane, where a major task of his had been giving the 'customer' D-types their shake-down test at MIRA. He knew Lyons from this period: 'If ever he saw me come in the gate, he would stop and ask how it was going...' That was some three years previously and now Bottrill was on the Jaguar stand in New York, having been sent to America as a service engineer. To Bottrill's surprise, Lyons broke away from the group he had been talking to 'and came over and chatted to me for about 20 minutes... Then he said to me, "How's your son? He must be..." and he said his age and he was exactly right.' Les Bottrill would describe Jaguar as 'like a family';[12] it was – and still is, in many ways. Not one without typical family tensions but a family nonetheless and that feeling was inculcated by the founder.

Lyons and his own family then embarked on a typically packed schedule, which included Mexico City. This destination featured because Jaguar had taken up the idea, put forward by the Mexican distributor Maria Padilla, to assemble Jaguar 2.4 and 3.4 saloons locally from parts. Using local labour and materials, this incurred less import duty and between August 1957 and July 1960 214 Jaguars were assembled successfully in Mexico. The exercise demonstrates Lyons's willingness to sanction quite adventurous schemes if they were soundly based. The three-week tour further included Los Angeles and San Francisco (where the family enjoyed a round of golf with Kjell Qvale) before a return to New York.

Back in the UK, Lyons soon found Jaguar badly hit by a strike at Pressed Steel. Starved of saloon bodyshells, immediate intentions to ramp up production to 450 a week had to be shelved and by 16 May it was anticipated that some 400 employees would have to be given notice.

No wonder, then, that when Lyons gave his views on the North American market to the National Advisory Council meeting on 22 May, he identified failure to meet delivery dates to dealers as one of the biggest problems. 'Customers in the USA were being continually disappointed and some dealers were going out of business,' he said.

The Pressed Steel strike was hitting a number of manufacturers, affecting exports of British cars. With buoyant US sales, especially in California, it was tragic that supplies were so often interrupted. Jaguar too needed to take advantage of demand while it was there, especially as the competition was making its inexorable progress in North America – in June Lyons sent off a slightly panicky memo to Eerdmans asking why Mercedes-Benz sales were 'streaking ahead' in the US. Eerdmans replied that it was partly due to a boom in foreign car sales and partly because Studebaker-Packard dealers were selling Mercedes and were discounting, as was commonly done with domestic cars. 'I agree that they have streaked ahead of us,' said Eerdmans pointedly, 'but I am certain that if we had been able to obtain cars from the factory at the rate of our schedules of 632 per month, we might have shown approximately the same sales figures as they have done.'

On the other side of the coin, some people at Jaguar considered that the company's American sales arm (in January 1958 renamed Jaguar Cars Incorporated) itself needed improvement. These included 'Lofty' England and there was sometimes friction between him and Eerdmans. England sent a memo to Lyons noting there had been 23 new US dealer appointments and 34 cancellations in one month, which (in his view) meant prospective and existing owners were not likely to get any sense from dealers.

Meanwhile, Jaguar Cars Inc was still failing to receive the vehicles it wanted. This included the Mk VIII: the first examples with the vital US ingredient of power-assisted steering were not received until April and then just token quantities arrived until production ceased in September to allow the factory to change over to the Mk IX. Thus sales of the large sedans fell from 602 in 1957 to 363 in 1958. Of the 1,154 XK150 roadsters shipped, some 500 remained in stock at the year end and the future for this model was said to be 'rather uncertain'. Prospects, though, looked promising for 1959 in Jaguar's most important export market but the introduction of power-assisted steering was urgently required on the 3.4 if the compact sedan was to spearhead the sales drive.

Even before the introduction of the Mk IX, Jaguar was aware that its chassis, introduced back in 1948 and shared, in essence, with the

XK150, was outdated. A new independent rear suspension was, however, under development and, according to chassis engineer Bob Knight (who worked in the experimental department under the direction of Bill Heynes), it was first fitted to a saloon car in the spring of 1958 as a result of a bet with Lyons!

In his accustomed manner Lyons was doing his factory rounds and called in to see Knight. 'The conversation turned around to independent rear suspensions,' recounted Bob Knight, 'and he said he'd like to have an independent rear suspension on a saloon car. He said, "If you were to do it in the shop, in Experimental, and not do anything in the Drawing Office, how long would it take?"

'I said, "You could pretty well do one in a month." To which he said, "Bet you couldn't" and I said, "Bet you I can!" In the end bets were placed. It was only after he had left me for about a minute that the penny dropped that he was going to win both ways, 'cause he either won the bet or got a bloody car!'[13] Bob won his bet and Lyons got his first prototype saloon with irs.

That independent suspension had already appeared, in embryonic form, on a small, highly secret prototype sports car, code-named E1A; this had been lent to Christopher Jennings, then Editor of *The Motor*, in May for his opinion – a remarkable instance of Lyons's close relationship with certain sections of the press. Jennings was deeply impressed and considered that 'the new Jaguar is a potential world beater'.[14] E1A would metamorphose into the fabulous E-type, on which the new suspension would debut in 1961 (the suspension also featured on the Mk X saloon and would be in use for more than 35 years).

The AGM was held on 26 June and was an entirely orthodox one; Lyons had no awkward shareholders to answer! This was the norm as Bernard Hewitt testified: 'The AGM was held in the board room. Because it was a successful company, hardly anybody ever came to it. He'd say to me, "Hewitt, we're going to the Annual General Meeting. I'll give you 10 minutes. If it's not over in 10 minutes, do something." At the end of 10 minutes, he'd say, "Any other business?" Nobody would open their mouths, he'd get up and go. He didn't stop to talk to people. He was back at work and that was over and dealt with.'[15]

The 1957–8 financial year turned out to have been very successful. Profits were up 153 per cent at almost £1.5m, though tax still sucked out a massive £863,644 (58 per cent). A new profits tax with a flat rate of ten per cent had been introduced in April, on top of the standard income (company) tax. Successive Governments, it appeared, were continuing to bleed British companies dry of funds for re-investment.

The dividend was increased, at last, by 40 per cent but the management fees were up by 93 per cent! All borrowings were paid off and the company now had £2.1m in the bank, though creditors were up by £700,000 and there had been little investment. It was still quite a turnaround in one year with exports, up 47 per cent, leading the charge. In his report Lyons complained that purchase tax restricted home demand, something his foreign competitors did not suffer from, allowing them to plan for greater volumes.

Later in the year Lyons committed to paper his thoughts on purchase tax: 'If our industry is to maintain its present position as a principal contributor to the country's economy, production figures must continue to rise. If they do not, we shall lose ground to our competitors.'

He warned that a delayed relaxation by the Government 'may well be too late for the patient's recovery. What is required is that the injection should be given before there are any signs of disease.' Lyons emphasised the need for manufacturers to plan ahead and that a substantial home market 'should be our stable base...all this means that Purchase Tax should be reduced when the industry is at its flourishing peak, and not delayed until even the first signs of recession appear.' With hindsight, Lyons's conclusions appear to have been perceptive. Alas, British industry failed to retain the volume that Lyons considered was necessary to keep pace with the competition.

However, Jaguar itself was in good enough shape for Lyons to report at a July board meeting that he had re-opened negotiations with the Ministry of Supply for the purchase of Browns Lane by making an offer. This was under consideration, he said.

On 7 October Lyons responded, via Ernest Rankin, to motoring journalist Alan Brinton, who had asked him for his views on high performance motoring. In fact Brinton was to ask Lyons similar questions a few months later and his combined responses reveal the attitude of Britain's foremost producer of fast cars to speed and road safety.

Lyons felt that a 120mph (193kmh) car was safer at 80mph (128kmh) than one with a top speed of 80mph (128kmh) 'because the former car possesses characteristics of acceleration, steering, suspension and braking power, which give it a safety factor at 70–80mph [112–128kmh] equivalent to that of the slower car when driven at 35–40mph [56–64kmh].' Also, fast drivers were safer because they were more alert than slow ones, who took far greater risks when overtaking due to less performance. 'Speed is not the danger. It is stupidity and carelessness.' For the latter, Lyons advocated draconian punishment: those who passed on a blind bend or brow of a hill should serve six months' imprisonment! He evidently thought that few Jaguar drivers would end up in gaol as he told Brinton that British Jaguar drivers would finish 'high on the passing out list' of the Institute of Advanced Motorists.

Brinton supposed that the Mk IX, with a bigger engine, had just been introduced because Americans demanded a speedy getaway from the lights. Lyons agreed that Americans appreciated good acceleration but rarely drove 'really fast'. Asked what speed he drove at, Lyons stated that it depended on conditions and what he considered safe, 'which may be anything from 10-mph to 100+mph [16-kmh to 160+kmh] on the ideal road'.

Howard Hunt, later to be Jaguar's Service Manager, confirmed that Lyons sometimes drove at the top end of this speed range. Their routes to the Browns Lane factory in the 1960s coincided and sometimes he encountered his boss, who would soon leave him trailing behind at speeds approaching 120mph (193kmh)!

Daughter Pat, questioned on Lyons's road driving, confirmed: 'Yes, he was a good driver, though not as comfortable to drive with as my mother. Like all men he tended to be a bit erratic – lots of braking and accelerating, which is why I tended to feel a bit sick when I was young. But he taught me a lot when I was learning to drive – my mother actually took me through all the trying stages, the difficult bits, but he used to give me tips.'[16]

The 3.8-litre (230cu in) engined Mk IX mentioned by Alan Brinton was announced in October 1958. It was the final manifestation of the Mk VII series that, like the XK, was by then technically well overdue for replacement. It was probably a pleasant surprise to Jaguar that the 113mph (181kmh), disc-braked Mk IX sold in respectably large quantities, including in North America.

Looking back on the year 1958, it was both a successful and frustrating 12 months for Jaguar – especially in relation to North America. The US company and its distributors reported record sales in spite of starting the year deep in recession but, as ever, it could have been so much better. The real potential lay in sales of the high-performance 3.4 sedan and yet the strike at Pressed Steel had destroyed output in the middle of the year, to the extent that only 123 were shipped in April, 46 in May, 22 in June and 90 in July. Not a single XK150 roadster was received in the first three months of 1958 and then 106 arrived in April. Then, when supplies of 3.4 and

Mk VIII bodies were cut off by the strike, Jaguar shipped virtually nothing but XK150 roadsters (XK bodies were still built in-house) with as many as 303 in July alone, which flooded the market. This left the dealers considerably overstocked by the year end with an imbalance of models. Despite the body shortages, overall production in 1958 was up by 5,780 cars at 19,456 units. That at least must have been of considerable satisfaction for Lyons.

Mike Hawthorn, who had led the Jaguar team in 1955–6, became World Champion during 1958, driving for Ferrari. Always popular at Jaguar, he remained closely in touch with 'Lofty' England and Lyons and continued to drive Jaguars on the road. Alas, it was in the tuned 3.4 saloon, with which he had so entertained the crowds at Silverstone, that he died in a road accident on the Guildford bypass in January 1959.

So 1959 began with great sadness, especially, perhaps, for Lyons; the accident to Hawthorn cannot have failed to have evoked memories of the loss of John. 'Lofty' England told of the particular regard Lyons had for Mike. 'After his son John was killed, Sir William always showed a great interest in Mike Hawthorn. I only realised how alike they were when I went to Mike's memorial service with Sir William and it dawned on me that they both had the same names (John Michael), were the same age and both had blond hair and rather similar build.'[17]

England was as close as anybody at the factory to Lyons, and it is a letter from 'Lofty' to Jo Eerdmans that gives us a particular insight into how Lyons regarded his Service Director – and how Lyons coped with potentially disruptive situations within Jaguar.

England had written to Eerdmans on 5 January 1959, having taken exception to an article in a Jaguar Cars Inc sponsored club magazine. The offending matter had been written by John Gordon Benett, former Cunningham team driver and by then General Sales Manager for Jaguar Cars Inc; it was all about the 3.4 sedan that he had been running.

'Lofty' felt strongly that the feature contained 'certain statements far better not put in print' and spelled out his objections with typical England sarcasm. Firstly, he considered an article praising Jaguar's own product was about as meaningful as an article by Mr Budweiser in the Budweiser magazine saying his beer was perfect! He was perturbed that chassis numbers had been quoted after they had gone to considerable trouble to avoid giving any information that might allow customers to work out when their cars were actually built, owing to the inevitable delays before cars were sold in the US!

His next grumble was that Benett had said his car had been totally trouble-free, which was not true 'unless the four claims we have had and settled for the trifling sum of $73.60 are phoney'. Then he considered it 'misguided' for Benett to have revealed that his 3.4 was using just one quart (1.94 Imp pints/1.1 litres) of oil every 2,000 miles (3,218km) because 'it will only result in anyone who has a car on which the oil consumption is higher than that figure starting to complain'. 'Lofty' England's letter to Eerdmans concluded: 'Frankly, I would have thought that Benett would have known better than to write this sort of stuff and, secondly, that Martin would have checked the article before it was put forward for publication and vetoed the points I have mentioned.'

Jo Eerdmans was sufficiently concerned by this letter to cable Lyons personally. Lyons's response to Eerdmans is worth printing in full. The authors consider it demonstrates Lyons's ability to get to the heart of the matter, his considerable but far from blind regard for the man who would become his successor, and his desire to see a potentially explosive situation dealt with immediately and with finality.

Dear Mr Eerdmans,

I confirm my cable of this morning. You will, of course, appreciate why I sent it to your private address.

I read the copy of Mr England's letter dated the 5th inst., which I felt was unfortunate to say the least, as it could do no other than give rise to some bad feeling, and I should be glad if you would destroy it without showing it to Mr Benett or anyone else.

I am not concerned as to whether Mr England's criticisms are justified or not. I am only interested in ensuring amicable co-operation throughout the whole of the Jaguar organisation, and, psychologically, his letter could not do otherwise than have an adverse effect upon this.

You have, I know, previously had difficulty with Mr England. He is imperious and inclined to be unreasonably critical at times, but he has very high qualities which are of great value to the Company. I would like you to reply to him in light-hearted vein. I suggest you say you are sorry he has taken Mr Benett's article, which was calculated to be of some value to Jaguar, so much to heart, that you have noted the points he has raised and that, in future articles, any matters which might be subject to question will be considered before they are printed.

I am going to have a talk with Mr England about the letter today, and I will see that some good comes of his interview with me. I am sure you will understand why I wish you to adopt the tone I have suggested in replying. I want to settle the matter today, and therefore it would not be desirable for it to be raised again.

Yours sincerely,
W. Lyons

Not long after this incident, Lyons reported to the board that his offer of £1.25m for the acquisition of Browns Lane had been accepted. This was a great step forward and it was the purchase of the Browns Lane plant that later Lyons would count among his most satisfying achievements. At the same meeting he renounced £30,000 (some £375,000 in today's terms!) of his commission – Jaguar's increased profits had evidently triggered payments which Lyons considered too high.

During 1959 a committee was formed to discuss introducing and administering a Quality Incentive Scheme. Lyons considered it would be impossible to establish a formula to cover each department but that awards would have to be based on a general appraisal by the committee. There had obviously been a move to insulate the formula from 'the voice of the customer' (as the industry would put it today) but Lyons was having none of this. 'I do not agree that customer complaints should not be taken into consideration. It is simple to discriminate between those which are genuine, and those which are not.'

Lyons then sent out a firmly worded memo to all employees saying that quality must come first. Every skilled man was paid a skilled rate, he said, and must do the job expected of a skilled man and that any man who did not would lose his job. This was not, perhaps, the most tactful way of wording a perfectly logical proposition – but then some of the workforce seemed intent on destroying their own employment prospects anyway.

A dreadful series of walk-outs began in April. On the 13th members of the Transport & General Workers' Union went on strike as a protest against actions of the National Union of Vehicle Builders. Two days later Lyons wrote on the subject of unofficial action and internal union problems. He found it difficult to understand why the unions did not put their houses in order 'for the unofficial action undermined the authority of their officials, while being compelled to join in futile stoppages depleted the wage packets of their members.

'The difficulty the unions are in is, of course, due to the policy of enforcing membership. If they enforce discipline by taking away membership, they virtually take away a man's livelihood, so the penalty could really take the form of a fine.'

He was concerned that the majority felt powerless and they preferred to use their leisure time in relaxation rather than attending union meetings. 'There are many, however, who would attend meetings if others, who think as they do, would also attend. They could then use their vote.'

Next day a statement was issued. 'Speaking in Coventry today, Sir William Lyons said, "The AEU is to be congratulated on the stand it is taking in disciplining its members. Unless our industry can keep its ship on an even keel, it cannot stay up in front in the race for world trade. If the crew will keep 'rocking the boat' we must fall behind. I do not think anyone, except those who captain the ship, realise how much our industry is put off course by the indifference of the crew to the ship's position. It is not true, as is often said, that our competitors' boats are 'rocked' as much as ours."'

Any strike led to a loss in output which in turn caused late deliveries. One aspect of this over which Lyons expressed his concern was 'the delay in completion of cars for delivery in this country to overseas visitors'. Many customers specified a date to coincide with their holidays. 'It requires little imagination to realise the tremendous disappointment and inconvenience which the delay will cause.' In fact Lyons would not have needed to use his imagination at all – his own daughter Pat would have been relaying the grisly details to him personally!

In the late 1950s, Pat was divorced from Ian Appleyard and, to fill the vacuum, 'Daddy suggested I went to work as a receptionist in the export department in Piccadilly, handing over the export cars to the Americans.

'And it was a nightmare job, because the Americans would buy their car in the States, and give all sorts of detailed specifications which the dealers accepted, and then they would arrive on their holiday, expecting this perfect car, exactly right, to be waiting for them in the middle of Piccadilly... But the worst thing of all was that very rarely was the car ready or right, and so I had women in tears and men in a rage, and I used to ring [the factory] and it was quite obvious that the car was miles from being ready, there wasn't a hope. Quite often I used to lend them my own car.'

This was no small part of the business – Dugdale reckoned that at one time around 1,000 cars worth $50m, some 20 per cent of the total US sales volume, were being collected personally each year by Americans in Britain.

Lost production also caused Lyons to write on May Day to Grice and Silver to say that it had been necessary to turn down an order for 400 Mk IXs. He said his main concern was the long-term effect because dealers would be short of stock and would have to turn down orders. 'This is just what our competitors, particularly the Germans, want. It gives them the opportunity to take our dealers away from us. It is only too obvious that if we lose our dealers, we lose business.'

However, the problems continued; in mid-June there was a mass walk-out of inspectors and final-line men resulting in 3,500 other workers being sent home and production ceasing. Yet the following Wednesday the 230 inspectors returned to work 'under precisely the same conditions as existed before they walked out'. Once again, nothing was achieved and much was lost. During the strike Lyons had requested a survey of the hourly rate for works inspectors and 20 companies had been telephoned, including the major motor manufacturers. Of these, 14 were paying under 7s (35p), two including Jaguar were paying 7s and four marginally exceeded 7s.

On 20 June Lyons chaired a meeting with union officials Chater, Lapworth, and Gallagher. 'My purpose in meeting you today is to register in the strongest possible way my disappointment and perturbation at the action that has been taken by your members in ceasing work on this issue. Press statements have been made suggesting this claim has been outstanding since November, implying that nothing has been done. You must know, as I do, that this is so far from the truth as to be almost libellous...'

Lyons may have sympathised with an industry attempt to go on the offensive against industrial unrest. A draft set of objectives of the British Motor Manufacturers' Association was compiled in June. The gist of this was that if a member firm was subject to unreasonable strike action, the other member firms would support it by 'unilateral action' (if for example body makers at one manufacturer took unofficial action, their equivalents at other association companies would be sent home without pay).

However, Lyons feared that any word of such positive action would result in 'a bombshell'. He concluded with two blunt practical questions: could such action ever be put into effect and would it stop wildcat strikes? The idea, of course, was never put into practice and Britain's manufacturers continued to operate individually in the field of industrial relations.

Mid-1959 saw something of a brake-failure scare in the US. Much investigation went on and Kjell Qvale wrote reassuringly to all the

US Jaguar distributors saying he had recently had a conference on quality issues with Lyons, Bill Heynes and 'Lofty' England. They discussed brake problems and oil leaks in particular and Qvale was able to tell his fellow distributors that the brake problems appeared to be solved and the other matter was being worked on.

Lyons, he said, had given him 'a complete tour of his new installations developed in an effort to produce an absolute trouble-free braking system. I can assure you it was extremely impressive, and I can personally say that I have never seen any other factory spend as much time and money on their brake installations.'

The brake problems appear to have been a storm in a teacup and Lyons was eventually irritated by it. At the beginning of September he wrote to Eerdmans saying that he felt the dealers were quick to complain about the factory but the factory rarely complained about them. The factory had tried to respond to complaints but he was wondering if it had been wrong to accept so much responsibility.

'An excellent example recently', said Lyons, 'is of course the tremendous scare about the brakes. I understand the investigation made by Bottrill [Jaguar service engineer] and Rowe [Dunlop engineer] disclosed very little justification for the panic which occurred. In fact, I understand when they arrived over there, it was even suggested that it was not necessary for them to make the service tour which had been planned.'

Sometimes opportunities to expand the American operation appeared. Two arose during 1959, both interesting in view of what eventually transpired with the companies and personnel involved. In July Lyons turned down a proposal put to Eerdmans to sell Rover cars. Eerdmans himself was not keen, feeling they would be competing with the 3.4 saloon.

Then later in the year came approaches from Leyland Motors, British commercial vehicle manufacturers. Eerdmans wrote to Lyons on 18 December: 'Mr Stokes, the sales director of Leyland Motors, came to see me and we had a further discussion in connection with marketing their products in the USA.' He explained that a survey of the truck market in the US was being prepared that 'should enable us to determine what the possibilities are for selling a substantial number of Leyland vehicles and to decide whether or not it would be worthwhile taking on the agency.'

Following the survey, Eerdmans recommended that Jaguar Cars Inc should sell Leyland trucks in the USA. It was an unfortunate time for this experiment as the US market was in recession. It proved unsuccessful (Lyons recalled that Eerdmans obtained the orders but the vehicles were unreliable) and in late 1961 Jaguar divested itself of its interest in Leyland Motors (USA). Little did any of those involved realise that in less than ten years, Jaguar would be part of Leyland and that Donald Stokes would be essentially in complete control of Jaguar.

Sometimes Lyons gave Eerdmans strange jobs to do. On 2 June Lyons sent a cutting from *The Daily Telegraph* on go-karts, saying he would like Eerdmans to get hold of one ('with the largest engine obtainable') and send it over. Whether or not it ever arrived is not known but certainly Shelsley Walsh hill climb was to witness the unlikely sight of the 6ft 4in (1.92m) tall F. R. W. England tackling the hill in one of these diminutive machines! In a similar vein on 11 November Lyons wrote to Jo Eerdmans: 'I find it impossible to get any vests the same as the ones I bought from Saks, Fifth Avenue. As I particularly like them, please get eight of these. I will be glad if you will send them as quickly as possible, as I am getting rather short.'

The previous summer Lyons had spotted an item also in *The Daily Telegraph* and had tackled Eerdmans about it. In the light of today's debate about such things, it shows Lyons eager to investigate any new avenues in road transport. 'If it [is] true that a battery is being produced, which will last over 1000 miles,' he wrote, 'there is a big opening for an electric vehicle. Will you please get me all the information you can on the vehicles which are being produced – details of design, if these are available, particularly information about battery capacity.' However, there are no records of Jaguar engineers being instructed to build an electrically powered car!

In his statement accompanying the 1959 annual accounts at the mid-year AGM, Lyons announced a record turnover – a word he could now use, as previously companies' accounts did not have to show turnover. Profit was up 75 per cent at a very impressive £2.6m. Cash in hand was still as much as £3m, in spite of spending £1.2m on purchasing the Browns Lane site and £875,000 on Tax Reserve Certificates (the company was paying its tax in advance and receiving interest). Tax, as high as ever, amounted to £1.2m. The dividend paid was up from £36,225 to £158,175 and the directors' fees were £205,000. Annual production in 1958–9 was 20,871 (1959 calendar year was 18,509) and break even was now 265 cars per week.

Jaguar's increasing worth during the late 1950s had provoked occasional speculation about possible takeovers but these had always been dismissed by Jaguar. However, on 26 April 1959 *The Sunday Times* had written: 'It is not easy to think of a British motor company that would feel it advantageous to acquire Jaguar, nor are there signs that any of the leading American companies are in the market.' Lyons wrote to the paper quite indignantly, asking if it was implying that Jaguars were not worth buying. 'From your subsequent favourable comments on the status of our company, it is obvious that you did not intend to infer that our company was not worth acquiring and, for my personal edification, I would be grateful if you would be good enough to let me know what you had in mind.' No reply from *The Sunday Times* is on file!

An improved version of the small Jaguar saloon range was now imminent. During his spring 1959 visit to Browns Lane, Eerdmans had been delighted to hear that production of the exciting new 3.8 would begin after the summer. He said that, in discussions with Cunningham and others, they favoured giving this model a distinctive name rather than merely calling it the 3.8 or a Mark III, as Eerdmans had proposed. They suggested 'a very attractive British name somewhat similar to, say, the Ford Thunderbird... I would also like to say that I was thrilled about the new 3.4 Litre [210cu in] Sedan which you showed me and I am sure it will meet with great success.'

Eerdmans concluded by saying he had noticed a 'a big improvement in the factory...and I think you have accomplished a great deal in the way of efficiency in the last six months.' Manufacturing was not, however, one of Jaguar's strongest points at this time, though Lyons continued to take a keen interest in the mechanics of the assembly line. During 1959 he wrote to John Silver: 'I have studied the sketch you sent for the elevated conveyor on the Final Line. It would seem that it does not provide big enough length of accessibility. In other words, the car should start below the operator so that they have access to the top, and should gradually rise providing a sufficient number of stations. There does not seem to be enough to give a gradual access to the whole of the body from top to bottom.' This practical approach by the Chairman of a multi-million-pound company to shop-floor working might seem surprising, until one remembers that it was Lyons who organised the series production of the Swallow sidecar in Blackpool and instigated the very first assembly line at SS Cars back in the mid-1930s...

Early October saw the launch of the Jaguar Mk 2 with 2.4 and 3.4 (151 and 210cu in) models – plus the 125mph (201kmh) 3.8-litre (230cu in) version intended primarily for the US. This introduced the larger-capacity XK engine to the compact range; it was also made available for the XK150 and XK150 'S' sports cars in a further effort to stave off competition until the E-type was finally ready. This remodelling of the old 2.4/3.4 saloon range was masterful and the success of the Mk 2 models was to be fundamental to Jaguar's fortunes in the 1960s.

The year 1959 saw developments in Lyons's private life too, with Bob Robinson joining as farm manager; it was the start of a long and enjoyable relationship. Bob Robinson remembered the usual routine: 'When he was at home on a Sunday morning, he would ring me up – never failed – about 10 o'clock. "Meet you at the bottom, Robinson." I used to go down the field and meet him. We used to walk right round the farm and if he found a thistle or a nettle, if it hadn't been sprayed next time he went round... I reckon we were the cleanest farm in Warwickshire, without a doubt. Every gate on every field had to open perfectly and shut properly. I used to have to do a report on every gate every year. I think there was 134.'[18]

As for true recreation, golf remained the most important activity. Apart from his local club, Lyons made time to play at other courses and quite often drove with Greta to Hunstanton (they even bought a house there, though it was sold before long). In September 1959 they spent a weekend golfing in Scotland with their friends the McKeowns. On their return, with his customary courtesy, Lyons wrote to the hotel manager: 'May I say that we all felt Gleneagles is a great credit to this country, due to the excellence of your personal management. As one who has travelled all over the world, I feel it does one good to find a hotel in Britain superior to them all.'

'Golf was the next most important thing to the factory,' said Pat. 'I think that was one of the things he was terribly torn about, more than anything – the fact that his life at Jaguar prevented him playing golf as much as he would have liked to. I think that was the one thing he was really sad about. He was quite good, considering he couldn't play seriously.'[19]

After an exchange of gifts and cards at Christmas 1959, Lord Brabazon of Tara wrote to Lyons: 'What a perfectly lovely card portraying a really beautiful motor car from a very lovely person. Thank you very much.' This did not stop Lyons, with his eye for style and attention to detail, telling Rankin after New Year that he was not happy about the quality of either the company Christmas presents or the cards. He felt the gifts failed to convey the prestige value intended and that the card was 'very ordinary'!

Showing seasonal goodwill, Lyons had donated £1,000 to the Bishop of Coventry's 1958–60 Appeal. On a less happy note, it was calculated that during 1959 Jaguar's employees had lost wages, due to unconstitutional stoppages, worth £80,000. It was, incidentally, a year of zero inflation.

In 1960 it seemed as if the unique and important relationship between Lyons and the infamous Fred Gardner was threatened. During the first four months, one of Silver's men had been trying to investigate Gardner's area to tighten up piecework procedures. Initially he could not even gain access and, he reported, when questioned Gardner 'became rude and aggressive'. Any kind of work study was quite new to the sawmill, the 'haggle and barter' method of rate fixing having been applied before. By claiming 'tuition rate' Gardner had 'boosted gang earnings' by 'double payment for work done'. When questioned, he said that dockets had been passed to the wages department marked 'No Charge' but none could be traced. In other words, he and his 'gang' were on the fiddle and 'the operatives are doing much as they like without fear of any sort of reprimand'.

Furthermore there was a lack of co-operation with other sections. Gardner overruled the inspectors and failed to adopt modifications issued by the designers. 'For example, a modification was issued some weeks ago for incorporation in the Mark 2 cubby lid, being the addition of a handle and two ball catches. This is not being done, even now.'

Men had been summarily dismissed at Jaguar for much, much less than this. However, Fred Gardner remained another clear instance of Lyons's habit of assigning to a few chosen people who were valuable to him (and whom he liked personally) the status of 'protected species'. Fred Gardner may have abused his special situation and certainly caused widespread resentment in various areas of the company (his position was also unique in that he claimed to be both 'gaffer' and shop steward in his department!) but as this incident illustrates, he was inviolate. Though in his defence, he and other sawmill operatives often worked long and unsocial hours on Lyons's multifarious styling projects.

Lyons continued to keep an eye on the quality of the cars. On 22 February he wrote to Heynes about the 3.4 Mk 2 he drove. 'I do not believe there has been sufficient time spent in investigating the various causes of noises which develop in our cars after some mileage... An excellent example is the *Autocar* Road Test on the 3.8 YHP 790. This car was gone over very carefully before it was handed over for test. I drove it this weekend on an indifferent road. It sounds as though it is falling to pieces.'

Perhaps it was. An investigation carried out into body creaks on the Mk 2 had found that Pressed Steel was missing out vital welds: 'the lack of welding and general fitting of mating surfaces is really frightening...' stated the report. On the cantrail the number of welds was found to be '60 per cent short of designed requirements'.

A subsequent 2,000-mile (3,218km) continental excursion with Greta in YHP789 – taking in Geneva, Zürich, Frankfurt, Wiesbaden, and Brussels – was a happier experience. Lyons reported to Heynes: 'In general I was pleased with the car although I'd very much like to make a similar trip in a Citroën or a Mercedes because my opinion is expressed without comparison.' He found comfort and engine performance over 3,000rpm 'outstanding', but in the lower speed range, performance and acceleration compared unfavourably with many small Continental cars. Steering was 'fair', lacking in feel and directional stability. 'Bad – noises thrown up on bad roads give the impression of unsubstantial construction and loose assemblies. The elimination of this effect would double the value of the car.'

A 2.4 Mk 2 cost £681 to make, an increase of £60 over the 'Mk 1', and the retail price in the UK before tax was £1,082. The company's profit on a home market sale was £53, the difference being due to overheads and dealer margins. The average profit on an export sale was £40 but varied enormously, being as little as exactly £1 in Switzerland!

On 18 March 1960 came an unexpected loss, which was felt deeply by both Jaguar and the entire Lyons family. Alice Fenton died at the tragically premature age of 50 from a cerebral haemorrhage. A remarkable woman, she had given extraordinary service to Lyons ever since she joined him in Blackpool during 1926.

Lyons wrote to tell the dealers on 21 March in these terms: 'It is with the deepest regret that I have to inform you of the death on Saturday night of Miss Alice Fenton, a loyal and devoted servant of the company for over thirty-five years'. In a press statement, he stated that he had 'lost a colleague and a friend' and that 'her loyalty and enthusiasm for the company's progress were invaluable'. At the company's AGM a week later, he said he found it 'difficult to pay tribute to her in adequate terms'.

Alice Fenton had acted as a focal point in the company. 'She was an absolute tower of strength...in the early days he [Lyons] relied on her tremendously,' said Pat. 'And she was so efficient. I remember thinking when I was young that anything in the world that went wrong, all one had to do was to get Alice Fenton and it would all be put right overnight.'[20]

Alice was the only woman in the Jaguar executive (and the highest-placed woman in the British motor industry) and she was there on sheer ability. In her office next to Lyons's, she not only directed home sales but somehow managed to continue as his secretary. Their interaction was exclusively verbal – there exist no memos between them. She would keep Lyons informed about what was going on in the trade. He undoubtedly sounded out her opinion on many things.

'Being of the generation he was, he didn't regard women as being in the same category as men,'[21] said Pat, explaining the lack of women on Jaguar's staff. Those few women that did impact on her father, considered Pat, were those with masculine thought processes. The somewhat theatrical Joska Bourgeois also fell into that category, Pat said.

During the early part of 2001, Mme Bourgeois's close links with a later Jaguar Chief Executive, Geoffrey Robinson, were examined in a book (*The Paymaster*, London 2001) on him by investigative journalist Tom Bower. In relating Bourgeois's early career Bower asserts, in a single line reference, that in the process of acquiring the Jaguar franchise for Belgium in 1947 she had 'a brief fling' with Lyons. This assertion needs to be considered even though no evidence is offered by Bower and no one that the authors have ever interviewed, who might be expected to know about such an affair, has ever given any credence to the allegation.

The whole thrust of Lyons's life, consumed as it was by Jaguar, does not hint at any likelihood of, or need for, extra-marital affairs – quite apart from the fact that he had an extremely happy marriage with a wife that he adored. 'I just laughed because it was so ridiculous,' said his elder daughter Pat of her reaction on first reading Bower's claim.

'Joska's approach to business was masculine, and it was her business ability that appealed to him, that persuaded him to do business with her. The fact that she had perfume and jewellery completely went over his head!

'He would have run a mile if it hadn't been for the fact that [she was] a very important businessperson. Definitely she played a very important part…but I think an accurate picture has got to be drawn, and it's not of a fluffy, feminine person getting round someone, it's someone with a good hard head who comes up with the business. And this is why I think that the stories the press go for, trying to make a picture of her as a *femme fatale*, don't understand what she was like at all. She wasn't feminine, she was frightfully tough.

'Maybe you could say he only went for exceptional women, because Alice was exceptional in her way, though totally different of course. Alice wasn't all that feminine, really – they both thought like men. Their thought processes were masculine. Joska was extreme but he was mildly amused. He realised she was a clever businesswoman, and she was; that was why he took her on board. He made a point of getting on with people who were otherwise totally alien to him.'

'But she got quite fond of us as a family. I don't think she'd ever come across anyone like Daddy before, because he was always so straight.'[22]

Another 'theatrical' friend of Lyons, though this time male, was the entertainer Kenneth Horne, who was also a director of Triplex and fellow Royal Automobile Club committee member. Horne was famous for his radio shows and on one occasion he invited Lyons to a recording of *Round The Horne* at the BBC. According to scriptwriter Barry Took, Lyons slept right through the performance![23]

With Jaguar production increasing, the need for yet more factory space became acute. Further major building work at Browns Lane had been turned down – no more industrial development was being allowed in Allesley. Accordingly, Lyons sent teams to evaluate various development areas.

'My recollection,' stated Bob Berry, 'is that he was under heavy pressure from the Government of the day to move to one of the so-called under-developed areas. He was completely opposed to it for the very reasons that have proved so true subsequently, that the effect on manufacturing costs was so huge that he was not prepared to contemplate it and despite the pressure and the incentives, he was resolute that that was not the right way to go.'[24]

Lyons solved the problem in his own way. On 26 May 1960 came the shock announcement that Jaguar was to buy the Daimler company from BSA. With the famous name – it was Britain's oldest surviving car-maker – came Daimler's rather antiquated but extensive factory of one million square feet (92,903sq m) at nearby Radford; that was the reason.

The announcement came as a complete surprise to all; not least Lyons's own board! 'I remember how furious old Heynes was,' recounted Bob Knight. 'He was listening to the radio while shaving and on the 7 o'clock news it was announced that Jaguar had bought Daimler. It was the first he had heard of it! He immediately rang Whittaker, and dragged him away from his shaving, and Whittaker assured him, God's honour, he didn't know anything about it.'[25]

The deal that Lyons arranged with BSA Chairman Jack Sangster meant that Jaguar would pay a total of £3,110,000 plus the excess of Daimler's current assets over current liabilities – at a price to be jointly ascertained and certified by Jaguar's and BSA's accountants. While the basic agreement was formally ratified on 18 June, Lyons continued to bargain over various other aspects as he learned more about what he had bought.

Lyons must have known the basics, of which quite a lot was unpalatable. The cars were low volume and not profitable. The Majestic Major V8 saloon was just entering production but at only ten per week, and the old six-cylinder Majestic was coming to its end. Then when Jaguar investigated the US market where Daimler's SP250 sports car was being sold, it was discovered that the Daimler name was not registered. This left the company open to possible litigation from Daimler-Benz, though the German car-maker had never traded under that name in North America. Edward Turner, when Managing Director of Daimler, had been aware of this situation but had decided, perhaps wisely, that 'the best thing to do was do nothing'; attempts to register might have raised the sleeping dog.

However, on 17 August Eerdmans wrote that although The Daimler Corporation had been rejected by the Secretary of State for New York State, Daimler Cars Inc could be registered.

Meanwhile Jaguar's body engineers' report on the glass fibre-bodied, Turner V8-powered SP250 sports car was not encouraging. 'With a load applied by hand at the rear end of rear wing, the door opening can be closed or opened approx. 5/16in [8mm]. Windscreen mounting – there is considerable movement at top screen. The pillar can be moved over 1in [25mm] by hand.' The resin content of the glass fibre body was 75 per cent, whereas Jaguar worked on 40 per cent maximum. 'This will, of course, have the effect of seriously weakening the fabric of the material.' Steel stiffeners had to be fabricated at Jaguar to be incorporated in the bodyshells (in due course much of the car was redesigned).

Eerdmans wrote to warn Lyons that the SP250 situation in the US was pretty dire. The idiosyncratically styled cars were arriving in terrible condition, requiring $50 to $80 to be spent on them, and they were not selling. Out of 366 cars received, only 61 had sold by the end of June. He said the distributors were really 'down-hearted about the reaction of both dealers and public'. In mid-October Eerdmans reported on sales of SP250s by Daimler Inc in the USA during September. There were none! The same result was achieved in Canada. Later, the unsold cars had to be shipped home at huge cost for virtual rebuild.

The bus division had become so run down that it was making losses. Eerdmans sent Lyons an enquiry for 175 buses but Lyons replied that he was not sure whether it would be possible to accept such an order. He would find out. However, a new bus, the Daimler

Fleetline, had been designed and was introduced, to a very favourable reception, at the Commercial Motor Show in September, so some areas were showing promise (indeed Daimler was soon making more double-decker bus chassis than anyone else). Another profitable sideline was the Ferret armoured car contract, which Jaguar continued.

On 4 October 1960 Lyons and Jack Sangster of BSA met to discuss the supplementary payment to be made by Jaguar to complete the purchase. Lyons, not surprisingly, argued that Majestic sales were dying and the SP250 was a disaster. Dealers were stuck with cars they were unable to sell and the likelihood was that Jaguar would have to make them a considerable allowance and thus incur a heavy loss.

Following their meeting, Sangster wrote to Lyons to set out his final offer which, if not accepted, would go to arbitration. In that event, his claim would be for £193,124. On a without prejudice basis, he was prepared to accept a reduced amount of £140,000, making a total purchase price of £3,250,000. In his own hand, Lyons appended a note: 'Mr Sangster, agreed on telephone, Oct 12th £130,000. WL.'

On 23 November Lyons wrote to Sangster, enclosing Jaguar's cheque for £130,000 and confirming their agreement. The £10,000 discrepancy? It seems that when Sangster realised he had omitted to mention some outstanding pensions to the value of £10,000, they tossed a coin for this amount. Lyons had won!

In the meantime, development of Jaguar's own new large saloon, the urgently needed replacement for the Mk IX, was well under way. In late June Lyons was concerned that Zenith (as the Mk X was code-named) was slipping behind schedule. Lyons felt strongly that the engineering department needed re-organising along more logical and accountable lines with individuals taking responsibility for transmission, suspension, air conditioning, body structure, etc. 'There is no doubt that at the present time everyone is blaming everyone else for our deficiencies. If we go forward, everyone having responsibilities, the weaknesses will very soon show up.' He wanted 'complete co-ordination between Engineering and Planning from the moment the project is started'.

It is clear that Jaguar's small and, by any normal industry standards, under-resourced engineering team was beginning to feel the strain. In mid-November, Heynes wrote to Lyons about his engineers' heavy workload. They had a bewildering number of projects on hand or needing attention and there was no doubt that they were 'stretched due to lack of manpower'.

Meanwhile the new sports car was undergoing development but

several people have commented that Lyons, at first, appeared not keen on the car. 'He wouldn't look at the E-type,' said Jack Dunnett. 'That was Heynes and Sayer who initiated that... He walked past just to show he didn't approve. Suddenly this car clicked with him. I don't know what changed his mind, but he wanted to put a hard-top on it, which they roughed up.'[26] Tom Jones confirmed that the creation of the fixed-head coupé won Lyons around.[27] Maybe he felt this was his creation. It certainly had his incredible purity of line. In August Lyons must have been on holiday down at The Bolt because Norman Dewis drove a prototype E-type to Salcombe.

In September Rankin dictated a memo advising against the possible launch of the E-type at Earls Court the following month. He felt a last minute 'Show sensation' would be of dubious value and 'would be lumped in with gold-plated ashtrays and mink-trimmed foot-warmers and all the other gimmicks that abound at Show time'.

Financially, Jaguar was still doing relatively well. Lyons stated at a board meeting that in view of the increased profit and consequent large increase in directors' remuneration, he wished to renounce £50,000 of his commission; Whittaker and Heynes also renounced £5,000 each of their commission. Turnover for 1959–60 was higher at £25m but profit was down from £2.6m to £1.8m. Cash was down to £1.1m, reflecting the Daimler purchase, but creditors were up a massive 64 per cent to £7m.

By mid-June the body track was producing 60 Mk IXs, 415 Mk 2s and 35 XKs weekly. September saw record production at Browns Lane, while overseas the first Mk 2s were being produced from Browns Lane kits (plus some local materials) in South Africa. This was under a new agreement with Car Distributors' Assembly there. Production for the calendar year was a new record of 23,352 cars, including 903 Daimlers. The 20,000 barrier had been broken and since 1955 production had more than doubled.

In October's *Jaguar Journal*, the in-house Browns Lane publication that had recently been revived (not the club magazine of that title in the US), Lyons wrote of the recession that enveloped the motor industry. Predictably he said that everyone must do their best to keep costs to a minimum to remain competitive. 'The Chairman of the Shop Stewards' Committee said to me at the time of the fire, when most employees buckled to, to clear up the mess, "If we could get a spirit like this into producing cars, we could lick the world." How right he was. I am afraid that there is in some quarters a greater desire to lick the management rather than our competitors.'

He blamed the recession on purchase tax and the credit squeeze.

In the November issue of *Jaguar Journal*, Lyons answered the question 'Is industry right to expand?' He said that, with rising costs, a manufacturer had no choice even in a recession. 'Failure to do so puts him out of the race for the world's markets, and he joins the names of the past.'

Three days before Christmas Lyons had a meeting with the unions, at their request, to discuss future employment prospects in view of the economic downturn. He felt the recession had been caused by multiple factors but the introduction of the domestic compact car in the US, together with a semi-recession there, had contributed to a drop in sales for most companies. However, they had no choice but to go forward and regard the recession as a temporary one.

Finally, he talked of the importance of close co-operation. 'I would like to make it clear that we believe the unions can play a vital part in industrial relations...we, as employers, do not presume to be above criticism in our relations with your members, but at least I can say that the majority of us try very hard because we recognise we cannot afford to be wrong.'

Correspondence in November revealed that Lyons was a Lloyd's name. However, he prudently covered himself against the unlimited liability factor by taking out stop-loss insurance, which was quite unusual in the 1960s. During a busy year he had received various invitations from the Royal Society of Arts, which had appointed him a Royal Designer for Industry in 1954, but had had to 'regret' every invitation.

The year concluded with the announcement of a £2m investment plan to increase production and in December, no doubt through a contact made while holidaying at The Bolt at Salcombe, the Lyons attended a South Devonshire Conservative Ball.

CHAPTER 8

THE E-TYPE ERA

By the beginning of 1961 the new models under development were badly needed; while the new Mk 2 range was proving highly successful, the big saloon and the sports car were both living on borrowed time. However, as the XK150 model was being phased out, the E-type assembly jigs were being installed and soon the world would set eyes on one of the greatest Jaguar sports cars of all time.

The production programme in early 1961 was for 535 cars per week: 475 Mk 2s and 60 Mk IXs. However, of 442 cars tested in one week, 59 had been rejected with the worst problem being automatic transmissions. Industrial relations continued to dominate the agenda. The company was involved in a two-day conference with the unions on 2–3 January. An eight-page brief, almost certainly the work of Lyons, made the point again that it was necessary for the unions to be able to punish their own members 'who are out of concert with the Shop Steward'. Inter-union rivalry caused each union to consider its claims to be a priority. He considered that union officials should be employed by their unions, be better paid and answerable to the union senior management – not the rank and file with whom they had to court popularity to remain in office.

In much of industry, unions at this time were operating as employment agencies; Jaguar had had some success in breaking this but there still remained the problem of demarcation, where unions dictated what type of labour was used for a task. At the former Daimler plant at Radford, Lyons cited an example 'akin to some of the ridiculous practices' of the shipbuilding industry – the removal of boot trim to reach the petrol tank could not be carried out by the man who was to repair the tank; it was another man's job.

Lyons also suspected communist infiltration; he said direct evidence was hard to obtain but 'the Communist keynote of success was to wreck the economy and prosperity of the nation'. He singled out the electrical union and asked what the unions themselves could do about the subversive elements. 'You couldn't control,' said union convenor Ron Butlin, 'mainly because of International Socialists.'[1]

When the annual wage awards were being negotiated they told the workers to ask for a ridiculous amount and caused the union officials, and Jaguar, an enormous amount of trouble.

The January issue of *Jaguar Journal* carried a New Year message from Lyons, in which he once again underlined the need for the highest quality, but the publication opened with a statement from the Joint Shop Stewards' Committee. This urged their fellow workers to honour the letter and, above all, the spirit of their joint agreement with management. It emphasised the need for a spirit of co-operation if they were all to enjoy 'steady employment with maximum earnings and the uninterrupted output that will give us those things'.

In March Lyons's name was on four papers on various aspects of industrial relations, including 'Coercion', 'Antagonism to Work Study Techniques', 'Bad or Careless Workmanship', and 'Lack of Authority of Shop Stewards'. They all gave examples of incidents where production in the factory had been disrupted through industrial action, without any benefit to the workforce but resulting in loss of production.

The next month, 60 press shop workers walked out over rate fixing. The TGWU's full-time official persuaded the men to go back to work next day and it transpired that the men had been given a gross distortion of the company's promises. 'The Press Shop was officially condemned by the Joint Shop Stewards' Committee.' Some 120 employees were involved, 2,189 were affected, and 10,000 man-hours lost.

Lyons met with various members of the management to discuss labour relations in early May. He emphasised that the company should be as right and correct as it can be. He considered there were subversive elements engaged in discrediting union officials and undermining the relationship between management and unions, in order to bring chaos to the industry. He said it was 'up to all of us to do what we can to recognise and combat this common enemy by helping the union executives as far as we can'.

Moss Evans, former General Secretary of the TGWU, stated: 'Jaguar was very highly regarded within the Union. We had regular reports…and relationships were exceptionally good. They were much better than at Standard where they were rather rebellious. The good relationship was put down entirely to Sir William Lyons.'[2]

Another thorn in the motor industry's side was purchase tax, which since 1959 had stood at 50 per cent. The SMMT was lobbying the Chancellor in February. It was grateful for some easing in hire purchase restrictions but said that it was 'much more important to the long-term prospects to the British motor industry that a substantial and early reduction be made in the 50 per cent rate of Purchase Tax now applicable to cars'. The SMMT report forcefully illustrated the advantages West Germany, perceived as the main competitor, enjoyed; purchase tax there was just 13 per cent. On 1 March Lyons, together with four other senior members of the British motor industry, met the Chancellor to discuss the matter but far from reducing purchase tax, in July he increased it to 55 per cent.

In this continuing climate of industrial unrest, the company was gearing up to introduce vital new models. In early February, Lyons sent a memo to a large number of managerial colleagues regarding the build up to E-type production. 'It is absolutely imperative that this programme, which is already very much behind, is met. We have firm commitments to our distributors and dealers in America, and it is imperative that we do not break them. I appreciate it will require very special effort and concentration on everyone's part, but I must ask the programme be met... Mr Rankin has issued a programme for press arrangements. It is vital also that this is met.'

Lyons had a particularly significant appointment on 15 March in Geneva, where in the restaurant at the Parc des Eaux Vives he unveiled the stunning new E-type fixed-head coupé to the press. He was also photographed outside with the fixed-head, registered 9600HP. This had arrived with only minutes to spare after Bob Berry had had the epic drive of his life, motoring non-stop from Coventry and using all the performance. 'Good God, Berry, I thought you weren't going to get here,'[3] exclaimed Lyons!

In the Parc, Lyons was ringed by a swarm of press and photographers – from whom demand for test drives was so great that Norman Dewis had to drive out the open two-seater demonstrator, 77RW, with equal rapidity. A fixed-head coupé featured on the Jaguar stand at the Show, where it created scenes of excitement reminiscent of the XK120's debut in 1948. Once again Jaguar had produced a supremely beautiful two-seater with the performance of a racing car – the road tests published that same week by *The Motor* and *The Autocar* both recorded the magic 150mph (241kmh) top speed. Yet like the XK120, the E-type was affordable – if you could get one: production would be limited and was months away from commencement.

Patrick Mennem witnessed the press launch. 'I always think one of the cleverest things he ever did was to launch the E-type at Geneva. He knew all the motoring press of the world would be at the Geneva Motor Show. It was more important then than it is now.

He launched it at the Parc des Eaux Vives so the SMMT paid for the reception and everything else! He had the most fantastic reception I can recall for a motor car. Everybody thought it was breathtaking and he hadn't spent a penny. Very astute fellow.'[4]

Dealer and team entrant John Coombs remembered it well. 'I went to Geneva where Lyons gave a party. There was great excitement. It really was the most astounding sports car that has ever been produced.'[5]

'I used to go to all the motor shows around the world,' stated advertising man Bob Bett, 'and I was the first advertising man to do this. I well remember the E-type launch at Geneva. It was held in a great park and Eric [Colburn] and I sat in the car that was used for the launch. I got in by putting my legs in first, and then my bottom. Sir William said, "You don't do it like that, Robert. You put your bottom in first, and then your legs!"'[6]

Jaguar shares were tipped after the E-type launch. It was pointed out that 100 Jaguar shares bought in 1952 at 24s (£1.20) would have increased to 900 shares at 78s 9d (£3.94) by 1961. This rise in value was the major reason why shareholders, with rare exceptions, did not jib at Jaguar's none-too-generous dividend payments.

Stanley Sedgwick, President of the Bentley Drivers' Club, wrote to Lyons to congratulate him, claiming the new Jaguar was the complete answer to those who said that motor racing no longer contributed to production car development (the E-type's construction and styling were based firmly on the D-type's). He hoped this presaged the reappearance of a works team at Le Mans in 1962 and asked if he could be put on the bottom of the list of people clamouring to borrow one for a weekend. Lyons replied: 'Certainly we will be delighted to lend you one of these cars, when it will be I do not know. I am looking forward to being able to take one myself, but I cannot see any possibility of this for some time to come.'

At the 1961 AGM in March, Lyons announced a number of key appointments: Arthur Whittaker was created Deputy Chairman and Bill Heynes became Vice-Chairman (Engineering), Edward Huckvale continued as Company Secretary, John Silver and Bob Grice joined the board, and 'Lofty' England was made Assistant Managing Director. Of Silver, Lyons said: 'He has shown himself as a man of outstanding ability in the planning and works organisation and I feel we owe very much to what he has done during the past ten years and I am sure that these appointments will prove to be very beneficial to the company's future interests.'

No one could dispute the talent and experience of those promoted but the average age of Jaguar's top men – Lyons, Whittaker, Heynes, Huckvale, and England – was approaching 60 (Huckvale was aged 72!). Despite the acknowledged absence of a natural successor to Lyons following the death of his son, clearly no attempt was being made to bring in (or bring on) well-trained younger executives. This was to result in a weakened management structure in the critical years that were to come. However, at the AGM Lyons ignored the fault-line that was developing in his company. Quite correctly he could say: 'So far as the company's sales picture is concerned it has never been better. We have a full order book and demand continues to rise throughout the world markets.'

At the end of the meeting a Dr Catto asked a number of questions and stated his disappointment that the new car, presumably the E-type, was not available for inspection. The company, he said, had the reputation of producing some of the fastest cars in the world and of being one of the slowest in producing its balance sheet! Lyons replied briefly that no cars were available 'because we preferred one to be in Geneva where it would get some orders and prove beneficial to the company's position'.

Similar disappointment on the lack of E-types to be seen was expressed by Richard Logan, who wrote to Lyons on 14 April. While abroad he had read of the E-type and on his return went straight to the London showrooms. He was not impressed when he found none on display and even less so when the salesman told him there was not likely to be one for several months. 'I am a shareholder in your splendid company and feel entitled to say that, whatever the demand for the car, it is surely a great mistake not to have a single one on show in the capital city and greatest market in the land. One Jaguar in London is not going to spoil delivery schedules!'

In fact, only seven cars existed at this time, four of which were on their way to New York. There they were to be the stars of the Fifth International Automobile Show at the New York Coliseum in April. Far more people saw the E-type in New York than in Geneva, 330,000 crowding the show during its eight-day run. Most seemed to be round the Jaguar stand. On opening day, Jaguar Cars Inc had arranged for Miss Marilyn Hanold, *Playboy*'s Miss June of 1959, to adorn the sleek bronze fixed-head on the stand. She was scarcely needed, though; the E-type sold itself and 2,000 orders were taken. America's love affair with the Jaguar sports car was about to be refreshed.

In April the E-type made its racing debut at Oulton Park. Against credible Ferrari and Aston Martin competition, Graham Hill scored a fine win in the Equipe Endeavour roadster belonging to Tommy

ABOVE: *Lyons was interested in politics mainly as it affected the car industry but he was always a Conservative Party supporter. Here he shows British Prime Minister Harold Macmillan the new Mk 2 saloon at Earls Court in 1959.*

BELOW: *Bill Lyons with his chief engineer from 1935, Bill Heynes. Lyons rests a hand on the Austin Swallow Seven saloon which started his motor car career, while Heynes leans on the 2.4 which was to take Jaguar into the semi-volume market in 1955.*

ABOVE LEFT: *In 1956 came a knighthood – and a royal visit to Browns Lane. Here Sir William prepares to bid goodbye to HM Queen Elizabeth and Prince Philip, Duke of Edinburgh. Daughter Pat can be seen at the front of the rope barrier.*

ABOVE RIGHT: *Sir William enjoyed visiting overseas motor shows. This is at a mid-1950s Paris Salon and with him and Bill Heynes is David Brown (centre), industrialist and owner of Aston Martin and Lagonda.* (Bernard Cahier/JDHT)

BELOW: *An evocative photo of Sir William with the loyal Arthur Whittaker, who had joined him in Blackpool in 1923 and went on to become Jaguar's legendary purchasing manager. The date can be pinpointed as early 1957: through the window of Sir William's office can be discerned the wrecks of cars destroyed in the factory fire of February 1957.*

LEFT: *This photograph, dated 18 April 1957, is captioned in Sir William's own hand: 'Futile effort [to] persuade workers [of] importance of exports to company and country'.*

ABOVE: *Lyons hated public speaking and radio interviews – although he seems happy enough speaking to Richard Dimbleby here!*
(Mrs Pat Quinn)

BELOW: *Joska Bourgeois and Sir William Lyons at an official Belgian Motor Company dinner on 24 May 1957. Lyons had a high regard for this remarkable woman's business acumen; she is talking to Sir Peter Norton Griffiths, a Shell executive.*

LEFT: *A fine picture of Sir William Lyons in his prime.*

BELOW LEFT: *Jo Eerdmans helped Lyons exert more control on the North American market and build up a more effective sales and service organisation there.*

ABOVE: *Sir William confers at a motor show with the indomitable Harry Weslake, who was instrumental in developing the XK engine's cylinder head.* (Paul Skilleter collection)

ABOVE RIGHT: *The XK engine was behind Jaguar's biggest commercial and motor sport successes of the 1950s and 1960s. The men who designed it are (from right) Claude Baily, Bill Heynes and Walter Hassan. On the left is Harry Mundy, who joined the company's brilliant engineering team in 1964.*

BELOW: *Leonard Lee, managing director of Coventry Climax, which was purchased by Jaguar in 1963.*

RIGHT: *A Jaguar 'character' – the irrepressible Fred Gardner was Lyons's chief styling aide for some 25 years. This is at Wappenbury Hall with a styling prototype that would eventually evolve into the XJ6.*

ABOVE LEFT: *Alice Fenton, a tireless worker for Lyons and Jaguar, pictured with her boss at a mid-1950s dealer convention at Browns Lane.*

ABOVE RIGHT: *Lyons with his friend Freddy Richmond (the Duke of Richmond and Gordon, owner of the Goodwood race course), and Sir Leonard Lord (centre), formerly of BMC.*

BELOW: *Sir William pours tea on the terrace at The Bolt.* (Mrs Pat Quinn)

ABOVE: *Lyons's great regard for Bertie Henly comes through in this 1961 photograph; the occasion is the presentation of a new E-type in connection with the Motor Trades' Benevolent Fund. 'Lofty' England (second from right) watches.*

BELOW: *The Jaguar board in 1961: from left are F. R. W. England, E. F. Huckvale, A. Whittaker, Sir W. Lyons, W. M. Heynes, J. Silver and R. W. Grice.*
(Coventry Evening Telegraph/JDHT)

ABOVE: *Lyons and the Jaguar group. This photograph, taken c1962 in front of the Browns Lane office block, shows Daimler and Guy commercial vehicles plus the Jaguar range (Mk 2, E-type, Mk X), Daimler range (Majestic saloon and limousine, SP250), and the Ferret armoured car.*

BELOW: *The Browns Lane factory complex, seen in the 1970s. The main entrance was off the suburban street at the right.*

ABOVE LEFT: *Lyons with Colin Chapman of Lotus – one intended company acquisition that was not to be, probably for the better.*

ABOVE RIGHT: *Although not an expert, Sir William could dance. Here he and Greta step out, perhaps on board ship during one of their cruises of the late 1960s and early 1970s.* (Mrs Pat Quinn)

BELOW: *'Uncle Bill said "Let's have a look"!' During the early 1970s Lyons recalled his Blackpool piano shop days 60 years before and began dismantling a faulty piano. The girl on the right is Jane, Pat Quinn's youngest daughter.* (Alan Docking/Mrs Pat Quinn)

ABOVE: *Bill and Greta with their daughters Pat (left) and Mary on board* Sea Type *off Salcombe. Note the Cairn Terriers (Winkle and Jill) which Lyons adored.* (Mrs Pat Quinn)

BELOW LEFT: *Sir William Lyons and the BMC man he thought he could do business with – Sir George Harriman. Unfortunately Harriman became ill and departed the scene, leaving Lyons without the ally at BMH he needed as British Leyland entered the picture.*

BELOW RIGHT: *Sir William and Lady Lyons threw magnificent parties at Wappenbury Hall, taking extreme care over the preparations. This is on the occasion of Mary's 21st birthday, 23 July 1958.* (Mrs Pat Quinn)

ABOVE: *Toasting the bride, November 1961: Mary Rimell's wedding reception at Wappenbury Hall. To the right of the bridegroom are Fred Rimell and Greta. Far left is Mercy Rimell.* (Mrs Pat Quinn)

BELOW LEFT: *Leyland's Lord Stokes appreciated Lyons's experience but failed to use it or capitalise on Jaguar's strength as a brand. The relationship between the two men was uneasy.*

BELOW RIGHT: *The XJ6 of 1968 was probably the finest and certainly the best-value luxury car of its time. It was the culmination of all that Jaguar engineering had learned and it set new world standards. Sir William and Bill Heynes pose with the new car and some of those who developed it.*

FAR LEFT: *The XJ6 was a world-wide success even if its launch was blunted by lack of supply. Here Sir William shows the new Jaguar to French President Charles de Gaulle at the Paris Salon; with him are Charles Delecroix, Paris distributor, and John Morgan (far right).*

LEFT: *Sir William Lyons taking a breather, perhaps at a motor show.*

BELOW LEFT: *Lyons was proud of Jaguar's commercial divisions. An older Daimler bus sits alongside the latest Big J truck at this 1972 Jaguar club meeting.* (Paul Skilleter)

RIGHT: *Sir William the golfer. He was passionately interested in the game and could play quite well – but never as well as he would have liked…*

BELOW: *Farming became a growing interest for Sir William. This is his championship-winning flock of Suffolk sheep, with farm manager Bob Robinson (far left) and shepherd Robert Keys (far right).* (Mrs Pat Quinn)

221

ABOVE: *Sir William and Lady Lyons enjoying a cattle show in the 1970s.* (Mrs Pat Quinn)

LEFT: *John Morgan continued to visit Sir William in his old age. This photograph, taken in the porch of Wappenbury Hall, dates from 1983.* (John Morgan collection)

ABOVE RIGHT: *The final production Jaguar with which Sir William was involved during his retirement was the new XJ6 (XJ40) that appeared in 1986, the year after his death. Here he views the car at Wappenbury.*

RIGHT: *Towards the end of their lives Sir William and Lady Lyons visited South Africa regularly and made some good friends there. This photo, taken during one of those visits, shows the deep affection that existed between the couple.* (Mrs Pat Quinn)

ABOVE: *John Egan built up a fine rapport with Sir William, who in his final years was much cheered by the revival of the enterprise he had founded in 1922.*

BELOW: *Sir William Lyons with some of the many classic models he created, which are now cherished around the world by enthusiasts.*

Sopwith. Tommy drove the winning car to Wappenbury Hall on the Sunday where he had lunch with Lyons. 'He was thrilled as it was marvellous publicity.'[7]

Two cars had been made ready for Oulton only just in time, as Lyons explained when writing shortly afterwards to his friend the Duke of Richmond and Gordon at Goodwood. Thanking him for his congratulations, he expressed his regret that the E-types had not been ready for the Easter Monday meeting at Goodwood. 'Actually, they were hardly ready in time for Oulton and it is almost a miracle that they were so successful. They did not come off the line until Thursday night.'

The Daily Mail of 17 April carried an article entitled 'In the Lyons' Den' with a photo of Lyons relaxing in a garden chair with his dogs. It told how he had watched the Oulton Park race on television. 'I am now willing to consider putting my company back into motor racing as an official team – but only if the international climate is right. I am not interested in prototypes against prototypes. What I want to do is send out showroom cars that the public can buy to compete against similar production models of our rivals.'

The orders received from America for the E-type were most welcome in view of the difficulties experienced in this market due to the combination of a recession and competition from the new domestic 'compacts'. SMMT figures showed that exports of all British cars to the US, which had stood at 209,333 in 1959, had dropped to 132,492 in 1960 and crashed to a mere 30,519 in 1961.

Jaguar and Volkswagen were among the few imported brands to escape relatively unscathed. Amazingly, annual production of Jaguar cars, now including Daimlers, rose from 18,619 in 1959 to 23,352 in 1960 and 25,224 in 1961 (calendar year figures from the Jaguar Daimler Heritage Trust archives), compared with a drop in the British motor industry's overall output from 1.35 million cars in 1960 to just one million in 1961 (SMMT production figures).

On 2 May Lyons wrote to Jack Bryson in Australia saying that Jaguar was working at full production and had been the only company to maintain five-day working during the recession that winter. The US market had been taking fewer cars and so the company had had to rely more on Europe and the UK. He told Bryson that the E-type had not yet commenced proper production and that the factory was making nothing but Mk 2s. He was concerned at allocating a large proportion to the home market and wondered whether Australia could take some extra cars.

Things were also looking up at Daimler and the improved SP250 had revitalised demand. Production was being raised to 20 per week and would soon increase to 35. However, in June, Lyons wrote to Eerdmans about 60 of the original SP250s that were still on the West Coast. 'I appreciate you have done your best to persuade Mr Hornburg and Mr Qvale to reduce the number of cars to be returned, and, therefore, the only thing that remains is for them to be sent back and we will do what we can with them.'

The 3.8-litre (231cu in) Majestic had been dropped but production of the 4½-litre (278cu in) Majestic Major was being increased to 25 a week (though this would prove very optimistic and the rate was short-lived). A Majestic Major was supplied to Lord Brabazon of Tara, who relished its performance; it carried his distinctive registration FLY1.

Despite losses at Daimler as the company was integrated into the Jaguar organisation, the financial results for the year showed marginally improved pre-tax profits. Profits tax had been increased which meant post-tax profits were virtually unchanged. Cash was well up but stock and work in progress had also jumped considerably.

Some effort was being made towards modernising the Jaguar and Daimler plants, yet the 'new' body-finishing and paint plant was actually purchased from Mulliners Ltd in Birmingham, where it had previously been used to paint Standard and Triumph cars. Still, some £644,000 had been invested in plant and tooling, principally for the forthcoming Mk X. A lower foreign tax liability suggests the US and Canadian companies had a poorer year. In his report Lyons stated that National Insurance and pension contributions had been increased and taxes on fuel oil for industry introduced. He said the Majestic Major had been hit by the introduction of a £2,000 price limit for business car tax allowances.

In acquiring Daimler, Lyons doubled Jaguar's plant area and took on another 1,672 hourly-paid employees; he viewed it as a serious opportunity to break into the commercial vehicle market. Soon after the purchase, he made the key appointment there of Clifford Elliott, who had previously established a fine reputation at Dodge Trucks; his job was to design a new Daimler truck.

This was shelved only when truck manufacturer Guy Motors went bankrupt and Lyons bought the company from the receiver. The assets included a 23-acre (9.3-hectare) factory in the centre of Wolverhampton and a range embracing the 14-ton Warrior and 24-ton Invincible, plus three bus chassis. Founded in 1914, Guy employed 825 people but was said to be losing £300,000 a year.

The Guy acquisition revealed Lyons's bargaining talents at their best. The receiver valued the whole business at £2,220,299 but suggested £1,200,000 as a realistic purchase price. 'I again repeated we were not interested,' Lyons recorded, 'and he was about to go when he said would I make any offer at all. I considered this for some time, and I made an offer of £800,000 which to my surprise was accepted.'

Daimler could now concentrate on buses while Guy continued with trucks. Elliott was therefore transferred to Guy where he began work on a new range of heavy trucks. Daimler's own Chief Engineer, the veteran Cyril Simpson, stayed on well after retirement age to complete the Daimler Fleetline bus project.

During 1961 Lyons became involved with Daimler on almost a day-to-day basis. Copies of every bus enquiry were sent to him, he arranged pricing for various bus models, and he reverted to his old job of salesman when he personally entertained the Chairman of the Leeds City Transport Department, trying to clinch an order for 35 bus chassis!

Meanwhile, Jaguar's biggest-ever (in every sense of the word) saloon car project was coming to fruition. On 10 October a large convention was held at Browns Lane for the initial launch of the new Mk X saloon. Lyons praised his engineering staff for their achievements and Bertie Henly reciprocated by wishing Lyons as much success with Daimler and Guy as he had enjoyed with Jaguar. Behind the scenes, great efforts by management and senior shop stewards just avoided a highly embarrassing mass walk-out on the E-type tracks; as it was, 206 man-hours were lost over a simple accountancy error in a few men's wages computations. The 59 men involved gained precisely nothing.

The Mk X was one of those rare instances when a new Jaguar's styling did not meet with universal acclaim. William Towns, Rover and later Aston Martin stylist, said it looked as if Jaguar had listened to a marketing consultant. Side and profile were normal Jaguar, he thought, 'but in all other views, it's a great fat pudding'.[8] Bill Boddy of *Motor Sport* described it as 'portly' and even more worryingly, some pundits in the US were comparing it to a 1948 Hudson! Nevertheless, the Mk X had a dramatic presence on the road, surprisingly good handling, and acres of room inside. It caused a sensation at the time.

This was reflected by orders from American and Canadian distributors at the London Motor Show in October for $63m, representing a doubling of demand in North America. 'This order represents the biggest challenge in our career,' commented Lyons at Earls Court, 'and we will need every effort by both management and men in order to meet it. It presents an opportunity which we may never have again to establish an unassailable position in the American market. I am bound to say that the delivery dates which the distributors have specified leave no margin for any delays.'

Bob Berry had sat in on the meeting and saw a publicity angle. 'I went along to Sir William and I said, "How anxious are you to publicise this morning's meeting? I think we can make a good story out of it in the financial papers by actually talking about the sheer dollar value." He said, "If you think it's good publicity you'd better go and do it but let me see the draft."' Berry did so, making no reference to volumes and simply talking about the dollar value. Lyons approved it and suggested he add a couple of quotes from Hornburg or Qvale. Berry then phoned it through to all the papers. Instead of confining it just to their financial pages, the newspapers embellished the story and made it front page news! Berry was astonished. 'I went into the motor show and Sir William said, "Mm, not bad this morning, was it, Berry? All we've got to do now is make them." And with that he walked off.'[9] Berry found this low-key praise not unsurprising; when some truly exceptional success was achieved, he said, Lyons regarded it as merely natural. Anything less than a total triumph was slightly disappointing.

With its success in the bus field, Daimler was now second only to Leyland as a supplier to 'municipal undertakings', according to a *Commercial Motor* league table. Lyons wrote of this period: 'Later in the year we found ourselves in the position of being the only car manufacturer unaffected by the Purchase Tax and credit squeeze restrictions. These circumstances made for a "sober" attitude on the part of our workpeople. They were surrounded by those less fortunate than themselves and management "propaganda" they had heard previously, rang true.'

Lyons's normally robust health, though, had not been perfect. At the beginning of 1961, he had woken one morning with a severe headache and in subsequent months these became worse. The ever-helpful Bertie Henly recommended the appropriately-named Sir Russell Brain who in May 1961 arranged a lumbar puncture. However, this seemed to intensify the headache to an almost unbearable extent and, a few days afterwards, Lyons reported that the pain was so great he had to stop his car and vomit.

After further consultation, Brain told him to drink as much as possible to build up his fluid level. Lyons found that concentration made matters worse and even playing golf brought it on badly. He said that he had been taking things more easily and had taken three weeks' holiday in Portugal, when things improved a little. Perversely, he found that when he occasionally attended functions and had 'a lot [of] drinks, possibly wine and whisky, instead of feeling ill effects the next morning, I feel a lot better. I find that a whisky and water when I return home in the evening is helpful.' He even wrote to Dr Harold Wolff, Professor of Medicine at Cornell University Medical College, after being shown a *Reader's Digest* article.

A week before Christmas Jack Bryson sent a gift, which seemed to cheer Lyons up. Obviously not one to leave opening his presents to Christmas morning, he wrote back to Bryson at once: 'What an exciting present I received from you this morning. I am looking forward to a fine day during Christmas to try my skill. I have always been fascinated by a boomerang and I am sure I shall get a lot of joy from it, even if I am frustrated in my attempts to throw it successfully.'

However, Lyons was not able to bounce back. He could not keep his usual date with the Geneva Show in March 1962 because, as he explained to Marcel Fleury (co-distributor in Switzerland with Emil Frey), he was going to 'have some treatment for a little trouble I have had for some time. It is nothing serious, but until now it has been difficult for the doctors to fit me in with each other's arrangements.' On the recommendation of H. Clifford Holt, a Coventry estate agent, Lyons entered the London Clinic for treatment by Dr Leyton for what were termed migraines.

Subsequently, Lyons wrote to Dr Leyton: 'After two days at home I am still feeling optimistic that your treatment has had the desired effect.' Later he remarked to Clifford Holt: 'I must admit I am rather nervous as to whether or not the treatment has been completely effective, and am keeping my fingers crossed. Dr Leyton agreed that I should see how I feel in a month's time.'

Sadly, it did not prove effective. When Dr Leyton wrote asking for a donation to the Migraine Trust, Lyons replied: 'I am afraid the treatment I had did not have any lasting effect, I came to the conclusion that I am really not a migraine subject. I did, you will appreciate, invest quite a substantial sum in your cure, and as it did not have the desired effect I do not feel I can add to this.' The headaches returned after Christmas 1962. He then had deep X-rays and found treatment to his neck helped and, in 1964, found some relief after treatment by J. Bradley Hoskisson.

The true cause of those headaches was never established medically; Lyons was successful in keeping them hidden from his colleagues at work and indeed from his wider family. However, Pat Quinn was convinced that they were brought on by stress. In view of the enormous responsibilities on Lyons's shoulders as he single-handedly guided what was now the Jaguar group – including dealing with an often unco-operative workforce and facing an ever more competitive market – such a diagnosis appears credible.

This is a good juncture at which to recap on family history. In mid-February 1962 Lyons's mother had died. Universally known and loved within the family as Granny Lyons, she was well over 90. This was ten years after the death of William Lyons senior, who had died in 1952 after suffering a series of strokes.

In 1937 Lyons's parents had moved from Blackpool to Parkstone in Dorset. There they had a pleasant house in a quiet road near a well-known local landmark, the Blue Lagoon swimming pool, and were a few minutes away from Sandbanks and Poole harbour. Lyons, with Greta and the children, would visit them regularly there, often at Easter – though father sometimes had to dash back to Foleshill!

By 1950, William Lyons senior had suffered a particularly bad stroke, which affected his speech, and Minnie was finding it increasingly difficult to look after both him and the house, despite her daughter Carol staying with them mid-week. So that year the Parkstone house was sold and the couple moved to Sutton Coldfield to be near Carol (Lyons's sister had now married Charles Atkinson).

After her husband's death, in 1954 Granny Lyons moved to Borth, South Wales, because the Atkinsons liked to holiday there and had the use of a house on the sea front. This was Break House, bought by Lyons for his sister and family to use. It was (and still is) an interesting little holiday home right by the sea – so close that the water often comes in the back door and sweeps out of the front! Granny Lyons lived conveniently nearby in a bungalow, looked after by a Mrs Simpson; both received a monthly allowance from Lyons. When Granny Lyons died the bungalow was sold. Break House remained in Lyons's name and on his death was left to his niece Barbara. The family still enjoys it.

Lyons looked after his wider family too. He would help with relatively small items, such as when in 1962 he assisted his sister-in-law Gladys Docking to get a new Mini (via his old firm Brown & Mallalieu), and in more substantial ways too. When his elder daughter Pat married a widower, Norbert Quinn, he helped educate four of the eight stepchildren that Pat brought up. There are many more instances, big and small – and, one suspects, probably more than the Lyons family today can recall.

Various branches of the family were able to take advantage of The Bolt too. His niece Carol Smetham said that 'he used to lend us his house at Salcombe, and his boat, and let our four boys loose amongst all the Crown Derby! We used to go there quite a bit'. To Carol, he was always a favourite uncle: 'He was an absolutely wonderful man. He had very high principles and a lovely quiet sense of humour and he was very loving, kind and caring all through my life.' She recalled that he could tell a joke against himself, citing the Christmas hat story that had entered family lore. At the Jaguar staff Christmas party one year, crackers were pulled. Lyons told how he put on the hat that fell from his cracker, then realised that nobody else had! He was then faced with the embarrassing predicament of either leaving it on or taking it off...

It was Lyons's younger daughter, Mary, who provided him with his first grandchild. This was Katie, born in 1963 to Mary after she married Guy Rimell in November 1961. Guy was the son of the famous jockey and trainer Fred Rimell; Fred still holds the record for having trained the most Grand National winners – four in all. Mary later had a son, Tom, born in 1965, and another son, Mark, in 1970.

That Lyons had both the respect and affection of many of his shop-floor employees too is shown by the appreciative letters many wrote to him upon retirement. This extract is typical: 'Please accept the most grateful thanks of my wife and myself for your wonderful kindness to me during my employment with you and on my retirement. Wishing you, sir, and Jaguar Cars Ltd., every success.'

To return to Jaguar in 1962, Lyons was putting on paper some quite radical thoughts on wage structures; when finished, he sent a copy to Joe Edwards at Pressed Steel. His idea was for 'a new wage structure, which would abolish all existing rates and awards, and establish minimum rates for trades. No other factor would be involved, but this minimum rate could be allied to cost of living standards.' This would certainly have dispensed with the curse of piecework and the outdated working practices still jealously guarded in the industry. In reality, anything like this was still some 25 years away. Jaguar's weekly wage bill in 1962 was, incidentally, £150,000.

In 1962 there was a black market in Britain for E-types and even Mk Xs, such was their scarcity. Deliveries of the big saloon commenced in March, along with a stern warning from Lyons to the 56 distributors who collected their first cars that they must make every effort to ensure they were being sold only to bona fide customers for their own use, rather than profit-making purposes. This was at a time when the E-type Jaguar was virtually the hottest automotive property on the planet; all sorts of people tried to pull strings to get an early delivery. 'The one thing he detested was people taking advantage of him,' commented Pat. 'If there was a waiting list for a car, somebody well known would come along and manage to talk him into them jumping the queue, and then he'd find out that they'd sold it at a profit – that used to get him more angry than anything. I know George Formby once did that. Oh, he was so angry! George Formby persuaded him to let him have a car but they were like gold dust and he sold it within a month for a fantastic profit... It was against his sense of fair play.'[10]

So Lyons must have been pleased when Duncan Hamilton, his former Jaguar team driver, wrote to him in the autumn of 1962 saying that he had kept his E-type fixed-head coupé for 11 months but his back was playing up due to his Le Mans accident and would Lyons mind if he now sold it. Also he had been having rather a lot of dramas with the police and hoped he didn't lose his licence! What he would really like was a Mk X with a manual gearbox, if such a car was being made. Lyons agreed to him selling the E-type and thanked him for keeping his side of the bargain.

Lyons appreciated the funny side of Duncan Hamilton's letter but at work his sense of humour was not obvious. 'He had a sense of humour,' said Patrick Mennem, 'but he kept it well hidden. It wasn't his job to be amusing. It was his job to run Jaguar Cars.'[11] Lyons's response to a letter from Joe Edwards, boss of Pressed Steel, requesting a charitable donation showed his lighter side, though you sense he was still making a point. 'I am afraid, after the staggering blow inflicted by the company's body suppliers, I think it is better that I should go to the workhouse, rather than this company go into liquidation, so I am enclosing a personal cheque... I think you are doing a very worthwhile thing.' Presumably Pressed Steel had recently increased its prices!

Bob Berry confirmed that there was a humorous side to Lyons, even at Jaguar. 'His idea of humour was a very subdued sort of chuckle. I never knew him to laugh out loud... He was amused by situations... He could see the funny side even through a serious situation. He used to laugh with his eyes – he had eyes of a very steely blue, and unwavering. If he was annoyed with you he'd bore holes through you. If he was going to relax, you would see it in his eyes first; nothing else would change. He had a sort of twinkle in his eyes if he was amused by something.'[12]

March saw the appointment of Arthur Thurstans, another of the old guard, as a director. S. E. Aston of Daimler had now taken over as Company Secretary from Huckvale, who sadly had died in November. He had still been a director at 73, retained well after retirement age in another instance of Lyons's feelings of loyalty to his key people. His departure was keenly felt by Lyons; they had worked together since November 1928.

The 1961–2 accounts were unexceptional. Profit was five per cent up, though by only one per cent in real terms. Reflecting the Guy purchase, cash was down, investment in buildings and plant was up, and tax, with the benefit of Guy's tax losses, was slightly reduced. Stock and work in progress, though, was up a massive 32 per cent. Incomplete cars regularly had to be set aside due to shortages from component suppliers. It was taking time to turn Daimler round and the process had barely begun at Guy.

The August *Jaguar Journal* announced that Jaguar had been granted the Royal Warrant of Appointment, as Motor Car Manufacturers, by Her Majesty Queen Elizabeth, The Queen Mother. Lyons had sought this for some time and the royal crest was proudly displayed in the Browns Lane foyer and on the notepaper.

On 8 October, in time for the London Motor Show, those at a Daimler convention were told of the company's 1963 plans and inspected the new 2½-litre (155cu in) saloon – created by fitting the excellent Daimler V8 into the Jaguar Mk 2 body. After lunch for the 200 distributors and dealers, Lyons told them the hybrid had come about because of the need for a medium-sized Daimler saloon to sell in volume at home and abroad. He pointed out that the Mk X had taken nearly five years to develop and a completely new Daimler would have taken a similar time. He was confident that it would be perceived as a model in its own right and indeed, the Daimler 2½-litre V8 did find a useful niche in the model range.

'At Earls Court in those days,' said Pat Smart, 'we used to have an office suite, and a very small restaurant as well, for entertaining VIPs. Sir William used to take down a selection of his office equipment – there was the big blotter, the blotting pad, and also there used to be two bottles of barley water, a tin of Fox's Glacier Mints and a packet of biscuits. The packet of biscuits had to be unopened and the bottle of Robinson's barley water which was opened had a pencil mark on the label so he could see how far down it had gone. The other one had to be sealed. He'd also counted the mints!'[13]

Daughter Mary recalled an early 1960s Earls Court: 'I remember the Duke of Edinburgh going round the Motor Show and sitting in the Fixed Head E-type. He said it hadn't got enough headroom, which there wasn't. I remember Daddy coming home and saying, "Of course, he knows absolutely nothing about how to make motor cars!" Daddy, who wasn't particularly small, used to fold himself in two to get in.

He would try and talk himself into believing there was enough headroom in order to keep the line!'[14] This was another reminder 30 years on of Lyons's fury at Walmsley's raising of the SS1's roof!

On the last Friday of the Show, Lyons threw his traditional press cocktail party. It 'was one of the great occasions of the year,' said Patrick Mennem. 'An invitation to Sir William's party was fought over, really. I was chatting with him and I remember him telling me about a factory he was looking at in Coventry for pressings – the great problem, all his life, was body production. He said to one of the workers, "How many of these do you stamp out a day?" The chap said, "I don't know, but I tell you what, every time that goes bang, it's sixpence [2p] for me!" Old Bill Lyons thought that was terribly amusing.'[15]

Reflecting on the 1962 Motor Show, Lyons wrote that attendance figures were down and the car selling boom was definitely over. (He was wrong, for once; from 1962 to 1964, the home market would expand by 50 per cent!) For Jaguar the Show had been particularly difficult as people were complaining about slow deliveries. 'Despite the fact that, most of this year, there were at least three customers for every car, our inability to supply them at the right time has resulted in the loss of two of the three customers to other manufacturers.'

It had not been an easy year. One saving grace was that purchase tax was reduced in two stages to 25 per cent, which acted as a tonic to the home market. Production for the calendar year had fallen slightly, to 24,181 cars including Daimlers. While the Mk 2 was still the most popular range, even this had dropped from the 1961 record of 21,236 cars to 12,751 and would continue to fall. Of the new models, 6,266 E-types and 4,312 Mk Xs were made. The US market slowly picked up again, and total exports for 1962 had increased by 28 per cent. However, as production had fallen well short of the targets, the export figures had been achieved only at some cost to home market deliveries.

The question of whether Britain should join the Common Market was now becoming important to the motor industry. In March Michael Shanks, Industrial Editor of *The Financial Times*, told an audience of 900 members of the Motor Agents' Association that entry into the Common Market would mean increased competition. 'If you produce a really good model,' he said, 'as Jaguar have shown, you can swim successfully against the tide of the big battalions.' Jaguar issued a press release the next day, quoting Shanks and saying that, in the 1960–1 financial year, Jaguar's sales to Common Market countries increased by 78 per cent.

Before leaving for a holiday in Portugal in the winter of 1963, Lyons had received a confidential valuation of Coventry Climax's sites, the first indication on record that he was interested in this firm. On 7 March Lyons and Leonard Lee of Coventry Climax announced to their respective workforces that Coventry Climax Engines Ltd was to be taken over by Jaguar, by means of a share exchange. Lyons was to be Chairman and Lee would become Deputy Chairman and remain Managing Director. None of the directors of either company had been consulted and Wally Hassan – who had been at Coventry Climax ever since leaving Jaguar in 1950 – read about it in the *Coventry Evening Telegraph*!

It was not the reason for the acquisition but certainly, as Mary Rimell phrased it: 'Daddy was frightfully pleased he had got Wally Hassan back. It appealed to his sense of humour!' Hassan, in turn, hoped that Climax would retain its autonomy and it did. 'Once the first burst of interest in the takeover had died down, business seemed to carry on precisely as before... The only immediate advantage was that purchasing activities were rationalised. It seemed that this was almost a "marriage of convenience" as there were so few links between Jaguar and ourselves. It was almost a takeover without consequences.'[16]

It was rare for a parent to avoid meddling with its subsidiaries; history judges Lyons correct in resisting the temptation to do so with Coventry Climax. Its fork lift truck business was sound and since 1957 the company had produced a series of highly successful grand prix engines; these had gained Jack Brabham (Cooper-Climax) the World Championship in 1960, and Jim Clark (Lotus-Climax) achieved the same in 1963.

A communication to Eerdmans, his trusted lieutenant in the US, explains Lyons's private reasons for his latest acquisition. 'You'll probably have heard we have acquired Coventry Climax Engines by an exchange of "A" shares. It was felt that this company could be of considerable value to us by not only strengthening our engine division, but also providing an additional business which is operating on a good profit-earning basis, that is, the manufacture of fork lift trucks for which there is a growing demand... The company has a very good reputation... We ourselves have chosen them in preference to all others for a number of years. The company claim to be competitive in price, even in export markets, but there does not seem to have been much drive in that direction and we must obviously explore immediately the possibility of sales abroad.'

Climax was supplying Lotus with engines and, perhaps for that reason, a delegation from Lotus visited Browns Lane in May, including Colin Chapman (Chairman), Fred Bushell (Managing Director), and Ron Hickman (Design and Development Director). While there Lyons showed them the SP252 (or SP250 Mk II) prototype, which did not particularly excite them, but they were impressed by the Daimler engine and seriously considered fitting it in Hickman's M20 (Elan 2+2) prototype. 'It was envisaged the new Lotus would have a Daimler engine,'[17] said Hickman.

Following their visit, Chapman said to England, who later recounted the episode: 'What about coming to see my place?' So 'Lofty' went. 'When I got back I said to Sir William, "I reckon we could buy this lot for £½ million, complete with the motor racing side." He said he'd better have a look at it, so I took him down. "I think you're right," he said.

'So we then negotiated with Chapman and got to the point where they actually shook hands. It was a share deal. The Old Man then went off somewhere, and about a week later a letter came from Chapman saying that they'd reconsidered this and would we be good enough to let them withdraw. So I thought… "He's not coming in on the right foot if he doesn't want to do it."' So I said, without asking the Old Man, "fair enough".'[18]

Alan Newsome was involved in some of the Lotus meetings and met Colin Chapman; he was apprehensive about Chapman's character, so was not displeased when the transaction fell through. Bill Heynes, according to his son Jonathan, was plain furious. All in all, this would appear to have been one marriage that would not have been happy.

Now that the home market seemed set to expand after the reductions in purchase tax, attention was turned to export markets. A letter Eerdmans sent to Lyons revealed that the Mk X was selling very slowly indeed and he made the ominous comment: 'when the time has arrived that the factory can supply this model with a more powerful engine and new gearbox, we will have to evaluate the Mk X market again'. In other words, Eerdmans dismissed the Mk X so far as America was concerned – an unprecedented situation with a mainstream Jaguar saloon.

The Mk X did find favour elsewhere. On 23 February Lyon's oldest distributor, Emil Frey, wrote from Switzerland with some statistics. 'Due to the vivid interest you have always shown in getting informed of the sales figures for Mercedes in comparison to Jaguar on free market. I have included only the competing models which are of interest, i.e. model 220S plus SE and 300. Though the Swiss market

236

is a free market, Mercedes are enjoying big advantages, namely, the factory is only 110 miles [177km] away from Switzerland, the Mercedes marque is introduced on the Swiss market for nearly 50 years, 70 per cent of the Swiss population speaks German, many German people are living in our country. With regard to these facts, the success which we have been able to obtain is double worthy and pleasant for both of us.'

Emil Frey's figures compared sales on the Swiss market of equivalent Mercedes-Benz models (220S, 220SE, and 300) with Jaguars and quoted the percentage of Jaguar sales to Mercedes sales. In 1959 Mercedes sold 990 cars and Jaguar 296 (30 per cent). The following year Mercedes sales reached 1,646 compared with 476 for Jaguar (28.6 per cent). Peak year for Mercedes was 1961, with 2,092 sales against Jaguar's 688 (31.9 per cent). However, Frey's figures showed Mercedes sales almost halved in 1962 at 1,114 while Jaguar reached a peak of 691 (38.1 per cent). For Jaguar, more than doubling sales in the tough Swiss market over four years was a considerable achievement.

Lyons sent a copy to Eerdmans. 'I think you will be interested in the enclosed report from our Swiss distributor, Emil Frey because it shows the success of our competition against Mercedes in Switzerland, a very different picture to that which exists in America. Incidentally, I have tried one of the new 300 Mercedes recently and, in my opinion, it does not even start to compare with the Mk X. It is rough, noisy and I did not even find it a particularly pleasant car to drive. I do not know how it is selling against the Mk X. I do not even know the price comparison but I shall be glad if you will give me some information on this.'[19]

Eerdmans's comments on Mercedes must have cheered up Lyons. At least they weren't having much luck with big saloons either. 'Sales of the 300SE Mercedes was less than 100 in 1962. This proves again that with the great competition in the United States from the domestic manufacturers it is not easy to sell an expensive sedan. In comparison with Mercedes, we have not done too badly in 1962, as we imported and sold to our distributors a total number of 1079 [sedan] cars.'

In fact 1962 was to be the 3-litre 300 model's best year by far; Eerdmans's comparison oddly overlooked the smaller-engined 220 Mercedes sedan, a Mk 2 competitor, which sold in far greater numbers – 37,695 worldwide in 1962, or 13,514 more than all Jaguar and Daimler sales combined that year.

Eerdmans provided sales figures which showed that the E-type, at about 220 a month, was spearheading Jaguar's US attack. The Mk 2 now accounted for barely 25 per cent and just 12 Mk Xs had been sold in February. 'It is too early to say whether the reduction in price on the E-type will help sales.' They were having a big push but a three months' newspaper strike had not helped.

This price reduction now seemed to have been unnecessary and Lyons replied immediately. 'It is indeed a very serious situation. You say, of course, that the reduced price of the E-type has not yet had time to have effect but the indications are that we made a very serious mistake in taking notice of our distributors and reducing the price, even though the sales may have been quite a bit lower, because, had we retained the old price, we'd have avoided the serious losses we are now making.'

On 11 March Lyons cabled Eerdmans in something of a panic. 'Understand new Corvette and American sports car trend now four door. This contrary to emphatic wishes distributors London meeting. Please clarify.' In fact, Lyons was getting muddled and meant the Thunderbird. Eerdmans did some digging, and found that there were no plans to bring out the Thunderbird as a four-door model. They were trying to ascertain General Motors's plans. 'However, as the [Buick] Riviera [two-door] was introduced only six months ago and has been a great success, I doubt if they will consider changing this model to a four door sedan.'

Lyons was planning a trip to the US and told Eerdmans he would like to meet as many of the distributors as possible, 'indeed I am anxious to discuss with them the position. As regards the President's Luncheon given by the British Automobile Manufacturers Association Council [BAMA, with which John Dugdale was by then associated] on April 16th and the lunch being given by Mayor Wagner on the 17th, these will mean my remaining in New York a whole week. If I can do any good by doing so, I will stay that time.' From New York, Lyons was planning to go on to Jamaica and then possibly Puerto Rico.

On 4 April Lyons (and Lady Lyons, who hated flying) set sail for New York on the *Queen Elizabeth* to attend the Motor Show. He then had a packed schedule, including a visit to Washington. As planned, he spoke at the luncheon given by BAMA. He said that the US automobile manufacturers had made enormous progress in the past ten years with compact and sports cars and presented a formidable challenge. 'Had this rate of progress come ten years earlier, I doubt whether many of our businesses would have got off the ground.'

Don Iddon, writing his *Daily Mail* column from New York, reported that Britain had the largest display of any visiting nation. 'I had a drink with Sir William and Lady Lyons. The huge success of the Jaguar, the wealth and title have left them completely unspoiled. Our motor tycoons, led by Lord Rootes, have done more for Britain in the last few years than all the diplomats put together.' Afterwards, the Lyons spent ten days playing golf in Montego Bay.

On his return he was interviewed by the UK's *Jaguar Journal*. He spoke of how impressed he had been by US employees. 'I was surprised to find the man operating a machine or driving a truck regards his job as being of equal importance to that of the most senior executive of the company – which is, of course, as it should be. There is no feeling of antagonism towards management.' What a breath of fresh air that must have been to Lyons!

One employee at Jaguar joined the management when Lyons shrewdly appointed Harry Adey, who had been one of the sheet metalworkers' union's senior stewards, as Jaguar's Industrial Relations Manager. 'When Harry Adey went over to management,' said Butlin, 'Sir Bill came to me and asked if I would join the management. "I would like you to be my representative throughout the area." I said, "No thank you." He said, "These people don't care about you, you know." I said, "I know. I am well aware of that. That's one of my strengths..."'[20]

Another appointment was John Morgan, who had worked in exports with Rootes for 13 years. A gifted linguist, he had been educated for a time in Switzerland and so felt 'pretty European'. His father was, like Lyons, a great friend of Bertie Henly. One day Lyons spoke to him and said he had been watching his progress. 'I think you're the sort of person that would quite enjoy working with us, Morgan.' He replied: 'Yes, Sir William, I'd love to work for Jaguar.' Lyons responded: 'Oh, you would, would you. Well, we don't offer jobs in this company. People have to apply for them. But if you'd like to apply, I think there is a good chance of you getting a job here.' 'So I did, and I got it,'[21] recalled John with much amusement.

Always interested in others' opinions, Lyons invited his old friend Dick Hutchinson of Studebaker to cast his eye over the business. Hutchinson made some significant comments, according to John Morgan. 'One of the things he suggested was that he should get rid of the old boys. I came in one day from a little trip and I was suddenly told, "You are taking over tomorrow. Mr Hilton's been retired from Daimler."'[22] Ben Mason, who had been Jaguar's very first Export Manager and who was well past 65, also took well-earned retirement and Morgan found himself Export Manager for both Jaguar and Daimler.

In mid-July Lyons paid £129,250 for the Paget Works, a 150,000sq ft (13,935sq m) site adjacent to Guy in Wolverhampton; with the launch of the new Big J range of trucks not far off, the purchase provided badly needed additional space. The figures for 1962–3 showed that the Jaguar group's profits were slightly improved for the third year running but the increase was actually less than the rate of inflation. A cash balance of £703,256 had turned into a group overdraft of £132,797. Another 428,572 shares had been issued due to the share exchange deal with Coventry Climax and for the first time Lyons's percentage holding had been reduced. The emphasis appeared, from the accounts, to be on increasing the size of the business rather than maximising profitability. The dividend had been increased, which arguably was not a prudent decision on these figures.

Meanwhile, Lyons had been considering some major personal acquisitions. He obtained details of various large country estates, including the Kinlet Park Estate in Shropshire, and in October enquired with agents about the Lareen Estate, which had its own hotel, near Donegal in Northern Ireland. Early retirement was not in mind, however; Pat Quinn said that these were investments suggested by financial advisors but were vetoed, Mary thinks, largely by Greta as she did not want the restrictions and responsibilities of running a big country estate!

On 6 November Lyons wrote to his old friend, Sir Henry Spurrier of Leyland, saying he was delighted to hear from Bill Black (Sir William Black of ACV, who had taken over from Spurrier as Leyland's Chairman) that he was so much better and that they had all missed him during the Show. 'I was so pleased to see that Donald Stokes has been put into the position I know you always planned for him. I am sure he will make a great success of it, and it must be a comfort to you to know that Leyland is still in good hands.

'I think the new Triumph 2000 is going to be a winner. I had a good look at it at the Show and was very impressed. At its price I think it has the edge on its competitors. It looks as though your worries about Standard are over.' He gently chided him for not coming to Salcombe that year and hoped he would next year. Sadly, Spurrier died soon afterwards, a loss that probably had a crucial influence on what was to transpire with Jaguar and Leyland.

In earlier correspondence, Lyons had congratulated Black on becoming Chairman of Leyland and wished him every success. Black thanked Lyons: 'I hope we shall have lots of opportunities of co-operation to our mutual advantage.' Sadly, there would be a certain irony about that statement.

The Mk X again caused some anguish when an unfavourable road test report appeared in *The Motor* during November: the decorative woodwork was thought to have 'skin deep' quality, the sound damping and trim could have been better, the seats gave 'an absurd lack of lateral support' and body roll was considered 'excessive'. Lyons's old friend Christopher Jennings, no longer Editor, wrote to say that he disliked 'more than I can say, the attitude towards the Mark X shown in this week's road test in *The Motor*. All that I can say is, that if I'd still been in the chair and in the light of 12 months' driving of the car, things would have been very different, and, I am exceedingly sorry to read what I regard as a most unfortunate report.'

Next day Jennings sent Lyons a hand-written note from London, 'I came up here in the early hours with our telephone conversation much in mind. Without mentioning our talk, I've just had a spell with Bensted-Smith [Editor] and gave him my own views on the subject! I'm sure that there must be a "background" to all this and I intend, if possible, to find out what it is. I cannot accept that my own judgement of a car, based on 12 months and 12,000 miles, could prove so far removed from that of *The Motor* unless there exists some hidden cause.'

The 'background' was simply that Roger Bell, *The Motor* staffman who compiled the road test, thought the Mk X had serious failings! The sequel is that he was invited to Jaguar, only to find himself shown into a room packed with what seemed Jaguar's entire engineering executive – including Bill Heynes. He was given a good grilling but stood by his opinions.

This episode also illustrates Lyons's keen interest in magazine road tests, especially those of the two yardstick British weeklies, *The Autocar* and *The Motor*. As Bob Berry confirmed, after a new model had been submitted for test he might well ring the Editor for an opinion even before the test was published. This might have been an unconscious effort to 'steer' the report but it was as much due to his insatiable quest for information. An offshoot would be increasing care in the preparation of road test cars by Jaguar. Bob Knight would eventually take this to almost fanatical levels, the key press cars being almost hand-built to levels of perfection which, frankly, were not often found in the average production example.

September saw the introduction of the S-type, with a choice of 3.4- or 3.8-litre (210 or 230cu in) engines; it was a derivative of the Mk 2 saloon with Mk X-type independent rear suspension and a larger boot. It was well reviewed but, while initially outselling the now-elderly 3.4 and 3.8 Mk 2 models, it never approached the Mk 2's heyday sales of the early 1960s. The S-type was an effort to produce a new model economically and within a short lead-time; it was also the start of a wider but less focused model range as Lyons tried to cater for every niche and to compensate for a lack of truly new saloon models.

The S-type was, of course, displayed at the October Motor Show in London. As always, Lyons was able to include some relaxation among the rounds of receptions and meetings, including a visit to the theatre to see a new Peter Ustinov play at the Caprice. Maybe he was intrigued by its title: *How to Succeed in Business Without Really Trying*!

In November Heynes wrote a long report to Lyons on model policy. There seemed to be some indecision. The XJ6 project had started as a stretched E-type back in 1961, then gone through a variety of iterations. Their thinking had been influenced by the Ford Thunderbird and Buick Riviera – America's 'personal cars' with sporting pretensions yet with adequate seating for four persons. The E-type front had then been dropped for a four- headlamp set-up more akin to the Mk X. This body had been released to Pressed Steel on 1 April 1962 but clearly was not proceeded with and was then superseded by a frontal design showing Italian influence. There were suggestions of making a wider version with an E-type front and a V12 engine for the US market, and a narrower model with a squared front end and six-cylinder engines for Europe. Heynes suggested that they needed two models because one would not suit both markets. Ultimately, out of this mêlée would come two new cars – the XJ6 and the XJ-S – but it would take a long time.

Eric Kenny, a director of Henlys, wrote to Lyons to thank him for his Christmas gift and added a postscript, 'I didn't think you would ever get around to horse racing, or is it Greta's Department only? Congratulations on the win last Monday!' This was a reference to Jungle Beach, one of several racehorses owned by Greta for a while and trained by Fred and Mary Rimell. It won 12 races and was once second in the Mackeson Gold Cup at Cheltenham. But horse racing was not a mainstream hobby for Greta and as for her husband, Mary Rimell explained that 'Father wasn't in the slightest bit interested... He said it was like watching cars go round in second gear!' Though Mary did recall that her father had an uncanny ability to identify an outstanding horse, purely through his eye for line.

Jaguar also won something worthwhile in 1963 and that was the first ever European Touring Car Championship. Peter Lindner (Jaguar's importer in Germany) achieved this with co-driver Peter Nöcker and it proved that the 3.8 Mk 2 was still about the quickest four-door car you could buy in Europe.

In January 1964 Lyons and Grice had a telephone conversation on an oft-raised matter, that of leaving lights on unnecessarily. Grice contacted the heads of departments and sent Lyons copies of their replies. Most expressed their views forcefully, saying natural lighting was insufficient and quality could suffer. In this it would appear that Lyons was being petty but on reflection, he was simply ahead of his time in appreciating energy conservation: today's Jaguar plants have automated lights, which switch off when people leave an area.

John Morgan recalled: 'He had some little quirks on economy which were quite extraordinary.' Many wealthy overseas customers visited John's London office and the carpet, made in strips, was becoming very worn. There was no budget to replace it and so he had the carpet re-laid so that the worst parts were under cabinets around the edges of the room. The chairs were similarly worn and the stuffing was protruding. He had these re-covered by the Jaguar apprentices, who also made some stylish wooden covers for the metal desks.

'Sir William said to me one day, after visiting the London office, "Morgan, what have you been doing? The extravagance!"' Morgan pointed out the rearrangement of the carpet and Lyons said: 'That's very good, very good indeed. I like that. I must tell my wife. She must do the same with our carpet at home.'[23]

Then Lyons discovered Morgan had ordered a new chair for his secretary. He immediately came on the telephone: 'Morgan, what are you doing buying chairs? You're not taking on more staff, are you?' Morgan explained and Lyons said, 'Well, before you order it, you ought to go round and see if there are any.' Morgan found a spare one in the telephone office. Four days later, Lyons rang again: 'Morgan! What have you done about that chair?' 'I found one, Sir William.' 'There we are, you see. This is it. You young men are going to run this company. You've got to learn economy.'[24]

Again, this was not meanness: it was to further the culture of thrift, which ultimately helped keep the price of the cars down. Whether Lyons took this too far in important areas such as engineering is open to debate, however.

In about 1964 there was nearly a sales arrangement with BMW. Morgan explained: 'We had a joint distributor in Hamburg [Fendler & Ludemann] who said, "BMW are in real trouble. They've got to drop the V8. Why don't you get together with them? You could sell their small cars and they could sell your big ones.". They were almost bankrupt and Morgan thought this a good idea. 'I made enquiries and talked to BMW and they said, "Yes, We would be interested if you would distribute BMWs in the UK and we would distribute your cars in Germany, to start with." We were not doing terribly well in Germany.

'We had a meeting with the Managing Director, Herr Wilcke [Gerhard Wilcke, Quandt's legal adviser, who was a member of BMW's supervisory board from 1960 onwards, and Chairman of the management board from 1965 to 1969] in the Carlton Tower and he said he would be quite interested in going further with it.' 'Lofty' England was at the meeting, thought it looked promising and that they should talk to Lyons.

'So we did,' said Morgan. 'He sat there, blinking. No reaction whatever. Then he said, "Perhaps you might tell me, Morgan, who owns BMW?" I said, "The Quandt family. They've got the majority interest in it. Very powerful. They own a battery company as well and they've got 14 per cent of Mercedes-Benz."

'"What?" he said. "I'm not going to deal with anyone who has anything to do with Mercedes-Benz." That was it. Closed. Finished. We didn't discuss it any more. But it could have been a lovely tie-in.'[25] This story cannot be verified in the official BMW history, although indeed BMW had earlier looked at alliances with various firms, including Daimler-Benz, American Motors, Ford, Chrysler, Simca, Fiat, and Rootes.[26]

In late May, a takeover specialist had written to Lyons about Maserati, which it was claimed would be receptive to an offer from Jaguar. A set of accounts was enclosed but 'they do not represent, as is the case with practically all Italian companies, the real state of affairs'! Lyons was invited to Modena to be shown around by Adolfo Orsi and it was intimated that some American manufacturers were showing interest.

Lyons countered by asking for a list of the plant but the Italians were reluctant to provide this information and wished him to visit. It seems that Italy was suffering from a severe credit squeeze and they needed £300,000 to £400,000 to bring out their new models. A Jaguar loan for this amount was suggested, 'to be secured on the property, and an option to buy such proportion of the holding you may require. This would give the opportunity to assess the value of the company before taking a controlling interest.'

Maserati cabled to say it was not willing to disclose further information without an indication of 'concrete interest'. Again a visit was suggested or 'if helpful Orsi son willing fly'. Being completely objective, Lyons responded: 'I think it is very doubtful as to whether any company manufacturing in small quantities could survive in the industry today. However, when I have the full details of the plant, I will get in touch with you again.' Finally, Lyons concluded the negotiations with this statement: 'Having examined all aspects, together with our own future programme, I cannot visualise any advantages which would accrue from this project. May I, however, thank you for the opportunity.'

Having passed up opportunities to become involved with BMW and Maserati, a less glamorous takeover was completed by the end of the year. In February Lyons received a confidential unsigned memo about the Henry Meadows company, which had just been acquired by Quinton Hazell Ltd. His informant felt the business was badly run down due to lack of finance and had little product on offer apart from two engines and a gearbox. The main attraction was obviously the site itself; the total factory area amounted to 391,000sq ft (36,325sq m), of which Chubb Ltd occupied 81,000sq ft (7,525sq m) with a further 13 years to run on its lease. QH was considering asking £1.1m for the factory and £300,000 for the business but would buy back the gearbox side. There was a tax loss of £400,000 included.

Lyons must have done some negotiation, as in December Jaguar completed the purchase of Henry Meadows for £212,500. The premises were adjacent to Guy, making an island site. Meadows had been founded in 1919 and began by manufacturing its own design of transmission, followed by complete engines which were used in such cars as Invicta, Lea-Francis, Frazer Nash, HRG and Lagonda. The company then went on to make diesel engines and was involved in the 1950s with the Frisky bubble car.

In mid-May *The Financial Times* carried a report on Pressed Steel. Output was expected to rise from 520,000 bodies to 720,000. Its largest customers were Rootes and BMC, while 100,000 bodies were manufactured for Jaguar, Standard, and Rover in total. As Jaguar built the E-type bodies in-house, Jaguar's requirement was around 20,000 a year. Vital as they were to Jaguar, to Pressed Steel it was a fleabite. It was as well Lyons was on such friendly terms with Joe Edwards – or maybe Pressed Steel, which also made Rolls-Royce bodies, regarded Jaguar as a prestige job.

As if to reinforce the potential risks to a company of Jaguar's size, a few days later Lyons sent Silver a strongly worded memo: 'At your meeting this morning will you please stress that if the company is to remain in business, it is vital that we obtain a minimum average output of 600 cars per week.' That equated to nearly 29,000 cars per year, which would not be reached for a few years yet, although 1964 turned out to be Jaguar's best so far, with production of 25,862 cars.

In early October Lyons wrote to Lord Leigh. He agreed entirely with the need for a Conservative Party fighting fund and said that Jaguar had 'already made a very substantial contribution towards this'. However, in the general election the Labour Party under Harold Wilson came to power.

Meanwhile Jaguar's accounts showed that pre-tax profit was up eight per cent at £2.4m on turnover of £30m. The cash situation had improved by £½m. Tax for the year was lower, thanks to £83,000 in foreign tax due to be repaid to the company. Stock and work in progress were now running at almost a third of turnover, which seems high, and debtors had almost doubled in a single year, which suggests an uncharacteristic lack of control. The profit was claimed to be the best in the company's history but this was not correct in real terms. Adjusting for inflation it was actually 20 per cent lower than the 1959 figure.

The stimulating influence of Jaguar on the group's commercial division was seen in September with the launch of Guy's new Big J trucks and the Daimler Roadliner, a rear-engined single-deck bus. Both were fitted with V6 9.63-litre (587cu in) Cummins diesel engines and an agreement was announced between Jaguar and Cummins for the manufacture of V6 and V8 Cummins engines to be used in the company's products. They would also be offered for sale to others and Lyons looked forward to 'the substantial world sales which these engines are certain to enjoy'. However, it was not to prove plain sailing.

At the Motor Show the 4.2-litre (258cu in) engined Mk X and E-types were launched. The saloon needed a performance boost, as Eerdmans had said in early 1963. Cyril Crouch stated: 'The Mark X wasn't a success really. The body was very heavy. Bill Heynes insisted on 16-gauge sill panels and so on. The heating distribution was pretty poor. It was too large for this country really, and it wasn't quick enough off the mark for the Americans... The 4.2 engine made it a nice motor car, but by then it had got a name, and whatever we did to it, we couldn't do much of a rescue act on it. That was one of the non-successes of Jaguar – about the only one, I would think.'[27]

Jo Eerdmans called it the 'lemon'. 'The problem with the E-types,' explained Eerdmans, 'was that they couldn't make any more. I told Lyons of the possibilities in America and he said he would double the output. It took four or five years.'[28]

William Heynes would have agreed with Eerdmans's sentiments about the E-type at least. He had strongly urged Lyons to spend money on having the body fully tooled for quantity production. Lyons had refused to take what he perceived was too great a risk –

he did not believe the new sports car would sell more than a handful a week. So the E-type body was painstakingly assembled from small pressings at Browns Lane in a not dissimilar fashion to the XK series before it. The result was that, although profitable, it could have been much cheaper to make and, above all, could have been made in sufficient quantities to meet the big demand that existed, especially in North America, during the early- and mid-1960s.

Eerdmans appeared to be realistic about Lyons's evident limitations. 'I went over three times a year to Coventry. The organisation in Jaguar was not flexible enough. Lyons, of course, was the owner and he wanted to decide everything. I talked to Heynes, who in my opinion was an outstanding man, and Whittaker was a good man, and we decided what had to be done. Then we went to Lyons and he said he would think it over. It was always, "I'll talk to you next week, I'll talk to you next month".'

'Lyons was so conservative in his decisions. He wanted to make certain that everything he was doing was right. I told him that was tripe. "You have got to take your men at the right value, and give them more responsibility. How often do you take all the decisions?"

'He was a dictator. I knew that man inside out. His wife knew what he was like as well, and we discussed how to change his outlook on certain things. But you couldn't do it.'[29]

'He wanted to keep it as a specialist car,' said daughter Mary. 'One of the things he always used to say was, "We must always have a waiting list". As long as you have a waiting list, people want the car. The minute you've got them sitting in the showrooms, you've got problems. You must be very careful you don't produce more than you can sell.'[30]

'His whole idea,' said Alan Currie (who had followed Eric Warren as Home Sales Manager), 'was that nothing was available immediately. If somebody said, "Have you got a red one with five wheels?" you didn't say, "Yes, aren't we lucky, we happen to have one". You said, "Now I'm not sure about that" and the chap would say but there is one in the showroom. "I'm sorry, sir, that's spoken for, but I'll do my best to find one."'[31]

The counter argument here is, of course, that the wrong major investment decision or over-production might have jeopardised the whole business or at least Lyons's grip on it. Clearly, Lyons felt he was walking on a tightrope almost his entire business life. One big slip and it would all be gone. Far better, therefore, to err on the side of caution. There can be some sympathy with this outlook: after all, as his old Blackpool hand Jack Beardsley once remarked, 'he didn't have GM behind him'.

CHAPTER 9

LYONS MERGES
JAGUAR

A year earlier, in January 1964, Bertie Henly had written to say that
he had asked his wine merchant to put down for Lyons six dozen
Chateau Beychevelle 1959 and the same quantity of Chateau Lascombes
1959, which he said would be right for drinking in four or five years'
time. 'The Beychevelle you have had and the other one I am sure you
will enjoy drinking. Thanks for lunch the other day. We enjoyed it so
much as usual.' The same wine merchant wrote in April 1965 to
confirm that Lyons could accept delivery of the 12 cases. 'He appreciated
good wine,' confirmed Pat, though he did not consider himself an
expert. Alan Newsome confirmed that Lyons took a considerable
interest in good wines and laid down a fine collection in the cellars at
Wappenbury Hall. His drinking, however, was always in moderation.

Jaguar was no more prone to dishonesty or corruption than other
motor manufacturers – probably much less, in fact – but an event at
the start of 1965 undoubtedly shocked and saddened Lyons.

John Silver, the Production Director he regarded so highly, had
been foolish enough to have accepted inducements from one of
Jaguar's contractors. For example, Silver had not paid for the
installation of central heating at his house. There was a police
prosecution and, at a board meeting in early January, Lyons said the
company's solicitor recommended the termination of Silver's
directorship. Lyons spoke of the adverse publicity that had arisen
during the court hearing. After long discussion it was decided that
the directorship should be terminated at the earliest possible date.

Lyons went on to speak of his determination that no such situation
would occur again. A letter was to be sent to all suppliers and
contractors making it clear that no employees were permitted to
receive any gifts or favours and that a suitable notice would be
displayed in the works prohibiting any work other than to official
company orders.

On 19 January Silver resigned. It had been his 53rd birthday just
a week before and his expertise would be missed. Bernard Hewitt
commented: 'I liked John Silver but I hadn't got any sympathy.

The court dealt with him very severely. We were absolutely flabbergasted because other people were getting away with it quite lightly and the judge said, "An example must be set". I know that when it happened, Silver went to Sir William and I understand Sir William said, "I'm sorry, Silver, I can't help you".[1] In fact, Lyons had felt betrayed by Silver.

Another area of concern was the manufacture of the Cummins engines. As the British operation was not up and running, the possibility of having them made by Krupp in Germany was investigated. In early April Mr de Jong of the Guy Motors continental office wrote: 'You will understand no doubt that the general assumption is that any Vee engine fitted to Big J vehicles will be of British manufacture but in the beginning American engines may have to be used... I am afraid the position in Europe, where Krupp's reputation as engine manufacturers has never been too good, is rather different. Keeping it secret seems a dubious matter. If it would ever become known...our reputation is likely to be very seriously shaken.'

On 13 April Lyons sent a telegram to the Cummins Engine Co in the US: 'Thank you very much for your cable. We also look forward and share your enthusiasm for the success of our joint undertaking and assure you of our wholehearted effort to make it so.' A fortnight later the agreement was signed. A joint company, Jaguar-Cummins Ltd, was formed with capital subscribed in equal shares. Investment of £2.5m was planned, giving production of 50 engines per day with a workforce of 1,000. Production was to be built up in stages; first using imported components to make engines, with imported content being reduced over two years.

That the omens were not good, however, was indicated by a letter R. S. Crouch, Guy's Sales Manager, wrote to Cummins in June stating that Sunderland Corporation Transport Department, having run a Daimler Fleetline demonstration bus fitted with a Cummins V6 engine, 'were not happy with the consumption and engine was rough and noisy when idling'.

There were also disagreements between Jaguar and Cummins over a site for the joint venture, nor were Jaguar happy with what were termed 'design changes' to the engines by Cummins. The relationship was clearly not developing as had been hoped and would never come to fruition as intended.

In June a tiny incident occurred that would mushroom into one of the few really major strikes in the company's history. The inspection department found three window frames to be below the agreed standard and returned them to the three polishers responsible. One did the rectification, which was part of his piecework operation and took three minutes, but the others refused, saying they should be paid extra. The company refused discussions until work was resumed so the operators walked out and 2,500 other workers had to be sent home.

Five days later Lyons drafted (but did not issue) a letter to all manual workers. 'I have for some time been reluctantly compelled to accept the view that the workpeople in our industry have no interest other than that which affects their wage packet at the end of the week.' He added that if the company had to go on short time or close down, other companies might be in a similar position and unable to offer work. Strikes had already cost Jaguar over £600,000 that year.

The *Coventry Evening Telegraph* recorded that Jaguar would make no reply to the unions, which said they were keen to return to work but wanted assurances. The company line was that it had nothing to add and nothing to discuss until work was resumed.

Lyons received letters from American distributors and Jo Eerdmans all saying it was disastrous news about the strike. They had no cars. They were facing ruin and their dealers would be forced to take up other franchises. This was the ideal time for selling cars and they desperately needed the 4.2 E-type in particular.

Some three weeks after the incident that sparked it all, Jaguar took the highly innovative step of placing full-page advertisements in various Midland newspapers. Entitled 'THE STRIKE AT JAGUAR', the page was split into three sections which were headed (from the top) The Accusations, The Facts, and The Features. Each of the three accusations was comprehensively demolished.

Next day a large feature in the *Birmingham Post* was entitled 'SIR WILLIAM TAKES OFF THE KID GLOVES'. 'During the unhappy post-war history of labour relations in the motor industry, says our Industrial Editor, too many manufacturers have let their case go by default. Now one of them is setting an example for the less bold to follow.' The article stated that industrial history had been made the previous day with the advertisements. It mentioned that the statement was anonymous 'but no one who knows anything about Jaguar could possibly doubt that every word of it was carefully studied and finally passed by the man who created Jaguar – Sir William Lyons. In its meticulous phrasing, in its rigid adherence to the letter and spirit of agreements and its final uncompromisingly tough sentence – "It must be understood that the company now feels compelled to take such steps as it may consider necessary to protect its interests" – the statement reflects Sir William's attitude to business and to life.'

The article noted that Lyons had always had strong views about honouring agreements and quoted him on the theme in 1961, 1962 and 1963 to show his consistency. Concluding that too many manufacturers had been, in effect, feeble and weak principled, it stated: 'It may not be the least of Sir William Lyons's services to the industry that he has set a pattern for less bold spirits to imitate.'

After five weeks the Ministry of Labour intervened and recommended an immediate resumption of work, pending discussions. Thus the whole matter petered out with over £5m production lost and £600,000 forfeited in wages by the employees.

Thanking the Ministry of Labour for its help, Lyons wrote: 'we believe that concessions under duress are the cause of a great deal of trouble in industry today, which is having a materially adverse effect on productivity and our efficiency to compete in world markets.'

He also wrote to George Woodcock, General Secretary of the TUC, emphasising 'the tremendous hardship' imposed on 'manufacturers of the goods on which our country depends for its very existence as a successful exporter...due to the failure of the trade unions to enforce its members to conform to National Agreements.'

Lyons had in his private papers at home a newspaper cutting, which wrote of the setting up of a Royal Commission on trade unions and employers' organisations. Ron Smith, General Secretary of the Union of Post Office Workers, stated that this was the last chance for the labour movement to put its house in order voluntarily. Lyons circled a paragraph, which quoted Smith as saying there were too many inter-union rivalries and demarcation disputes in British industry.

Thanks to the strike, 1964–5 turnover was up only three per cent which was less than inflation. Profit was static, with inflation at five per cent that year, and stock and work in progress were up by 17 per cent and now 37 per cent of turnover. Cash was down and, thanks to the overdrafts of subsidiary companies, the group was now £361,051 in the red. There appeared to be little investment. However, despite the strike, production for the 1965 calendar year was another record, at 26,905 cars. The S-type had had its best year at 9,741 cars, the Mk 2 range augmented by the Daimler version reached 8,277 cars, while over 5,000 E-types and 3,000 Mk Xs were made.

During 1965 Alan Currie and Lyons made a journey together. 'We were sitting in the back of an aircraft, and...got down to a very serious discussion about our suppliers – SU, Pressed Steel – and our franchise set-up – distributors, dealers, overseas, who represented us and what were their other interests. Basically, he said he couldn't stand Stokes but in view of the fact that there were only going to be four or five motor manufacturers in a few years time, we had got to get together...

'He liked Harriman, he'd like to get tied in with him, because apart from anything else he made the bodies, the carburettors and so forth. What was impressive was how far ahead he was looking. I don't think many people were saying, in the sixties, that the motor industry would compose of four or five [companies] Europewide, or worldwide.'[2] Indeed, Lyons had been predicting there would be a coming-together of British motor manufacturers since at least the 1950s.

This was a period of some indecision in Jaguar product planning. As we have seen, there were thoughts of four-seater versions of the E-type to tap other, and larger, markets. In essence, the small saloons had now been in production for ten years but, supplemented by the S-type, demand was holding up well. The four-seater E-type design was gradually metamorphosing into what would be the XJ6 but it would be another three years before this finally made its appearance.

'It took a long time to come out,' said Jo Eerdmans of the XJ6. 'We had a big distributors' meeting in New York with Lyons, and then in London. We told him what type of a car we wanted, and brought photographs of Buicks and other cars, and told him what we liked on each car. We told him what was the ideal car we would like from Jaguar. So then they designed the XJ6. If they could have done it a little quicker, we would have had a far bigger part of the market.'[3] Most appropriately, in late 1965, Johannes Eerdmans was made an Honorary CBE for his services to Anglo-American friendship and understanding.

The postponement of the XJ6 launch provoked Lyons into taking sudden action during the autumn of 1965. 'Sir William had hoped that sales of the S-type would be good enough to keep production up to the required level until the introduction of the new car,' recorded 'Lofty' England, 'but with that date put back one year he was watching the situation closely.

'I well remember going to the 1965 Motor Show at Earls Court where we were again showing the S-type, and on the second day Sir William said to me, "There is not enough interest being shown in the S-type – we must do something quickly". So next day he went back to Coventry for one day and got the styling of the 420 started...'[4]

Such was Jaguar's product planning in the mid-1960s: no

committees on advanced concepts, no feasibility studies, no market research consultants, no customer clinics. Lyons could decide that a new model was wanted one day and start on its design literally the next. On paper it was a hopeless and chaotic way of managing, yet – in those circumstances and with that team – it usually worked.

Thanks, that is, to the troops in the trenches. Bob Knight had the nightmare job of managing what was to be the 420 project – Lyons's vision of an S-type with a Mk X type front end and the 4.2-litre (258cu in) engine. Lyons told Pressed Steel Fisher (as the body manufacturer had become within BMC) he wanted it by the following July. PSF was horrified, Bob Knight recalled: 'They said it was quite impossible as there were not even any drawings at this stage, simply a mock up. He said, "If you are not prepared to do it in seven months, I will have the first 2000 made by hand." They agreed to do it.'[5] So 1965 ended even more frantically than usual.

The year 1966 was to prove a momentous one in Jaguar's history and Lyons would face the biggest decision of his career. Now in his mid-sixties, he had carried all the worries and pressures virtually alone for so long. Only his great love of 'the business', and above all, 'his' business, had kept him going. But could it last?

A letter written at this time to Andrew Wenzel, retiring Chief Executive of Firestone, suggested that Lyons was envious of someone about to take it easier: 'What a lucky man you are to be freed from responsibilities [and] the trials and troubles of today...'

Perhaps Lyons should have made life easier for himself by finally distancing himself from the routine of the business but the habit of a lifetime was not easily discarded and he was still consulted on detail matters to an extraordinary level. 'I think he was very interested in detail, almost too much so...' said Morgan. Lyons and 'Lofty' 'took too much notice of little matters' instead of using a broad brush and leaving 'the managers to deal with the detail.'[6]

For instance, in September 1966 England sent Lyons a memo marked Urgent: 'Will you please take a look at the 420G (Mark X) in the Final Line area which is fitted with fluted valve covers. YOUR APPROVAL IS URGENTLY REQUIRED.'

Tom Jones explained: 'Even a switch in Sir William's day had to have his personal approval. Anything visual on a car had to be OK'd by him. If he saw something he didn't recognise on a car on the track [the production line], he'd say, "Where's that come from?"'[7]

Lyons was certainly aware of weaknesses in other parts of Jaguar as can be seen from a memo he sent Heynes on 12 February 1966, about the way the whole engineering department was proceeding and the need for drastic improvement. He did not pull any punches. Because of delays at Jaguar, Pressed Steel would have to postpone the XJ6 programme again – 'an indictment against our engineering capabilities,' he wrote – which would in turn disturb PSF's programme. 'We shall be called upon to meet very substantial excess costs resultant from their changed programme.' Lyons referred Heynes to his note of 8 December 1964, which had stated: 'I have given considerable thought to the very unsatisfactory manner in which our organisation is operating...the almost chaotic state...[is] entirely due to our inability to introduce a new model into production within many months of the target dates... It is vital to our future that steps are taken to correct this critical state of affairs.'

In addition to work on future models, Lyons continued, engineering staff had to deal with problems on current models, creating 'a vicious circle which must be broken. We have failed because we have believed that we have no suitable people within our Engineering Division to whom responsibility can be entrusted... these people will HAVE to be found if Jaguar Cars is to continue to be a successful company...'

The supply departments were hampered by late releases and multiplicity of units. 'Initial design and development must come under the control of two different teams, one concentrating on design and the other on development. They must be given responsibility and not held up by waiting for decisions from above.' He accepted mistakes would be made but stated: 'In this way projects can be stepped up, and although it may mean some of them will have to be discarded, the full time of the design team will be employed on producing something new...a tremendous amount of brain power and time is wasted as we are operating today.'

He said it was essential to have a forward programme which would also assist in 'the commonising of components, and generally in the rationalisation of specifications, thus dealing with the problem of multiplicity of components which is such a handicap to our production'. Lyons conceded that since writing the December memo, some changes had been made, such as extending Bob Knight's responsibilities; yet schedules were slipping again and 'we are quite obviously now going to have little time for XJ.4 [XJ6] development.

'I am sure you must agree that it is imperative we should once again have a new look at our design organisation. It must be obvious to you, as it is to me, that the lack of regard to the time factor cannot do other than result in calamity at some time in the future.'

One delayed model, the E-type 2+2, was duly introduced in March 1966, after many false starts over the preceding five years. It gave the car a 'family' appeal and would sell well, particularly in the US, but the shape was compromised. 'He didn't like the 2+2,' stated Mary, who recalled he used the same description he had applied to the original SS1: 'He said it looked like a conning tower!'[8]

In late February Lyons had told Grice that it was imperative Jaguar acquainted the US dealers with the true situation: '...if deliveries are going to be poor they may wish to cancel all their publicity and announcement arrangements for the new [2+2] model... I have informed Mr Eerdmans quite frankly that the position is very black, because the present indications are that piece work negotiations will not be resolved for a long time because we have no intention of making concessions which will force up still further already high earnings which are so largely responsible for the fact that the American business is almost unprofitable to us... Fortunately, Mr Eerdmans appreciates this position, but he does insist that we let him know one way or the other about deliveries by the 2 March...'

Lyons was in New York by 4 April. The 2+2 had been well received at the Show there and next day England cabled to say the factory was increasing 2+2 production to meet demand. Production had reached 80 a week and should be 120 by 20 May. However, in late May Lyons was told that the increased E-type output would not be achieved due to a shortage of bodies because of a delay in agreeing rates on metal finishing 'after weeks of negotiation and operator resistance' and 'the engagement of additional labour in the Body Shop to meet demand has been blocked by the Shop Floor...' In June, Lyons took a 2+2 home. He found it generally acceptable apart from the transmission and a lot of wind noise. 'I think it imperative that new cars are continually checked, and I propose to take a car home at least once a week...'

At a board meeting in February 1966 Lyons had announced his intention of holding board meetings more regularly. In March, F. R. W. England and R. W. Grice were appointed Deputy Managing Directors and Leonard Lee and Ralph Lockwood (a partner of Haworth, the auditors) became directors; five executive directors were also appointed. On 10 May Alan Newsome was appointed a director. For many years he had been, and would be, a trusted advisor and also a personal friend. 'He would do nothing without Newsome,' said John Morgan. ' I used to have to go down and tell him about things we were doing the other side of the world. It just made Sir William feel better that the man he trusted knew about these things.'[9] As life became ever more complicated at Jaguar, this source of advice would be an ever greater comfort.

The question of a return to motor racing had resurfaced. Bob Knight recollected a conversation, the gist of which was that Heynes could build a Le Mans contender if Lyons could have a new limousine![10] The latter became the Daimler DS420 of 1968, a car much loved by the 'carriage trade' and even royalty. Just one XJ13 mid-engined sports racing car was built, in great secrecy.

Berry sent a memo to Lyons recommending keeping the car under wraps. Lyons then wrote to Heynes: 'Until a definite policy is decided regarding the XJ.13, will you please ensure that in no circumstances does it leave the shop'.[11] It did, of course; Norman Dewis tested it at MIRA and was subsequently carpeted by Lyons, who then proceeded to ask anxiously how the car had performed!

Bob Berry put together the arguments for and against a return to racing. He acknowledged that Jaguar owed its fame to racing, that it badly needed an image boost, and that employee morale would benefit. Against that he suggested that competition was far greater now, so it would have to be much better planned and professionally executed than in the past, and that advertising any success would cost as much as the racing programme itself due to the British success prevalent in Formula 1. Above all, he stated that the greater priority was to concentrate the engineering staff on creating the next generation of production cars.

Lyons arranged a meeting of senior personnel to discuss the question. Matters to be resolved included the fact that 'we must be satisfied that our new car programmes, which are already seriously behind schedule, do not suffer in any way. This is a most crucial matter and must be fully and satisfactorily resolved before any racing programme can be undertaken.'

On the engine front, Hassan, Baily, and Mundy (under Heynes) had been working on Jaguar's first new engine since the XK was launched in 1948. With racing, production cars, and technical prestige in mind, it was to be a V12, to be launched in the forthcoming XJ saloon.

In late June Lyons put together a four-page document setting out the matters for discussion at a model and engine meeting. He stated that the home market must always come first and a car of S-type dimensions was the most popular in its class. Thus it was hoped that the XJ, in both two- and four-door forms, would be ideal. He discussed a possible smaller sports saloon but said the XK engine was physically too large and the Daimler V8 would be more suitable.

As to engines, he felt the XJ with the 3-litre engine was feeble and that the performance must be 'noticeably better' than the 3.8 Mk 2. Therefore the larger XK engine had to be fitted, as they could not rely solely on the V12. Also he felt it was essential that a derivative engine, either V8 or slant six, should be able to be produced from the V12 tooling, which involved a 'considerable expenditure'.

Elsewhere, inexorable external forces were moving that would alter Jaguar's entire future.

Before going into detail of how Jaguar and the British Motor Corporation came together, it is worth examining the background. Postwar, the smaller motor manufacturers were increasingly aware of how dependent they were on their body suppliers. Ford had taken over Briggs Bodies and then declined to make a new body for Jowett, effectively forcing that small specialist company out of business – Bob Berry recalled this made a deep impression on Lyons.

Then also in the early 1950s BMC (formed from the merger of Austin and Morris in 1952) acquired body supplier Fisher and Ludlow, which had provided bodies for Standard-Triumph as well as for BMC. Subsequently, Leonard Lord of BMC refused to supply bodies when Standard-Triumph wanted to produce the Triumph Herald, causing the firm severe difficulties.

So it was of tremendous significance to Jaguar when, during 1965, BMC had acquired the other major body supplier, Pressed Steel, which made Jaguar's bodies. Lyons now became seriously concerned about his future supplies, especially as BMC work at Pressed Steel began to be given ever-greater precedence over Jaguar's much smaller requirements.

Additionally, the consolidation of the British motor industry, predicted long ago by Lyons, had been proceeding apace. In 1960 Standard-Triumph had fallen victim to a takeover by an aggressive and expanding truck manufacturer – Leyland, which had bought Albion and Scammell, then wanted to diversify into car manufacture and had seen the vulnerable Standard-Triumph concern as the route. Then in 1964 the Rootes Group was sold (to Chrysler) and it seemed that the whole British motor industry was going to end up in the hands of just a few players; so, to Lyons, Jaguar's long-term viability as an independent specialist producer must have appeared in doubt. George Harriman, who became Chairman of BMC after Len Lord retired in 1962, is credited with conceiving the 'grand design' for the British motor industry: a merger of the British Motor Corporation with Leyland, Rover and Jaguar.

Talks began between BMC and Leyland in the summer of 1964 but

Harriman was by then also in discussion with Lyons, who appeared happy with the idea of a merger involving Jaguar, provided that he retained executive control. 'Lyons had previously been wooed, at one time or another, by just about everybody – Sir John Black of Standard, Lord Hives of Rolls-Royce and Spurrier [of Leyland], who had been an old friend,' recorded Graham Turner in his book *The Leyland Papers* – which gives the best account to date of the machinations that were to result in the British Leyland Motor Corporation.

According to Bill Heynes, Lyons respected Spurrier and he thought that Lyons would have voluntarily joined up with Leyland had Spurrier not retired in 1963. After all, John Lyons had served his apprenticeship at Leyland, which was also a major supplier to Jaguar of XK engine castings. As recorded, the two companies had worked together briefly in the US in the 1950s when Donald Stokes had been Sales Director. Now, at 52, Sir Donald Stokes (he had been knighted in 1965) was the Leyland Motor Corporation's Chief Executive. Lyons, however, described Stokes to Heynes as being 'only a salesman',[12] not a manufacturer. From the start it appears there was little empathy between the two men.

Nevertheless, in 1965 Lyons met with Sir William Black (then Chairman of Leyland and another old friend) and Stokes. The proposal was that Lyons would run the entire car business but the downside was that he would lose overall control of Jaguar. This was not acceptable to Lyons and, as a result, Leyland decided to pursue Rover instead.

Then Harriman approached Lyons in 1966. He offered to buy Jaguar, in which Lyons held 54 per cent of the voting shares (260,000 out of 450,000), but would let Lyons retain operational control. On 17 May 1966 a letter was sent on Lyons's behalf to John Pears, the senior partner of Cooper Brothers, BMC's accountants. This stated that the Chairman was 'keenly interested in the mergers of the leading British companies to combat the overseas giants' and financial gain was of less importance. Nevertheless he valued the Jaguar shares at 50s (£2.50), which Pears considered 'highly excessive'.

At the same time, discussions were held between BMC and Leyland with a view to forming a joint holding company and then acquiring Jaguar. However, Joe Edwards, the recently appointed Managing Director of BMC, having held the same position at Pressed Steel, was not prepared to be number three to Harriman and Stokes; Stokes was not willing to share number two position with Edwards. Negotiations ceased and BMC lost its chance to be the major partner.

BMC then moved quickly to firm up the matters already in progress with Lyons. On 6 July it decided to make an offer that was close to Lyons's price and Pears found himself advising both sides as, according to Graham Turner, neither side trusted merchant bankers. Keen to wrap matters up, Harriman and his Finance Director, Ron Lucas, drove to the Browns Lane plant, entering by a back gate. They saw Lyons and agreed terms. The final figure was 38s (£1.90) per share.

A Jaguar board meeting was held on 11 July to discuss the BMC/Jaguar merger. Lyons recalled a previous discussion on this subject, which had taken place after the board meeting of 24 February. For the benefit of the new directors, he recounted the circumstances leading to his talks with the Chairman of the BMC, the progress made during their discussions and the final conclusions, which they mutually agreed.

Later that day, a press conference was held at the Great Eastern Hotel, Liverpool Street, London. There Lyons and Harriman jointly announced that the 'Jaguar Group of companies is to merge with The British Motor Corporation Ltd., as the first step towards the setting up of a joint holding company to be called British Motor (Holdings) Limited'. This would comprise BMC, Jaguar, and Pressed Steel. 'The Chairman will be Sir George Harriman with Sir William Lyons as a director. Jaguar Cars Ltd. will continue to operate as a separate entity and with the greatest practical degree of autonomy under the chairmanship of Sir William Lyons.'

Harriman emphasised that he and Lyons regarded the merger as a 'joining of forces'. He continued: 'Finally, I would like to say…how thoroughly gentlemanly and how, dare I say, British has been the co-operation and the frankness of the discussions which Sir William and I have had over the past weeks to enable this merger, shall I call it, or joining of forces, to have the success it has today.' Lyons added it was something they had talked about for a very long time. He had had some reluctance but had convinced himself it was in the best interests of Jaguar.

To questions, Lyons replied that he and his family trust owned over 50 per cent of the ordinary shares. That did not include the non-voting 'A' shares. When pressed on the proportion of these shares that he held, Lyons said that he had no idea because his only concern had been to retain a controlling interest 'to avoid being taken over by an American company.' This provoked some laughter.

It was stated that BMC had 42–44 per cent of the UK market, Jaguar 1–2 per cent. BMC capacity was 20,000 vehicles a week,

Jaguar 600 cars. BMC employed 120,000 worldwide. Lyons was not sure how many Jaguar employed but thought it was 12,000 worldwide. The UK market shares given were exaggerated: BMC in 1965–6 held little more than 35 per cent of the car market (this later dropped below 30 per cent) and Jaguar's best figure was 1.25 per cent in 1967 (SMMT figures). Production of Jaguar and Daimler cars was fairly static throughout the 1960s, averaging little more than 24,000 cars per year and, after a peak of 26,905 in 1965, actually declined in 1966–7 (calendar year statistics, JDHT archive).

After being pressed, Harriman said Schroder Wragg and Cooper Brothers had advised BMC. Lyons, perhaps crucially, had not retained advisors. Harriman was asked if increasing market share to over 50 per cent would involve joining forces with anyone else. He did not think so! Lucas stated the total value of the offer was £18.2m. Harriman, having said that existing dealers and distributors would be unaffected, was asked if there would be rationalisation once those contracts ran out. 'No, no. No rationalisation,' he answered. A questioner stated it was understood Lyons was one of the highest paid executives in the land. Would this remain so? He replied: 'I have not given it a thought.'

In concluding, Harriman again stressed twice that it was a joining of forces and said it would be the largest wholly owned British company. Lyons concluded by saying it had been done 'because I believe it is the right thing to do. There are no potential implications of any kind. This is just what is wanted to put the British motor industry in a position to compete abroad.'

The deal was done by BMC issuing shares and loan stock but effectively BMC paid £17,485,027, of which Lyons himself received only £1.7m, as he had sold or transferred over 3.5 million non-voting shares – though it is likely a good proportion had gone into his charitable/family trusts.

On the day of the merger, Lyons wrote to various Jaguar group executives. 'I am taking the earliest possible opportunity of advising you of a development which will be of immense benefit to the entire Jaguar Group, namely that after lengthy and cordial discussions with Sir George Harriman, we have mutually agreed to a merger of our two organisations... I am sure you will agree that this is a far-sighted and wise move, and I am sure that I can continue to count on your loyalty and service.'

Apart from his concerns about ongoing body supplies and the trend towards automotive giants, what else influenced Lyons in his decision to join forces with BMC?

One reason was undoubtedly that he was very friendly with Harriman and respected Edwards, according to Berry. Lyons was given assurances, and believed them, that he would remain his own boss. He, perhaps naively, saw it as a genuine amalgamation or merger of equals, rather than a takeover. However, there was another factor, as daughter Mary explained: 'I think my father was a stronger character than George Harriman. There was no question that he [Lyons] wouldn't be in complete control. George Harriman would not have been capable of standing up to my father.'[13]

Then there was the simple fact of his age: Lyons was 64 and moreover was not in good health – those awful headaches were continuing and the pressures, if anything, were growing with seemingly no end in sight to labour disputes and punitive taxation. Greta was pressing her husband to, as Mary put it, 'let go, let go...'

Above all Lyons's decision can be traced back to the fatal accident in 1955. Certainly that is what his farm manager of 25 years standing, Bob Robinson, believed: 'If his son had lived, nobody would ever have got Jaguar. He told me that many times.'[14]

Had John lived – and proved capable of managing the business in the face of all the same problems, which was by no means certain – it is quite possible that Lyons would have sanctioned Jaguar establishing its own body shop. That was something Bob Berry was keen on, though he was realistic in acknowledging that Jaguar was getting far more than just bodies from Pressed Steel, which was contributing much expertise too. The body shop proposition featured in family discussions at this time; it would have been costly and not without risk but Jaguar's lack of borrowings and its assets meant that raising money from the City would not have been difficult.

As it was, with no John to help, 'I think my father just felt too old to embark on such a project,' said Mary. She also considered that after John's death 'he should have been looking for a John Egan, but he only looked towards his own organisation... A lot of his ideas were 100 per cent and 30 years ahead of his time, but basically he was too old to go on doing it, and he just couldn't bring himself to head hunt somebody else.'[15] Poaching people went against the grain for Lyons, ever since he 'stole' that sheet metalworker back in the Swallow days. Finally, the lack of a successor had come home to roost.

Lyons received letters both for and against the merger. One long-standing Jaguar dealer expressed his disappointment that Lyons had chosen BMC rather than Leyland. Another dealer, Lyons's old friend Sam Newsome, wrote to congratulate him on 'a very wise and clever decision' and added that 'BMC should be congratulated equally on an acquisition...' One senses that, good friend though Newsome was, Lyons would not have appreciated the word 'acquisition'! So even some of Lyons's friends misunderstood the situation; or perhaps more precisely, they didn't and he did.

The financial press was less than ecstatic at the 38s (£1.90) share price. One newspaper wrote: '...it is hardly the glittering prize which would have justified years of hopeful waiting on a 2 per cent or less dividend.' Lyons also received letters from a number of disgruntled shareholders and in late August a Mr Lawton wrote to fellow shareholders saying that consideration was being given to forming a shareholder's committee to oppose the bid. Mary Rimell commented: 'Father had decided the merger would go through – the shareholders were so furious because basically they didn't get a say. That was it. Father had made up his mind...'

To another correspondent, he wrote, 'I note you are somewhat concerned that following the merger with BMC, the cars we produce may lose their identity. However, as you may have seen in the press, it is intended that Jaguar should continue to operate with the greatest possible degree of autonomy.' He also wrote to his old friend and advisor, Dick Hutchinson in Florida. 'I am glad you think our merger with BMC is a very good thing. I believe the British motor industry must get together in order to provide sufficient strength to combat competition and I hope eventually that more will join us.'

The Jaguar financial results were disappointing with 1965–6 group sales up 10 per cent but profits slightly lower (five per cent lower in real terms). Profit in America was a record at £176,000, mainly due to the 47 per cent increase in the number of cars sold there (thanks to the launch of the 2+2 E-type). Coventry Climax profits improved, while Jaguars Cars, Daimler buses and Guy declined. A comparison of pre-tax profits as a percentage of net assets showed Jaguar at 18 per cent was impressively ahead of the motor industry average of just five per cent.

The home market was depressed and although the US distributors had forecast they would take 10,000 cars during the year, Lyons had had to agree to supply the new 420 range at a very low price. He felt total car production should be cut back to 480 cars per week to avoid losses. For the year ending 31 July 1966 exports were 27 per cent higher. Sales to the Common Market were up 21 per cent 'despite the increasingly severe tariff barriers with which exporters are having to contend'.

On 3 August Lyons sent a memo to Whittaker, Heynes, England,

Brown, and Langley informing them that a meeting would be held on 10 August to discuss the practicalities of the merger. 'Although the company will continue to operate autonomously, the objective behind the merger is obviously to implement mutual aid in the best interests of both companies...' Another memo the same day stated that it was 'now essential that we should prepare a realistic programme for the development and introduction of the XJ... This to include completion of the six prototypes, the progress of which is most disappointing.'

Heynes, as requested, gave his views on how the merger should work. He suggested that Jaguar should be responsible for all saloon and sports cars over 3 litres (183cu in). He felt no attempt should be made to integrate chassis layout or engine designs, or styling. The exceptions to this would be items such as gearboxes, axles, overdrive units, and particularly heaters and air-conditioning equipment.

Ever the motor racing enthusiast, Heynes also thought that they should discuss competition work 'to combat Ford supremacy'! However, at the next board meeting Lyons said he considered it would be unwise to proceed with any new motor racing project, pending the exchange of ideas with BMC, and it was decided not to continue the scheme for the time being.

Lyons wrote to thank Harriman for a 'brochure' setting out his thoughts for implementing the merger and said these broadly coincided with their own. 'Some of the items, as I am sure you will agree, are outside our understanding of autonomy...' He said they had in mind that the next step would be a meeting of individual directors with their counterparts. He then listed 20 suggestions for areas of collaboration and discussion.

In late August Lyons wrote a revealing personal letter to Maurice Smith, Editor of *Autocar*, concerning an article in the magazine: 'It is quite untrue that, in the sense described, B.M.C. took over Jaguar, or the inference that Jaguar was in the market without bidders. There was never any question of Jaguar seeking an offer, on the contrary, many approaches had been made, including one from Leylands: earlier there had been Rootes and Rolls Royce. The deal with B.M.C. was done with an agreement that each partner would have full autonomy, and to this end, the holding company B.M.H. was formed, with the intention that it should be an umbrella for the two companies. In the event, entirely due to the tax position, it was found to be sensible for B.M.C. to acquire Jaguar shares, I did not like it very much, but it would have been stupid of me not to have accepted it. You may remember Sir George Harriman trying to make the position clear at the Press meeting at the Great Eastern Hotel, when he stressed "this is not a takeover, it is a get together".' Lyons, privately and publicly, consistently stuck to this view.

On 11 October 1966 the press launch took place of the new 420, the 420G (basically an embroidered Mark X) and Sovereign (a Daimler-radiatored version of the 420) at Kensington Close Hotel. Lyons, in his speech, said that in spite of Government restrictions they were cautiously optimistic.

On 1 November Lyons sent Heynes, England, and Thornton a graph showing the sales of 'pillarless bodies' in America. In 1965 this reached 4,250,993, which was almost double that of four-door sedans, five times that of two-door sedans and station wagons and more than eight times that of convertibles. Thoughts turned to a two-door, pillarless XJ.

In January 1967 there was a shock when BMH's first six months' trading results were announced: they showed a loss of £7.5m after a profit for the same period the previous year of £5.8m. Production was down from 435,750 to 347,179 – the former BMC division had been badly hit both by a three-month strike by delivery drivers and by the credit squeeze, which damaged sales. The poor figures made people at Browns Lane begin to wonder what Lyons had let the company in for.

Clearly, having set his mind on the merger, Lyons had assumed from his knowledge of the group, his trust in George Harriman, and from previously issued figures that BMC had been substantially in good health. This had persuaded him – probably against the advice of friends – not to take the precaution of having the business examined by professional advisors, largely, his daughters believe, because he never liked paying professional fees and would have faced a very large bill for such an investigation.

This lack of what we would now call 'due diligence' was, in Mary Rimell's opinion, 'one of the biggest mistakes he made'. Yet in the years that followed, as the situation deteriorated and his life's work appeared to be near ruin, never once did family, friends, or colleagues hear Lyons complain or attempt to spread the blame. 'I think that at the end of the day he probably realised he should have looked at BMC more,' said Mary. 'He never admitted it to us, but I bet he admitted it to himself. And he was very good at looking at himself very objectively and very honestly, and he wouldn't blame anybody else for something where he knew he'd taken sole decision... OK, he talked to other people about what they thought, but he was the one that made the decision.'[16]

With BMH weakened there was speculation that Leyland, 'smaller and livelier,' would do a reverse takeover or that 'the government, not content with its small stake in one loss-making motor group, Rootes, would take a stake in this one, or in the combined British motor company dreamed of by empire-building politicians,' as one unattributed cutting in Lyons's personal papers put it. 'A rejuvenated BMH could be the share bargain of the decade at 10s. [50p] or below.'

It was stated that for the first time ever Lyons had had to drop his claim that 'we can sell every car we can make'. This had arisen occasionally before but, this time, the fall off in home demand was said to be approaching 30 per cent and a market research survey had shown that one third of potential Jaguar customers were buying cheaper cars. Exports were also struggling with troubles in France, high tariffs in Italy, and recessions in the EFTA countries. 'The result brought Jaguar on to a short spell of three-day working. It's now back to four days but even that is only kept going by a sudden 30 per cent pick-up in shipments to the US.' Credit for this was given to the 420 and the 'four-seater E-type'. Nevertheless, the situation does tend to support the view that Lyons mostly got the balance right and that volume should not be regarded as an end in its own right.

In April, brighter news came when it was announced that Jaguar had won the 1967 Queen's Award to Industry for export achievement. This was based on a substantial rise in exports from 1963 to 1966 and a large increase in export sales proportional to overall sales, which was higher than the industry average. Jaguar was selling into 126 countries.

At February's board meeting, Lyons reported an uplift in car demand, which he thought would continue for six weeks to two months, but recent restrictions imposed on production might present difficulties in raising output. Grice was asked to consider ways of increasing production in spite of the trade unions' embargo on overtime. Lyons then referred to the overdraft, which had increased dramatically, and the cost of this. Steps had to be taken to reduce it. By March it had dropped from £7.60m to £7.47m. Jaguar's pre-tax profits for the six months to March had tumbled to £424,481 or just £217,481 after deducting bank interest.

Nor were the financial results for 1966–7 encouraging. Profits for the Jaguar group were over 50 per cent lower, at £1.2m, and were not helped by Daimler making a loss of over £500,000. Guy contributed a useful £233,000 and the tiny Climax concern, at £405,000, made almost half as much as Jaguar Cars! Net cash was now £3.4m in the red. BMH decided to pay a dividend, in spite of making a massive loss, and so Jaguar had to contribute £900,000 towards this, which hardly helped. Contrary to Lyons's policy of low yield and high retention, BMC paid out 58 per cent of its available earnings in the years 1961–5.

One of the big bugbears for at least two decades had been use of piece-rates to remunerate the workforce. In November Financial Director Arthur Thurstans wrote to colleagues Ball and Jenkins about Lyons's request to have prepared, in broad outline, 'an alternative method of paying our pieceworkers, based on a guaranteed rate per hour'. The general idea was to have a lower basic rate that would be supplemented by a bonus for effort and savings in scrap, rectification, and warranty costs.

On the merger front, Leyland now came back into the picture. Sir William Black of Leyland wrote to Lyons in February: 'George Harriman, Donald Stokes and I were asked to go along this morning to talk to Grierson of the Industrial Reorganisation Corporation. This followed a statement made by the Minister of Technology [Wedgwood Benn] when he announced the Chrysler/Rootes deal, and when he said he was going to try and get the leading British Companies to co-operate in overseas markets, in view of the predominance of the Americans in this sphere.' The IRC was a new Government body, formed to encourage regeneration and amalgamation in British industry, with £150m to spend. Donald Stokes was a founder member of its board.

'We had the usual somewhat ineffective discussion, but I think some good will emerge, because Donald and George Harriman had a heart to heart, which I think will bear fruit, however long delayed.' Lyons replied that he was pleased to hear the discussion between Harriman and Stokes had been 'so encouraging'.

An agenda was drawn up for a product meeting to be held on 1 March. The model range still included a new small Jaguar, which was now illustrated as a shorter 2+2 coupé. This was to be discussed in relation to the Jaguar range but, even more significantly, in relation to the BMC range.

In fact, Heynes and his engineering team were struggling to cope. Apart from the crucial XJ saloon and the two-door pillarless version – aimed at taking advantage of the massive escalation in demand for such models in America (though this would turn out to be a mirage for Jaguar) – there were E-type facelifts, the new limousine, a new family of V12 and V8 engines, the possible small saloon, and a five-speed gearbox to consider.

Just to add to the pressure on the ridiculously small team, there was now a long and ever increasing list of US safety and emissions regulations to satisfy with the existing models. One could argue that Lyons should have been recruiting engineers but – with wildly fluctuating North American demand, a Labour Government inflicting a squeeze that was destroying the home market, a massive overdraft, and a parent in trouble – that was hardly to be contemplated.

In September Heynes had to inform Lyons that Pressed Steel had advised that work on the two-door XJ had now been stopped 'due to other BMC projects of high priority'. It would now be 12–18 months behind delivery of the first XJ saloon. Heynes had made it clear that this was unacceptable as the Americans were not interested in the four-door and the two-door was likely to be the big seller there. 'It appears the programme has been so loaded with the BMC new models, all at a high priority for early delivery.'

Foreman Bill Cassidy glimpsed the human side of Lyons during this time. 'We always used to get a yearly bonus because we weren't paid for any overtime, and I used to do very well on the yearly bonus. Then I had a heart attack in 1967 and I was off work for 26 weeks. It happened over Easter and the day after the holiday, he was in the shop and somebody told him. "Oh," he said, "why wasn't I told?" I was in hospital and the sister came and asked if I knew anybody named Lyons. I replied that he was my boss. Apparently he had been on the phone asking how I was, and every day his secretary rang up. After a while I went back, not to work, but just to have a wander round the factory, and I saw him. Now in those days you only got paid for the first six weeks you were off and then it was up to Lyons. He said to me, "Don't worry about hurrying back and don't worry about your salary". I got paid the whole time I was away. He even said to me, "Are you happy with your treatment? If you're not, I'll send you down to Harley Street." He had been known to send his foremen to Switzerland when they've been ill, for a week's holiday.'[17]

Lyons continued his work at Jaguar at an undiminished rate but all around, or so it must have seemed to him, his contemporaries were taking well-earned retirement. Sir William Black retired and on 17 May Lyons wrote to Sir G. Edward Beharrell of Dunlop: 'How very wise and fortunate you are... I would like to make this an opportunity of thanking you for the great help you have always given to my company. It has always been greatly appreciated. As you know, I have always endeavoured to reciprocate.'

As a result of the BMH merger, in August it was announced that the previous US importers (Jaguar Cars Inc and BMC-Hambro) would be replaced by a new company to be known as British Motor

Holdings (USA) Inc, with Graham Whitehead as President. Jo Eerdmans was at a meeting in the UK soon after the merger and 'Ron Lucas got up and said, "Don't forget Sir William, we did not merge with Jaguar. We bought Jaguar. You are just part and parcel of us, and of course the bosses are the bosses of BMC."[18]

'Then Lucas said, "we want a BMC man to run the business in America."' Eerdmans was 63 and had agreed with Lyons that he would have a pension in the US, could remain on the US board until he died and would be paid a monthly fee. The agreement also stated that Lyons would remain on the US and English boards until he died. So Eerdmans proposed that BMC man 'Graham Whitehead become my successor and take over the whole caboodle in America, as I knew him very well and I thought he could do a damn good job. I said I would help him all I could and that was accepted. I said this was on one condition, that I could remain on the Board, as I had agreed with Lyons, and have my fee. Lucas and the others said this was OK and I asked them to put it in the minutes. Sir William never wanted to put anything in writing. We were old friends and I trusted him completely. But when the company was taken over, things changed. It was a drama!'[19]

Commercial opportunities still presented themselves and Lyons gave most his usual serious consideration. Joe Bamford, of JCB excavator fame, made an approach in the summer of 1967 with a view to a strategic partnership with Climax in the fork-lift truck field. Bamford and his son visited Lyons, showed him some of their products and asked for more details of the Stacatruc and Climax operations. However, Leonard Lee of Climax got to hear about the conversations and, perhaps because of sensitivities there, matters were never taken any further.

The unhappy Cummins venture came to an end in 1967. Cummins accepted 'that the new engine was not a viable proposition for operators in this country. Development had ceased and they were prepared to meet the abnormal expenditure involved in this venture.' It had proved to be an expensive and unfortunate exercise for Jaguar and appears to have badly delayed the resurrection of Daimler and Guy. Cummins agreed to purchase Jaguar's shares in Jaguar-Cummins Ltd for £1 and Jaguar undertook to buy the remaining built up engines, though Lyons refused to pay for the 40 installed in Guy vehicles until they were sold, pointing out that it might be necessary to fit alternative engines. This was very frustrating for Lyons as he had been championing the cause of the Daimler Roadliner single-decker but so far sales had been handicapped by the Cummins engine failures. By March 1969, Cummins agreed to reimburse tooling costs of £131,000.

Lyons went to Italy for the Turin Motor Show in October 1967, and also visited a number of coachbuilders, including Bertone and Pininfarina. John Morgan joined him. 'During the visit to Bertone, he said, "You know, if I was twenty-five years younger, I wouldn't be building motor cars. I would be doing this. This is wonderful." At that time Bertone was building a few thousand Spyders. It was just what he liked doing.

'I'll never forget when he was with Sergio Farina, they were looking at the Austin Maxi and it looked dreadful. He was saying, he didn't know what to do with it. "They won't let me do anything. They want me to use the doors from this and the doors from that." Then Sir William said, "Let's have a look" and the two of them went to work with strips of silver paper on the top of the roofline and that sort of thing. And they were having a lovely time. They were totally immersed and I stood back and watched. I had never seen him work before.'[20]

In December Berry made a survey of the use the press was making of the title BMH. He felt it had largely been used as the new identity of BMC. Although motoring journalists knew the difference, labour, industrial, and city journalists did not and thought of Jaguar as a subsidiary of BMC, and BMH as BMC in another guise. The initials were too similar. He reminded Lyons of his strong opposition the previous year on those grounds. He suggested that BMH needed an identity, to be promoted, and have its own channel of communication. On occasions Jaguar matters had been handled by BMC people and caused Jaguar great embarrassment. 'For several years Jaguar has successfully avoided or deflected firmly and politely all enquiries about our multi-cylinder engines. It falls to BMC to confirm not only the existence of a V12, but also to provide gratuitous and negative information that the Jaguar V12 engine had been tested but no decision made as to its potential.' Then when Harriman was given a briefing note for the BMH AGM, the suggested answer to the anticipated question 'How have BMC's results been affected by the acquisition of Jaguar?' was 'The acquisition of Jaguar proved to be a worthwhile investment'. The use of the word 'acquisition' was rather different from the language of a year earlier.

Lyons was still keeping in personal touch with his old-established overseas distributors and in September wrote to Jack Bryson in Australia, who had had a difficult year, saying that he was optimistic about the future.

In the autumn, Lyons told the board he expected the recent price reductions of the Mk 2 and S-type to result in improved demand. Sales of the 420 were good and he hoped a reasonable volume would be maintained until the introduction of the XJ model. However, an analysis of US sales for 1967 showed that Mercedes-Benz was now selling almost four times as many cars there as Jaguar and even Porsche sold about 20 per cent more.

In fact Mercedes-Benz total production for 1967 was 200,414; Jaguar was a minnow by comparison, producing just 21,961 cars that year. Even BMW had now left Jaguar far behind with a 1967 total of 87,816 – the Bavarian company had overtaken Jaguar way back in 1955, when it had made 17,478 vehicles against Jaguar's 10,868.

At the end of year board meeting, Lyons stated that, following the Earls Court Show, trade had improved and production was now being built up to 485 and later 555 cars per week. He said the recent Government measures of devaluation and tax impositions had added to the difficulties but XJ production was now planned for March 1968, with sales starting in July. Investigations were continuing on a two-door model. The E-type continued to be popular and would be retained in the range, though probably with changes to the bodywork.

At the first board meeting of 1967, the Chairman broached (seemingly for the first time at this level) the question of successions in the higher management of the company. He felt they should be providing for, or even nominating, successors and there were a number of talented men whom he would like to see developed and encouraged. Now almost 12 months later, Lyons's thoughts on the future had crystallised. 'With the appointment of Mr England and Mr Grice as Deputy Managing Directors in March, 1966, there was an intention that they should, in time, relieve me as Managing Director, as it is my sincere desire that the management of the company shall be in competent hands before the time comes for my complete retirement. (I am now 66.)'

England and Grice were appointed Joint Managing Directors from January 1968 but Lyons made it clear he was to continue as Chairman and Chief Executive. Whittaker, who was in poor health, gave up his executive role but had asked to remain a director and non-executive Deputy Chairman. Following BMH practice, the Jaguar directors would in future have a fixed salary rather than salary and commission.

Staff salaries were about to change too because salaries determined which grade of restaurant staff ate in and Jaguar grades were near the bottom. 'Until we joined BMH, none of us got a decent salary,' said Morgan. 'I was hauled in with Bob Berry and Alan Currie and we were told we were going to be upgraded. Then I was allowed to talk to the Export Director of BMC and dine with him, and use his lavatory!'[21]

'Lofty' England once described a typical Jaguar job as: 'You worked seven days a week, 24 hours a day, for nothing!'[22] This was true for those not on the old profit-sharing scheme, certainly. On the other hand, Jaguar had always offered a special excitement that made up for a relatively meagre pay packet, as Bob Berry explained: 'You never really thought about it – there was so much going on, there was never a dull moment. You couldn't wait to get into work in the morning because something interesting was going to happen. And it was extraordinary, the feeling it gave you. You either enjoyed working at Jaguar or you didn't... But very, very few people left.'[23]

However, that board meeting did nothing to truly solve the succession issue. Neither England nor Grice were that much younger than Lyons, yet there was still no talk of recruiting from the outside. Bob Berry put it this way: 'There was nobody at Jaguar that could run Jaguar in a different way to that which had been taught them by Sir William.'[24] That was the very reason Lyons gave for choosing England over an outsider...

CHAPTER 10

THE LEYLAND
FACTOR

By 1968 it could be argued that Jaguar was losing its way. The products were still good and popular but the range was sprawling and mostly ageing. In 1967 production was less than 22,000 cars; the newest models, the 420/Sovereign twins, reached 7,722 and the Mk 2 range still achieved 6,432 but the S-type was dying on its feet with production of just 1,008, many of which were sold as police cars. The 420G, at 1,640, had its niche but its market had shrunk dramatically; the E-type at 4,989 was down almost 2,000 from 1966.

Though it might be claimed that the wide range of saloons catered for every sector of their market, this was not quite so. With so many models made in such small volumes, the manufacturing challenge was a nightmare, while the dealers must have cursed the lack of new product. Lyons needed to address the situation. However, no longer could he decide at a motor show what was required and go away and build it; his freedom of movement was now heavily constrained by his 'partner', the former BMC. These constraints would get worse and the result was to be a violent swing from a multiplicity of saloons to, essentially, just one – the XJ6, which was slowly coming to fruition.

Before that new car arrived on the market there was to be a dramatic intervention by yet another partner. The seeds of the merger between BMH and Leyland had been sown over a period of several years but germination was proving to be a problem, due in part to a clash of personalities. However, in 1967 the highly interventionist Labour Government under Harold Wilson felt under pressure because of Chrysler's takeover of the Rootes Group. Government talks with Stokes and Harriman with a view to Leyland and BMH staging a joint rescue attempt of Rootes had come to nothing. In October 1967 the Prime Minister invited Stokes and Harriman to dinner at Chequers, where political pressure was brought to bear. Both men agreed in principle to a merger, 'in the national interest'.[1]

The Industrial Reorganisation Corporation offered an inducement in the form of a £25m loan and that November a merger, on a 50/50 basis with the adoption of immediate central planning, was agreed in principle. On independent advice from merchant bankers the possibility of a holding company had already been ruled out. Ominously, on 14 December Stokes made it clear to Harriman that, amongst other things, he did not favour fully autonomous subsidiaries.

During the protracted negotiations the financial position of BMH worsened to such an extent that Stokes and Leyland seriously considered pulling out and possibly launching a hostile takeover for BMH. However, a deal was finally struck, representing a clear victory for Leyland. On 17 January 1968 the merger was announced.

That day the two boards held a meeting and a document was produced entitled Principles of Management and Organisation. It had several ominous sounding clauses. 'The company will operate as a single integrated company and not as a holding company with autonomous subsidiaries... The subsidiaries of both the present parent companies will largely disappear as operating units and will be reorganised into divisions of the integrated company. This will not necessarily mean the disappearance of long established names such as AEC, Austin, MG, Morris, Triumph and others – many of these will be retained in the market as distinct model names...[but] parallel ranges of cars with different badges would not be continued.'[2]

A shareholders' meeting was called for 25 March to ratify the agreement, which would become effective on 13 May. Meanwhile it was decided to hold a 'dummy' board meeting on Monday 12 February. It was not a pleasant meeting and there was considerable friction between the two sides. Lyons's notes in his own hand make fascinating reading: 'Whilst the BMH board has full regard for the image which Sir Donald Stokes has built up as a very successful exporter of commercial vehicles... Sir Donald has not in the opinion of the BMH board the expertise to virtually go it alone.' In the meeting, Lyons expressed his concern that Jaguar might lose its autonomy and felt, as Chairman, he should remain in control. He was accustomed to operating the company as he thought fit and, though he would collaborate, he did not wish to be questioned about the management of the company or have people visiting the accounts department. No instructions were to be given over his head and he thought it best to make his position clear from the outset. Stokes said it would be imprudent to lose either the individuality of Jaguar or the involvement of Lyons and thus any comments he had to make would be made only to Lyons.[3]

Then a further problem developed. Leyland had been investigating

BMH's financial figures and was not impressed. BMH also drastically revised its predictions and did not feel able to issue a profits forecast. In the evening of Thursday 15 February, a crisis meeting took place at the flat of merchant banker Sir Siegmund Warburg, who had advised Leyland. Stokes felt Leyland should pull out. A crucial deadline was rapidly looming because a decision would have to be made before Leyland's AGM took place the following Tuesday.

Sir Frank Kearton (Chairman of the IRC) supported a Leyland takeover bid for BMH and it was suggested that Harriman should step down as Chairman and become the nominal President. Various people were suggested as Chairman including Lyons. Eventually Verey of Schroders, Warburg, Kearton, and Stokes agreed that Stokes should become both Chairman and Managing Director. BMH was given 24 hours to reply when the meeting concluded at 2.45am in the morning.

The BMH board met the next day but, after two hours, reached no conclusion. Lyons offered to mediate and met that evening with Stokes, his Finance Director John Barber, Warburg, and Verey. Lyons said he thought 'the financial figures were secondary and the human factor all-important'.[4] He apologised for the behaviour of certain members of the BMH board and suggested a fresh start. Stokes and Barber were not easily swayed but Lyons said he felt it was not right for his board to have been told the deal was off if Harriman did not resign and he had the impression this had come from Stokes, which made Stokes very angry. On being assured that it had not emanated from Stokes, Lyons was happier as this had rankled with the BMH board. Lyons offered to seek the assurance of every BMH board member to co-operate in the fullest manner but this was now not enough for Stokes and Barber and a full takeover by Leyland was the only option that interested them. Lyons, with great reluctance, agreed to investigate the possibility of Harriman resigning.

Next day (Friday 16 February), Lyons and Harriman went to Leyland's headquarters in Berkeley Square. There South African Leyland director Jack Plane applied shock tactics and tore into the BMH financial figures using very strong language. He 'told Harriman that the best thing he could do was "to get the hell out of it"; if the merger was to go ahead, he had to resign immediately.'[5] Once again Lyons spoke up for Harriman, who was far from well, partly due to the stress.

Stokes, who was still not totally sure the merger was a good idea, saw the top job in the motor industry within his grasp. On the Sunday Harriman offered to go, though at a meeting that night

Lyons continued to argue his side. Finally it was agreed that Harriman would remain as Chairman until November and then take the nominal title of President. He was by now quite ill and was rushed to the London Clinic where, at 8.30am next morning, he had to sign his letter of agreement 'in a state of semi-consciousness'.

A British Leyland board meeting was held on 19 February. Lyons then made a statement regarding his insistence on no interference in Jaguar management and his comments were so strong that it was decided to omit them from the board minutes! Stokes replied that he wanted Lyons to remain Chairman and retain control.

Sir Siegmund Warburg wrote to Lyons about the months of negotiations: 'I shall always remember that evening when you tried in such a warm and dignified way to introduce a strong element of human understanding and tolerance into a situation where bitter feelings seemed to cloud the fundamental issues. I have no doubt that you have rendered invaluable help at a rather critical moment.'

On 27 March Lyons and Stokes had a meeting and agreed that Jaguar should remain as a separate accounting and operating unit. Lyons would remain as Executive Chairman, fully responsible for the general policy of Jaguar, subject to the overall policy of the British Leyland board. Any group activities concerning Jaguar would be conducted through Lyons, or his nominee. It was further agreed that they would have short monthly meetings and Stokes would become a Jaguar director. Lyons was appointed a Deputy Chairman of British Leyland, and worked increasingly closely with Stokes.[6] Apart from Lyons, no Jaguar people held any of the senior appointments.

On 1 April Stokes addressed the BMC executives, telling them: 'Your first and only loyalty is to British Leyland...' He also stated that all expenditure would be scrutinised; there was to be no further capital expenditure or engagement of extra staff without his written authorisation.

Around this time several members of Jaguar management received a BL document with which Lyons was very unhappy. Accordingly on 9 April Lyons wrote to Stokes: 'Some people in our organisation have received a document entitled "Policy Instruction". As this is contrary to the agreement we have made I would be glad if you will be good enough to ensure that this does not recur.'

Lyons welcomed Stokes to his first Jaguar board meeting in June. He said Sir Donald had the wholehearted support of the board in 'the arduous tasks' that lay ahead. He believed Jaguar had an important role to play within BLMC and it was their intention to contribute fully towards its success. Stokes thanked him, paid tribute to Jaguar and said, he was 'confident that Jaguar would contribute appreciably to the success of the Corporation, whilst retaining its independence in character and products'.

Naturally, there were consequences of the merger. An important question concerned overseas distribution. In the US market Jaguar and BMC interests had already been amalgamated. On 11 April Lyons wrote a long letter to Stokes on the matter of dispensing with their American distributors and setting up a joint BLMC organisation. Lyons argued a strong case for retaining the status quo. He quoted Hornburg and Qvale as having done a particularly good job and he clearly felt a strong sense of loyalty to the people who had supported Jaguar for so long – but irrespective of that it made good business sense. Interesting in view of the difficulties Lyons had experienced with Hornburg in the early days of their association!

In May 'Lofty' England wrote to BMC (Australia) that 'it was clearly understood within BLMC that we are responsible for our own distributor arrangements'. He went on to say that they had long-standing arrangements and were not contemplating any changes. Nevertheless, at September's board meeting, it was resolved that Jaguar Cars' operations in the US and South Africa would be handled by Leyland Motor Corporation companies. Eerdmans in the US claimed he was very badly treated and Lyons, though he tried continually, could do nothing about it. One outcome of the reorganisation overseas was that the profits from the South African company would no longer accrue to Jaguar. Lyons asked his Finance Director, Arthur Thurstans, to take this up with BLMC to establish a similar arrangement to that of the US company 'as it would have a very bad effect on this company's morale if these profits were to be lost'.

Then there was the question of corporate identity, perhaps a trivial matter but one which caused a great deal of unhappiness to both employees and customers. In April 1968 Stokes issued Policy Instruction No 7 regarding the new corporate symbol, the so-called 'mangle handle', which was to be used throughout BL. In July a new British Leyland badge was required to be fitted to all commercial vehicles produced by the group, including Daimler and Guy. Shortly before Christmas 1968, Bob Berry wrote to Lyons concerning British Leyland Motor Corporation, warning that it was the corporate image that was being promoted in exhibitions and advertising and not the individual marque names. He concluded: '...we are beginning to get our attitudes mixed between the requirements of corporate and marque publicity. We are tending to promote BLMC as if it is a product which can be bought instead of promoting it as it ought to be – a large powerful umbrella under which some famous marque names are to be found. It is the success – or failure – of these names that will ultimately decide the fate of the Corporation. If they succeed, the Corporation will succeed, and nothing should be allowed to diminish or overshadow their stature.' This was a far-sighted point of view – but one not to be implemented within BL until more than ten years later, after Michael Edwardes arrived.

Product rationalisation within British Leyland was also under way. At the Rover-Triumph Home Sales Policy Meeting in April it was minuted that Triumph was to build quality cars up to 2,000cc (122cu in), the Rover (P6) models would remain much the same but Jaguar would replace the Rover 3.5 (P5) and upwards, thus giving Jaguar a monopoly within BLMC on the largest type of car. This suited Jaguar in many ways but still left a big hole in its model range. There would be no replacement for the Mk 2.

Lyons has been criticised for not producing such a key model but in fact such a car had already reached mock-up stage by 1967 at Browns Lane. 'Lofty' England explained: 'Having discussed it with Sir William I got his agreement to make a start on a car similar in size to the Alfa Romeo Giulia Sprint which would look like a Jaguar, go like a Jaguar and be priced like a Jaguar...' The car would have used a V8 1.5- or 2-litre (91 or 122cu in) engine based on the Coventry Climax grand prix engines, with chassis components (suspension etc) from BMC. In an uncanny parallel with the 'new' S-type some 20 years later, the body was to have been 'made, painted and trimmed by PSF Castle Bromwich and...priced at about £1250 including purchase tax on an output of 50,000 per annum'. It was not to be. At the first management meeting with the new BLMC, 'Lofty' was told by Stokes: 'you can forget that – your job is to make cars for the top of the BLMC range – the small car you were planning is to be handled by Triumph'.[7] That is how Jaguar lost its highly profitable medium-size sports saloon slot in the luxury car market for many years. It was regained only when the new S-type was announced in 1998 – to be built at Castle Bromwich! On the other hand, Jaguar had managed to get a new large Rover, the 4.5-litre (274cu in) P8, cancelled at a late stage. Ostensibly, it would have been in XJ6 territory.

Routine production, meanwhile, continued to be dogged by problems. In February came a letter from a US dealer (Franklin D. Roosevelt, Junior, son of the wartime President) complaining about 'the factory's total inability to ship us cars in accordance with our orders'. Lyons replied that he regretted the shortage of cars but it was entirely due to the new Federal regulations 'which required a considerable re-design of our models, putting us out of production'. He said it was a tragedy that a longer time was not given to manufacturers to comply with the new regulations but claimed Jaguar 'were one of the first, if not the first, to get off the mark with cars complying...'

Throughout the year, there were reports of component shortages holding up production. Lyons spoke to Lucas to increase deliveries of lamps for the E-type and Borg-Warner automatic transmissions were in short supply. By July car output was increasing but had now also been affected by a one-day national strike. Sales continued at a high level, with strong demand for the E-type in America. The profit rate was good on the scheduled programme, providing output could be maintained.

Jaguar Group turnover for 1967–8 (a 14-month period, adjusted to British Leyland's accounting year) was £62.7m, with profits at £2.34m, double the previous year's figure but still less than that recorded in 1959, despite 34 per cent inflation over that period. It seems that at least half the profit was actually from car spares, well up from the previous year. The overdraft had increased by £½m to £3.9m. The reason was that most of Jaguar's profits went towards paying dividends to BL shareholders, just as had been the case with BMH in the previous year. Out of £1,311,575, the dividend taken by BL was £1,011,575. Jaguar was left just £300,000 with which to invest in, and finance, its future. So much for the advantages of a larger partner!

Regarding Jaguar's own product development, the most important question was the introduction of the new XJ model range. At February's Jaguar board meeting a resolution was passed, for investment grant rules, confirming that although Jaguar contributed 100 per cent of the cost of tools to Pressed Steel, ownership was vested in Pressed Steel. This suggests that Jaguar's inability to pay for the XJ tooling, which has sometimes been given as the real reason for the BMC Jaguar merger, is not correct. The relationship with Pressed Steel was not entirely happy. In the June board meeting, discussion took place on the varying quality of bodyshells being received from Pressed Steel and the heavy cost of rectification.

There was also the question of which engines to fit in the new car. At a directors' meeting in May Lyons reluctantly accepted that the V12 engine would not be ready in time for the XJ launch and the announcement should be phrased, the range 'will include the 4.2 litre engine'. England said this would seriously change the layout of literature but Lyons felt this could be overcome by carefully extracting inappropriate text and illustrations.

In June the new Daimler Limousine was launched. At the end of his speech to the press, Lyons added an 'off the record' note: '...this is the first of the presentations we shall be making to you during 1968. We have some exciting things in store and I believe that, by the time 1968 draws to a close, you will agree that it has been Jaguar's year. We shall, therefore, be making a major contribution to the picture of BLMC.'

At August's Board meeting a delay was reported in the V12 pre-production run owing to receiving unsatisfactory engine blocks. August production was crucial for the build up to the XJ6 launch but it had been very disappointing due to strikes at Pressed Steel and at the manufacturer of the radiator grille. With Jaguar about to launch its most important model for a very long time, the company had been let down. Only some 160 XJ6s were completed in time for show and dealer use. 'This involved considerable effort on the part of management and supervision, and moreover without the surplus of manual labour arising from the strike lay-off position, these cars could not have been completed.'

On 26 September 1968, the XJ6 was proudly launched by Lyons at the Royal Lancaster Hotel in London to great and widespread acclaim. Full-page advertisements appeared in newspapers, with a photo of Lyons standing behind an XJ6. The caption began, 'In the long history of Jaguar, this is the very first time that I have appeared in an advertisement for one of our cars. But it only seems right that I should personally introduce the XJ6 to you. Not out of vanity, but as a tribute to the designers and engineers who have worked so hard over the past four years to produce something so much in advance of its time. I believe the XJ6 is the finest saloon car Jaguar have ever made, and one that challenges comparison with any in the world. Inevitably, I am prejudiced! But I hope you will take an early opportunity to try the XJ6 for yourself. When you have, I am confident you will understand and share my enthusiasm.'

Bob Bett of Nelson Advertising added: 'Sir William didn't like being projected himself. He was a bit backward about that. That's why, at the XJ6 launch, Bob Berry dreamed up the idea of recording his voice, instead of him having to speak at all the sessions, which went on for four days. His image was projected up on the screen, the lights went out and the recording started. It was a good idea.'[8]

At November's board meeting, Lyons reviewed the position of XJ production, stating it was not possible to produce more than ten per day due to the short delivery and unsatisfactory state of bodyshells being received from Pressed Steel. Grice stressed that economic piecework rates could not be established on the XJ cars at this low quantity and considerable negotiating difficulties must be expected.

In the same board meeting, the question of the succession was raised again. 'The Chairman stated that, as a further step towards his retirement, he wished to appoint Mr F. R. W. England as Deputy Chairman and it is his intention to delegate his day-to-day duties to the Deputy Chairman and his co-Managing Director but he would keep in close consultation with all matters of main policy.'

Lyons said he had advised Stokes that certain executives were concerned about their future after his retirement and he had been asked to convey Stokes's assurances 'that it is his desire that Jaguar should continue with its present management and retain its own entity. The board expressed appreciation of this message.' In view of his ongoing illness and inability to attend board meetings, it was resolved (with his complete agreement) that Arthur Whittaker would now fully retire. He had joined at the age of 17 in 1923, had risen from salesman to Deputy Chairman, and had been a key member of Lyons's original team.

Bill Heynes, with whom he always enjoyed a close relationship, would later write to Lyons: 'There is no doubt the Company is badly missing Mr Whittaker who was responsible more than anyone in the organisation for welding the various departments into a single unit. He could, and did, discuss with all the Directors the various day to day problems without any personal aggrandisement, and was virtually the second step in the ladder, which gave cohesion.'

Jaguar entered 1969 with tremendous demand for virtually all its products and a total inability to meet that demand due to situations completely beyond its control. It must have been so frustrating for Lyons, after several hard years, to see the pot of gold at the end of the rainbow yet not be able to reach it. There is an added irony in that major problems were caused by the body suppliers – the main reason for Lyons deciding to give up his independence in 1966.

However, from a lowly production figure of 23,351 in 1968 – a difficult year because of the problems of getting the new XJ6 into production – 1969 would see a welcome improvement with a new Jaguar production record of 28,614 cars. The XJ6 accounted for more than 13,700, the revised E-type Series 2 for almost 10,000. Most of the remainder was from models discontinued during the year – the 240, the Daimler V8-250 and the 420-type Daimler Sovereign; only the 420G stayed in production into 1970. In December, England reported there were no signs of a revival in 420G sales and an assessment was being made of an economic run out of this model.

As to car output, in February Lyons had expressed his concern and 'insisted on having a day-to-day review' – so much for handing over the reins! For the first time, night shift working was to start to meet the increased demand. E-types were being produced at a record rate of 220 per week, with 90 per cent going to America. It was believed a night shift would enable production to rise from 693 to 825 units per week. In the preceding weeks Jaguar had recruited and trained over 600 assembly track workers and some 150 personnel to operate the allied supply departments.

In March, there were still shortages of bodies from Pressed Steel and castings from Leyland. In mid-April, Louis Rosenthal, the Director of Manufacturing who had been appointed in 1968, told Lyons that production facilities should now be able to cope with 800 cars a week if only they could get bodies and other supplies. Lyons stated that car prices had been based on volumes that had not been achieved and, with further cost increases likely and the strong demand, the prices should be increased immediately to produce a margin to set against the lost volume.

After his return from a two-week holiday in Europe in May, Lyons wrote to all Jaguar's suppliers saying the situation regarding parts was most unsatisfactory and should be followed up at the highest level. As a result a number of companies wrote directly to him outlining the action they had taken to improve the situation. As an example, during the first half of 1969 production of the 420G was held up by a lack of brake calipers. When they became available, there was a shortage of bumpers.

A strike at Leyland in June caused a shortage of cylinder heads and blocks and, ironically, Stokes suggested Jaguar should look for an alternative supplier. Jaguar would perhaps have done so, as already in the previous year McMillan had queried the high price that Leyland charged for engines for Guy and Daimler, leading to a loss of profit for Jaguar! He was still very concerned about the cylinder block supply position in July. Unless there was a considerable improvement on the promises given, a complete collapse of the future XJ6 programme was likely. Lyons said every pressure must be brought on Leyland for a permanent improvement in its supplies. Rosenthal brought up the capital expenditure required to increase production to 1,000 cars a week and asked for a decision shortly.

Despite the problems of sustaining and increasing the level of production, during 1969 the Jaguar board turned its thoughts to the question of expanding the company's activities to a hitherto unseen level. Alan Newsome had been in dialogue with the Coventry Corporation regarding building on land adjacent to the Browns Lane factory. There was a proposal to swap land but the local authority was dragging its feet and being indecisive. Lyons wanted to make it clear that Jaguar's future development plans depended on this decision and if it could not be resolved shortly, the company might have to consider moving elsewhere. However, the following year Jaguar declined Stokes's suggestion of moving to a development area.

When Rosenthal, the Director of Manufacturing, asked for guidance on the future volumes and types of car to be produced, Lyons suggested any schemes should be based on a similar production pattern and expanded progressively to 100,000 cars per annum. This level would indeed be reached – but 30 years later, with an extended model range, additional factories and the might of Ford behind the company!

The board also discussed using Radford for the spares division of BLMC's Specialist Car Division (Jaguar, Rover and Triumph) and developing Browns Lane. For this an Industrial Development Certificate was required and that might prove a problem because the scheme would not necessarily lead to a considerable increase in employment. Lyons, perhaps naively, urged that the case be argued on the grounds of improved efficiency and be based on 50,000 cars rising to 100,000, with the emphasis on the high proportion that would be exported.

For many months there had been ongoing discussions with the Coal Board about mining under the Radford Works and the subsidence being caused. An impasse had been reached and Lyons said he would write to Lord Robens and point out that the assurances given were not being fulfilled. In December Lyons spoke of his recent informal talks with Wedgwood Benn about re-zoning the area around Browns Lane for industrial development. A BLMC document proposed development of Browns Lane to increase production from 37,500 to 75,000, including an extension of 1,755,000sq ft (163,044sq m). The Coundon Wedge Road was planned at this time, with a new assembly hall where the main entrance is now. At least there was a measure of agreement between Jaguar and BLMC about future expansion.

The 1968–9 financial results showed a lower turnover of £57.6m, as the previous year had been a 14-month period, but in fact sales were seven per cent up on a pro rata basis. Profit had recovered somewhat to £2.8m, though again almost half was accounted for by profits on car spares. The Jaguar group overdraft was down by almost £900,000 to £3m but stock and work in progress was up a massive 32 per cent, no doubt because of unfinished cars having to be held due to shortages. There appeared to be minimal investment but net current assets had grown from £2.9m to £6.5m, which made the picture look healthier. Jaguar contributed £1m, about half of its post-tax profits that year, to the BL dividend. There were now some 9,000 employed by the old Jaguar group companies. Lyons's pay increased from £35,000 to £45,000.

Stokes wrote to Lyons in December about controlling salary increases, requesting that increases over £2,500 go through him. Lyons replied, politely but pointedly: 'The principles you are anxious to establish in respect to salary increases have always applied at Jaguar...'

British Leyland was re-assessing the future rationalisation of its commercial vehicle range during 1969. For nearly a year England had been attending monthly meetings of the corporation's Truck & Bus Committee, which was supposed to be producing a plan for the disparate companies, but had made little progress. At the February board meeting Lyons stressed the urgency of having a decision from the committee on the centralisation of bus manufacture. In September, Lyons reported that the decision had been made not to integrate Guy with Leyland but to leave it 'undisturbed at Wolverhampton'. However, should the company be transferred to Leyland Motors, Stokes (now Lord Stokes) had assured him that Jaguar would be recompensed completely for its investment.

Bus profits were improving and the bus order situation was the best ever but, as with the cars, production was badly hampered by component shortages. Lyons spoke about the supply of buses to Edmonton in an attempt to break into this market in North America. Using the Cummins engine – despite the previous unhappy relationship with Cummins – and Allison (General Motors) transmission, all parties had agreed to work closely to make it a success. The results had been otherwise and complaints had been routed via the Ministry of Technology to Jaguar and 'he now felt that General Motors had undoubtedly failed and had also broken the confidence Jaguar formerly had in them...'

Stokes reiterated that, in the event of Guy being transferred to the Truck and Bus Division, Jaguar must receive 'an equitable transfer price. He further asked Sir William to remain as Chairman of Guy Motors Ltd., as counsellor and to keep a watching brief on their activities – Sir William agreed to do this.' Lyons then asked Thurstans to prepare a valuation and agree the figures with John Barber.

In November England reported that the Truck & Bus Committee had been disbanded! On bus production, Lyons said he appreciated the difficulties but must insist on the production management exercising more pressure on increasing output. A letter from the BL board was read confirming Lyons's suggestion that Henry Meadows (which had been gradually integrated with Guy since 1968) should now, after all, be transferred to the Truck & Bus Division together with Guy for the net asset values, which were respectively £460,000 and £2.4m.

Repeatedly during the year, Lyons enquired after progress of the new V12 engine. In April, Heynes had been asked to report when production would start, but three months later Lyons was still waiting for a proper production schedule. In October, Lyons again expressed his disappointment at the lack of progress with the V12 engine project 'which was having a devastating effect on the programme for this car' and Hassan explained that the delays had been caused by the difficulty in meeting the 1970 US emissions requirements. A decision had only been taken two months previously to use the Brico fuel injection equipment but they were hampered by the fact that it was not yet in production. At this stage production looked possible by April 1970 with the launch of the XJ12 in June. Concerns over the Brico fuel injection were voiced again in December and Lyons insisted that an alternative carburettor scheme be prepared urgently.

Heynes received a CBE in the 1969 Queen's Birthday Honours List and, congratulating him on this, Lyons said it was 'very gratifying to know that Mr Heynes's services to the industry had been so well and graciously recognised'. Lyons said that Heynes was due to retire at the end of June but had agreed to stay on for a further month. 'Sir William then paid tribute to Mr Heynes, speaking of his 34 years of work for the company and of his personal disappointment in losing a very close and trusted colleague; he felt the company owed him a great debt.' In thanking the Chairman and other board members for their sentiments, Heynes said he was very appreciative of the support he had always received from Lyons. It had been a long time since, in April 1935, Lyons had told the young man that he intended to build one of the world's finest luxury saloon cars. Surely, culminating in the XJ6, William Heynes had helped him achieve exactly that.

'Lyons was a good chief to work for,' said Heynes a few years later. 'He was always approachable and in later years, when we had board meetings of a sort, he had become more considerate towards the views of the committee. Although it did not often alter his actions, he perhaps put things in a different way.'[9] With the retirement of Heynes, Walter Hassan and Bob Knight became directors. In 1969 Lyons added to his growing list of distinctions the award of an honorary doctorate by Loughborough University of Technology. In May 1970, Lyons was also given the Coventry Award of Merit, for his outstanding contribution and personal leadership in the field of automotive engineering.

The theme throughout much of 1970 was the worsening situation in production, often owing to external industrial conflict affecting supplies of parts to Jaguar. At the January board meeting, Rosenthal said the company was deprived of £400 every time a car was lost in production. Lyons stressed that maximum effort should be exerted to produce every car possible, although not at the expense of meeting excessive wage claims which, once established, are long-term.

Pressed Steel was still letting the side down badly. Over the past year a weekly average of 329 usable bodyshells had been received. The previous week just 237 good bodies were received against a promise of 500. Once again one can sense the frustration Lyons must have felt. What did he need to do to succeed? His company had produced a winner in the XJ6, with the demand for it strong and the car profitable.

The statistics were worsening, too. In January 45,000 man-hours were lost at Jaguar, 50 per cent due to a strike at British Road Services and the remainder due to acute shortages of bodies and parts. There was only one full week worked during February and output reached 51 per cent of target. Failure to deliver XJ6s was causing a loss of goodwill in many export markets where distributors had spent a great deal on promotion and were then embarrassed by the inability to supply. 'The great danger of this situation is the long-term repercussions it may have on future sales, particularly as our competitors, Mercedes and BMW in particular, are consolidating their positions at our expense,' said Lyons.

During March labour disputes at Girling and Adwest caused the loss of 389 E-types (brake shortages) and 315 saloons (no steering racks). De-rusting Pressed Steel bodies caused delays and there were absenteeism and lateness during heavy snow. Some 66,861 man-hours were lost.

By April 1970, Jaguar had experienced only four full weeks of work since Christmas due to industrial disputes, mainly at suppliers. Grice said that this inconsistent working was causing the loss of some of his best men. More strikes were to follow at Pilkington (manufacturers of Triplex glass) and Lucas. Some 800 or 900 cars had to be assembled without glass while alternative supplies from Italy were being arranged and cars were being sent out with temporary Perspex windows. By June 1,300 cars were held due to shortages. Lyons called for a special effort from everyone to try and retrieve the situation before the year end.

The General Election brought the Conservatives back into power under Edward Heath. It was a priority for the new Government to tackle the industrial relations problem and in 1971 a new Industrial Relations Act was passed by Parliament.

As Deputy Chairman of British Leyland, Lyons made a couple of suggestions in January 1970 to amend Stokes's draft Chairman's statement. He wrote: 'In the short term, restricting the home market may squeeze a few extra cars into export markets but when restrictions are of the severity and duration of those in this country, they have a profound effect on our modernisation and expansion plans. A comparison of capital expenditure by the major British and European motor manufacturers over the past five years shows how we...lag behind in this vital area.'

Relations between the two men were not always easy. Stokes included Lyons on the mailing list for a letter, which stated that too many senior people were 'spending an exorbitant amount of time visiting overseas Shows and exhibitions, and that they should travel economy class'. To infer that this went on at Jaguar was to show ignorance of the way Lyons had run the company over the years. Lyons, however, replied to Stokes with his usual politeness: 'I am completely in agreement with you that it is very necessary to keep control of senior people and, indeed, all people visiting shows. We have always done this.'

During discussion of costs at the April board meeting, it was noted that the £48,000 increase in sundry expenses was mainly due to the new BLMC head office charge of £40,000. Lyons mentioned the heavy extra load imposed by paperwork for head office and the strain on management, which was already having to cope with expansion and the problems of shortages. At the close of this meeting, Stokes congratulated the Jaguar management on doing a very good job of work.

However, in mid-June Stokes wrote again. 'The figures supplied to me of your salaried staff from 1 October 1969 to 16 May, 1970 show an increase of 52 for Jaguar and 43 for Coventry Climax... I have no doubt that certain of the additions may be desirable but certainly some of them seem questionable. I would like to bring the overall number of staff down to at least pre-October 1969 figures.' No reply from Lyons has been traced.

Ironically, in view of this memo, Walter Hassan later said in a report to Lyons that 'Present R & D effort is not adequate but is conditioned by the availability of spending power and manpower'. Hassan also spoke of the increasing demands of the US authorities on air pollution and the increasing number of countries creating legislation, all with varying requirements and procedures. The existing facilities, recently doubled, were now in urgent need of further expansion.

The US market had its own problems. Despite the E-type, sales were suffering during a recession.

As regards the expansion programme, in April Stokes had mentioned that he would be seeing Wedgwood Benn shortly to discuss BLMC factory developments and the Minister might suggest that Jaguar should build an entirely new factory in one of the development areas. Lyons responded that this proposal could not be considered and the board was unanimous in its support of his statement.

A report dated 1 July 1970 detailed the 'Proposed Expansion of Jaguar Manufacturing Facilities'. Plans had been scaled down from the original concept of 75,000 cars per annum to 65,000. The existing Browns Lane and Radford factories were to be developed exclusively for car production. Spares and service were to be in a new building alongside the Browns Lane factory; bus and fighting vehicle manufacture would be transferred to Bristol and Alvis. At 50,000 cars per annum, profit would be £14.7m and net profit as percentage of capital employed would be 28 per cent. At 65,000 per annum the profit would be £21.7m. The planned expansion foresaw a gradual rise in weekly output to 1,350 cars by 1974–5. In September, a 'Profit Plan 1971–5' was put together by the Market Research Group at Berkeley Square (BLMC's headquarters). The aim now was further reduced to 52,000 cars a year by 1974–5.

A discussion, in late August, on spare parts was concluded by Lyons emphasising the importance of maintaining an efficient spares service to owners. He pointed out that the sale of spare parts yielded a high proportion of the total profit of the company. A comparison between Jaguar, Rover, and Triumph showed that gross margins as percentages of sales were 31, 26, and 23 per cent respectively, the higher figure for Jaguar being mainly due to the company's lower overheads.

In spite of all the difficulties, Jaguar had had a very good financial year in 1970. Turnover was up by 17 per cent, at £67m, and profit up an impressive 42 per cent at £4m. While tax was just 34 per cent compared with the much higher rates Lyons had had to pay in the 1950s, 82 per cent of the post-tax profits went towards BL's dividend. The overdraft was up to £4.7m and fixed assets, including the value of plant and tooling, were greatly reduced. At least buses were in profit now and had made £1.5m for the first four months of the financial year. Lyons's faith in the Daimler bus operation was finally proving well placed; 2,308 Fleetline buses were on order in December and another 1,600 were ordered by London Transport.

As a further illustration of the difficulties encountered, car production during 1970 rose only by 994 – to 29,608. With the demise of the 420G, Jaguar now had one of its slimmest model ranges since the early 1950s – basically the XJ in four models, together with the E-types, and a small number of Daimler limousines (built at the Vanden Plas factory in London). The XK-engined E-type was being phased out. Production of the V12 E-type finally began with the aim of having a fair quantity available by the 1971 launch but inevitably output was behind schedule due to limitations imposed by operators, pending settlement of rates.

At BLMC the financial situation was now serious and Jaguar was the only division not to have increased corporate borrowings. In fact, 1971 saw a new record for Jaguar with 31,549 cars produced but 1972 and 1973 were to prove disappointing.

David Jenkins had now succeeded the long-serving Arthur Thurstans and brought in more modern accounting methods. On 1 July 1971 Jenkins sent Lyons his comments on Lord Stokes's letter to Lyons on reducing manpower, stocks, work in progress, capital and revenue expenditure. He queried how they could reduce manpower by ten per cent while being urged by BLMC's HQ to increase production to 1,000 cars a week. Jaguar's recently submitted budget for quite heavy capital expenditure on badly needed plant appeared to have been accepted but if that was now in danger they needed to know urgently. He felt they needed a positive lead from HQ so that they were progressing 'in the manner agreed by all'.

Next day Lyons received a memo from Rosenthal, agreeing with Jenkins. 'In some areas extra people must be brought in if we are to meet our new model programmes. These, and the annual changes involved in meeting [the US] Safety Regulations, are producing complexities never before encountered.' He concluded: 'The only way of making any real impact on the profit situation, as I see it, is to increase the output to get a better overhead recovery per vehicle.'

In January 1971 John Barber had put together a paper on the

future management of BLMC. In it he wrote: 'I am beginning to wonder whether Jaguar should not be kept somewhat separate.'

Lyons sent a copy to England, who was particularly strong in his comments about Filmer Paradise, Managing Director of British Leyland Europe. 'Setting up individual companies, dispensing with distributors, etc., has been done in accordance with a plan put up by Paradise, and has cost BLMC a stack of money, quite apart from the disruption which has occurred in the loss of sales... My opinion is that we should have top people who are respected and in whom our distributors and dealers have confidence.'

The reorganisation of the international dealer network, carried out by Paradise and Jack Plane, involved spending a lot of money buying out individual distributors to create national sales companies. Sadly, in the process many long-standing and effective relationships between Jaguar and its distributors in the UK and internationally were broken. Most of the severed dealers took rival franchises, producing collateral damage for BL.

In April Stokes sent his fellow BLMC directors a copy of his report on a recent visit to South Africa, one of the first territories where Plane had merged the networks. At the end of a long paragraph on the car division, he wrote, 'The Jaguar has been a great success and without it I think our whole distribution system would have fallen apart. This is a profitable vehicle which has made up some of the leeway which we have lost with some of the smaller ranges of cars' (meaning ranges of smaller cars).

While one important issue was the question of how to achieve the desired increase in output, in a situation when there was little capital available for investment, the other problem was the post-merger overhaul of the British Leyland sales network. In Lyons's mind the two were linked, shown by a 'Private and Confidential' letter written to Lord Stokes in July 1971. It is worth quoting at length because it illustrates many points, including Lyons's attitudes and policies, in the international climate at the time.

'With regard to Jaguar, I have always aimed at maintaining a close relationship between liquidity and profits...it is better to have lower profits than build up a high bank interest burden which may put the Company at risk. This policy has resulted in the growth of this Company's asset value rising from nil to approximately £20m with the introduction of only £350,000 outside finance. In this context, I think we should take a very hard look at the advisability of expanding Jaguar at the present time beyond the 42,000 cars we have planned for the next year, which is

certainly the maximum we can achieve without a very considerable capital outlay which, indeed if expended, may offset substantially the value of the greater production which would accrue.

'I appreciate that this is not a modern outlook and it may be that it is right to go ahead with a big scheme, but there are more important factors which should be considered.

'In the light of the present uncertainty, not only at home, but also in the export markets, there is evidence that optimism for greater sales is not warranted. South Africa, Europe, Australia are all requiring substantially fewer cars than originally predicted and [the] USA market must be acknowledged as hazardous in view of the constantly changing legislation and our precarious price position. Even the UK market is showing signs of a reduced demand and, whether it will absorb cars at a greater rate predicted for next year is, I think, dependent solely upon an improvement in the country's economic condition. We may have run into the danger zone with our prices and we can only hope the increases we have just made do not seriously affect sales.

'On the other hand, if we go into the Common Market, the outlook may change drastically.

'That is one side of the sales picture by which to judge our future expansion policy. The other is that our sales, in the main, have been self-generating. I do not think that the present sales set up has established a sound basis from which to sell Jaguars. The sales organisation which Jaguar built up has, to a large extent, been destroyed and there is no evidence that it is being replaced by the type of specialist sales organisations which we have always regarded as being essential for a prestige car. Jaguar sales cannot be affected [sic] by run of the mill organisations, and it may be that we can take a more optimistic view of Jaguar's world sales.

'To achieve the 42,000 cars per annum, we shall, of course, have to incur considerable expenditure, but to go higher than this would involve further outlay which may not prove to be justified if sales do not absorb the increased output.'

The same day Berry also wrote to Stokes and was more upbeat on Jaguar's sales potential. He felt that, except on one or two occasions, Jaguar had never had to make any serious attempt to sell its cars. As a result it had no sales organisation. What it had was, effectively, a franchising and distribution organisation. He felt that with a proper sales organisation Jaguar could sell substantially more cars. There were more models to come with the XJ12, two-door coupé, and XJ-S but he was concerned they should be planning an XJ6 replacement for three to four years' time. 'British Leyland appear to be realising that specialist cars cannot be treated in the cavalier fashion of the past. I consider that our European position has been put back at least five to ten years by the total neglect of Jaguar by British Leyland during the past three years.'

In late August Lyons wrote to Stokes about the five-year sales forecast he had just received from Berkeley Square. 'Much as I would like to give it my blessing, I do not believe it to be realistic and I am quite sure it would be a serious mistake to regard it otherwise.'

This letter summed up where Lyons felt that BL was going wrong and how it affected Jaguar. Though in his 70th year, Lyons was still as sharp as ever. In polite terms he made it clear he had no faith in the HQ sales forecasters who were overly optimistic.

'As you know, from the outset I have been against the destruction of our distributor and dealer network, which took us so many years to build up. I think it is obvious the present set up has failed because of lack of understanding of the specialist business, and it is essential that it is replaced by people experienced in specialist sales and service facilities, and who are divorced from the volume side. I advised you how pleased I am that you had put Morgan in charge of Specialist Cars and [hope] that you will vest him with the necessary authority so that he can operate effectively.

'I have been told that the failure to achieve sales forecasts is due to poor quality. Whilst I am never satisfied that we achieve the standard at which we aim, I cannot do other than regard this as a lame excuse.' He stated that his view was proven by the strong demand in other markets where they had good representation, by the very high reputation that the XJ6 had achieved in three years, and that 52,000 examples had been sold. He made a number of pertinent and detailed criticisms of BL national sales companies in Europe: '...sales have suffered, dealers have become frustrated due to poor support, and many have become involved in other makes'.

In view of this climate he advised against any heavy capital expenditure. 'Also we must not overlook the fact that an increased programme inevitably puts up total overheads and, if it is not met by sales, it creates immediate availability which results in a substantial mark down in second-hand values, the biggest deterrent to cars in the highest price bracket. At the present time, on the home market, the XJ6 has the lowest depreciation by a long way except for Rolls-Royce...'

The build up of stocks of V12 E-types before launch was being seriously affected by a lack of blocks and heads to the standard required. The high rejection rate was also making it difficult to agree piecework prices, which had been a limiting factor in increasing production. Meanwhile, to add to the challenges, a decision had not yet been received from the American Federal authorities as to which type of rear crash test would have to be met by the 1972 models.

In late March, Lyons went over to Palm Springs for the launch of the Series 3 V12 E-type. It was to be his final visit to America. British Leyland launched the Triumph Stag at the same time but it would not be anywhere near as successful in the US as the new E-type. In the UK and US the order position was very good for Series 3 E-types but very disappointing in Europe as no special launch publicity had been issued by British Leyland Europe, which had not included this car in its marketing plans!

On 4 September 1971, Lyons reached the grand age of 70. BL's in-house newspaper *Teamwork* devoted the front cover to a photo of Lyons and his wife to celebrate. They were pictured with two small dogs – 'latest additions to the household, Norwich terriers, Buttons and Peppy'. The Editor interviewed Lyons and the following are the more interesting and revealing answers to the questions asked.

What was the secret of his success? 'To succeed one must be able to offer a product or service for which there is a need, or potential need, at a price commensurate with its value and related to what the consumer is prepared to pay. This must be backed up by intensive effort and the right decisions. Any business seriously lacking in any one of those areas is doomed to failure.'

Could he have succeeded in any other business? 'Right from the very beginning I have always wanted to be involved in the car industry... I have always had a clear idea of what I wanted to do and have pursued it to the best of my ability.'

He had been criticised by City Editors for his modest dividends but replied that it was important to reinvest profits. 'I have never doubted that we followed the correct course of action with regard to profits and dividends. The Company owes its success to the fact that the maximum possible profit was retained in the business in order to finance its expansion and growth. Those shareholders who retained their shares in Jaguar over the years reaped a substantial reward for their confidence in us.'

How did he keep his prices so low? 'We have always tried to produce our cars as economically as possible – this, I believe, is of fundamental importance. In addition, I have always preferred to operate on a modest profit margin, rather than the maximum the market would stand, in order to ensure a certainty of demand throughout the year and thus provide fulltime operation of the factory.'

When asked if he could see a future with a four-day week and retirement at 45, he said he thought this could do enormous harm to the community. 'Too much leisure time is bad for the individual... I consider that a wholehearted effort put into working a reasonable number of hours is good for everyone. Frankly I see very little wrong with the current 40 hour week; it provides a reasonable schedule, a disciplined life and added enjoyment to the periods of relaxation.'

His favourite model? 'Without any doubt at all, the XJ6 is my personal favourite. It comes closer than any other to what I have always had in my mind as my ideal car.'

Was it lonely at the top? 'Perhaps I haven't climbed high enough! I certainly have never felt lonely!'

Had he found decision making had been a nightmare? 'Decision making has never been exactly a nightmare, but it has been very worrying indeed on many occasions and for long periods at a time. That is the price one must pay for responsibility.'

What qualities did he look for in senior management? 'Briefly, I would say integrity, a sound knowledge and understanding of the task one is called upon to do, and a dedication to work.'

Noting that there was elegance in Wappenbury Hall but not ostentation, the questioner asked what money meant to him. 'Very little. Even in the very beginning when I worked every hour possible and earned a very small salary indeed, I was overwhelmingly concerned about the progress and success of the business. This success has earned money for me but it has always been of secondary importance. I think the value of having money and what it can provide in life is very over-estimated. You don't have to be rich to be happy – frequently the reverse is the case.'

Had he ever wished he had opted for a less strenuous life? 'No, never. Despite the endless worries, the problems and the difficulties – some of which, on occasions, appeared insuperable – I would not have chosen any other life. To me, the daily challenge of running a business of this type has no equal in any other sphere. The Motor Industry is the most exciting of all and I am sure that most of those engaged in it share this view.'

The financial results in Lyons's last full year as Chairman were a record by some distance. Turnover, at £82m was up 22 per cent, which was well ahead of inflation at 9.7 per cent. Profit was up 45 per cent at £5.9m. Investment in plant and tooling had increased by £1.1m but the overdraft was only fractionally reduced at £4.5m.

Why was the overdraft not tumbling after such a profitable year? The answer once again was simple. Most of the profit went in tax or dividend. The post-tax profit was £3,682,437. The dividend was £3,682,423, which left Jaguar £14...

Stokes wrote to Lyons to thank him 'for the very substantial contribution that has been made by Jaguar under your direction'. He added: 'We are going through at the moment rather a difficult period through no fault of management.' Lyons replied, thanking Stokes. 'I am sorry that our contribution was not more; this was entirely due to the delay in stepping up the E-type production because of a shortage of cylinder blocks, and then our problems with track labour on the usual pay question. I will most certainly pass on your message to 'Lofty' England and all concerned and I am sure it will be greatly appreciated, for they are, as you say, an enthusiastic and, I consider, a very good team. It is a great pity that, due to the toolroom strike, we have made such a bad start to this year, but you may be assured that no effort will be spared to retrieve our lost production as much as possible.'

To prepare for his retirement, Lyons had created a styling department in the late 1960s. Oliver Winterbottom, a former apprentice, was an early member of that small team. 'Bill Thornton and those sorts of people gave up their area of responsibilities reluctantly. Fred Gardner did particularly... Lyons I saw quite a lot of and I always liked him a lot. There was great respect and we all quaked, because he was the big boss. He was an awfully nice man – he was a gentleman, and there aren't too many of those about.

'He used to do these so-called drawings if he was trying to explain that a line on a model, or whatever, wasn't quite what he wanted. He used to get the pen and he couldn't draw a normal line – it was always little wispy strokes, so the whole thing looked like a groundhog, or something, when he'd finished it. You can imagine an XK120, which by the time it was finished actually looked as if it was made of nylon fur! He didn't have that one-stroke purpose that you'd expect him to have. What he really was, was an incredible judge of good taste.

'He got to know who I was and when I left the company, he actually called me up to his office and asked me why I was going. I said, "I've been here for ten years now. I'm not going to make much more progress, whereas going to Lotus will be a tremendous opportunity, broaden my experience and, perhaps, one day I could come back to Jaguar." He said, "I think you're absolutely right."'[10]

CHAPTER 11

LYONS BOWS OUT FROM JAGUAR

To some extent Lyons was now, finally, doing less at Jaguar. His farm had always been an outside interest and, together with golf, his main activity outside Jaguar. However, he did not treat farming as a hobby, taking it seriously and becoming more involved as he approached retirement.

In 1967 Lyons had founded the Wappenbury flock of Suffolk sheep, making his first purchases at Ipswich and Banbury. 'He liked his Jerseys and he liked his sheep,' said his long-serving farm manager, Bob Robinson. 'He always used to say to me, when I went to Jersey to buy cattle, "When you buy anything for me, Robinson, we want the best". He never thought anything was expensive if it was good.'[1] A precept, in fact, which Lyons applied in almost every field.

In January 1971 an article on Lyons and his farming appeared in the *Coventry Evening Telegraph*. Robinson was quoted as saying: 'He is keen that every inch of his farm should be producing something.' He had recently spent £20,000 on a grass-drying and cubing plant at Barn Farm which, with Manor Farm and Hill Farm, made up the 463-acre (187-hectare) unit. It was stated that the farm paid its way despite steeply rising costs. 'We're out to beat the terrific rise in the cost of feeding stuffs,' said Robinson. It was planned to make the three farms self-supporting in feed stuffs.

Lyons obviously believed in investing in state-of-the-art equipment at his farm, which rather contrasted with the archaic plant at Jaguar. At Hill Farm last year's wheat harvest was in a fully automatic grain drier, which had cost £8,000 six years before. The barley and oats crops from 80 acres (32 hectares) were turned into stock feed in an automatic corn mill and the Jerseys were milked in what was the latest state-of-the-art milking parlour in Warwickshire. At milking time 106 of the herd of 200 queued for eight milking units. Daily, 200 gallons (909 litres) were piped straight to the dairy and cooled in a refrigerated tank.

The newspaper journalist mused on what Lyons – with all his

drive, determination, vision, and scientific-outlook – might have done for farming in Britain had he chosen it as his career.

His Wappenbury flock won the Suffolk Sheep Society's Cup in their annual flock competition three times between 1969 and 1976 in different categories. 'I am delighted,' he was quoted as saying in October 1976 in the *Coventry Evening Telegraph*. 'But really it's a great credit to my farm manager, Mr Robert Robinson and my shepherd Mr Robert Keys that they have won the competition.'

The year 1972 would mark the 50th anniversary of the formation, by young Billy Lyons and his partner, of their tiny company. That year would see the retirement of Sir William Lyons, who had created a motoring empire and a make of car that was known and admired the world over.

In January, his colleague Leonard Lee retired, having made such a valuable contribution with his Coventry Climax company. Whether Lyons himself would have chosen to retire, we will never know but he was well past the normal company retirement age. Unquestionably, he had earned his retirement and on 4 February a company press release announced it. At least he was handing over the reins to a true 'Jaguar man' in 'Lofty' England, a man he had nurtured and trained, and was genuinely fond of. 'Lofty' had, and would continue to have for the rest of his life, the most enormous respect for Lyons.

Three days later an internal communication from BLMC stated that the parent board had approved the formation of a one-company structure that would take over all the trading companies, including Jaguar. The new company was to be called British Leyland UK Limited. By the end of the year Jaguar Cars had ceased to exist as a separate company.

In mid-February Lyons had written to John Dugdale in America, thanking him for his letter and good wishes. He concluded: 'I shall be retaining my office here, but intend to take no active part other than give any advice which may be required, as I am anxious that "Lofty" England should take complete control.'

Everyone had abiding memories of Lyons. One such was Bernard Hewitt. 'He was a man for whom I have the very highest regard and respect. I consider it was an absolute privilege to have worked with him. He was always immaculate in a dark blue suit, black shoes, white shirt with double cuffs, cufflinks, never one hair out of line. Always looked very smart and set a great example. Many people in his position are looking for, and enjoy, "yes" men. In my opinion, he didn't. He'd ask me my opinion on something. Some people would have turned round and said, "You fool. How can that be right?" He'd say, "All right, Hewitt" and that was it. This attitude of allowing you to express an opinion and not shout you down, to me showed a great quality in the man. He would always listen.'[2]

On 2 March, Stokes wrote to Lyons: 'It would give all your colleagues on the British Leyland Board very great pleasure if you would join us for dinner on Tuesday, the 2 May, in a private room at the Savoy at 7 o'clock.' On 3 March Lyons ceased to be a Director and was given the title President.

Writing to thank Stokes for the dinner party, Lyons said he was glad to have been of some help, honoured to have been appointed Deputy Chairman but only wished he could have made a greater contribution to resolve the difficulties. 'The merger, of course, changed things for me, but I have greatly appreciated your understanding of my position and views and, also, the arrangements for my retirement. I am happy that the delegation I have exercised in the past two years is working out so well. I believe, under 'Lofty' England, Jaguar can continue to make a substantial contribution to the Corporation, providing its image is maintained.'

He concluded: 'If, at any time, you think that I may be of any help to you in your deliberations, please do not hesitate to call on me, and I will continue to do all I can for Jaguar'.

At retirement, Lyons had to undergo a round of interviews. Typically, he did not feel comfortable about personal publicity: 'But Berry tells me I've got to do it – it wouldn't do Jaguars any good if I were just to fade out.'[3]

'I have never, I think, flinched from what I consider to be my duty. I have never hesitated to sack someone if I felt the situation warranted such extreme action. If you really want to credit me with anything that I am proud of it is not falling below a 50 per cent export ratio.'

On the subject of retirement, he said he would probably give more attention to his farm. 'Otherwise I will play an indifferent game of golf.'[4]

For another interview he wrote out his answers. 'I do not visualise revolutionary changes in the foreseeable future in respect to power units and transmissions but I do see, good as they are today, advances in such important things as braking – anti-lock braking will be perfected, also suspension will be still further improved, ride levelling will play an important part. What I believe to be the most important characteristic which must be achieved is a reduction in driving fatigue, relief of driving tension by improved ride and handling and noise reduction. This will all add to personal safety but occupant protection in case of accident must feature as a high priority.'

'It is difficult to identify a single period in the company's development which has given me the greatest personal satisfaction, so I would say the substantial step forward we made in 1952 when we moved to Browns Lane, then the acquisition of Daimler, Guy Motors and Coventry Climax. It was during this period we had such success in racing, particularly at Le Mans, our first victory establishing the first British win for [this left blank!] years.'

He told Peter Garnier, Editor of *Autocar*: 'My sincerest wish is in the continued success of Jaguar. For the last two years, I have been delegating responsibility so that I feel I can now retire with confidence that Jaguar will be well managed under my successor Mr. England... Any influence I may have will be confined to advice which I may be asked for. It would certainly be wrong for me to interfere...

'I have no regrets that I shall be able to take things more easily. It is something I have never been able to do and I am sure I shall enjoy the opportunities it will give to spend more time with my wife, and to take holidays without the feeling that I am leaving the ship.'

When asked which of his many designs had given him the most pleasure, he replied: 'At the time the XK120; but without hesitation I can say the XJ6 – a car which we took six years to develop – has pleased me the most.'

On a rather more sobering note, he stated: 'I have enjoyed building up Jaguar, but I would certainly not like to start again today, if only because I am sure present day conditions would make it impossible to achieve the same result.'[5]

Treating the rival weekly motoring magazines with equal favour, as ever, he also gave Philip Turner of *Motor* an interview. 'I get all sorts of cars to drive, American, German, French, Italian... They are all good cars for I am not interested in other than good cars, but I always feel after trying one of them and getting back into an XJ6 that the XJ6 is the better car. I always enjoy driving it more.

'I drove a Ferrari a short time ago and it brought back the little boy feeling – it was terrific. It was good fun, you know, roaring away from corner to corner with a racing car feel. I don't think I've developed into an old man sort of driver and I can still drive reasonably fast. It was a different sort of motor car. It was a fun motor car, and I did get quite a bit of fun out of it, but to be perfectly honest I wouldn't like to drive it down to Salcombe. I was almost glad to get back...'

Turner suggested that to have someone at the top who enjoys

driving has a very definite effect on the product: 'Oh, I'm certain it does.' Was he sad to be retiring? 'No, I don't think so. I feel I have had a good span – 50 years – it's a long time. I think it is the right thing to do, for I am anxious to see it go on without me. To see it from the outside, you have just got to get out and let somebody else run the company.'[6]

In another interview he was asked if he felt any affinity with the men who worked for him. He said he did but used to feel much more so years ago, 'when we did not have "them and us". We all worked together to make the company prosperous and we had some good bonus schemes which made up some good wages.'

Courtenay Edwards conducted an interview for *Motor Industry* magazine. Lyons told him: 'Autonomy is not as complete as it was before, for obviously all the different companies are working towards the implementation of corporate policy. Jaguar and Daimler cars will certainly continue to retain their individual identity and I am satisfied that the future management – upon the establishment of which I have concentrated in the last few years – can maintain the company's success.'

When Edwards said that he had prevented his management structure from becoming top-heavy, he replied: 'Yes, I think I can claim that. We have vested responsibility in a small group of managers and let them get on with it. To do otherwise would destroy the great enthusiasm and sense of initiative of the individual members of our team.'

Asked if his story could be repeated, he said, 'Fifty years ago, when I started, and for many years afterwards, the labour content in most manufactured goods, in particular, was considerably greater than it is today, so that plant and tooling was by no means so expensive. I suppose the spirit of enterprise is as strong as ever, but to succeed, one has to overcome far more frustration than in the past.'[7]

In July he attended the XJ12 press launch, but did not address the 150 journalists and senior management present. Stokes spoke first and said Lyons would still play an important part and the identity and individuality of Jaguar would be encouraged. The main speaker was 'Lofty' who said he felt something of an interloper as he was about to do something that had only ever been done by one man.

The press reaction to the XJ12 was overwhelming. Many compared it with models from Rolls-Royce and Mercedes-Benz and speculated that the XJ12 might be the best car in the world. Others just stated it. Sadly, a ten-week official strike occurred soon after the launch. Lyons issued a statement to the *Coventry Evening Telegraph* outlining his 'deep concern' for the company. The paper's editorial said it was a 'masterly exposition of the fundamentals of industrial economics... it sets out in faultless logic everything that needs to be said about prices and wages. Anyone in Coventry who does not now understand does not want to'.

In spite of England's attempts – supported by Lyons – to prevent it, the big distributor break up began in America. Several long-standing firms were sacked and others, such as Hornburg, had their status reduced to mere dealers. The policy was moving inexorably towards total centralisation and the elimination of distributors. In July Lyons wrote to Stokes thanking him for an invitation to dinner in Paris on 3 October. 'Incidentally, whilst I am writing to you, I would like to say that I entirely agree with England's letter to Whitehead of 3 July, regarding Qvale and Hornburg, in spite of my old feud with the latter, but he can sell Jaguars.'

In September the company's Golden Jubilee was celebrated with an exhibition in the Herbert Art Gallery in Coventry, which was to prove the best attended exhibition in the gallery's history. Another exhibition was mounted in Blackpool. Lyons and his wife opened both.

During 1973 Frank Adam joined Lyons as 'a sort of chauffeur and gardener because he went to London perhaps twice a month. He didn't go out a great deal.' Adam recalled that on golfing holidays to Scotland they would stay at Gleneagles. 'He made sure I had a room with a colour television and a bathroom. Whereas other drivers I spoke to were sent down to a village to book into the pub, he insisted that I stayed in the same place as they did.'

Adam detected a closeness between husband and wife. 'Holding hands. They didn't like obvious extrovert displays of affection. They kept it very much between themselves. But being out with them in the car, you'd notice little things. You just thought, "Oh, that's nice."'

Adam sampled Lyons's quiet generosity: 'In my living room there was a cupboard with a wooden top and I asked if I could get a piece of wood from the chap who did the maintenance work for him to make a larger top. He said, "Why do you need that?" I said I was thinking of renting a colour television and he said, "Oh, it's terribly expensive. It costs a lot of money. Let me make some enquiries, but you can have the piece of wood and do that." I did that and a week later a colour television was delivered and installed. I mentioned this to him and he said, "Ah yes, renting is far too expensive. I thought you'd better have one."'[8]

Back at his beloved company, some three months from the end of the financial year Jaguar was on course for profits of £7.6m and the man-hours lost were the lowest for two years. England was proving he had been well taught by the Old Man. Meanwhile, Geoffrey Robinson had returned from running Innocenti in Italy and Stokes appointed him Managing Director of Jaguar in September. 'Lofty' became a titular Chairman. It would prove to be a difficult time for Lyons's chosen successor. Shortly afterwards, at the end of January 1974, he retired at the age of 62.

Lyons was very disappointed as farm manager, Bob Robinson, recalled. 'He liked "Lofty". He was one of his favourites. Never very struck with [Geoffrey] Robinson. He said, "He's too familiar with the workforce." That was what he used to tell me.'[9]

Geoffrey Robinson wrote to Lyons to thank him for his letter following his appointment. 'No one who takes on the job can do so without strongly sensing your extraordinary achievement in building from scratch such a fine and internationally famous company. It ranks, to my mind, amongst the most outstanding British industrial achievements.'

For a glimpse of Lyons in active retirement around this time, Alan Docking (whose mother was Greta's sister) was a frequent visitor to Wappenbury and also met up with his uncle in Belgium, where Docking was working. He tells the following story. 'My uncle was a keen golfer, though not as good as my aunt, who I seem to remember played off single figures and represented her county. We played quite often together, and I remember one incident which I think gives an insight into one of his major characteristics – the determination to win in everything he did. We were playing on my home course at Royal Zoute in Belgium, as usual for some very minor wager. I had the advantage, playing at home, but started slicing badly when I was three up with five to play. My uncle said, "I know what you're doing wrong and can correct it in an instant." I said, "Fine, what is it?" He replied, "I'll tell you after the game!"'

Things were starting to deteriorate badly at Jaguar but, however bad they got, Lyons rarely expressed an opinion. Adam does remember him once saying 'It's so sad to see it going down hill. We seemed to be doing so well. Now it's all going down the drain.'[10] As quality became appalling and production erratic, Mike Dale, British Leyland's US sales supremo, 'was wont in his frustration to call Jaguar "the worst car in the world", much to the distress of the few loyal Jaguar people still around'.[11]

John Morgan had kept in touch with Lyons. 'I used to go and see them and have tea with them. He was quiet, very quiet. He was still interested in what was going on. He'd say, "Dear, dear. Dear, dear", when I told him one or two of the horrors. "Good gracious," he'd say, but he'd never say more than that. It was obvious he was horrified by it all. Of course, he had a lot of money involved.'[12]

The industry had certainly not forgotten him. On 23 October 1975, Lyons was made an Honorary Fellow of the Institution of Mechanical Engineers.

In December 1974, with BLMC facing a cash crisis, Anthony Wedgwood Benn arranged a £50m guarantee and appointed Sir Don Ryder, the Chairman of a paper company, to produce a definitive report on the corporation. This was issued, in several parts, from April 1975. It advocated total centralisation and, effectively, the loss of individual company management. The Jaguar board was disbanded, Stokes became British Leyland Ltd's President, and Barber left. Alex Park was appointed Chairman of BL. Geoffrey Robinson resigned from Jaguar in May and Derek Whittaker was made Managing Director of the new Leyland Cars Division. At Jaguar, an operating committee had been set up under Cowley manufacturing man Tony Thompson though it was able to do little. 'I was furious with the Ryder Report,' said Lyons later. 'I went down to London to plead with him to keep it [Jaguar] separate but he wouldn't.'[13]

During this period, though divorced from the factory, Lyons nevertheless maintained his interest, as Adam remembered. 'He would sometimes go up into the stable block and you'd find him with his car, at that time an XJ6, and he would have some pieces of thin wood and string and tape and he was trying to work out what would be a good shape for an estate car. He said that there wasn't really enough room for carrying luggage for a family in the XJ6 and it would be a good idea to build an estate car. "But it's so difficult to get the shape right."'[14]

Bob Knight had to spend far too much time playing politics and fighting for Jaguar's very future during this period. Almost single-handedly, he contrived to keep Jaguar engineering intact and so preserved the heart of the company for better times. In this he had behind-the-scenes support from Lyons, who shared his distress at the apparent destruction of Jaguar. It was at this time that Greta was at her most supportive.

'In those days when he was very depressed during the awful time with the Leyland business,' said Pat, 'and he was terribly upset throughout, I think my mother helped him a lot, mostly by being quite tough with him – you know, "Stop being so sorry for yourself" sort of thing. Because to him it was almost like having a child taken away from him; and she encouraged him not to show it too much and to keep a stiff upper lip. But he was desperately upset.'[15]

Some distraction from the misfortunes that were afflicting his company was provided by a number of voyages to South Africa during this period. They both made good friends there and enjoyed relaxing aboard the cruise ships and meeting interesting fellow passengers. Nevertheless, it seems that Lyons was seldom able to forget about Jaguar entirely.

In this climate the XJ-S had been introduced. The controversial styling was, it seems, a combination of Sayer, who tragically had died in 1970, and Lyons at different times. It was certainly no successor to the E-type, nor was it intended to be. It was aimed at a wealthier and more mature customer. Oliver Winterbottom commented: 'I have a theory that as people get older – when management in general gets older – the products start to appeal to an older and older man. You don't get 20-year-old people designing stuff for 60-year-old men, and you don't get 60-year-old people designing stuff for 20-year-old people.'[16]

Lyons himself was quoted at the US launch as saying, 'We decided from the very first that aerodynamics were the prime concern, and I exerted my influence in a consultative capacity with Malcolm Sayer. Occasionally I saw a feature that I did not agree with and we would discuss it... I took my influence as far as I could without interfering with his basic aerodynamic requirements and he and I worked on the first styling models together. We originally considered a lower bonnet line but the international regulations on crush control and lighting made us change and we started afresh.'[17]

During 1976 Lyons had the first of several strokes. 'He made an enormous effort to get himself fit,' stated daughter Mary. 'He bought himself an exercise bike. It did affect his speech very slightly, but that got a lot better.' Pat remembered that he went very thin. 'My mother was very possessive about him...'[18] Less able to be so physically active, Pat told how 'he became passionately interested in professional golf, and you daren't say anything when he was watching a tournament on television. There mustn't be a sound – he watched every ball.'[19]

He continued to maintain contact with Jaguar, mostly through Bob Knight but also with Andrew Whyte, by then Product Press Officer at Jaguar and who, as the company's unofficial historian, appreciated as much as anybody exactly what Lyons had achieved. At a meeting to discuss the Series III XJ, Knight was asked if he ever heard from Lyons. 'Perhaps too much,' he murmured, adding that

Lyons seemed to phone him almost daily, once threatening to come over to discuss something he felt was going awry![20]

However, visits to his retired former directors were not frequent; Bill and 'Dutch' Heynes, for example, had expected to see more of him in retirement, especially as there had been a certain friendly rivalry between the two men with their farms. (Heynes also ran an exemplary farm at his home near Snitterfield, only a short drive from Wappenbury.) But visits and reciprocal invitations to Wappenbury were few; Lyons continued to keep his personal life very private, though his deteriorating health probably affected the situation too.

In November 1977 Michael Edwardes was appointed Chairman of what he renamed BL. It was realised that centralisation was unworkable and a move was made to give the companies, and in particular Jaguar, their identities back. An American, William Pratt Thompson, was put in charge of Jaguar Rover Triumph for two years but made no mark on Jaguar. Indeed production in 1979 dropped to an abysmal 14,283 – the lowest since 1958. Thompson was moved to another post and Percy Plant briefly took up the reins. Meanwhile the determined and brilliant engineer, Bob Knight had been made Managing Director. On 9 April 1980 the Jaguar workforce went on strike over grading and pay. Edwardes told the strikers to return to work or lose their jobs.

In that atmosphere John Egan was appointed Chairman. Edwardes was threatening to close Jaguar down. Egan later said he thought, 'I was going to be the only chairman of a car company who never made a single car'.[21] After three long days of persuasion, the unions agreed, by a small majority, to resume work and Egan's awesome challenge began.

Meanwhile, back at Wappenbury, Lyons had appointed Tom Sage as his new head gardener. He replaced his predecessor, Jack Meddings, who had been at Wappenbury for 40-odd years and who had been regarded very fondly by Lyons and his wife. They were both extremely upset when he collapsed and died in the garden.

Sage himself soon experienced Lyons's generosity. 'We'd been here about a year and we got on quite well. We had the thatched cottage down by the church, which was always the head gardener's house. We weren't very happy there – we'd got two small children and my wife didn't drive. There was no community, just a farm and two cottages, and the bus service round here is pretty poor. I liked the gardening job but my wife didn't like it here. So I went to Sir William and said I thought I was going to have to leave because the family weren't happy here. "All right, Sage," he said, "let me think about it," and off he went. Whenever you saw him about anything, he never gave you a decision there and then but always came back to you within a few days.

'A couple of days later, Sir William and his wife went down to see my wife and spent the afternoon down there just talking. Nothing happened again for another couple of days and then he called me and said, "Right Sage, if you don't like living down at that cottage, find yourself somewhere where you do like to live and I will buy it for you." And he did, as a tied cottage. We found a semi-detached house in Leamington and he came to look at it. He sat outside in his car and said, "Go in and see if you can get a bit of a discount off the price. See if you can get the price cut down and I'll consider it." So I went in, had a word with the lady and she reduced it by about £500. So I went back out to Sir William and he said, "Oh right. If it's all right, we'll have that." And he bought it for me.'[22]

In May 1979 Margaret Thatcher had defeated the Labour Party and her belief in the enterprise culture had influenced Egan to take on the challenge at Jaguar. There would be some pain to suffer as Margaret Thatcher grappled with, but finally overcame, the unions and radically overhauled industrial relations in Britain. Not surprisingly Lyons was a great admirer and he must have wondered how much easier life would have been, and how much more successful he could have been, if she had arrived on the scene 20 years earlier.

'When I started,' said Egan, 'the company was in pretty poor shape. I think they'd had five or six Managing Directors between his retirement and my arrival. The Company had been stripped of most of its functions and indeed one of the things I had to work on as soon as I got there was that they [were] trying to get the design team out of there as well. So I didn't have many allies. The only one I had to start with was Michael Edwardes. He said we could have as much independence as we deserved.

'So I started putting the company together again. Fairly quickly I went to see Sir William because he had been very disillusioned by what had been going on. For example, he had even, at one stage, taken away some of his own personal effects. He thought that people might steal them! Paintings and stuff like that.

'I went to see him and I had an idea in my mind that I would like to put on our letter heading, as part of our winning our independence, that our President was Sir William Lyons. I went along to see him and he was very pleased to see me and we sat down and talked. I asked if he would become President and he looked at me for some time and then he said, "Lad, I already am". Nobody had told me. Everybody had forgotten! So I said, "Let's reinstate the whole idea" and he said, "I'm very pleased with that."'[23]

Frank Adam remembers Lyons's reaction. 'He wasn't very impressed with Geoffrey Robinson. Didn't think he was the right man for the job. But when John Egan came out to the hall and Sir William met him for the first time – he used go out for a walk round the gardens with the dog, and he stopped and I was probably cutting the grass – and he said he'd just met the new chap who was going to take over Jaguar and he said, "That's the man for the job. He'll sort it if anybody can."'[24]

Mary Rimell was not surprised that her father took to John Egan – he was confident and determined, qualities that Lyons admired. He also appeared to have understood Lyons's careful husbandry of Jaguar – a contrast, in Mary's opinion, to Geoffrey Robinson, who once remarked to her that Lyons was the meanest person that he had ever met. 'He obviously did not know my father very well or understand his philosophy on how to run a business,' she commented.

Bob Knight was not happy with the new arrangement and resigned. His contribution to the company in his role as development engineer had been tremendous. In his time he was probably the world's foremost expert on noise suppression and ride quality and helped Jaguar to set world standards for luxury cars.

Egan kept in touch with Lyons. 'I used to meet him from then on, I suppose, about once a month when we would chat over where things were going. He was always invited into our styling studios whenever he wanted to come. If anything was happening, I would ask him to come. It was really quite amusing. He was really quite an old man when he was walking towards the studio but as soon as he got in there he seemed to almost metaphorically throw his stick away. He lost about 20 years. He was absolutely alive. I remember on one occasion him saying, "It's no good. We can't have this." I said, "I know, but I don't know what to do." He said, "I do and I'll show you." He really was quite a determined person when he was in absolutely his own element.'[25]

During these years the farm had been the main beneficiary of that determination, stated Bob Robinson. 'He liked to be up-to-date. In 1980 he scrapped the milking sheds and went in for cubicles and a circular parlour, which was top of the tree for that time. They used to come from miles away to watch this circular milking... The schools used to come. We had a platform built and they could watch the milking through a glass panel.'[26]

Tom Sage remarked: 'There had been a big fire in a listed barn just before I came. It burnt down and a lot of damage was done by the fire engines. He wanted a lawn putting back in front of the wall and it had to curve with the drive. I laid all the turf and I curved it round. He used to come out and say, "That's not quite right. You want a little bit off here and a little bit off there" and then he'd come back later and have another look. This must have gone on for several days and he said, "I did not get where I am today without knowing a good line!" It was the same with the hedges. I used to cut the hedges and he would kneel down and look down the line. "Very good, Sage." He loved lines, whether they be straight or curved. He didn't want an informal garden, he liked a formal garden.'[27]

When Lyons retired, the mantle of unofficial styling supremo had been taken up by Knight, assisted by Jim Randle. Knight recalled asking Lyons about his styling process: 'I asked him, "How would you say you go about evolving a new style?" And he was completely non-plussed. That was the amazing thing – he didn't know. "Well, all I try to do is make nice cars."'[28]

Knight's successor as Engineering Director was Jim Randle, another passionate Jaguar man, who was working on the successor to the original XJ6. 'Jaguar has unique style and it required people who were sympathetic to that style. As the years went by and we moved away from BL, his interest in the company grew again, and I used to see him a great deal. He'd be in here at least once a month and usually once a fortnight, and helped us with this car [XJ40] and the next car. It was usually small details. He'd come and look at it and say, "Now Randle, stand over here. I don't think that looks quite right, do you?" We used to argue quite frequently about the motor car. He never actually said, "Do this". He'd always say, "What do you think? Do you think that's quite right?" And usually when you went and thought about it for a while, you agreed with him. I loved that man dearly, I must say. I miss him now. But he left a good legacy.'[29]

One of the men in the department was Bill Jones, brother of Tom. 'In his latter years when he came into the Department, he recognised people who had been loyal to him and stuck with him. There was someone younger with a responsible job but he wouldn't recognise him so he would come straight over [to me].' Jones recalled an occasion when Lyons was chauffeured to the factory in a car with rise and fall seats. 'He sat in the back and he could see the mechanism. He was out of that car, even though he'd had a fall, called me and he went spare, as if it was my fault! In his day, you would never have seen anything like that.'[30]

A young man who came into contact with Lyons at that time and upon whom he made a deep and lasting impression was designer Keith Helfet, who went on to style such cars as the XJ220, XK180, and the F-type concept car. 'He was an incredibly special person. He was one of the most talented designers the world has ever seen. I was, as it were, touched by God and consider myself as extremely lucky.'

'He would come in and ask about everything. On XJ41 [a stillborn sports car project] he would come along, "Oh, I don't like that".' Initially Helfet would think he was wrong. 'Then I would really look at it and he was always right. He had the most incredible eye. He was eighty-odd, he was quite wobbly and his voice was not strong, but my God was he decisive and sharp. He never missed a trick. The XJ41 was really the last car that he had a direct hand in.

'He understood form so well. I learnt…a lot from him. He had such a good eye for line, for form, for the way surfaces moved and accelerated. He was great. In design terms, he was absolutely sharp to the end.'[31]

Knight stated, and Helfet confirmed, that he would stand for a very long time, just staring at each aspect of a shape. 'He spoke through his walking stick. There are some wonderful pictures of him pointing with his walking stick. He made the decision of which theme to pick for XJ41. There were various proposals. Jim liked mine but Egan was concerned that it looked what he considered old-fashioned because it was all round and flowing. We are talking 1980 when all cars were square and boxy. Egan called Lyons in and he just said, "You must do this one. That's the Jaguar." I felt very confident that soft, flowing shapes would come back, which they did. I felt things were going that way so it would lead fashion rather than follow it. He operated as if he was the Chief Designer!

'I remember he was once very concerned about the lower screen finisher on the XJ40. He said, "You know, I've been thinking about this part all night. Kept me awake, you know." It really had been bothering him…

'Occasionally he would try and illustrate a point, especially when his speech was getting more difficult, by trying to sketch, but by this stage his hand was very shaky and he would draw a line very slowly. You could see he was really struggling.' Even previously, 'He didn't draw. He'd just use lines to illustrate a point. He didn't sketch anything. He was a sculptor, rather than a painter.'[32]

As for the family, by now Lyons had a number of grandchildren. As already recounted, the first had been Katie, born to Mary and Guy Rimell in 1963. Then when Pat married Norbert Quinn, who already had eight children, she brought up four of them – Carol,

Sally, David, and Jeremy. They, like all the grandchildren, became close to their step-grandfather. A favourite family rendezvous was always The Bolt at Salcombe.

Pat then had Michael in November 1964. Michael Quinn now works for Sid Creamer, the Kensington Jaguar dealer, and has fond memories of his grandfather. At Wappenbury or Salcombe 'he was relaxed and easy going, but one knew one had to be on one's best behaviour.' It was Lyons who gave Michael his first car, a Morris Minor Traveller that had been used by Meddings the gardener. Michael was 17 and thinks the rationale was that it was safer than a motor cycle! 'It's funny – I've got five motor bikes now – a couple of old ones and three new ones,' he said; his grandfather's enthusiasm for two wheels is perpetuated!

Michael can vouch for Lyons's sharpness even in old age. He had to turn down an invitation to attend the 1984 Le Mans race through ill health but sent the young Michael in his place. Adam, the chauffeur, drove him to Birmingham airport and was waiting there to bring him back to Wappenbury afterwards. Lyons was 'quite poorly' but sitting up in bed and expected a detailed report of how the Group 44 XJR-5s had gone and was asking about speeds. 'I was younger then but it still makes me cringe,' said Michael. 'I was telling him they were doing 300mph [482kmh] – absolutely ridiculous, it was 300kph [186mph]. He could not even speak very well, and there was me insisting it was 300mph, and he was shaking his head and saying, "No, 200mph [321kmh] maybe." So he knew exactly what was going on.'[33]

Michael Quinn recalled that, as a very young child, he would sometimes tell people that his grandpa 'invented Jaguar' – which really isn't a bad way of putting it.

The last grandchild of all was Mark, born to Mary in 1970. Having previously bought Mary's younger son, Tom, a go-kart that he had much enjoyed, Lyons – assuming all boys would want such things – now presented Mark with a schoolboy scrambler motor cycle when he was aged about 14, somewhat to Mary's initial horror! However, Mark found scrambling much harder than he anticipated and, she recorded, 'fortunately it got motor cycles out of his system'.

Pat Quinn's last child was Jane, born in June 1966. Jane studied art after leaving school and is a sculpture graduate of the Royal Academy of Arts – not entirely surprising with her grandfather more than once being described as a sculptor! Lyons always took an interest in his grandchildren – including their progress at school – and would sometimes attend sports days, his distinguished presence creating quite a stir.

CHAPTER 12

LYONS TAKES
HIS LEAVE

Since retirement and his increased interest in the farm, Bob Robinson had become like a companion for Lyons, who found great enjoyment in visiting the agricultural shows and sales.

'We used to go to Edinburgh and the ram sales. We went up to Scotland once and the chauffeur was driving. After a while he said, "Oh, Adam, you must be feeling tired. Let me have a spell."' They pulled in at some motorway services and Adam then sat in the back. Robinson continued: 'He was doing 130mph [209kmh]. He was 80 then.' Lyons pulled in at the services at Lancaster and asked how far they had to go. He was told about 140 miles [225kmh] and asked how long it would take. Robinson replied: 'It depends on who's driving!' "Well," he says, "I didn't frighten you, did I?" I thought, bloody hell, not much!'[1] Adam added: 'I think maybe he was trying to prove something, that he could still do it.'[2]

Even today, everyone speaks highly of Lyons in the village of Wappenbury. In the 1960s, he served as Chairman of the Parish Council. Without any airs, he was very much the squire in that he looked after everyone and was exceptionally generous. Many who had only known him at Jaguar might have been shocked to hear of this side of his character.

'When it became time for me to retire,' said Bob Robinson, 'I didn't but kept working. He said, "Whenever you want to retire, Robinson, go and find yourself a bungalow and I'll buy it for you. If you want to go back to Lancashire, you can do." I came from Lancashire, as he did.

'Later on he said, "Have you done anything about this bungalow?" I said I hadn't but I thought I'd rather stop round here. He said, "All right, I'll build you one." There used to be an old garage here, all piled up with scrap cars and he bought that just to do away with it. I think he paid this chap £25,000 for it. This bloke had a permit for a dwelling to be built. He paid for the building of it and every time the builder said, "Should I do this, should I do that?" he always said, "You go and see Mrs. Robinson, she's going to live in it." The missus had it just as she wanted it.'[3] It had been an eyesore that Lyons had objected to as spoiling the village back in 1967, writing to complain to Warwick Rural District Council!

One day, out of the blue, 'Lofty' England, who had retired to Austria, received a phone call. 'England, we're fed up here. We'd very much like you to drive us around Europe on a quiet trip.' 'Lofty' replied that he would be delighted but should they not seek medical advice first. Sadly the advice vetoed the idea.

Jaguar historian Andrew Whyte and his wife visited Wappenbury one day and Wendy admired the flowers. 'Yes,' said Lyons, 'you can buy some from my gardener.' John Morgan had a similar experience. 'He said to me, "If you want to buy some good geraniums for your garden, I have an arrangement with the gardener. He can sell them." So I went round and got some magnificent geraniums from these super greenhouses.'[4]

However, this is as not as mercenary as it sounds. Tom Sage was employed as a gardener with a normal salary but, Pat Quinn explained, as a bonus he was allowed to run the greenhouses on a commercial basis for himself. So in fact Lyons was encouraging visitors to support Sage's 'business'. The running costs of Wappenbury Hall were, as the family discovered later, 'phenomenal'.

Tom Sage runs a commercial nursery there to this day. 'It was his idea. He said sell things and use the money to buy plants for the garden. So when we first started, we opened up for a weekend and the cars parked on the drive. He was out there with his stick, parking the cars because he didn't want them to touch the grass edges. The grass edges, at that time, used to be absolutely immaculate, dead square and kept clean. He'd play merry hell if anyone drove on his lawn edges.' Like everyone else, Sage has nothing but respect for him. 'He was a gentleman. He was always very polite, he would always doff his cap to any ladies.'[5]

Lady Lyons was popular as well but there was quite a turnover of domestic staff. 'She was a bit tough on the indoor staff. Sir William used to try to mend things and smooth things over. He often became an arbitrator in some fall out. He was a remarkable man. What used to impress me – he wasn't very well and yet he used to come out and whatever the weather he used to go round this kitchen garden. He couldn't walk very well, but he'd get faster as he went. This was his morning constitutional and he'd go round and round and round. If it was raining hard, he would go in the stables and walk round the stables inside. Most mortals would have given up and died long before he did.

'He seemed to go up and down with Jaguar. If Jaguar were going well, he seemed to be up and out and bright. Then things went down and he'd take to his bed and we wouldn't see him for a fortnight. It was amazing.'[6]

In January 1984 during an XJ41 styling session outside Wappenbury Hall, John Egan, Jim Randle, and Keith Helfet (to his surprise) were invited inside for a sherry. 'It was my first view inside Wappenbury,' stated Helfet. 'It was the height of good taste – everything looked in keeping with the man who created Jaguar.'[7]

'We had a lot of fun,' recalled Egan. 'We'd take new models round for him to see. Often he used to say, "Well, bring it round and let's put it in front of the house. Sometimes I get a different view of it when I see it here." We'd walk around it and spend time over it. In the rough hurly-burly of me trying to save the company, it was a nice thing to be able to go and talk over its future with him in a calm and sensible way.'[8]

By now Jaguar had been back in profit for a couple of years and the Conservative Government decided to privatise it. 'He was excited that we were going to get out of British Leyland,' said Egan, 'but he had misgivings as to whether we could survive on our own, because he had come to the conclusion that he couldn't. Interestingly enough, I had conceptually that same worry, even right from the very start. On the other hand, we had decided that survival meant getting out of British Leyland. We did not think we could survive as part of British Leyland. I said, "I'm just going to have to get out of there and you're going to have to help me." He agreed with me that getting out of British Leyland was absolutely vital. At least he did live to see the company privatised.'[9]

In September the Lyons celebrated their diamond wedding anniversary. John Morgan continued to visit. 'He wasn't a fit man the last few months I saw him. He was a frail man. He used to sit in the sitting room at the front of the house. He was still mentally sharp.'[10] Tom Sage added: 'His speech was very difficult. You didn't help, that was not done. If you tried, he would jump on you. Sometimes, he found it difficult to find the right word.'[11]

The end was drawing closer, as Adam recalled. 'The first indication that he had Hodgkin's disease [he thinks it was] – my first wife used to do his washing and ironing and he accused her of shrinking his shirts because his collars didn't fit any more. She said they couldn't possibly have shrunk. There must be some other reason. I think it was just after that that he went to the doctor and they discovered something like cancer of the thyroid. That was causing his neck to swell, which was why his shirt didn't fit. Then he started going for treatment for that.'[12]

'He had shingles before he died,' said Robinson. 'I went up to see him one day in his bedroom and he rolled the sheets back and said, "Look at this mess, Robinson!" He had scabs all round his stomach... it was a mess.'[13]

Frank Adam recalled a day in early 1985. 'He came up through the garden and stood just outside the potting shed, by the greenhouse, and looked over the garden and said, "Good morning" to everybody and had a little chat to them. One or two said, "It looks as if he's having a last look round." He wasn't walking very well. He went back into the house and that was the last time he came out.'[14] 'Then he had a fall on the landing,' stated Robinson, 'and he damaged his brain, I think. That's what ended him. The doctors had said that he'd always be a cabbage. There was no hope of him recovering from this brain damage.'[15]

On Friday 8 February 1985 Lyons passed away.

Jaguar's press release quoted John Egan as saying, 'Sir William has had a magnificent career in the motor industry. He created this wonderful company and will be sadly missed by his great many friends in Jaguar and throughout the industry. He has been a great friend to me personally and a great ally in the renaissance of this company. I shall miss his wise counsel.'

Andrew Whyte wrote: 'His pleasure over the past few months, culminating in the news of an all-time record for output and sales – plus, of course, the return to the private sector – was plain to all who met him.'

Ted Loades, whose Abbey Panels firm was so closely linked with so many of Jaguar's key models, stated: 'I wish we had him here today. I've been right through the industry, Rover, Ford, the lot, but the one man I admired the most at the time was Sir William Lyons. I personally think he should have been made a Lord, not a Sir.'[16]

'Today you have got to have billions,' said Patrick Mennem. 'He only did it in his day because he was so shrewd, so careful and his husbandry was so marvellous. He produced these motor cars at a price that nobody, relatively, is matching today.'[17]

'He obviously had wonderful taste,' said Jackie Stewart whose father was a Jaguar dealer, 'because whoever was in there designing...at the end of the day, I think it all went down to Sir William, when it came to that style. The man was so unassuming and so mild. He always had his dark blue suit on, with his light blue tie and his white shirt. He was a wonderfully elegant man...and almost an introvert within the industry.'[18]

A Thanksgiving Service was held at Coventry Cathedral at 3pm on

27 February. It was conducted by the Bishop of Warwick, with readings by John Egan and Jim Randle. The Coventry City Jaguar Band played in the entrance to the Chapel of Unity. 'Lofty' England flew in to give the address. Among a packed congregation were Connie Teather, Jack Beardsley and George Lee from the Blackpool days, Emil Frey (86) from Switzerland, and Joska Bourgeois from Belgium. 'The post-war story of Jaguar has become,' said 'Lofty', 'through his leadership, a piece of British history.'

In May it was reported that he had left an estate valued at £3,356,278 net (£3,417,111 gross). Most property was bequeathed to Lady Lyons and the majority of his wealth had already been put into his family and charitable trusts. He left approximately £18,000 to his local retainers, including £3,300 to stockman Ron Mace, who had looked after his Jersey cows for 35 years before retiring the previous year.

Referring to the house Lyons built for him, Bob Robinson said: 'I've got this for life, me and my wife, for five pence a year. So that's how generous he was. And he left me £10,000 in his will. He was one of the best.'[19] Also, to his surprise, he has a pension of £60 week from Jaguar, towards which he had never paid a penny, so it had been funded by Lyons. He never mentioned it and Bob knew nothing about it until after Lyons died.

Not surprisingly, as they had been so close, Lady Lyons was deeply affected. 'She was very upset,' said daughter Pat. 'She was very lonely afterwards. She missed him dreadfully.' Some 13 months later she passed away. 'One couldn't help thinking it was the best thing for her.'[20]

Greta had always been a wonderful support and given him strength behind the scenes. She has never received the public acknowledgement that her contribution deserved. 'I think at times she must have been a very lonely woman...' Lyons observed when he retired. 'But she understood. I don't think I always appreciated just how much, although I have always realised she had exceptional qualities as a woman. She once said to me that she sometimes wondered if I remembered if I had children. I saw them all the time and knew what they were up to but I rarely had time to take them out, or play with them.'

As we have seen, against amazing odds and almost overwhelming obstacles, Lyons built a very large and successful business. He created a make of car that is known, revered, and loved throughout the world. But perhaps the most remarkable thing is that he achieved it all with honesty and honour, without making enemies.

He did not break the rules, as so many successful people have done.

Lyons could appear aloof and cold in public but he was never unkind or unfair. All knew that everything he did was for the good of Jaguar. If he seemed mean at times, it was with good purpose; that such was not his character was proven by his generosity to close associates and to his family. He did not often choose to show it but there was also a very human side to this authoritative man.

He earned the respect, admiration, and affection of his competitors, his senior colleagues, his management, most union officials and the vast majority of his workforce. He proved that the old fashioned virtues of honesty and hard work could indeed bring the highest rewards.

'Success;' Lyons once pronounced, 'comes from you, from believing in what you are doing.'[21]

BIOGRAPHICAL
NOTES

APPLEYARD, IAN
Son of a Leeds Jaguar dealer, Ian Appleyard achieved Best Performance in an ageing SS Jaguar 100 in the 1948 Alpine Rally. Thus selected to have one of the semi-works XK120s; his was registered NUB120. Married Pat Lyons in 1950 (later divorced) and together they took many international honours in rallying.

BAILY, CLAUDE
After working for Anzani and Morris Engines, Baily joined the company in 1940 as an engine designer. He was a key member of the legendary teams who designed both the XK and V12 engines.

BERRY, BOB
Cambridge graduate, who joined the Publicity Department in 1951 as assistant to Rankin, becoming PR Manager in the 1960s. Meanwhile, had enjoyed a successful amateur career in racing until Lyons told him to choose between motor sport and Jaguar. Worked closely with Lyons and later held senior positions within BL.

BLACK, CAPT (LATER SIR) JOHN
Managing Director of Standard, he agreed to supply engines and specially designed chassis to the renamed SS Cars. This arrangement allowed the young Swallow company to evolve a step further towards the complete manufacture of cars that would come later. Relations would become strained for a while.

BLACK, SIR WILLIAM
Former Chairman of AEC, he was appointed Chairman of Leyland in February 1963. Not to be confused with John Black of Standard.

BOURGEOIS, JOSKA
Madame Bourgeois became the Belgian Jaguar importer in the late 1940s and built up an extremely successful business. It has been stated that she and Lyons enjoyed a brief relationship but this seems highly unlikely. Her name hit the headlines in the 1990s in relation to Geoffrey Robinson MP, who was briefly MD of Jaguar in the 1970s.

BRYSON, JACK
Became Jaguar's Australian importer just after the war and was a most loyal supporter of the growing Jaguar business. Lyons had great affection for and loyalty to Bryson, whom he rated highly. Bryson built Australia into Jaguar's third most important market, after the USA and UK.

CURRIE, ALAN
Joined company at start of 1950s to introduce some young blood and concentrated on sales. Gradually progressed up the ladder to become Home Sales Director and thus worked closely with Lyons for many years.

EDWARDES, SIR MICHAEL
Former Chief Executive of Chloride, appointed Chairman of BL in 1977. Introduced strong management, broke the union domination, closed plants, reduced workforce, and revised new model programme. Appointed John Egan as Chairman of Jaguar in 1980.

EERDMANS, JOHANNES
London-based Dutchman, who moved to the States and set up Jaguar's American company for Lyons. Played a very major role in creating and maintaining Jaguar's most important market and enjoyed a unique relationship with Lyons.

EGAN, SIR JOHN
Appointed Chairman of Jaguar by Sir Michael Edwardes in 1980, he fought for Jaguar's identity and autonomy, extracting the company from BL and restoring its independence. Regularly sought Lyons's advice as he rebuilt the image and returned the company to profit.

ENGLAND, 'LOFTY'
After gaining experience as a racing mechanic with Sir Henry Birkin, Dick Seaman, Prince Bira, and Whitney Straight, plus a spell with Alvis, England joined Jaguar in 1946 as Service Manager. When the company officially entered motor racing, he became a highly effective and legendary Team Manager. Gradually promoted to the higher management echelons as Lyons groomed him as his successor. Became Joint Managing Director in 1968, Deputy Chairman later that year and Chairman upon Lyons's retirement. England retired in 1974.

FENTON, ALICE
Joined in the early Swallow days and became Lyons's invaluable secretary. For the next three decades she single-mindedly devoted herself to Jaguar and Lyons, effectively being his personal assistant and being given the title of Home Sales Director as an indication of her importance within Jaguar. Tragically died in 1960 at the age of 50.

FREY, EMIL
One of Lyons's earliest customers and one of his first overseas agents, Frey would remain the Jaguar importer for German-speaking Switzerland for several decades and build a successful conglomerate business.

GARDNER, FRED
Superintendent of the wood mill and in charge of the body development shop, Gardner enjoyed an unusually close working relationship with Lyons and was one of the very few people to be addressed by his first name. Like Holland before him, played a crucial role in translating Lyons's styling ideas into reality.

GRICE, BOB
Rejoined company in 1957 and appointed Works Director, responsible for labour relations and quality. Later promoted to Joint Managing Director in 1968 and retired in 1972.

HAMILTON, DUNCAN
Larger-than-life character, who raced an XK120 before joining the works team in 1952 and winning Le Mans with his 'partner-in-crime' Tony Rolt in 1953. Raced D-types for the factory (he and Rolt missed a debut victory at the French classic by just 104 seconds) and a friend of Lyons.

HARRIMAN, SIR GEORGE

Managing Director of British Motor Corporation (BMC) from 1956, Harriman succeeded Sir Leonard Lord as Chairman in 1961. Engineered acquisition of Jaguar by BMC to form BMH in 1966. Honoured pledge to Lyons regarding Jaguar's autonomy but forced to stand down when British Leyland formed in 1968.

HASSAN, WALTER

Apprenticed to Bentley, Wally Hassan joined SS Cars before the war as a development engineer. During the war he took part in the famous fire-watching sessions when the XK engine was planned. In 1950 he joined Coventry Climax where he was responsible for designing the successful GP engines. After Jaguar acquired Climax in the mid-1960s, Hassan took charge of the V12 engine project and became a director in 1969.

HAWTHORN, MIKE

Works team leader in 1955 and 1956, he won the tragic 1955 Le Mans with Ivor Bueb in a D-type. Very popular at the works, Hawthorn was much liked by Lyons. He also raced Jaguar saloons and, a few months after becoming World Champion, was killed in his 3.4 on the Guildford bypass.

HENLY, BERTIE

A leading London car dealer, who formed his business with Frank Hough in 1917, he gave Lyons his first big commercial break, thus beginning a business relationship that would continue until retirement. Henly became a loyal friend and trusted advisor who helped Lyons to build the business into such a success story.

HEWITT, BERNARD

Taken on by Lyons as his personal assistant but would be more accurately described as looking after special projects, investigating Lyons's many ideas and suggesting his own. As one of the few members of his personal staff, Hewitt had a close view of Lyons at work and has immense respect for him.

HEYNES, WILLIAM

After a grounding at Humber, Heynes was selected by Lyons in 1935 to be his first Chief Engineer. Played an absolutely crucial role in designing and developing every model of Jaguar, promoting a pioneering engineering spirit, until his retirement as Vice-Chairman in 1969. Lyons relied on Heynes entirely on technical matters and Heynes created a pre-eminent team that built the production and competition cars, which enjoyed such success for so many decades.

HOFFMAN, MAX

Austrian-born car dealer in New York, who became Jaguar distributor for the East Coast after the war. Regularly accused of sharp practice, he and Lyons fell out acrimoniously in the early 1950s.

HOLLAND, CYRIL

Master craftsman, who joined in 1926 and translated Lyons's conceptual ideas into practical reality. Reluctant to move from Blackpool to Coventry, he was eventually persuaded to do so and was repeatedly invaluable to Lyons, who might never succeeded without Holland behind him.

HORNBURG, CHARLES

Appointed Jaguar distributor for the West Coast of America, he established a dealership on Sunset Boulevard. Though very successful at selling Jaguars, relations with Lyons cooled and his status was gradually reduced.

HUCKVALE, EDWARD
Joined in 1928, shortly after the move to Coventry, as Company Secretary. Helped Lyons to control costs and remained a director until his death, at the age of 73, in 1962. Highly rated by Lyons, as shown by his remaining with the company well past normal retirement age.

JONES, JACK
Local Coventry Transport and General Workers' Union representative (and also Secretary of the Confederation of Shipbuilding and Engineering Unions), Jones later became the regional organiser based in Birmingham and the national General Secretary and leader of the union.

KNIGHT, BOB
Brilliant development engineer, who specialised in the suppression of noise and vibration. Designed the C-type chassis, then later Jaguar's first independent rear suspension and played a major role in creating the XJ6. Succeeded Heynes as Engineering Director in 1969, was later briefly Managing Director and is credited with saving the company from extinction during the worst BL period.

LYONS, JOHN
Born in 1930, John Michael Lyons went to Oundle public school, followed by a three-year apprenticeship at Leyland Motors. After completing his national service with the REME, he joined Jaguar in 1955. A few months later he was tragically killed in a car accident in France. William Lyons thus lost his only son and heir.

MORGAN, JOHN
Linguist, who was part educated in Switzerland, Morgan joined Jaguar in 1963, after 13 years with Rootes. He was soon appointed Export Manager, replacing the ageing Ben Mason, and was then given responsibility for Daimler as well. Later became Export Director and held senior positions within BL. Battled to retain Jaguar's identity and was a member of John Egan's team in the 1980s.

MOSS, SIR STIRLING
Considers his victory in the 1950 Tourist Trophy at Dundrod in Tommy Wisdom's semi-works XK120 to be have been the first major victory of his amazing career. As a result of this extraordinary drive in appalling conditions, Lyons asked Moss, who was 21 next day, to lead the Jaguar works team. Drove for the company from 1951 to 1954. Clocked up many victories in sports, sports racing, and saloon Jaguars.

QVALE, KJELL
San Franciso-based dealer, who formed British Motor Car Distributors and claims to have sold more British sports cars than anyone else. Built an extremely successful Jaguar dealership and was highly respected by Lyons.

RANKIN, ERNEST 'BILL'
Advertising and Publicity Manager, who did so much to create the SS and Jaguar images. One of the many intensely loyal people within Jaguar who deserve great credit for helping Lyons to build such a successful business.

ROBINSON, BOB
Joined Lyons as his farm manager in 1959 and earned his trust and respect. In Lyons's later life, after his retirement from Jaguar, Robinson would become something of a 'companion' to his employer. Lyons showed his gratitude in several acts of great generosity.

ROLT, TONY
Ex-Colditz prisoner, Major Tony Rolt was drafted into the works team after putting up an impressive drive in the 1951 TT. Together with Hamilton, he took a famous victory at Le Mans in 1953, setting the first 100mph (160kmh) average for the race. Worked for Harry Ferguson and later built up FF Developments, the four-wheel-drive and transmission specialists.

SAYER, MALCOLM
Eccentric but brilliant aerodynamicist who joined Jaguar in 1950 and designed the Le Mans-winning C-type. Subsequently designed the D-type and E-type and thus created the image of the 'modern' Jaguar sports car, since perpetuated in the XJ220 and XK8. Influence on Jaguar styling was second only to that of Lyons.

STOKES, LORD
In 1949 appointed General Sales Manager of Leyland Motors at age of 35. Appointed Managing Director in 1962 and later replaced Sir William Black as Chairman. Led amalgamation of Leyland with BMH to form British Leyland and became first Chairman. Did not enjoy a comfortable working relationship with Lyons.

THURSTANS, ARTHUR
Thurstans joined SS Cars in 1943 as company accountant. He was responsible for setting up many internal systems and would give Lyons wise counsel. He was rewarded by being appointed a director in 1962 and was later given the title Financial Director. He retired from Jaguar in 1971.

WALMSLEY, WILLIAM
Lyons's original partner, he created the Swallow sidecar that was the basis of their business. Initially a reluctant partner, Walmsley came from a wealthy background and did not need to work. Older and less ambitious than Lyons, relations became strained and, in 1934, upon the flotation of the company, Lyons bought out Walmsley.

WESLAKE, HARRY
Irascible consulting engineer, who specialised in combustion and developed an overhead valve head for the original Standard power unit, transforming it into a more powerful engine for Lyons. Later advised on cylinder head design for the XK engine and ongoing development for racing use.

WHITTAKER, ARTHUR
One of the very first Swallow employees, he joined in 1923 at the age of 17. Taken on initially to handle sales, he soon transferred to buying at which he excelled, building an impressive reputation in the industry as the small company grew into an industrial force. Lyons's second-in-command worked tirelessly behind the scenes and his important contribution is not always recognised. Retired in 1968 as Deputy Chairman.

Bibliography

Clausager, Anders Ditlev, *Jaguar – A Living Legend* (Brian Trodd, London 1990).
Clew, Jeff, *Lucky All My Life – the biography of Harry Weslake* (J. H. Haynes, Sparkford 1979).
Dugdale, John, *Jaguar in America* (Britbooks, Otego, New York 1993).
Edwardes, Michael, *Back from the Brink* (Collins, London 1983).
Hassan, Walter, *Climax in Coventry* (Mercian Manuals, Coventry 1975).
Hughes, Les, *Jaguar under the Southern Cross* (Melbourne, 1980).
Long, Brian, *Standard – The Illustrated History* (Veloce Publishing, Godmanstone 1993).
Daimler & Lanchester – A Century of Motoring History (Longford International Publications, UK 1995).
Montagu, Lord, *Jaguar – A Biography* (Cassell, London 1961).
Porter, Philip, *Jaguar – The Complete Illustrated History* (Frederick Warne, London 1984).
Jaguar Project XJ40 – The Inside Story of the New XJ6 (Haynes Publishing, Sparkford 1987).
Jaguar – History of a Classic Marque (Sidgwick & Jackson, London 1988).
Jaguar E-type – The Definitive History (Haynes Publishing, Sparkford 1989).
Jaguar Scrapbook (Haynes Publishing, Sparkford 1989).
Jaguar XJ220 (Osprey, London 1994).
Jaguar Sports Racing Cars (Bay View Books, Bideford 1995).
Jaguar XK8 – The Authorised Biography (Bay View Books, Bideford 1996).
The Most Famous Car in the World (Orion, London 2000).
Skilleter, Paul, *Jaguar Sports Cars* (J. H. Haynes, Sparkford 1975).
(with Andrew Whyte) *Jaguar Saloons* (Haynes Publishing, Sparkford 1980).
Thomas, Sir Miles, *Out on a Wing* (Michael Joseph, London 1964).
Turner, Graham, *The Car Makers* (Penguin Books, Harmondsworth 1963).
The Leyland Papers (Eyre & Spottiswoode, London 1971).
Underwood, John, *The Will to Win – Jaguar and John Egan* (W. H. Allen, London 1989).
Whyte, Andrew, *Jaguar – The History of a Great British Car* (Patrick Stephens, Cambridge 1980).
Jaguar Sports Racing and Works Competition Cars to 1953 (Haynes Publishing, Sparkford 1982).
Jaguar Sports Racing and Works Competition Cars from 1954 (Haynes Publishing, Sparkford 1987).
Jaguar – The Definitive History of a Great British Car (Haynes Publishing, Sparkford 1994).
Wood, Jonathan, *Wheels of Misfortune* (Sidgwick & Jackson, London 1988).

JAGUAR FINANCIAL ANALYSIS 1935–71

Year	Sales revenue £	Pre-tax net profit £	Tax £	Tax percentage	Post-tax profit £	Net current assets £	Cash at bank £	Bank overdraft & loans £	Net cash £
1935	454,301	27,960	3,751	13	24,209	105,249	45,852	—	45,852
1936	685,059	30,258	2,891	10	27,367	103,783	40,326	—	40,326
1937	971,473	41,632	7,339	18	34,293	110,452	86,650	—	86,650
1938	711,649	29,727	7,509	25	22,218	113,917	79,377	—	79,377
1939	1,414,095	48,787	17,564	36	31,223	117,566	86,860	—	86,860
1940	292,819	-22,660	1,363	—	-24,023	17,942	177	23,377	-23,200
1941	—	40,419	9,444	23	30,975	55,711	330	70,841	-70,511
1942	—	67,152	28,930	43	38,222	113,414	520	88,495	-87,975
1943	—	118,314	82,230	70	36,084	229,761	471	50,127	-49,656
1944	—	164,919	124,255	75	40,664	322,432	21,274	—	21,274
1945	—	78,269	36,856	47	41,413	267,261	38,042	—	38,042
1946	—	32,717	9,865	30	22,852	330,073	1,006	127,465	-126,459
1947	—	190,424	76,979	40	113,445	317,697	91,019	—	91,019
1948	—	264,229	127,968	48	136,261	291,694	129,519	—	129,519
1949	—	125,000	61,108	49	63,892	187,404	41,841	—	41,841
1950	—	311,000	152,234	49	158,766	277,012	192,275	—	192,275
1951	—	336,000	186,022	55	149,978	200,935	199,940	—	199,940

Year	Sales revenue £	Pre-tax net profit £	Tax £	Tax percentage	Post-tax profit £	Net current assets £	Cash at bank £	Bank overdraft & loans £	Net cash £
1952	—	396,000	240,503	61	155,497	759,857	422,675	—	422,675
1953	—	438,000	247,813	57	190,187	863,295	349,286	—	349,286
1954	—	558,000	341,070	61	216,930	922,848	703,996	—	703,996
1955	—	526,000	265,939	51	260,061	775,833	684,139	—	684,139
1956	—	551,008	224,332	41	326,676	680,180	26,647	561,977	-535,330
1957	—	589,638	274,317	47	315,321	1,266,995	235,703	319,149	-83,446
1958	—	1,488,000	863,644	58	624,356	2,530,282	2,119,985	—	2,119,985
1959	—	2,604,000	1,220,541	47	1,383,459	2,361,512	3,075,384	—	3,075,384
1960	25,372,896	1,846,000	806,402	44	1,039,598	244,729	1,142,851	—	1,142,851
1961	21,437,961	2,062,000	976,463	47	1,085,537	719,969	2,859,388	780,142	2,079,246
1962	—	2,171,000	836,006	39	1,334,994	605,310	1,199,710	496,454	703,256
1963	—	2,253,000	1,017,669	45	1,235,331	1,291,129	576,423	709,220	-132,797
1964	29,973,413	2,430,000	933,153	38	1,496,847	3,138,978	1,225,730	762,411	463,319
1965	30,891,551	2,434,273	770,784	32	1,663,489	3,136,271	588,876	949,927	-361,051
1966	26,868,285	2,424,749	915,518	38	1,509,231	3,397,479	372,437	1,584,442	-1,212,005
1967	—	1,165,000	123,527	11	1,041,473	4,377,929	1,497,688	4,888,078	-3,390,390
1968*	62,673,272	2,339,532	1,027,957	44	1,311,575	2,915,604	1,209,186	5,118,517	-3,909,331
1969	57,603,244	2,867,955	910,433	32	1,957,522	6,453,822	702,180	3,733,694	-3,031,514
1970	67,308,190	4,064,159	1,398,997	34	2,665,162	4,127,322	237,593	4,357,126	-4,719,533
1971	81,852,836	5,891,054	2,208,617	37	3,682,437	5,561,620	71,260	4,519,382	-4,548,122

Note: Until 1966 the Jaguar financial year ended on 31 July. The date 1957, for example, refers to the annual accounts for the year 1 August 1956 to 31 July 1957. In 1967 Jaguar's year end became 29 July (to align with the BMC year) and was changed to 30 September in 1968 (to align with British Leyland's financial year). *The year ending 30 September 1968 was a 14-month period.

JAGUAR PRODUCTION 1931–73

By major model ranges: prewar figures by model year, postwar by calendar year.

Year	SSI & SS2	SS Jaguar & 'MK IV'	Mk V	XK inc C-, D-type	Mk VII, VIII & IX	2,4, 3,4 & MK 2*	Mk X & 420G	E-type	S-type & 420*	XJ*	Other Daimlers	Total per year
1931–2	777	—	—	—	—	—	—	—	—	—	—	777
1932–3	1,526	—	—	—	—	—	—	—	—	—	—	1,526
1933–4	1,791	—	—	—	—	—	—	—	—	—	—	1,791
1934–5	1,724	—	—	—	—	—	—	—	—	—	—	1,724
1935–6	235	2,232	—	—	—	—	—	—	—	—	—	2,467
1936–7	—	3,637	—	—	—	—	—	—	—	—	—	3,637
1937–8	—	2,277	—	—	—	—	—	—	—	—	—	2,277
1938–9	—	5,320	—	—	—	—	—	—	—	—	—	5,320
1939–40	—	893	—	—	—	—	—	—	—	—	—	893
1945	—	141	—	—	—	—	—	—	—	—	—	141
1946	—	2,928	—	—	—	—	—	—	—	—	—	2,928
1947	—	4,346	—	—	—	—	—	—	—	—	—	4,346
1948	—	4,243	8	—	—	—	—	—	—	—	—	4,251
1949	—	311	3,782	97	—	—	—	—	—	—	—	4,190
1950	—	—	5,679	1,519	8	—	—	—	—	—	—	7,206
1951	—	—	1,030	1,329	4,137	—	—	—	—	—	—	6,496
1952	—	—	—	3,002	5,966	—	—	—	—	—	—	8,968
1953	—	—	—	3,405	6,694	—	—	—	—	—	—	10,099
1954	—	—	—	3,440	6,454	—	—	—	—	—	—	9,894
1955	—	—	—	4,749	6,087	32	—	—	—	—	—	10,868

Year	SS1 & SS2	SS Jaguar &, 'Mk IV'	Mk V	XK inc C-, D-type	Mk VII, VIII & IX	2.4, 3.4 & Mk 2*	Mk X & 420G	E-type	S-type & 420*	XJ*	Other Daimlers	Total per year
1956	—	—	—	3,317	1,859	8,029	—	—	—	—	—	13,205
1957	—	—	—	1,503	3,653	8,520	—	—	—	—	—	13,676
1958	—	—	—	4,599	3,252	11,605	—	—	—	—	—	19,456
1959	—	—	—	2,201	4,977	11,331	—	—	—	—	110	18,619
1960	—	—	—	1,359	3,555	17,535	—	—	—	—	903	23,352
1961	—	—	—	2	603	21,236	4	2,182	—	—	1,197	25,224
1962	—	—	—	—	1	12,751	4,312	6,266	—	—	851	24,181
1963	—	—	—	—	—	12,697	6,572	4,065	43	—	546	23,923
1964	—	—	—	—	—	12,043	2,458	3,942	7,032	—	387	25,862
1965	—	—	—	—	—	8,277	3,296	5,294	9,741	—	297	26,905
1966	—	—	—	—	—	5,935	2,023	6,880	8,032	—	212	23,082
1967	—	—	—	—	—	6,432	1,640	4,989	8,730	—	170	21,961
1968	—	—	—	—	—	7,497	1,653	7,072	6,434	639	56	23,351
1969	—	—	—	—	—	1,915	1,617	9,948	1,041	13,769	324	28,614
1970	—	—	—	—	—	—	600	6,686	—	21,833	489	29,608
1971	—	—	—	—	—	—	—	3,746	—	27,517	286	31,549
1972	—	—	—	—	—	—	—	4,014	—	20,240	287	24,541
1973	—	—	—	—	—	—	—	4,686	—	22,913	294	27,893
Totals	**6,053**	**26,328**	**10,499**	**30,522**	**47,246**	**145,835**	**24,175**	**69,770**	**41,053**	**106,911**	**6,409**	**514,801**

*Mark 2, 420 and XJ ranges include Daimler models. Source: Jaguar Daimler Heritage Trust archive, production statistics.

JAGUAR EXPORTS

Ten best markets and overall export/home sales performance by sales year, prewar and postwar periods.

Prewar period 1931–40

Year	Switzerland	Australia (TKM)	Holland	India	Spain	South Africa	Malaya	Argentina	Portugal	USA	Total of ten markets	Total all exports	Home market sales	Total all sales	Exports as % of all sales
1931–2	5	5	1	4	0	—	—	0	4	0	19	40	736	776	5.15
1932–3	6	15	26	17	9	—	—	0	17	0	90	131	1,394	1,525	8.59
1933–4	2	29	43	16	43	—	—	23	8	0	164	226	1,567	1,793	12.60
1934–5	15	51	25	5	31	—	—	19	4	8	158	214	1,506	1,720	12.44
1935–6	24	9	22	6	9	15	4	7	5	29	130	177	2,292	2,469	7.17
1936–7	66	23	9	4	0	17	12	6	9	9	155	234	3,320	3,554	6.58
1937–8	45	9	7	12	0	16	10	6	5	1	111	174	2,035	2,209	7.88
1938–9	50	19	1	27	0	19	24	2	0	0	142	226	5,228	5,454	4.14
1939–40	11	9	0	12	0	5	18	4	2	0	61	77	746	823	9.36
Market total	224	169	134	103	92	72	68	67	54	47					

Note: Figures for Australia 1931–5 are in fact deliveries to TKM (Tozer, Kemsley and Millbourn). It is thought that some of these cars went to South Africa and Malaya.

Postwar period 1945–73

Year	USA	Australia	South Africa	France	Switzerland	Canada	Belgium	Italy	Germany	New Zealand	Total of ten markets	Total all exports	Home market sales	Total all sales	Exports as % of all sales
1945-6	0	19	13	2	53	0	37	0	0	6	130	305	827	1,132	26.94
1946-7	9	103	69	21	196	0	114	0	0	16	528	910	3,432	4,342	20.96
1947-8	245	517	79	26	191	0	389	0	0	66	1,513	2,104	2,082	4,186	50.26
1948-9	135	404	23	15	70	12	66	0	2	9	736	1,191	2,122	3,313	35.95
1949-50	729	1,675	6	76	156	225	88	0	22	77	3,054	3,926	2,721	6,647	59.06
1950-1	1,553	867	12	70	95	182	34	4	83	117	3,017	4,273	1,532	5,805	73.61
1951-2	3,243	1,250	39	278	222	96	225	16	288	327	5,984	7,978	1,001	8,979	88.85
1952-3	5,218	257	17	175	62	313	139	19	93	92	6,385	7,643	2,471	10,114	75.57
1953-4	2,834	622	1	235	54	217	88	24	107	173	4,355	5,335	4,796	10,131	52.66
1954-5	3,239	596	4	167	41	183	121	9	118	209	4,687	5,438	4,462	9,900	54.93
1955-6	3,871	484	5	230	197	351	164	29	138	212	5,681	6,847	5,305	12,152	56.34
1956-7	3,592	279	50	267	180	348	173	50	93	227	5,259	6,614	6,338	12,952	51.07
1957-8	4,607	537	583	314	274	512	247	77	119	335	7,605	9,177	8,375	17,552	52.28
1958-9	5,596	690	359	303	299	814	251	99	144	26	8,581	10,476	10,400	20,876	50.18
1959-60	4,934	507	171	389	322	524	251	121	201	103	7,523	9,677	9,564	19,341	50.03
1960-1	3,422	747	359	755	707	612	345	348	323	189	7,807	10,174	13,844	24,018	42.36
1961-2	5,716	448	163	645	589	444	240	456	349	122	9,172	11,135	10,895	22,030	50.54
1962-3	4,113	924	317	997	932	212	370	721	556	246	9,388	12,235	12,754	24,989	48.96
1963-4	4,037	1,021	357	735	316	227	309	314	351	487	8,154	10,206	14,142	24,348	41.92
1964-5	3,669	880	340	617	534	241	288	245	302	430	7,546	9,560	15,041	24,601	38.86
1965-6	5,418	864	741	675	491	351	355	389	369	459	10,112	12,098	13,838	25,936	46.65
1966-7	6,715	631	485	508	399	323	258	469	257	305	10,350	12,026	10,624	22,650	53.09
1967-8	4,430	602	666	426	363	382	293	127	336	209	7,834	9,800	14,515	24,315	40.30
1968-9	6,833	527	629	493	633	418	423	502	379	247	11,084	13,531	11,105	24,636	54.92
1969-70	7,384	1,100	2,238	906	842	433	392	1,323	425	310	15,353	18,422	12,001	30,423	60.55
1970-1	5,500	1,784	1,633	996	1,453	217	900	1,317	982	426	15,208	18,406	12,183	32,589	56.48
1971-2	4,734	506	1,375	551	124	297	395	143	253	439	8,817	10,945	12,043	22,988	47.61
1972-3	7,650	803	1,227	512	656	475	988	507	408	489	13,715	16,943	12,932	29,875	56.71
Market total	109,426	19,644	11,961	11,384	10,451	8,409	7,943	7,309	6,698	6,353					

Note: Daimlers are included from 1962–3 onwards. Source: Jaguar Daimler Heritage Trust archive, sales statistics.

ENDNOTES

Introduction
1. F. W. McComb *The Story of the MG Sports Car* (London 1972), p4.

Chapter 1
1. W. Lyons, prize-giving speech to British Leyland apprentices, c.1971.
2. Ibid.
3. Interview by P. H. Porter and P. Skilleter with P. Quinn and M. Rimell, Nov 2000.
4. Ibid.
5. W. Lyons, draft autobiography, 1976.
6. Ibid.
7. W. Lyons, untitled reminiscences, 19 April 1961.
8. Ibid.
9. Ibid.
10. A. J. A. Whyte, *Automobile Quarterly*, Vol 18 no 4 1980.
11. P. Turner, *Motor*, 4 Mar 1972.
12. W. Lyons, untitled reminiscences, 19 April 1961.
13. Interview by Miss McGowan, published 15 Feb 1972.
14. W. Lyons, draft autobiography, 1976.
15. Ibid.
16. Ibid.
17. Interview by P. Skilleter, Aug 1992.
18. W. Lyons, draft autobiography, 1976.
19. Ibid.
20. Ibid.
21. Ibid.
22. Ibid.
23. Ibid.
24. W. Lyons, speech at Motor Trades Luncheon Club, 25 June 1947.
25. Ibid.
26. W. Lyons, draft autobiography, 1976.
27. Ibid.
28. Interview, *Supercat* documentary Channel 4, 1984.
29. W. Lyons, draft autobiography, 1976.
30. Ibid.
31. Ibid.
32. Interview by G. Griffin, 1986.

Chapter 2
1. W. Lyons, draft autobiography, 1976.
2. Ibid.
3. Ibid.
4. Ibid.
5. Ibid.
6. Ibid.
7. Ibid.
8. Ibid.
9. Ibid.
10. C. Teather, memoirs, 1990.

11. Interview by G. Griffin, 1986.
12. C. Teather, memoirs, 1990.
13. Ibid.
14. W. Lyons, draft autobiography, 1976.
15. Ibid.
16. Ibid.
17. Ibid.
18. H. Teather '35 not out', *Jaguar Journal* (UK), 1958.
19. Interview by P. Skilleter, 1993.
20. Interview by G. Griffin, 1986.
21. W. Lyons, draft autobiography, 1976.
22. Ibid.
23. Ibid.
24. Ibid.
25. Ibid.
26. Interview by G. Griffin, 1986.
27. W. Lyons, draft autobiography, 1976.
28. Ibid.
29. Ibid.
30. Ibid.
31. Ibid.
32. Ibid.
33. Ibid.
34. Ibid.
35. Ibid.
36. W. Lyons 'The History of Jaguar and the Future of the Specialised Car in the British Motor Industry', Lord Wakefield Gold Medal Paper, 28 April 1969.
37. Interview by G. Griffin, 1986.

Chapter 3
1. Interview by P. Skilleter, Aug 1992.
2. Interview, *Supercat* documentary Channel 4, 1984.
3. Interview by G. Griffin, 1986.
4. Ibid.
5. W. Lyons, draft autobiography, 1976.
6. Interview by P. Skilleter, 1973.
7. W. Lyons, draft autobiography, 1976.
8. Ibid.
9. Ibid.
10. W. Heynes 'Milestones in the Life of an Automobile Engineer', paper, Oct 1960.
11. W. Lyons 'The History of Jaguar and the Future of the Specialised Car in the British Motor Industry', Lord Wakefield Gold Medal Paper, 28 April 1969.
12. W. Lyons, draft autobiography, 1976.
13. Interview by P. H. Porter and P. Skilleter with P. Quinn and M. Rimell, Nov 2000.
14. Interview by P. Skilleter, July 1997.
15. Ibid.
16. Interview by G. Mond, 1981.
17. P. H. Porter *Project XJ40 – The Inside Story of the New XJ6* (Sparkford 1987), p.37.

18. W. Lyons, draft autobiography, 1976.
19. Ibid.
20. Ibid.
21. Interview by P. Skilleter, 1973.
22. W. Lyons, draft autobiography, 1976.
23. Ibid.
24. Ibid.
25. W. Lyons 'The History of Jaguar and the Future of the Specialised Car in the British Motor Industry', Lord Wakefield Gold Medal Paper, 28 April 1969.
26. W. Lyons, speech at Motor Trades Luncheon Club, 25 June 1947.
27. Interview by P. H. Porter and P. Skilleter with P. Quinn and M. Rimell, Nov 2000.
28. Ibid.
29. Letter from E. Turner to W. Lyons, 13 April 1942.
30. W. Lyons 'The History of Jaguar and the Future of the Specialised Car in the British Motor Industry', Lord Wakefield Gold Medal Paper, 28 April 1969.
31. Ibid.
32. P. Turner, *Motor*, 4 Mar 1972.
33. W. Hassan *Climax in Coventry* (Coventry 1975), p.61.
34. W. Lyons 'The History of Jaguar and the Future of the Specialised Car in the British Motor Industry', Lord Wakefield Gold Medal Paper, 28 April 1969.
35. Ibid.
36. W. Lyons, draft autobiography, 1976.
37. W. Lyons 'The History of Jaguar and the Future of the Specialised Car in the British Motor Industry', Lord Wakefield Gold Medal Paper, 28 April 1969.
38. W. Lyons, draft autobiography, 1976.

Chapter 4
1. W. Lyons, draft autobiography, 1976.
2. A. J. A. Whyte, *Jaguar – The Definitive History of a Great British Car* (Sparkford 1994), p.124.
3. W. Lyons 'The History of Jaguar and the Future of the Specialised Car in the British Motor Industry', Lord Wakefield Gold Medal Paper, 28 April 1969.
4. W. Lyons, speech at Motor Trades Luncheon Club, 25 June 1947.
5. Interview by P. Skilleter, July 1997.
6. Interview by P. H. Porter with J. Jones, Jan 2001.
7. Ibid.
8. Ibid.
9. Ibid.
10. Letter from F. R. W. England to P. Skilleter, Feb 1990.
11. Ibid.
12. Ibid.
13. J. Dugdale, *Jaguar in America* (New York 1993), p.5.
14. Ibid.
15. Ibid., p.7
16. Ibid., p.8.
17. Ibid., p.8.
18. Ibid., p.9.
19. Interview by P. H. Porter with R. Robinson, Feb 2001.
20. Interview by P. Skilleter, May 2001.
21. Ibid.
22. Ibid.
23. Ibid.

24. Interview by P. H. Porter and P. Skilleter with P. Quinn and M. Rimell, Nov 2000.
25. Ibid.
26. Ibid.
27. W. Lyons, draft autobiography, 1976.
28. Ibid.
29. Interview by P. H. Porter, Nov 2000.
30. W. Lyons, draft autobiography, 1976.
31. Letter from W. Lyons to P. Skilleter, 1974
32. C. Edwards, *Motor Industry*, Sept 1971.
33. Interview by P. H. Porter, 1978.
34. Interview by P. H. Porter with W. Jones, 1986.

Chapter 5
1. Speech by W. Lyons, 6 Jan 1950.
2. Memo from W. Lyons, 24 Jan 1950, JDHT archive.
3. W. Lyons, draft autobiography, 1976.
4. Letter from C. H. F. D. McCarthy OBE, British Consulate General, New York, 6 June 1950, JDHT archive.
5. Works notice, 19 May 1950, JDHT archive.
6. Memo from J. Lyons to Newcombe and Orr, 16 June 1950, JDHT archive.
7. Letter from F. R. W. England to P. Skilleter, 7 April 1990.
8. Interview by P. H. Porter and P. Skilleter with P. Quinn and M. Rimell, Nov 2000.
9. Interview by P. H. Porter, 1980.
10. Letter from W. Lyons to W. M. Miller, Ministry of Supply, 18 Aug 1950, JDHT archive.
11. Interview by P. Skilleter, Aug 2000.
12. Interview by P. Skilleter 1974.
13. Letter from A. Brittain, published in *Jaguar Journal*.
14. *Jaguar Journal*, Feb 1951.
15. Letter from W. Lyons to G. E. Beharrell, 1 Feb 1951.
16. Leaflet issued by the Strike Committee, point 4, 12 Mar 1951, JDHT archive.
17. Management's reply to Strike Committee, point 4, 23 Mar 1951, JDHT archive.
18. *Jaguar Journal*, May 1951.
19. Letter from W. Lyons to Sir A. Rowlands, 1 April 1951, JDHT archive.
20. Memo from Heynes to Huckvale, 10 May 1951, P. H. Porter archive.
21. *The Daily Express*, 19 Oct 1962.
22. Interview by P. Skilleter, 1974.
23. P. Turner, *Motor*, 4 Mar 1972.
24. Interview by P. H. Porter, Dec 2000.
25. Interview by P. H. Porter and P. Skilleter, Jan 2001.
26. Interview by P. H. Porter, Jan 2001.
27. Interview by P. H. Porter and P. Skilleter, Jan 2001.
28. P. H. Porter *Jaguar Scrapbook* (Sparkford 1989), p.105.
29. W. Lyons, draft autobiography, 1976.
30. P. H. Porter interview, USA, 1988.
31. W. Lyons, draft autobiography, 1976.
32. Ibid.
33. Ibid.
34. Interview by P. Skilleter, June 2001.
35. Interview by P. H. Porter, Jan 2001.
36. Interview by P. H. Porter and P. Skilleter with P. Quinn and M. Rimell, Nov 2000.
37. Interview by P. H. Porter and P. Skilleter, Jan 2001.

38. Minutes of a meeting held at St James's House, 1 July 1953, JDHT archive.
39. Letter from W. Lyons to H. Ferguson, 13 Nov 1953, JDHT archive.

Chapter 6
1. Letter from Sir J. Black to W. Lyons, 28 Jan 1954, JDHT archive.
2. Interview by P. H. Porter, Dec 2000.
3. Ibid.
4. Ibid.
5. P. H. Porter *Jaguar Scrapbook* (Sparkford 1989), pp.105–6.
6. Letter from W. Lyons to M. Hoffman, 31 Jan 1955.
7. J. Dugdale *Jaguar in America* (New York 1993), p.53.
8. Ibid., p.35
9. NAC meeting, 15 Mar 1955.
10. Interview by P. Skilleter, July 1997.
11. Interview by P. H. Porter and P. Skilleter with P. Quinn and M. Rimell, Nov 2000.
12. Memo from W. Lyons, 17 Mar 1955, JDHT archive.
13. Interview by P. H. Porter and P. Skilleter, Jan 2001.
14. Interview by P. H. Porter, Dec 2000.
15. Interview by P. H. Porter and P. Skilleter, Jan 2001.
16. A. J. A. Whyte, *Jaguar Sports Racing & Works Cars from 1954* (Sparkford 1987), p.87.
17. Letter from F. R. W. England to P. Skilleter, 27 Nov 1992.
18. Interview by P. H. Porter and P. Skilleter with P. Quinn and M. Rimell, Nov 2000.
19. Interview by P. H. Porter, Feb 2001.
20. Interview by P. Skilleter, July 1997.
21. Memo from W. Lyons to W. Thornton, 7 June 1955, JDHT archive.
22. Interview by P. H. Porter, 1988.
23. Memo from W. Lyons to E. Rankin, 14 June 1955, JDHT archive.
24. Letter from H. Weslake to W. Lyons, 25 June 1955.
25. Address to Jaguar clubs, Australia, April 1986.
26. Interview by P. Skilleter, 1974.
27. Interview by P. H. Porter, Jan 2001.
28. Ibid.
29. Letter from W. Lyons to S. Elwes, 6 Jan 1956, JDHT archive.
30. Interview by P. Skilleter, July 1997.
31. Interview by P. Skilleter, 1985.
32. Interview by P. H. Porter and P. Skilleter with P. Quinn and M. Rimell, Nov 2000.
33. Interview by P. Skilleter, May 2001.
34. Board meeting, 5 Jan 1956.
35. Memo from W. Lyons to all executives, 16 April 1956, JDHT archive.
36. Press release, 29 Nov 1956, JDHT archive.
37. Interview by P. H. Porter, Jan 2001.
38. Interview by P. H. Porter with F. R. W. England, Austria, 1994.
39. Interview by P. H. Porter, Mar 1998.
40. A. J. A. Whyte, *Jaguar – The Definitive History of a Great British Car* (Sparkford 1994), p.147.
41. Interview by P. H. Porter and P. Skilleter, Jan 2001.
42. Notice signed by W. Lyons, 1 Oct 1957, JDHT archive.

43. Letter from W. Lyons to 'the NUVB Shop Committee and for all other employees to see', 9 Oct 1957, JDHT archive.
44. Statement by W. Lyons, 9 Oct 1957, JDHT archive.

Chapter 7
1. Interview by P. H. Porter, Dec 2000.
2. Ibid.
3. Interview by P. H. Porter and P. Skilleter with P. Quinn and M. Rimell, Nov 2000.
4. Interview by P. H. Porter, 1988.
5. Interview by P. H. Porter, Nov 2000.
6. Interview by P. H. Porter and P. Skilleter with R. Berry, Jan 2001.
7. Interview by P. H. Porter and P. Skilleter with P. Quinn and M. Rimell, Nov 2000.
8. Ibid.
9. Ibid.
10. Interview by P. H. Porter and P. Skilleter with P Smart, Jan 2001.
11. P. H. Porter *Jaguar Scrapbook* (Sparkford 1989), p.98.
12. Interview by P. H. Porter, USA, 1988.
13. P. H. Porter *Jaguar E-type – The Definitive History* (Sparkford 1989), p.59.
14. Memo from C. Jennings to R. E. Dangerfield, 14 May 1958.
15. Interview by P. H. Porter, Dec 2000.
16. Interview by P. Skilleter, July 1997.
17. Letter from F. R. W. England to P. Skilleter, 4 May 1993.
18. Interview by P. H. Porter, Feb 2001.
19. Interview by P. H. Porter and P. Skilleter with P. Quinn and M. Rimell, Nov 2000.
20. Ibid.
21. Ibid.
22. Interview by P. Skilleter, May 2001.
23. B. Took *Round the Horne – The Complete and Utter History* (London 1998).
24. Interview by P. H. Porter and P. Skilleter, Jan 2001.
25. Interview by P. Skilleter, 1985.
26. Interview by P. H. Porter, 1987.
27. Interview by P. H. Porter, Mar 2001.

Chapter 8
1. Interview by P. H. Porter, Jan 2001.
2. Interview by P. H. Porter, Feb 2001.
3. P. H. Porter *The Most Famous Car in the World* (London, 2000), p.89.
4. Interview by P. H. Porter, Nov 2000.
5. P. H. Porter *Jaguar E-type – The Definitive History* (Sparkford 1989), p.134.
6. P. H. Porter *Jaguar Scrapbook* (Sparkford, 1989), p.131.
7. P. H. Porter *Jaguar E-type – The Definitive History* (Sparkford 1989), p.181.
8. Interview by P. H. Porter, 1988.
9. Interview by P. H. Porter and P. Skilleter, Jan 2001.
10. Interview by P. H. Porter and P. Skilleter with P. Quinn and M. Rimell, Nov 2000.
11. Interview by P. H. Porter, Nov 2000.
12. Interview by P. H. Porter and P. Skilleter, Jan 2001.
13. Interview by P. H. Porter and P. Skilleter with P. Smart, Jan 2001.
14. Interview by P. H. Porter and P. Skilleter with P. Quinn and M. Rimell, Nov 2000.
15. Interview by P. H. Porter, Nov 2000.

16. W. Hassan *Climax in Coventry* (Coventry 1975), p.136.
17. Interview by P. H. Porter, Oct 2000.
18. P. H. Porter *Jaguar Scrapbook* (Sparkford 1989), p.124.
19. Letter from W. Lyons to J Eerdmans, 8 Mar 1963, JDHT archive.
20. Interview by P. H. Porter, Jan 2001.
21. P. H. Porter *Jaguar Scrapbook* (Sparkford 1989), pp.98–9.
22. Ibid., p.99.
23. Interview by P. H. Porter, Nov 2000.
24. Ibid.
25. Ibid.
26. H. Mönnich *The BMW Story – A Company in its Time* (London 1991), pp.481–2.
27. P. H. Porter *Jaguar Scrapbook* (Sparkford 1989), p.127.
28. Ibid., p.139.
29. Ibid.
30. Interview by P. H. Porter and P. Skilleter with P. Quinn and M. Rimell, Nov 2000.
31. Interview by P. H. Porter, Nov 2000.

Chapter 9
1. Interview by P. H. Porter, Dec 2000.
2. Interview by P. H. Porter, Nov 2000.
3. P. H. Porter *Jaguar Scrapbook* (Sparkford 1989), p.139.
4. Letter from F. R. W. England to P. Skilleter, 16 April 1993.
5. P. H. Porter *Project XJ40 – The Inside Story of the New XJ6* (Sparkford 1987), p.15.
6. Interview by P. H. Porter, Nov 2000.
7. Interview by P. H. Porter, 1987.
8. Interview by P. H. Porter and P. Skilleter with P. Quinn and M. Rimell, Nov 2000.
9. Interview by P. H. Porter, Nov 2000.
10. P. H. Porter *Project XJ40 – The Inside Story of the New XJ6* (Sparkford 1987), p.14.
11. P. H. Porter *Jaguar – The Complete Illustrated History* (London 1984), p.149.
12. Interview by P. Skilleter, 1985.
13. Interview by P. H. Porter and P. Skilleter with P. Quinn and M. Rimell, Nov 2000.
14. Interview by P. H. Porter, Feb 2001.
15. Interview by P. Skilleter, June 2001.
16. Ibid.
17. P. H. Porter *Jaguar Scrapbook* (Sparkford 1989), p.107.
18. Ibid., p.145.
19. Ibid.
20. Interview by P. H. Porter, Nov 2000.
21. Ibid.
22. P. H. Porter *Jaguar Scrapbook* (Sparkford 1989), p.123.
23. Interview by P. H. Porter and P. Skilleter, Jan 2001.
24. Ibid.

Chapter 10
1. G. Turner *The Leyland Papers* (London 1971), p.121.
2. Ibid., p.150.
3. Ibid., p.156.
4. Ibid., p.169.
5. Ibid., p.170.
6. Ibid., p.175.
7. Letter from F. R. W. England to P. Skilleter, 19 July 1993.
8. Interview by P. H. Porter, 1988.

9. Interview by P. H. Porter, 1987.
10. Ibid.

Chapter 11
1. Interview by P. H. Porter, Feb 2001.
2. Interview by P. H. Porter, Dec 2000.
3. Interview by Miss McGowan, published 15 Feb 1972.
4. Ibid.
5. P. Garnier, *Autocar*, 16 Mar 1972.
6. P. Turner, *Motor*, 4 Mar 1972.
7. C. Edwards, *Motor Industry*, Sept 1971.
8. Interview by P. H. Porter, Feb 2001.
9. Ibid.
10. Ibid.
11. J. Dugdale *Jaguar in America* (New York 1993), p.145.
12. Interview by P. H. Porter, Nov 2000.
13. *The Daily Express*, 19 Oct 1962.
14. Interview by P. H. Porter, Feb 2001.
15. Interview by P. H. Porter and P. Skilleter with P. Quinn and M. Rimell, Nov 2000.
16. Interview by P. H. Porter, 1987.
17. Press release for Jaguar XJ-S launch, 1975.
18. Interview by P. H. Porter and P. Skilleter with P. Quinn and M. Rimell, Nov 2000.
19. Interview by P. Skilleter, July 1997.
20. J. Dugdale *Jaguar in America* (New York 1993), p.202.
21. J. Wood *Wheels of Misfortune* (London 1988), p.230.
22. Interview by P. H. Porter, Feb 2001.
23. Interview by P. H. Porter, Jan 2001.
24. Interview by P. H. Porter, Feb 2001.
25. Interview by P. H. Porter, Jan 2001.
26. Interview by P. H. Porter, Feb 2001.
27. Ibid.
28. P. H. Porter *Project XJ40 – The Inside Story of the New XJ6* (Sparkford 1987), p.37.
29. Interview by P. H. Porter, 1986.
30. Ibid.
31. Interview by P. H. Porter, Feb 2001.
32. Ibid.
33. Interview by P. Skilleter, May 2001.

Chapter 12
1. Interview by P. H. Porter, Feb 2001.
2. Ibid.
3. Ibid.
4. Interview by P. H. Porter, Nov 2000.
5. Interview by P. H. Porter, Feb 2001.
6. Ibid.
7. Ibid.
8. Interview by P. H. Porter, Jan 2001.
9. Ibid.
10. Interview by P. H. Porter, Nov 2000.
11. Interview by P. H. Porter, Feb 2001.
12. Ibid.
13. Ibid.
14. Ibid.
15. Ibid.
16. Interview by P. Skilleter, July 1997.
17. Interview by P. H. Porter, Nov 2000.
18. P. H. Porter *Jaguar Scrapbook* (Sparkford 1989), pp.158–9.
19. Interview by P. H. Porter, Feb 2001.
20. Interview by P. H. Porter and P. Skilleter with P. Quinn and M. Rimell, Nov 2000.
21. Interview by Miss McGowan, published 15 Feb 1972.

INDEX